Sparks of Liberty

Sparks of Liberty

An Insider's Memoir of Radio Liberty

GENE SOSIN

THE PENNSYLVANIA STATE UNIVERSITY PRESS
UNIVERSITY PARK, PENNSYLVANIA

Library of Congress Cataloging-in-Publication Data

Sosin, Gene.
     Sparks of liberty : an insider's memoir of Radio Liberty /
Gene Sosin.
          p.   cm.
     Includes bibliographical references and index.
     ISBN 0-271-01869-0 (alk. paper)
     1. Radio Liberty (Munich, Germany)—History.
     2. Propaganda, Anti-communist—Soviet Union—History.
     I. Title.
     HE8697.8.S67   1999
     384.54´06´543364—dc21   98-35718
                                                                  CIP

It is the policy of The Pennsylvania State University Press to use
acid-free paper for the first printing of all clothbound books.
Publications on uncoated stock satisfy the minimum
requirements of American National Standard for Information
Sciences—Permanence of Paper for Printed Library Materials,
ANSI Z39.48—1992.

To Gloria

Я помню чудное мгновенье . . .
—Пушкин

I remember the wondrous moment . . .
—PUSHKIN

Contents

Acknowledgments

For their encouragement, advice, and support at various stages during the long gestation of this book, I would like to thank:

In the former New York Programming Center of Radio Free Europe/Radio Liberty: Albert Arkus, Irene Dutikow, Sara Hassan, and Irina Klionsky. In Washington: at RFE/RL Jane Lester was continually cooperative in responding to my questions and requests; Paul Goble offered valuable suggestions after reading the first draft of the manuscript; Larisa Silnicky shared her insights and concern about the current state of the Radio's Russian service; Mark Rhodes and Susan Gigli of InterMedia briefed me about current evaluations by focus groups inside the new nations of the former Soviet Union.

Anatole Shub drew on his lifelong expertise in Russian affairs to give me incisive comments on the manuscript. Nicholas Scheetz and Lisette Matano of the Georgetown University Library's Special Collection Division made Jon Lodeesen's papers available to me. Dorothy Sargeant invited me to examine her late husband's files before sending them to the Truman Library. Scott Shane of the *Baltimore Sun* contributed sound recommendations for revising the manuscript.

I am especially grateful to Kevin Klose for asking me to be a consultant for Radio Liberty's fortieth anniversary and to join the elite contingent that celebrated in Moscow. After RFE/RL moved to its new headquarters in Prague, he endorsed my trip there for further research and interviews. Members of the Prague staff deserve mention: Margaret Rauch, Vaclava Kosikova, Lechoslaw Gawlikowski, Bonnie Mihalka, Robert Gillette, Donald Jensen, Goulnara Pataridze, Yuri Handler, Mario Corti, Lev Roitman, Wladimir Tolz, Tengis Gudava, Roman Kupchinsky, and Richard Cummings. Gene Parta shared with me a wealth of background information about the audience research and program evaluation project he directed over the years. My thanks to Natasha Zuber in Munich, where she was assistant to the director of the Radio, and who was my secretary in New York in the early 1960s.

In Moscow, Sonya Berezhkova of Radio Moscow (now Radio Voice of Russia) contributed her dissertation on Radio Liberty at Moscow State University and kept me informed about post-Soviet reactions to the broadcasts. Nina Kreitner, the biographer of Aleksandr Galich, was helpful too.

In Israel, Evgeny Lein was one of the most articulate of the many Jewish émigrés who stressed the importance of Radio Liberty's broadcasts in sustaining their morale and resistance to Soviet repression. Collective thanks to the Soviet émigrés of different ethnic origins, some of whom worked for the Radio, and to their courageous dissident compatriots in the homeland. They strengthened my conviction that we were on the right wavelength in more ways than one.

In the American academic community, I am most appreciative to my dear friends Robert V. (Bill) Daniels and Maurice Friedberg. Throughout the turbulent history of Radio Liberty, both scholars lent their considerable authority to the defense of the Radio against our domestic opponents and contributed directly to raising the quality of the broadcasts in their reviews of programming and their interviews on the air.

At Penn State Press, I credit Editor-in-Chief Peter J. Potter for his persistence in urging me to shape the book into a memoir of Radio Liberty that combines an objective documentary account with my personal perspective; and Peggy Hoover, Senior Manuscript Editor, whose painstaking care resulted in a considerably improved text.

Closer to home I want to thank Thomas P. Lewis for his professional advice as a writer and editor and for his careful compiling of the index; Barbara Wenglin and Margaret Harper of the White Plains Public Library, who always found the answers for my myriad queries; Edward Kasinec of the New York Public Library; Arch Puddington of Freedom House; Arlene Leiter; Sheila Simon; and Dr. Philip J. Guerin Jr., who helped make my retirement years a time of creativity.

Thanks to my family who cheered me on—my son, Donald; my daughter-in-law, Joanna; and my grandson, Nicky (who now has the answer if he ever asks me "What did you do in the Cold War, Grandpa?")—and to Joyce and Adrian Hirschhorn, my sister-in-law and her husband. Very special thanks for her expert input go to my daughter, Deborah, a professional copy editor whose eagle eye helped me turn in a manuscript to my editors that made their work easier; and to my wife, Gloria, who has shared with me fifty years of studying Russia and writing and lecturing on this endlessly fascinating subject. Her editorial skills and passionate Javert-like pursuit of *le mot juste* reaffirmed her role as my best friend and severest (constructive) critic. *Ne sluchaino* ("not by accident," as the Russians say), I dedicate the book to her with gratitude and love.

Everyone has the right to freedom of opinion
and expression; this right includes freedom
to hold opinions without interference and to
seek, receive and impart information and ideas
through any media and regardless of frontiers.

—Article 19 of the UN Universal Declaration of
Human Rights, 1948

 INTRODUCTION

It would be difficult to overestimate the
significance of your contribution to the
destruction of the totalitarian regime in the
former Soviet Union. No less important are
the efforts which you are making today to
inform radio listeners in Russia about events
in our country and overseas.

—Message from Boris N. Yeltsin, President of
the Russian Federation, to Radio Liberty on its
fortieth anniversary, March 1993

This book is the story of how Radio Liberty
(RL), an American radio station, engaged
in a protracted conflict with the Soviet
superpower, pierced the Kremlin's seemingly invulnerable propaganda machine,
and helped win the Cold War. Since March
1953, the Radio has been broadcasting continuously to the Soviet Union and its successor states. (The name was changed
from Radio Liberation to Radio Liberty in
1959.) Radio Liberty played a major role in
the erosion of the Communist Party's con-

trol of information and thereby helped to accelerate the ultimate demise of the Soviet regime. From a weak voice in 1953, the Radio became the most powerful medium of communications to penetrate the Iron Curtain, influencing millions of Russians, Ukrainians, and other ethnic groups in the major populated areas of the Soviet Union. To this day, Radio Liberty contributes to the democratic education of the newly independent nations.

I joined the staff a few months before it went on the air, and for thirty-three years I took an active part in the development of programming and policy as director of the New York radio division, senior adviser to the director of Radio Liberty (at times acting director) in Munich headquarters, and director of broadcast planning for Radio Free Europe/Radio Liberty (RFE/RL) in New York after the merger of the two stations in the 1970s.

Many of the documents I quote, some of which were confidential, have not been previously published. Most are from my personal files, and some are the only extant sources for an account of the history of Radio Liberty. They include broadcast tapes and scripts, policy papers, and highlights of RL-sponsored conferences attended by American and West European educators and journalists specializing in Soviet affairs. Excerpts are quoted from broadcasts by leading Americans and Europeans in the political, scientific, cultural, and academic world, whose broad spectrum of ideas challenged the rigid Marxist-Leninist doctrine of the Kremlin.

Radio Liberty faced many crises during its history. The KGB actively interfered with the work of the Radio in an effort to terrorize and discourage its employees, including in all probability the murder of two members of the Munich staff during the 1950s. Over the years, the Radio was infiltrated with "plants" in the person of alleged defectors, who later returned to the Soviet Union and branded the Radio as a haven for Nazi collaborators and CIA agents. There was some truth to those accusations, because early recruits from among the émigrés in Western Europe included former Soviet citizens who had fought on the German side. It is also a fact that the CIA secretly funded Radio Liberty during its first eighteen years. The greatest threat to the Radio came in 1971, when its cover was blown and the raison d'être of RL itself was questioned by the powerful chairman of the Senate Foreign Relations Committee, J. William Fulbright.

The Radio staff's unique mixture of Soviet émigrés from different ethnic origins, all with their own political agenda, often resulted in the explosion of tensions within the Radio among Russians and non-Russian national minorities. These prejudices and conflicts crept into the broadcasts themselves, including anti-Semitic sentiments from some of the Russian and Ukrainian émigrés.

Many problems arose in adjusting American-directed policy and programming in response to the shifting phases of Soviet post-Stalinist history during four turbulent decades: from Khrushchev's thaw to Brezhnev's freeze-détente-stagnation; Gorbachev's *glasnost* and *perestroika,* which ended with the dissolution of the Soviet Union; and the advent of Yeltsin's inchoate democratic Russia and the emergence of independent nations of the former empire. What was perhaps Radio Liberty's finest hour came in August 1991 at the time of the attempted putsch against Gorbachev and Yeltsin. Correspondents of the Radio, standing side by side with the democratic leaders inside the "White House" parliament building in Moscow, reported to the outside world and, more important, to the vast audience inside the Soviet Union. As Andrei Sakharov's widow, Elena Bonner, put it, "You boys were on the barricades with us."[1]

Actually, Radio Liberty (then Radio Liberation) took its place on the barricades on March 1, 1953, the first day of its broadcasts. By a strange historical coincidence, Stalin suffered a stroke that night and died on March 5. Few of us on the original staff dreamed that we would see many of our goals realized: the end of censorship, full exposure of Stalin's crimes against the people, assertion of ethnic identity and self-determination on the part of the national minorities, and the resurgence of religion. Most important were the development of genuine public opinion that was influenced by ideas and information from the West and by the struggle for human rights on the part of a small band of courageous dissidents inside the Soviet Union; and, finally, the repudiation of the Soviet regime, of the Communist Party, and of Lenin himself.

It was little short of a miracle that a group of Americans, mostly inexperienced in the art of international communications, managed to combine their talents and energy with a similarly untrained group of embittered victims of Soviet tyranny bent on revenge against the power that had wronged them and their families. During years of dramatic changes within and outside the Soviet Union, this improbable alliance built a permanent bridge that linked the outside world with millions of listeners who grew to depend on the Radio's broadcasts as the voice of their secret thoughts, frustrations, and hopes. Soviet leaders from Gorbachev and Yeltsin on down, including a KGB general, have acknowledged the impact of the Radio. Of particular significance were the endorsements of Andrei Sakharov, Aleksandr Solzhenitsyn, and other prominent opponents of the dictatorship. They risked their freedom and sometimes their lives to reach public opinion abroad and, primarily via Radio Liberty, to deliver to their own people *samizdat* ("self-published," uncensored documents) articulating their demands for civil and human rights that the regime denied its citizens.

As the world enters the twenty-first century, Russia and its "near abroad" neighbors face an unstable period of social and economic problems. Radio Liberty's mission as a medium of democratic education is still relevant in helping to exorcise the specter of xenophobic nationalism and oppressive one-party control that stalks the former Soviet Union and threatens the hard-won independence of a long-suffering people.

My Road to Radio Liberty

Radio Liberty did not yet exist when I entered the field of Russian studies soon after the end of World War II. Soviet-American relations were already prominent in the international arena, offering career opportunities for specialists in Soviet affairs.

In 1947, I enrolled at the Russian Institute at my alma mater, Columbia University, under the G.I. Bill, which offered free education to World War II veterans. The two-year graduate master's program required taking courses in five disciplines and majoring in one: economics, history, law and government, political science, and language/literature. As an undergraduate, I had majored in French language and literature. The Navy taught me Japanese at the University of Colorado and sent me to Washington, D.C., where I served in the cryptanalysis section of communications intelligence. In my spare time, I tried my hand at Russian and was intrigued, so it was natural for me to major in language/literature at Columbia University's Russian Institute.

In 1949, after completing the two-year program, I received the Russian Institute certificate and at the same time received a master's degree in Russian language and literature from the Department of Slavic Languages, where I continued to work toward a Ph.D., and passed the orals in 1950. The chairman of the department was Ernest J. Simmons, a noted specialist on nineteenth-century Russian authors and on twentieth-century Soviet literature. It was in his course on Dostoyevsky that I met Gloria Donen, another former G.I. in graduate studies. I pursued both her and further language training at the Middlebury Russian Summer School in 1948 and 1949.

We were married in June 1950, and two months later moved to Munich, Germany, as members of the Columbia Bureau of Applied Social Research (BASR) team working with the Harvard Project on the Soviet Social System. The Project was sponsored by the U.S. Air Force and conducted under a contract with Harvard University's Russian Research Center. The purpose of the Project was to assess the social and psychological strengths and weaknesses of the Soviet system from interviews with refugees, in view of the impossibility of obtaining such information inside the Soviet Union.

Most of the hundreds of émigrés questioned were former Soviet citizens who were living in camps in West Germany. Brought to Germany as prisoner laborers by the retreating Nazi armies, these "displaced persons" had remained in the West after the end of World War II. Graduate students of the Harvard Russian Research Center formed the nucleus of the American team of interviewers. When the BASR's work ended, Gloria and I worked directly for Harvard. The rich experience of a year abroad meeting Soviet "displaced persons" provided firsthand insights into the reality of life under Stalin and invaluable training in the living Russian language.[2]

Under the genial direction of Raymond Bauer, a specialist on Soviet psychology, our staff included many future experts on the Soviet Union in the academic world.[3] We were given the simulated rank of captain by our military sponsors, with many of the perquisites of American officers in occupied Germany. Two other important nonmilitary American activities began during our service in Munich: On July 4, 1950, Radio Free Europe (RFE) initiated its broadcasts to the satellite nations of Eastern Europe that had fallen under the control of the Kremlin after World War II; and the Institute for the Study of the USSR was established, staffed by displaced persons and defectors from the Soviet army and later joined to the parent organization of RL. After the Radio began broadcasting in 1953, the Institute assisted it by providing research material and organizing academic conferences in Munich that attracted American and Western European experts. The Institute also helped the Radio recruit staff writers, editors, announcers, technicians, and researchers.

The Harvard Project interviewees were not only Russians, Ukrainians, and Belorussians, but also representatives of non-Slavic national minorities of the Soviet Union. In the spring of 1951, I traveled with Frederick Wyle, a spokesman for the Project, to Ulm, the city near the source of the Danube River where Albert Einstein was born. We met with leaders of the Idel-Ural (Volga) Tatar refugee community in their ramshackle barracks in Neu-Ulm on the outskirts of the city. Sitting on their cots in makeshift rooms separated by blankets, we two Americans communicated with these proud descendants of the ancient Asiatic conquerors of the Slavs in the lingua franca, Russian. Two years later, some of them began broadcasting over RL from Munich to their compatriots inside the Soviet Union in their native Tatar tongue, along with other émigrés from Soviet Central Asia and the Caucasus.

The Project terminated in June, and we returned to New York in the summer of 1951. I began to look for a job that would utilize my academic skills while I continued work on my Ph.D. dissertation. In 1952, I applied to the New York headquarters of the recently formed American Committee for the Liberation of the Peoples of Russia Inc., soon renamed the American Committee for Liberation from Bolshevism (abbreviated Amcomlib), which was organizing a new radio station, then called "Liberation," based in Munich, like Radio Free Europe, but with the Soviet Union as its target.

A small unit was set up in New York staffed by Russian émigré writers who prepared scripts to supplement the Radio's program schedule once it went on the air. Boris Shub, the American head of the unit, was impressed with my qualifications in the Soviet field, especially the experience in Europe with former Soviet citizens and my fluency in Russian, and hired me as his assistant. I embarked on a fascinating career with an international radio that ignited the closed Soviet society with sparks of liberty.

Stalin was swimming alone at his dacha outside Moscow when he started to drown. A peasant who happened to be passing by jumped in and pulled him out of the river. In gratitude, Stalin offered to grant the rescuer anything he wished.

"Comrade Stalin," the peasant pleaded, "please don't tell anyone I saved you!"

1 RADIO LIBERTY'S CONCEPTION AND BIRTH

Visionary American statesmen under President Harry Truman in the State and Defense Departments in the late 1940s realized the potential value of an American-sponsored radio station in the ideological struggle against communism. By harnessing the talents of refugees from Eastern Europe and the Soviet Union, they could reach their compatriots beyond the "Iron Curtain,"[1] a curtain that the Cold War had frozen into an impenetrable sheet of ice.

George F. Kennan, America's outstanding expert on Russia who had served in the 1930s in the U.S. Embassy in Moscow (became ambassador in 1952), was the policy planning adviser to the secretary of after the war. The containment of the inist regime was first proposed by K in his seminal article "The Sources of Conduct," published in the July 19 of *Foreign Affairs* under the pseudonym Thanks to his initiative, and with eration of other influential citizens government and private life, two

tions were soon created: Radio Free Europe (RFE), which began in 1950 to communicate with listeners in the Soviet-dominated countries of Eastern Europe, and Radio Liberation (RL; later renamed Radio Liberty, also RL), which began broadcasting to the Soviet Union in 1953. Both Radios received their funds via the CIA from congressional appropriations, and both were located in Munich, but they were distinct from each other and operated separately until their merger in the mid-1970s.

The funds for Radio Liberation were disbursed to Amcomlib, which was formally incorporated on January 18, 1951, in the state of Delaware as the "American Committee for Freedom for the Peoples of the USSR, Inc." In May 1951, it was changed to the "American Committee for the Liberation of the Peoples of Russia," to placate Russian exile leaders who opposed the recognition of the Soviet Union implicit in the title. In March 1953, it was again renamed the "American Committee for Liberation from Bolshevism," reflecting the common cause for which the multinational émigré groups were fighting. In 1956, "from Bolshevism" was dropped; the abbreviation "Amcomlib" was used throughout this period until 1964, when the American Committee for Liberation became the "Radio Liberty Committee." The station had been renamed Radio Liberty in 1959.

The facade of a private company was supposed to establish greater credibility for the Radio as an independent voice rather than as an official arm of the U.S. communications network that included Voice of America. Thus, when Soviet diplomats confronted their American counterparts at international conferences with the accusation that the émigré radio was "interfering in the internal affairs of the Soviet people," they were simply informed that it was a private station not subject to government control. To preserve the fiction, a board of trustees had been appointed that included several distinguished Americans, three of them famous journalists who had reported from Soviet Russia: William Henry Chamberlin, Isaac Don Levine, and Eugene Lyons.[2]

Eugene Lyons, for many years a senior editor of *Reader's Digest,* was the first president of Amcomlib. He had returned from the Soviet Union in the 1930s completely disillusioned with the socialist experiment he had once greeted with enthusiasm. After a brief tenure, he resigned, but joined the board of trustees. Admiral Alan G. Kirk, a former ambassador to the Soviet Union, became president in February 1952. Because of ill health Kirk soon left, but not before he had supervised the hiring of émigrés in Munich and New York to form the nucleus of the Radio's staff. He was followed later in 1952 by Vice-Admiral Leslie C. Stevens, who had served in Moscow as naval attaché. Stevens was president at the birth of the Radio and remained for another eighteen months, when he was succeeded by Howland Sargeant in October 1954.

Our New York office, located above a bank at 6 East Forty-fifth Street in Manhattan, hardly resembled a radio station. It was more like a city desk at a small newspaper, since we had no studios in those days. Only when I visited RL headquarters in Munich in 1954 did I begin to feel part of an active radio network. My new boss, Boris Shub, manager of the New York Program Section (NYPS), was the American-born son of a well-known writer and publicist, David Natanovich Shub. The elder Shub had known Lenin, Trotsky, Bukharin, Plekhanov, Zasulich, Axelrod, and other pre-revolutionary Marxist leaders of the Russian Social Democratic Labor Party, which split in 1903 into two factions: the radical Bolshevik majority and the moderate Menshevik minority. He considered himself a "European social democrat" rather than a Menshevik, although he was close to leaders like Plekhanov. Boris used to boast to his friends that he made his first political decision in 1916 at the age of four: when his father introduced him to Trotsky, Boris refused to shake his hand, saying, "He looks like the devil." However, he enjoyed the piggyback ride Bukharin gave him. Both Bukharin and Trotsky were living in New York before the 1917 revolution, and the elder Shub's house served as a meeting place for assorted rebels and foes of czarist tyranny.[3]

In his youth, Boris met anti-Soviet political leaders such as Alexander Kerensky, prime minister of the Russian provisional government of 1917, and grew up determined to help the Russian people get rid of the dictatorship, which he believed was a threat to peace in the world as well as an oppressive burden on its subjects. By the time he was forty years old, in 1952, he had gained a reputation in Western political circles as a skillful propagandist. He was the political adviser in Berlin to RIAS (the acronym for "Radio in the American Sector"), the U.S. government's German-language station broadcasting to East Germany. In addition, he had collaborated on a book with Walter Krivitsky, a high-level defector from Stalin's secret police. Most important, he had written a provocative book called *The Choice,* published in 1950, in which he argued that if Americans "restore our wartime alliance with the Russian people" by communicating our ideas and ideals, together we might achieve the goal of liberating them from the Kremlin's yoke.[4]

Initially, in 1952, my title was Research Coordinator of the New York Program Section, but I soon became Shub's de facto deputy. I was responsible for helping the Russian writers by establishing a reference library of appropriate books and periodicals. In those days, the Soviet press refused our request for subscriptions, so I would go to the nearby office of Frederick Praeger, a publisher who approved of our fledgling organization, to pick up the Moscow newspapers he obtained for us. Our mission in the NYPS was to prepare scripts in Russian for transmission to Munich, where Radio Liberation was building studios and hiring personnel in anticipation of launching broadcasts to the Soviet Union. His close ties with émigré intellectuals enabled Shub to recruit a talented corps of Russian staff members and freelancers in 1952. A few of them had taken an active part in the prerevolutionary struggle against czarism, including his father, who was best known for his unauthorized biography of Lenin (whom he disliked), published in several languages but banned in the Soviet Union. Later, in the 1970s, another of David Shub's books (in Russian), *Russian Political Leaders,* found its way to Soviet dissidents in Moscow and other cities, smuggled into the USSR along with other forbidden works published in the West. Among former Mensheviks the most prominent was Yuri P. Denicke, who had been active in early postrevolutionary politics in the ancient city of Kazan on the Volga and had more recently worked in a research section of the United States Information Agency (USIA) in Washington.[5] He was deeply respected by his fellow writers.

Roman B. Goul, the chief editor, was a non-Marxist who was also an editor of *Novy Zhurnal* (The New Review), a respected émigré *tolsty zhurnal* (thick magazine), as Russians call such periodicals on political and cultural themes.[6] Two of the writers were former Red Army officers who had defected at the end of World War II: Mikhail M. Koriakov, a captain and former journalist from Siberia, who defected in Paris; and Vladimir I. (Volodya) Yurasov, a Soviet lieutenant colonel who escaped from occupied Berlin to West Germany and who had been one of our interviewees at the Harvard Project in Munich.[7]

Among regular freelancers was Father Alexander Schmemann, a Russian priest and dean of the St. Vladimir Orthodox Academy in Westchester County, New York. Together with Boris Shub, Schmemann conceived a weekly "Sunday Talk" aimed not only at secret believers but also at people who were dissatisfied with the Marxist-Leninist atheistic *Weltanschauung* and were seeking spiritual inspiration to fill the void in their lives. He avoided strident sermonizing or a formal liturgical service; instead, he calmly discussed ethical and religious issues for Soviet believers and receptive nonbelievers. Father Schmemann's weekly fifteen-minute talks continued for more than thirty years and attracted a wide audience of admirers, especially members of the Russian intelligentsia that included Aleksandr Solzhenitsyn before the writer's forced exile in 1974. Solzhenitsyn told Western reporters in an interview in Moscow in the early 1970s that the talks were for him "the temple in which I worship." Schmemann spoke in a quiet, reassuring baritone, as though talking to an individual friend.[8] Occasionally he would come to the studio with his young son, Serge, who went on to Harvard and a career in journalism as a Pulitzer Prize–winning foreign correspondent of the *New York Times* and its Moscow bureau chief. It came to pass that this son of the Russian people's favorite radio priest, who long challenged Soviet official atheism with eternal Christian values, reported the demise of the Soviet Union in 1991.

In my relations with my émigré colleagues, I tried to speak Russian most of the workday, absorbing their insights about Soviet reality and empathizing with their implacable hostility to the regime. My eagerness to think and feel like a Russian went to such an extreme that once, on the Monday after the Russian Orthodox Easter, when Koriakov came to work and greeted everyone with three kisses on their cheeks and a solemn *"Khristos voskres!"* (Christ is risen!), I joined in, despite my Jewish heritage.

Under Shub's inspired direction, our NYPS produced a backlog of "timeless" feature scripts that would accompany the daily newscasts, giving the audience information about subjects forbidden by Soviet-censored sources. Several series were created that remained on the air for years: "Missing Pages" restored the writings of Russian authors repressed by Stalin—for example, Babel, Olesha, and Zamyatin; "How They Were Cured of Communism" quoted from the confessions of disenchanted former Communists in the West, such as Arthur Koestler; "For Your Freedom and Ours" cited passages from Alexander Herzen and other prerevolutionary Russian democrats, whose opposition to the czarist autocracy was relevant as a critique of the Soviet stifling of freedom; "Speaking Precisely" exposed the Orwellian clichés of Soviet Newspeak; "Our People Abroad" refuted propaganda about the miserable fate of Russian émigrés by offering them our microphone to describe their successful adjustment to life in America and to express their nostalgia and love for their motherland.

Shub and Volodya Yurasov also created a series called "Colonel Panin." It consisted of short messages ostensibly from a former lieutenant colonel in the Soviet army, addressed both to civilians and to Soviet troops in Eastern Europe, in which Yurasov/Panin excoriated the dictatorship and invariably concluded by declaring that the only solution for Russia's ills was a "government of freely elected representatives of the people." The messages effectively combined Shub's sharp political analyses with Yurasov's own life experience; as a Soviet citizen he had been an inmate of the gulag before he managed to escape, conceal his identity, and serve as an officer during World War II. Boris would pace the floor, exploding with ideas and phrases that Yurasov put into colloquial Russian. The two of them made an odd couple: Shub was short and frenetic, and Volodya was tall and solidly built, resembling somewhat the German boxer Max Schmeling. Although they respected each other, their collaboration was often stormy; I once witnessed them punctuating their writing session by wrestling on the office floor like schoolboys. I thought they were fighting—until they got up, burst out laughing, and resumed their script-writing.

Within a short time Boris shared with me his approach to editing the scripts, based largely on political rather than stylistic criteria, which he usually left to Editor Goul. Shub's goal was to shape the future broadcasts into effective weapons of psychological warfare. When I was put in charge of the NYPS a couple of years later, I tried to apply his subtleties and nuances. Ultimately, by 1960, the section expanded into a division with its own state-of-the-art studios, taping programs that we airmailed by pouch through special arrangement with Lufthansa in those days before telexes and faxes. Once communication satellites were launched into fixed orbit in space, urgent programs were transmitted immediately and could be broadcast instantaneously to the Soviet Union. And, of course, the computer age introduced the e-mail link.

From the early days, the New York output was integrated into the total program schedule in Munich, which included newscasts, press reviews, and features prepared by Radio staff there. In the beginning, we had to rent recording time at an independent audio-video studio on nearby Madison Avenue whenever we supplemented the written scripts with special recorded programs. Shub coached Sergei Dubrovsky, an actor from Moscow who later became a leading RL announcer (in Russian, *diktor*), in the proper recitation of the lyrics to the famous prerevolutionary song of the workers, "You Fell Victim." Played and sung at the funerals of comrades, it easily evoked deep emotions: "You fell victim in the fateful struggle, / With selfless love for the people, / You gave up everything you could for them, / For their life, their honor and freedom."[9] The song describes the suffering of the victims of the czar's cruel regime, wasting away in chains in dank prisons. The dirge concludes on a note of hope:

The despot feasts in his sumptuous palace, drowning
    his fear with wine—
But menacing letters were drawn on the wall, long ago
    by a fateful hand:
"Arbitrary rule will fall, and the people arise, great,
    powerful, and free."
Farewell, brothers, you have honorably trodden a noble
    and shining path.

Shub revived the song to use as a weapon against Stalin, because its message is that the people will ultimately prevail. Dubrovsky gave an emotional rendition of the lyrics, and Boris, ever the perfectionist, made him work repeatedly on the lines about the despot in his palace, zeroing in on every plosive consonant, like a Hollywood director who demands many "takes."

A new world of political indoctrination opened as I became acquainted with other well-known revolutionaries who had escaped Soviet tyranny: Vladimir Zenzinov, considered by some a "saint," was a leader of the Socialist Revolutionaries (SRs), who had defeated Lenin in the 1917 elections to the Constituent Assembly; the distinguished Menshevik leader Irakli Tsereteli and his colleagues Boris Nicolaevsky, Solomon Schwarz and his wife Vera Alexandrova, and Rafael Abramovich. The Mensheviks were closely associated with the *Sotsialisticheski Vestnik* (Socialist Herald) and the *New Leader*, the American liberal anti-Communist magazine. The New York Program Section became the center for intellectual ferment as the time drew near for Radio Liberation to take to the airwaves.

One of my first purchases for our library at the NYPS was the complete set of the *Bolshaya Sovetskaya Entsiklopediya* (BSE, the Large Soviet Encyclopedia), published in Moscow in 1950. It was a treasure trove of Soviet disinformation and distortion. The fifth volume, containing the biography of Lavrenty Beria, the notorious chief of the secret police and Politburo member in Stalin's final years, filled several pages of encomium, accompanied by an idealized full-page photograph. In 1953, within a few months after Stalin's death, Beria was arrested and all subscribers to the encyclopedia received substitute pages describing the Bering Sea, together with explicit instructions to take a scissors or razor, cut out pages 21–24 and the portrait (not otherwise identified), and paste in the new pages. Beria went down the Soviet memory hole, but I kept both versions in the library and for years would amuse and shock visitors with this vivid illustration of the post-Stalin regime's revision of its own recent history.[10]

At forty, Boris Shub was still an *enfant terrible*, contemptuous of authority, brutally frank in his criticism of the staff's efforts, but earning our respect for his innovative methods and brilliant insights along with his profound commitment to the cause of a democratic Russia. At countless lunches together, I listened as an eager apprentice while he shared his thoughts about how the Radio could make a significant contribution to changing Soviet listeners' attitudes and prejudices. He understood that the audience we were preparing to reach would be suspicious of any messages we might send that would simply project a mirror image of their domestic media. He appreciated their pride and sensitivity as members of a superpower that had successfully repelled the Nazi invaders at a staggering cost of twenty million dead. He was also aware that many of them were imbued with the socialist ideals proclaimed by Lenin and were hostile to the capitalist world. He spoke of our need to attract the "loyal Soviet citizen," not merely those who were already enemies of the regime.

Boris realized the tremendous odds against us in our attempt to exdoctrinate people daily exposed to an unending barrage of official propaganda. They faced reprisals if they sought other sources of information, especially from a radio station staffed by émigrés whom many Soviet citizens resented for having chosen a comfortable life abroad. But Boris was convinced that millions of Soviets were dissatisfied with the quality of their lives; that they had expected meaningful improvements in their spiritual and material condition after the victory over Germany but instead were plunged into a dangerous Cold War struggle with their erstwhile allies. He believed that they would be attracted by voices that spoke pure, unaccented, contemporary Russian and other Soviet languages, not Americans or Englishmen, but compatriots who expressed their genuine aspirations for lasting peace, freedom of expression, and a higher standard of living. Unlike Voice of America and the BBC, which focused primarily on life in the United States and Great Britain, Radio Liberation would be an *internal* radio even though it was situated beyond the borders of the Soviet Union.

In December 1952, Shub went on temporary assignment to Munich, where he worked with the newly hired émigrés and the Radio's American adviser, Manning Williams, preparing for the inauguration of the broadcasts on March 1, 1953. Williams was a former "Moscow hand," a member of the U.S. Embassy staff after World War II. He had been editor of *Amerika*, a slick *Life*-like Russian magazine produced by the USIA. (During the war, other Americans served in Moscow, including Isaac Patch, Thomas P. Whitney, Frederick C. Barghoorn, and Robert C. Tucker. They went on to carve careers as Soviet experts in the academic and communications fields, and in various ways made positive contributions to the Radio.)

The Radio's offices and studios were located on Lilienthalstrasse in northern Munich in the former administration building of the Oberwiesenfeld airport. It was there that Great Britain's Prime Minister Neville Chamberlain, and France's Prime Minister Edouard Daladier, landed in September 1938, en route to the conference with Adolf Hitler that doomed the independence of Czechoslovakia and thereafter gave the name "Munich" a pejorative association.

After the Radio went on the air in March 1953, it operated with six studios. If you entered the control room of, say, Studio One and watched through the soundproof window, you would hear an announcer speak Russian into the microphone. First he would give the latest newscast, followed by a review of the Western press and several feature programs— many of them sent from New York, others prepared by the local Russian section, and all of them recorded by the engineer for delivery to the transmitter in another part of West Germany. In the other studios, you would see a similar setup but hear another of the Radio's many languages. The atmosphere resembled a mini–United Nations, where Slavic faces could be seen along with Georgians and Armenians, as well as Oriental-looking colleagues from Soviet Central Asia. Russian and German were most frequently used for communicating among the various ethnic groups, and American and British executives needed to know at least one of those languages.

At daily meetings each language desk discussed the priorities for the topical segment of the program, based on screening the early-morning Western wire services, plus a pirated duplicate of a machine that punched out the news from TASS (Telegraphic Agency of the Soviet Union). RL, along with TASS's legitimate subscribers, had swift access to the official Soviet version of the latest events and could sometimes scoop domestic clients, who received the dispatches more slowly.

The staff also received the transcript of the previous night's monitoring of internal Soviet radio stations. On my first visit to Radio Liberation in 1954, I was especially fascinated by the monitoring section, where a solid wall of receivers operated around the clock, recording shortwave broadcasts captured from RL antennas turned eastward to the major cities of Russia and other Soviet republics. The early archives contained tapes of such historic events as Stalin's funeral, which included speeches by Khrushchev, Malenkov, Beria, and other members of the "collective leadership," who professed fealty to one another and to the legacy of their dead leader while they secretly jockeyed for power. Excerpts from such monitored Soviet broadcasts provided us with dramatic "sound bites" for interpretation and commentary at those stages of the regime's evolution when the past was rewritten and abruptly shifted to conform to the new Party line.

Who were the principal members of the Munich staff in those days? Two Russian-speaking Americans who began their careers with Radio Liberation in Munich worked with Manning Williams and played vital roles in shaping its image over the years: Francis S. (Ronny) Ronalds and James Critchlow. Ronalds, formerly with *Time* magazine, alternated working for the Radio and Voice of America and was Radio Liberty's director in the 1970s. I was always impressed with his love of Russian culture and by his ability to recite from memory the lengthy *Verses About the Beautiful Lady* by the great Symbolist poet, Aleksandr Blok. Critchlow had great rapport with his émigré colleagues and wrote with verve about many of them in an entertaining and informative memoir about his years with the Radio and his subsequent activities on the staff of the Board for International Broadcasting in Washington.[11] Like me, Ronalds and Critchlow were ardent disciples of Boris Shub and his advocacy of democratic education of the Soviet audience. Paraphrasing Dostoyevsky's famous statement about the debt he and other Russian realists owed to Gogol, "We all came out of Gogol's *Overcoat*," one of us quipped: "We all came out of Shub's *shuba*" (*shuba* being the Russian word for fur coat).

The heterogeneous group of émigrés of the newly formed Russian service, many of whom Boris and Ronny recruited, included Wladimir Weidle, a respected art historian and literary critic from Paris who became the Radio's first Russian program director during the early years. Weidle had just published a perceptive monograph, *Russia: Absent and Present,* which the well-known Oxford professor and critic Isaiah Berlin lauded in the *London Sunday Times* as "the most balanced, civilised, and informative account of Russia's position in the world during the last three centuries."[12]

Another of Shub's "finds" was Victor Frank, son of Semyon Frank, the famous Russian religious philosopher, who, like Weidle, was expelled from the Soviet Union in 1923. Victor came from the BBC, where he had been head of the Russian service, and he worked for RL for almost twenty years in Munich and London as our bureau chief. As senior commentator, he infused his broadcasts with his profound knowledge of Russia. He liked to compare the construction of his radio talks to wooing a woman from foreplay to climax. In my opinion, Frank came the closest among all of the

Radio broadcasters to Anatoli Maximovich Goldberg, the BBC's veteran Russian commentator who was generally considered to be the voice from the West most respected by the vast audience of Soviet shortwave listeners. Frank's brother Vasily, long a member of the RL news desk, compiled a book of tributes by émigré and American colleagues after Victor's death in 1972.

Gaito Gazdanov came to Munich from Paris, where he had arrived with the first wave of postrevolutionary émigrés after 1917. A gifted writer, with a barbed wit and a French cigarette always dangling from his lips, he had eked out a living by driving a taxi at night, leaving him time to write and to achieve success with his first novel, *An Evening with Claire* (1930), which made him famous in the Russian community in Paris. From 1953 to his death in 1971, he was an editor with the Radio in Munich and later in Paris. In post-Soviet Russia, Gazdanov has attained long overdue recognition: more than fifty editions of his work have appeared, including a three-volume collection in 1996.[13]

Other members of the emigration recruited for the Radio included Boris Orshansky, a Soviet army captain who defected to the West after the end of the war, and Alexander Bacherach, former secretary to Russia's first Nobel Prize laureate in literature, Ivan Bunin, who lived in exile in France. A colorful reinforcement to this largely intellectual group was Leonid Pylayev, a hard-drinking proletarian who used his sharp satirical mind to record hilarious and coarse political monologues as "Ivan Ivanovich Oktyabrev"—a kind of Russian Joe Six-Pack or Archie Bunker.

The non-Russian staff of the Radio in Munich included many dedicated writers and editors equally concerned about the fate and the future of their respective homelands, such as Carlo Inasaridze, chief of the Georgian desk, and Garip Sultan, head of the Tatar-Bashkir service.[14]

In Shub's absence, I was left in charge of the NYPS, working closely with the writers before their scripts were sent to Munich. It was excellent training for my subsequent job as Shub's successor a couple of years later, when he assumed a position as policy adviser on Amcomlib's executive staff. By then, Radio Liberation was a going concern, and although woefully lacking in transmitter strength, we soon incurred the wrath of the Kremlin, which attempted in various ways, some of them sinister, to discredit and frighten us.

*There is no Pravda [truth] in Izvestiya,
and no Izvestiya [news] in Pravda.*

2 WE ARE ON THE AIR!

*"Govorit Radiostantsiya Osvobozhdeniye
. . ."*—"This is Radio Liberation speaking,
the free voice of your compatriots abroad."
With these words in Russian, Radio Liberation went on the air for the first time on
March 1, 1953. It was not a strong voice, with
only two 10,000-watt transmitters in Lam-
pertheim, Germany, purchased from Radio
Free Europe. The studios in Munich
recorded the daily programs, which were
then rushed by train and motorcycle couri-
ers to the transmitter site almost two hundred miles to the north. We never found
out whether the first broadcast fell on any
sympathetic ears inside the Soviet Union,
but the regime's monitors were certainly
listening. Ten minutes after the program
began, their jammers zeroed in on our
shortwave frequencies. Unlike the BBC and
the Voice of America, which enjoyed periodic respites from jamming during the Cold
War, depending on the relaxation of tension between the Kremlin and the West, the
Radio was interfered with continuously for

the next thirty-five years, until Mikhail Gorbachev ordered it stopped on November 29, 1988, consistent with his policy of glasnost.

Jamming

The most effective way for shortwave radio to broadcast over a long distance is on wavelengths between 10 and 100 meters, corresponding to the frequencies 3–30 megahertz. Shortwaves, generally speaking, can travel along the surface of the earth, and also reflect off the ionosphere, a gaseous layer of nitrogen and oxygen molecules activated by the movement of ultraviolet and x-rays of the sun. The ionosphere stretches from 60 to some 300 or 400 kilometers above the surface of the earth and comprises several layers that reflect radio beams, depending on the time of day and season.

The Radio directed its signals to the ionosphere from Western Europe at angles that enabled them to be reflected back to earth at specific target areas in the Soviet Union. In order to obstruct (jam) transmissions, the Soviet regime used radio stations that operated on the same or nearby frequencies as the broadcasts they were attempting to block. The signals generated had to be stronger than those of the message to be suppressed. Just as one person may try to drown out another's voice by speaking louder, the jammer produced noise—a persistent, irritating buzzing or howling that was later called "KGB jazz" by Soviet dissidents.

"Sky-wave" jammers operated like the Radio's transmissions, sending signals from inside the Soviet Union to be bounced back into the target area. Thanks to the variations in the ionosphere's height between Western and Eastern Europe during the day and night, the signal was able to penetrate at times when the Soviet signal escaped into space. This type of interference was not as effective as local "ground wave" jamming within cities. Magnifying the kilowatt power of the broadcasting signal improved audibility. Soviet citizens used various methods: some of them tuned to the edge of the frequency; others bought foreign-made receivers or export-model sets that incorporated meter bands not produced for the domestic market. Even Soviet sets could be secretly adapted by persons with enough technical skill; they were known as "radio doctors." Listening was easier away from urban centers, so people with automobiles would drive out of town to hear the Radio; those with dachas would frequently tape-record the broadcasts there.

The regime could have saved millions of rubles in electronic costs and man hours simply by confiscating all radios and using loudspeakers exclusively, as was done on the rural *kolkhozes* (collective farms). But this was impractical because the vast land mass of the Soviet Union, extending from Eastern Europe to the Pacific across eleven time zones, required shortwave radio for the transmission of Soviet propaganda. Furthermore, permitting individuals to own radios created the illusion of democracy even if this meant that the regime faced competition from uncensored media abroad. Jamming served to discourage people from listening to hostile voices, as did the Soviet criminal code, which threatened punishment of citizens if they disseminated anti-Soviet information and ideas. Nevertheless, since jamming was not totally effective twenty-four hours a day, courageous or just curious people who were determined to seek the forbidden fruit of objective news and heretical ideas frequently managed to catch all or part of foreign broadcasts.

Soviet citizens who were tuning in to the shortwave frequencies that first day in March might have heard our opening statement. Here are excerpts:

ANNOUNCER: This is Radio Liberation. Listen to us on shortwave in the 31–meter band. Our half-hour broadcasts are repeated every day on the hour during March from 10 A.M. to 10 P.M. Central European Time. Listen! Listen! Today a new radio station, Liberation, is starting its broadcasts.

Fellow countrymen! For a long time the Soviet regime has concealed from you the very fact of the emigration's existence. Only rarely is it mentioned in the press, and then it is tied to some scandalous case of a well-known person deciding not to return home, or some other event unpleasant for the Soviets such as the trial of Kravchenko [a famous defector]. The rest of the time nothing good or bad is said about us. We have been covered with a gravestone of silence, but we have not died. We are well aware why the Soviets have decided not even to rail against us in written or verbal attacks. That would mean constantly reminding the people about the existence of an anti-Bolshevik Russia which did not find a place in the motherland, about a Russia which took arms against Bolshevism and to this day has not ceased its struggle, and awaits its hour. Every intelligent person in the Soviet Union is sure in the depths of his soul that the Bolshevik tyranny in Russia, which is so monstrously abnormal and defies reason and humanitarian principles, cannot endure forever. Only that certainty gives us the energy to bear the hardships that have befallen us. You suffer from unheard of oppression and physical torture, and we suffer the bitterness of exile and dispersal throughout the world.[1]

The broadcast went on to refute the distorted image of the emigration, which Soviet propaganda presented to the public in labeling those abroad as "white bandits, restorers of the monarchy, and hirelings of Anglo-American imperialism." To the contrary, "the preponderant majority of the emigration stands for democratic principles, have not forgotten their duty to the motherland, and do not intend to cease the struggle until the complete annihilation of the Communist dictatorship."

Radio Liberation spoke in the name of a "Coordinating Center of the Anti-Bolshevik Struggle," which had been established on November 7, 1951, under the aegis of Amcomlib at a conference in Wiesbaden, Germany, where representatives of Russian and non-Russian émigré political organizations promulgated their goals for the "liberation of all their peoples from the Bolshevist dictatorship."[2] The declaration was timed to the anniversary of the "seizure of power by the Bolshevist usurpers." The first broadcast recapitulated those goals:

> We oppose that regime with the principle of consistent sovereignty of the people that was first proclaimed by the February Revolution. We are enemies of the restoration of the absolute monarchy, as well as any sort of new dictatorship in place of Bolshevism after it has finally been destroyed. For all the nationalities situated on the territory of the present Soviet Union, we recognize their right to freely choose their fate on the basis of democratic self-expression. We are for full freedom of conscience and religious preaching. We are not only for the liquidation of the exploitation of man by man, but also for the liquidation of the exploitation of man by the Party and the state. We are in favor of subordination of state policy to the interests of the free development of the human personality and the raising of the material and cultural living standard of the peoples. The happy life about which our enslavers shout is unthinkable until the elimination of the system of terror, force, and all forms of slave labor, until the monstrous concentration camps are removed—that shame and horror of our times, until the kolkhozes are broken up and the peasants are offered the right to choose their own form of agriculture.

The statement condemned as one of the most criminal acts of the Soviet regime "the coercion of the people's creative activity and the culture of the country":

> The once great Russian literature, music, art, science—all forms of manifesting the Russian genius—have been put in the service of an anti-

popular regime and stifled by the iron press of Party policy. Cultural values, accumulated for centuries, are being ruthlessly destroyed, and new bearers of culture are being destroyed even more ruthlessly. We raise our voice against this trampling down and crushing of culture.

With regard to foreign policy, the statement continued:

We who are living abroad clearly see the terrible danger threatening Russia and all humanity because of the greedy, aggressive foreign policy of Bolshevism. . . . All the Russian people living abroad are strongly influencing the foreign world by means of the press, speeches at meetings, and letters to government leaders in Europe and America that Communism and the Russian people are not one and the same, that the Russian people are secretly inimical to Communism and hate their enslavers.

These efforts have already borne some fruit. There are many signs that foreigners are beginning to understand this, and evidence of this is the message of the American Congress to the Russian people. But understanding it is not everything. In the minds of many people in the West, the peoples of Russia are still seen as bearers of the idea of world Communism and that external expansion which has made all free Western states stand up against our country. We must bear witness before all humanity that Communist aggression is not our cause, not our Russian cause, not the people's cause, but the handiwork of the Kremlin maniac who dreams of going down in history in an aureole as the spreader of Communism throughout the world. How much have our peoples endured and paid for as a result of the criminal Stalinist policy and his great experiments! But may all the defenders of the Russian land save us from the final reckoning: a third world war.

The Coordinating Center will always struggle for the liquidation of the Soviet Union's aggressive foreign policy and for a resolute refusal to recognize acts of this aggression. We are well aware that this can be achieved only by means of the overthrow of the Soviet regime and the liquidation of Bolshevism. It stands to reason that we cannot give you ready-made recipes and instruct you how to overthrow the hateful tyranny. When the decisive hour arrives, you yourselves will sense better than we can how you must act. But we who are here in freedom are convinced that the Soviet regime is concealing from its subjects a great deal which the whole world knows—secrets of the Kremlin, secrets of the MGB [predecessor of the KGB], secrets of foreign and domestic policy that are well known to a greater degree abroad than in the Soviet Union itself.

Free thought is so stifled that they do not let you speak. . . . Our task is to tell you about what you never will hear in the Soviet Union, to provide you with truthful information, and to help liberate you from that web with which Soviet propaganda is enveloping your souls. We know that it is forbidden to speak to a Russian person, that it is permitted to listen only to what pleases the regime. But one thing cannot be taken away—the possibility of thinking freely!

Listen to our radio station! Listen to the truthful voice of the Coordinating Center of the Anti-Bolshevik Struggle![3]

From the perspective of the 1990s, the militant tone of this broadcast is striking but not surprising. After all, the Radio was being financed by Americans who authorized a group of political émigrés to voice their opposition to the dictatorship. Even after the American sponsors decided a year later to reject that concept in order to exercise tighter control over what went on the air, it would be several years before the clarion call for "liberation" was muted, especially after the Soviet suppression of the Hungarian revolution of 1956 made it clear that the policy of "rolling back Communism" proclaimed by the Eisenhower administration was empty rhetoric. By 1959 the very name of Radio Liberation was changed to Radio Liberty.

Despite the shrill and sometimes apocalyptic prose of this inaugural program and similar broadcasts in the Radio's early days, many of its fundamental and enduring themes were already clear: the identification of the broadcasters with the listeners as fellow Russians; their obligation to bring truthful information to compatriots who were denied that opportunity by the regime; the unequivocal expression of the need for a democratic system to replace the Soviet Communist order; the condemnation of forced labor and collectivized agriculture; the condemnation of the dictatorship's taming of culture and imposition of censorship; the emphasis on the threat of Soviet aggression and another world war; the prediction that a regime that did not fulfill the needs and aspirations of its subjects was ultimately doomed. The broadcasts were in fact relatively restrained in that they avoided inciting listeners to rise up against the Kremlin rulers. The closest the Radio came to imparting such a message was to say "when the decisive hour comes," but we also insisted that it could not offer "ready-made recipes," and we left it to the Soviet peoples to determine how to act.

Our cautious approach resulted from the close cooperation of the émigré writers and editors with their American supervisors. Boris Shub, who had arrived from New York to help launch the broadcasts, was convinced that the Radio would be effective only to the extent that it did not promise more than it could deliver and that we must take into consideration the complex psychology of average Soviet citizens, who had many gripes against the regime but at the same time were proud of their homeland's victory over the Nazi invaders and suspicious of voices from the capitalist world abroad.

The news broadcast that followed the inaugural declaration led off with information meant to capture the interest of the audience: a dispatch from Washington reported the appointment of Charles Bohlen by President Eisenhower as the new ambassador to the Soviet Union. The item described Bohlen as fluent in Russian, having served as interpreter for the late President Franklin D. Roosevelt at the Teheran and Yalta conferences during World War II, and for President Truman at Potsdam. He was replacing George Kennan, described as "a well-known American diplomat who has an excellent command of Russian and is an expert on Russian culture and history."

We explained the change in ambassadors as the result of the Kremlin's demand that Kennan be recalled after a statement he made to the world press during a trip to Berlin in October 1952. He had asserted that the Stalin regime was making it impossible for Western diplomats to carry on normal social and cultural contacts with the Soviet population. Further, Kennan had compared the isolation with that of the interned diplomats in Nazi Germany after war with the United States broke out. The broadcast continued: "At the time, specialists on Soviet life expressed the opinion that the Kremlin had simply been looking for a pretext to demand his recall because his knowledge of the Russian language and well-known sympathy for the democratic aspirations of the Russian people made him an undesirable witness to Soviet reality." The dispatch then quoted from an article by Kennan published in *Foreign Affairs* in April 1951:

> The fact that national greatness exists is obvious. And there is no doubt that the Russian people possess that greatness. This is a people whose path from darkness and poverty was difficult and marked by enormous suffering and tragic failures. Nowhere in the world has the fire of faith in man's dignity and charity withstood such a struggle with the whirlwinds that strove to blow it out. And everyone who studies the struggle of the Russian soul during the course of centuries can only bow his head in admiration before the Russian people who managed to preserve that fire despite all the sacrifices and suffering.[4]

We informed the Soviet public that the Committee on Foreign Affairs of the House of Representatives had unanimously adopted Eisenhower's resolution condemning the Soviet Union for violating treaties signed during the war.

The newscast then turned to events in Paris, where a Russian biochemist named Sergei Vinogradsky had recently died at the age of ninety-six. Vinogradsky was a former director of an institute of experimental medicine in Petrograd (later Leningrad). "After the seizure of power by the Bolsheviks in 1917, he lived in France and was elected in 1924 to the French Academy of Sciences." The item conveyed the message that among the members of the Russian emigration were people who made a significant contribution to mankind after going abroad. The phrase "seizure of power," as well as "Bolshevik coup d'état," were used in the Radio broadcasts for many years in a conscious effort to avoid dignifying the October 1917 events as a popular revolution.

As additional evidence of the false claim of the Bolsheviks to represent the people, the Radio devoted the rest of the first broadcast to a commentary marking the anniversary of the Kronstadt uprising by sailors of the Baltic fleet in March 1921. Kronstadt, the great naval fortress near Leningrad (called Petrograd between 1914 and 1924), had originally been one of the early Bolshevik strongholds in 1917. Its sailors and workers had supported Lenin and his cause, but by 1921 they had become deeply disillusioned. When the workers of Petrograd went on strike to protest their desperate living conditions, martial law was imposed. In solidarity, the Kronstadt sailors and workers defied the regime and demanded "soviets without Communists." Lenin and Trotsky replied by declaring Kronstadt a city of counterrevolution, supporting their charge with fantastic lies. They ordered the fortress to surrender or to be taken by force of arms. The insurgents refused, Kronstadt was stormed, and in a sea of blood those who had fought for the Bolsheviks in 1917 were killed by the Bolsheviks.

The Radio brought out all the facts about the uprising, along with a dramatic account taken from the *Izvestiya* of the Kronstadt rebels, the daily newspaper they printed and circulated during the days of the struggle. With our access to archives in the public and private libraries of the West, we were able to restore historical truth by providing listeners with these and many other "missing pages," or "blank spots," as the Soviet media later called them in Gorbachev's era. The commemoration of events in Russian and Soviet history, which were ignored or distorted by the Soviet media, became a permanent feature of RL programming during the next four decades. The truth about Kronstadt was finally revealed to the Russian population in 1994, and Yeltsin's government pardoned the insurgents.

I was exhilarated by the report from Munich that our first broadcast had already been pounced on by the Soviet jammers. Clearly, the regime was aware of us and was determined to prevent the people from being exposed to any information, particularly from "traitors" abroad, that deviated from the official propaganda line. At the time, the aggressive spirit of the RL statement did not bother me, since I fancied myself a "Cold Warrior" actively engaged in a rather heroic struggle against a formidable dictatorship. Shortly after Stalin's death, when my friend Abraham Brumberg of the U.S. Information Agency visited our NYPS office during a visit from Washington, I predicted to him that the Soviet regime would not last much longer. He chuckled at my naive enthusiasm.

The introduction that Boris Shub planned for the first day of the Radio's Russian broadcasts illustrates his flair for the dramatic. Listeners would hear the ticking of a clock followed by a solemn voice intoning, "Today, Josef Vissarionovich Stalin is 73 years, 2 months and 9 days old [pause and more ticking]. . . . The time of Stalin is drawing to a close." The plan was to open each subsequent day's broadcast with the same reminder of the "immortal" Stalin's mortality. However, after a dry run of the announcement in January, it was vetoed by those who argued that it would bore the listeners if it were repeated day after day, perhaps for several years. Who could predict that Stalin's time would abruptly end within a few days after Radio Liberation went on the air?

Actually, this was not just a clever gimmick on Shub's part, but rather it derived from his instinctive feeling that, as he told his brother Anatole at the time, "this guy's on his last legs." Based on various signs that Shub's sharp political antenna picked up, such as recent photographs of Stalin, his unexplained absence at some ceremony, and Malenkov's delivering a report in his place, Boris considered it entirely appropriate to suggest that the leader's days were numbered.

Moscow Radio informed the world of Stalin's impending death on March 3, and he died two days later. Boris sent an urgent message from Munich asking that I cable him immediately the names of the people who had been pallbearers at Lenin's funeral in January 1924. He planned to mount a program that consisted of reciting the names of the Bolshevik leaders—Bukharin, Kamenev, Zinoviev, et al.—who were vilified in the Soviet press for years and finally tried and executed as traitors during Stalin's purges of 1936–38. The implicit message of the program was to remind the audience that the despot's victims were loyal comrades-in-arms of Lenin.

Our research archives in the office were still far from complete, so Mikhail Koriakov and I went to the Slavic section of the New York Public Library for the information. The program broadcast later that week consisted of a solemn roll call of each of Lenin's pallbearers, followed by a statement about his fate (for example, "Bukharin, Nikolai Ivanovich . . . executed in 1938").

If there is any word that best characterizes the programming policy the Radio developed under Boris Shub and continued by his successors, it is *glasnost*. Long before Gorbachev encouraged Soviet media to fill in the "blank spots" of censorship (although the truth about the past remained selective, despite the Communist reformer's vaunted claim of openness), glasnost was the driving force of several Radio series prepared in New York. For example, "Missing Pages," mentioned earlier, was devoted to restoring taboo writings of prerevolutionary publicists, banned Bolsheviks, and anti-Stalin social democrats. Shub drew on the expertise of his father, as well as that of Boris Nicolaevsky, the renowned Menshevik historian, and Mark Vishniak, a *Time* magazine editor. Vishniak had been secretary of the ill-fated Constituent Assembly, which Lenin dispersed in January 1918 after his Bolsheviks received only 25 percent of the votes. Boris instructed his writers never to "get even" with the Soviet regime or to incite listeners to foolhardy action; the Radio should reach not only the citizens who hated the regime, but also those who were defensive and apologetic yet disturbed by the obvious discrepancy between the regime's propaganda and the reality surrounding them, which was marked by continued stifling of creativity and the poor quality of everyday life.

The Radio later serialized Boris Pasternak's *Doctor Zhivago* as soon as the original Russian became available in the West. Early postrevolutionary satire by Mikhail Zoshchenko, and Yevgeni Zamyatin's *We*, his pre-Orwellian vision of a future totalitarian society, was broadcast. Shub produced a suspenseful radio adaptation of Arthur Koestler's *Darkness at Noon*, to the accompaniment of Beethoven's "Appassionata" sonata, which Lenin admitted had moved but unnerved him because it evoked "bourgeois" emotions ill befitting a hard-boiled Marxist revolutionary.

Mikhail Koriakov was one of the most innovative of our NYPS writers. A newspaperman in his hometown in Siberia before the war, he served in the Soviet army as a captain. Disillusioned with the Stalinist regime, he defected to the West while attached to the embassy in Paris, came to the

United States, and later joined the Radio. He quickly adapted his journalistic skill, and for the next twenty years he turned out thousands of "radiogenic" programs written for the ear—that is, short, pithy sentences that could be caught through the jamming, with frequent variations on the principal theme of any given script. During the course of his writing feature scripts, he proposed a series he called "Glasnost," years before anyone had heard of Mikhail Gorbachev. Like any well-educated Russian, Koriakov knew the positive associations of that word in nineteenth-century Russian liberal publicistic writings. His programs were devoted to underscoring the importance of openness as the prerequisite of a civil society.

Another series Koriakov created was inspired when he read a letter the Radio received in the early 1960s. (Soviet listeners sent mail to Western "accommodation" addresses, which we regularly broadcast.) A sixteen-year-old listener in Serpukhov, near Moscow, praised the Radio, then added: "Listening to you makes me want to know more about our history. Could you put on a program that you would call 'Russia Yesterday, Today, and Tomorrow'?" Koriakov came into my office with a copy of this letter and, with his usual ebullience, suggested that he respond to the young man's request by starting such a series. That program became a permanent fixture of the schedule and endured into the 1990s, many years after Koriakov left the Radio and the Soviet Union left the world stage.

Shortly after Radio Liberation went on the air, we created a musical signal that would identify the Russian program in the minds of the listeners and help home in on the frequency as the sharp tones penetrated the jamming. Boris led the search for an appropriate tune. Yuri Petrovich Denicke suggested the theme from Borodin's opera, *Prince Igor,* that accompanies the words "O, daite, daite mnye svobodu" ("Oh, grant me, grant me liberty"). In hindsight, this would have been an excellent choice, since Radio Liberation was destined to become Radio Liberty within a few years. However, another old melody was selected, less well known but equally resonant in its musical and psychological impact: "Hymn to Free Russia," written by Alexander Grechaninov, who emigrated from Russia in 1917 and lived to the age of ninety in New York. The composer had taken the words from a poem by Konstantin Balmont written not to celebrate the Bolshevik victory but earlier, at the time of the short-lived democratic revolution of February 1917 that replaced the centuries-old Romanov monarchy with the Provisional Government under Alexander Kerensky.

The opening words to the tune were "Da zdravstvuyet Rossiya, svobodnaya strana" ("Long live Russia, a free country"), and the music was

played on a celesta to achieve maximum clarity, although many instru-
mental variations and tempos were subsequently employed, including a
full orchestra. For thirty-eight years, millions of Soviet listeners to the Russian service throughout the USSR heard that signal many times during the
day and night, and while ignorant of its provenance, it meant for them the
"free voice" beaming in from the outside world. Long after the Cold War,
the theme is still being used.

Non-Russian Services

Broadcasts in other languages of the peoples of the Soviet Union began
on March 18, 1953, in Armenian, Azerbaijani, Georgian, and several North
Caucasian tongues, including Chechen and Ingush.[5] The languages of
Soviet Central Asia were represented by Uzbek, Kazakh, Kirghiz, Turkmen, and Tajik. Broadcasts in Tatar-Bashkir began in December 1953.
Ukrainian and Belorussian were not yet included among the non-Russian
languages in which the Radio broadcast in the first year; they were inaugurated in 1954. The editors and writers on each language "desk" adopted
the general line of the Radio, calling for liberation from the Kremlin dictatorship and for presentation of truthful news from abroad and from inside
the Soviet Union. In addition, of course, each desk tried to reflect the special needs and interests of their ethnic brothers and sisters. The first Radio
Liberation broadcast in Ukrainian, on August 16, 1954, expressed this spirit:

> Dear brothers and sisters! Ukrainians!
> Today, for the first time, we address you over Radio Liberation. We
> live abroad, but our hearts and thoughts are with you always. No iron
> curtain can separate us or obstruct that. Today is a day of joy for us, for
> over the air our vibrant word of greeting, joy, and hope will reach you.
> Over one million of us Ukrainians are living abroad. For a long time
> we have been telling people in the free world the truth about life in our
> country. The beginning Ukrainian broadcasts over Radio Liberation
> entrust us with a new task. We shall speak *to* you and *for* you, fellow coun-
> trymen, because there in our homeland you have neither freedom, nor
> a democratic press, nor a free radio.
> Wherever we may be, . . . our paths all converge toward our own
> Kiev and the towns and villages of the Ukraine. . . . Kiev Rus, which
> became the cradle of our Ukrainian national existence, was an impor-
> tant cultural center, the focus of ancient democratic freedoms in East-

ern Europe. Through Kiev, the "mother of Russian cities," our culture spread to all corners of Eastern Europe. Later, in Khmelnytsky's time [the seventeenth century], the Cossacks gave the Ukraine glamour and might.

In the fire and storm of the Revolution of 1917, the Ukraine was reestablished as an independent state. Our people, longing to be masters of their own destiny in their own country, proclaimed the Ukrainian Democratic Republic. That was done in a democratic way—the manifestation of the sovereign will of the Ukrainian nation. It took place in accordance with the principles of self-determination of peoples. But the Ukrainian Democratic Republic fell victim to Bolshevist aggression. To deceive the Ukrainian people, to persuade them that nothing had happened, the aggressors converted the Ukrainian Democratic Republic into the Ukrainian Soviet Socialist Republic, which the Communist dictatorship made an instrument of oppression of the Ukrainian people.

In the struggle against Communism, our native land has made great sacrifices on the altar of liberation. But we have faith in God's justice. We are convinced that those sacrifices were not made in vain and that God will reward the Ukraine for all her sufferings. The struggle of the Ukrainian people will achieve their purpose.

And you, the Ukrainian people, "master in your house," will take your seat in the "circle of free peoples." The words of Taras Hryhorovych Shevchenko [the beloved Ukrainian national poet of the nineteenth century] will come true: "And there will be a son, and there will be a mother, and there will be justice on earth." Because "in our house there is truth, and strength, and the will for freedom."[6]

Unlike the Slavic services, which could be checked more easily by qualified Americans, it was almost impossible in the Radio's early days to monitor the content and tone of broadcasts in the exotic languages of Central Asia and the Caucasus. Unbridled anti-Soviet—and anti-Russian—invective undoubtedly reached the airwaves. Indeed, it took many more months before the relationship between the American sponsors and the émigré broadcasters was more clearly defined in favor of tighter American control. I soon learned who really was behind Radio Liberation.

"Comrade, why didn't you show up at the last meeting of the Party?"

"If I had known it was the last meeting, I sure would have been there."

 ## 3 THE SPARKS BEGIN TO KINDLE

When I joined Radio Liberation in the fall of 1952, I was told that the parent organization, Amcomlib, was a private company, although I had heard rumors that it was a "CIA outfit." The CIA did not yet have the negative reputation it later acquired when its many rogue elephant activities were revealed. Even if it were clandestinely involved, I thought, there was nothing unsavory about working for an agency dedicated to combating the Stalinist one-party dictatorship. My experience in Munich during 1950–51 interviewing displaced persons from Stalin's country had left me with a deep sympathy and clear appreciation of the suffering of émigrés, exiles, and defectors. Some people may have thought that we had a lot of gall to mix in the affairs of another country, but I felt that I was embarking on a crusade, assisting victims of Communism who could reach their brothers and sisters by radio with truthful information and spiritual sustenance.

After a few weeks at work, my curiosity

got the better of me, and I asked Boris point-blank whether there was any CIA connection. He bristled and indignantly barked at me, "That's a very indiscreet question!" His overreaction convinced me, but nothing further was said until exactly six months after I had joined Amcomlib.

It was March 17, 1953, and I was working in a crowded loft on West Forty-seventh Street, in the heart of the diamond district, a street more reminiscent of the old world than of fashionable Fifth Avenue around the corner. Shub and I, together with the staff of émigré writers, had been segregated from Amcomlib headquarter's WASPy executive and administrative staff on East Forty-fifth Street. The reason for separating us may have been security, because there were confidential documents on the premises. Or perhaps it reflected a latent prejudice against the "Russkies."

Ted Steele, the assistant to Admiral Stevens, then president of Amcomlib, asked me to come to the main office. I snaked my way through the St. Patrick's Day parade that was marching down Fifth Avenue and entered Steele's office. He greeted me with a grin on his ruddy face and said, "Gene, I have good news and bad news for you." My first thought was what kind of bad news. That I had not passed the security check? This was difficult to believe, since I had served with distinction in Naval Communications Intelligence in Washington, handling "top-secret" codes and ciphers in Japanese and sharing in the unit citation we were awarded by the secretary of the navy at the end of the war. Steele quickly explained, "The good news is that you passed the security check. The bad news is that you are now going to be made 'witting.'" I guessed what was coming. He confirmed that Amcomlib and the radio station under its control were indeed "assets" of the CIA, which received funds from annual appropriations of the U.S. Congress, secretly disbursed with the knowledge of only a few senators and representatives on the Hill. Steele requested that I sign a paper pledging that I would not reveal this secret. I kept the faith, with one exception: I told Gloria.

In the first two decades of the Radio's existence, before the American public at large learned of the government's involvement, I lectured before various social and academic groups and described us as a private operation. I was uncomfortable concealing our CIA connection, but I believed that the deception was justified if it protected us from Soviet efforts to undermine our mission.

However, I found it especially distasteful in April 1961, when our handlers in Langley, Virginia, requested that I fly to Cornell University with Valerian Obolensky and Isaac Patch to speak with Urie Bronfenbrenner, an expert on Soviet education. Bronfenbrenner had traveled to the Soviet Union on grants from the Human Ecology Fund, which he learned was covertly supported by the CIA. After he visited Radio Liberty in Munich, our supersensitive sponsors became concerned that he might also connect us to the Agency and wanted us to allay any suspicions.

We spent the better part of a day with Bronfenbrenner and some of his colleagues, acquainting them with our activity and our admirable goals, and we went home satisfied that we had scotched any further repercussions. Indeed, nothing further occurred. Nevertheless, I could not help seeing the anomaly of working for a medium that was communicating "THE TRUTH" to the Soviet peoples while we were lying to our own people. Coincidentally, when we went for lunch in the Cornell faculty club, we watched President John F. Kennedy on the television screen addressing the nation concerning his embarrassing anti-Castro fiasco in the Bay of Pigs. I was secretly more embarrassed at my own performance.

After the government's involvement in our operation finally became common knowledge, it was easier for me to lecture without having to pretend that we were a private organization. I never encountered any hostility, although once when I entered the classroom at Colorado College in Colorado Springs I saw on the blackboard an admonition scrawled in chalk: "Don't come—it's CIA." Ironically, it occurred many years after the CIA connection ended.

In 1971, Senator Clifford Case blew the cover and demanded that Radio Free Europe and Radio Liberty be funded openly by Congress if we were deemed worthy of being continued. Senator J. William Fulbright, on the other hand, argued that the Radios be terminated as "relics of the Cold War" (see Chapter 9). This aroused vigorous protests in the American press, and President Richard Nixon appointed a special commission of inquiry, headed by Milton Eisenhower, which concluded that the free flow of information from these radios should be maintained in the long-range interests of American foreign policy. In 1976 the Radios merged and continued to be funded by Congress. A newly created Board for International Broadcasting (BIB), whose members were distinguished Americans appointed by the U.S. president, was charged with overseeing the operations of the newly merged RFE/RL Inc.

Like most Amcomlib employees, I was never directly connected with the CIA. In fact, only a handful of the executives were actually CIA staffers during the years before all ties with the agency were severed. Nevertheless, I was to a certain extent caught up in the conspiratorial atmosphere of the early days. Shortly after I was made "witting" (a favorite word of the spooks), I was asked to sign a hush-hush document in which I was assigned a pseudonym, Alden Goheen, a name I imagined they had plucked out of a London telephone book. I can't recall just what I was supposed to do with this *nom de guerre froide,* but the whole idea was scrapped within a short time. On a few occasions I did visit the CIA headquarters in Langley, Virginia, and also debriefed a couple of Russian defectors in safe houses in Washington, D.C., and Connecticut.

One employee of the committee, Elizabeth (Beb) Pond, was brought into the inner family of witting staff members but refused to sign the pledge of secrecy and promptly resigned, asserting that it was against her moral principles. Beb later joined the *Christian Science Monitor* staff and went to Moscow as their correspondent, where she filed splendid dispatches.

A Visit to the Radio's Munich Headquarters

In the spring of 1954, I went back to Munich, this time as a member of Radio Liberation's New York staff to work for a few weeks at the center of broadcasting operations. The president of Amcomlib was still Admiral Stevens, who had a deep love for Russia, its land, history, culture, and literature. He wrote about his experiences in his book *Russian Assignment.* He was a dignified, courtly person, and I enjoyed the brief period of his tenure.

On the eve of my departure, Stevens made two requests: go to the U.S. Army PX in Munich (where RL employees could still shop) and buy him a bottle of his wife's favorite perfume. The other was to act as courier. He handed me a confidential document that, he explained, could not be entrusted to the international mail. It contained his (and presumably the CIA's) instructions to the American executives in Munich to curtail the status of the Radio as the mouthpiece of the Coordinating Center of the Anti-Bolshevik Struggle.

When the Center was established in 1951, Amcomlib quoted Eugene Lyons's hyperbolic description of the event as "historic" and "of tremendous importance" because it would "strike fear in the hearts of Stalin and his Politburo" when they learned that refugees from the Soviet prison state, despite different political convictions and nationalities, were capable of uniting in the struggle to break the "red chains" holding their countries. "The Kremlin will not be able to conceal this news from their much suffering subjects, who will be given hope for ultimate liberation from their hated yoke."[1]

To achieve that aim, Amcomlib had established Radio Liberation as the voice of the Coordinating Center and invested it with a large degree of autonomy. It became clear, however, within a year of the initial broadcasts, that the deep-seated ethnic tension and enmity among the disparate groups of political émigrés was resulting in uncoordination. The Center split into two hostile "coordinating centers," each claiming legitimacy; one represented the Russian organizations, and the other spoke for the heterogeneous national minority groups. Amcomlib received brickbats from extremists on both sides: the Russian nationalists accused the Americans of wishing to "dismember" Russia by favoring the separatist aspirations of the nationalities, while the non-Russians charged that Amcomlib was a tool in the hands of "Russian chauvinists." Tighter U.S. control was necessary, and that was the import of the message I carried to Robert F. Kelley, deputy to Admiral Stevens in Europe.

Kelley deserves special praise for his contribution to the Radio. In his role of Amcomlib's senior representative in Munich, almost from the time the Radio went on the air until the mid-1970s, "Uncle Bob" Kelley, as he was affectionately (and secretly) called by his subordinates, was a wise and benevolent supervisor of our operation, as well as of the Institute for the Study of the USSR. A graduate of Harvard magna cum laude, and of the Sorbonne, he had been the head of the State Department's Division of Eastern European Affairs (commonly known as the Russian Division) almost from its inception in 1924 until 1937, when it was suddenly (and stupidly) abolished shortly after the politically unsophisticated Joseph E. Davies became U.S. ambassador to the Soviet Union. In his supervisory position, Kelley encouraged the careers of several young diplomats who later became experts in the Russian language and Soviet affairs, among them two future ambassadors to Moscow: George F. Kennan and Charles Bohlen.[2] Kelley was not only a diplomat but also a scholar in Russian language and history, as well as an astute observer of the contemporary Soviet scene. He mingled easily with Westerners and Soviet émigrés and tried hard to reconcile the various warring factions in Munich's multinational emigration. He carried out Amcomlib's instructions, and by the time Howland H. Sargeant took over as president in October 1954, the brief era of authority of the Coordinating Center had yielded permanently to direct American control of the Radio, although the Center nominally continued for a short time.

Throughout the years of its existence, the Radio operated with minimum interference from Washington. Its remarkable independence was due in great measure to the personality and efforts of Howland Sargeant. Having served in Washington in the late 1940s as assistant secretary of state for public affairs under Harry Truman and Dean Acheson, Sargeant came to Amcomlib's headquarters in New York with the experience of a bureaucrat combined with deep appreciation of intellectual creativity. (Like President Bill Clinton many years later, Sargeant studied at Oxford University in England in the 1930s as a Rhodes scholar.) He remained at the helm until 1975, during the years of the Radio's transformation into Radio Liberty, nurturing its growth into a powerful network with several 250,000-watt transmitters beaming news and feature programs (political, economic, cultural, historical, religious, satirical, musical) into the Soviet Union.

Sargeant was determined that the Radio never be exploited or manipulated by American propagandists who might try to turn it into a "gray" or "black" operation to achieve some short-range tactical purpose. He was equally resolved that it not be used as a mouthpiece for vengeful émigrés to promote their own political programs on the air, thereby alienating many listeners who sought to make up their own minds about their future on the basis of full access to a broad spectrum of information and ideas. The government sponsors and Amcomlib's board of trustees firmly supported Sargeant's clearcut directive to the Radio: convey to listeners the genuine feelings of sympathy and friendship of Americans, but always speak to them from the viewpoint of Soviet citizens' genuine needs and interests. This approach also served the interests of the American people, because the evolution to democracy in the land of their chief adversary would reduce the threat of nuclear war between the superpowers and contribute to world peace. Sargeant was backed by Allen Dulles, director of the CIA, and his successor, Richard Helms. They and Cord Meyer, their principal officer responsible for supervising RFE and RL, appreciated that the effectiveness of the Radios could be vitiated by micromanagement from Langley.[3]

The Soviet Empire Strikes Back

In the twenty-one months between March 1953 and December 1954, the Soviet regime had maintained strict silence about the existence of the Radio. However, the uninterrupted jamming of the station offered evidence that the Kremlin was fully aware of us and was making every effort to drown us out. As mentioned earlier, thanks to the peculiarities of shortwave propagation via the ionosphere and to the steadily increasing power of the transmitters, the censors were never completely successful.

Jamming was accompanied by terrorism in the autumn of 1954, when two of our émigré staffers were found dead. In September, the body of Leonid Karas, a Belorussian writer, was found in the Isar River near Munich. Two months later, Abo Fatalibey, chief of the Azerbaijani desk, was garroted in his apartment by a suspected Soviet agent. Although the Karas case was never solved, the Radio also ascribed it to the KGB.[4] Other émigrés received telephone calls and letters from family members inside the Soviet Union who urged them to stop working for the enemy and to come home. The language of these entreaties was similar enough to convince us that Moscow Center controlled the operation.

Radio staff members were naturally very shaken by this grim evidence of the Soviet regime's interest in our operation. The émigrés in Munich were especially unnerved to realize that the KGB could reach into West Germany and threaten their safety outside the Communist orbit. Of course, a security system had been set up on the Radio's premises, but it was difficult if not impossible to protect everyone in his home or on the streets of the city. When I worked for four years at the Radio in Munich in the late 1960s, I was warned by one of the Russian writers, himself a former Soviet camp inmate, that I too should be careful. At first I dismissed his remark as overly alarmist, but a few days later, while driving the Opel sedan assigned to me by the Radio's motor pool, I pricked my finger on something sharp on the steering wheel. Until the cut healed, I was positively paranoid, thinking that I really was a target of the KGB.

Even in New York, my friend and colleague Volodya Yurasov often told me that he slept with a revolver under his pillow. After escaping from the gulag, he served in the Soviet army with false papers and defected to the West after the war. Back home, he was condemned to death in absentia and always feared reprisals at the hands of the KGB. Although Volodya lived until the age of eighty-two, he continued to blame his chronic gastrointestinal problems on a lunch in New York City years before, where he was convinced Soviet agents had poisoned him. But he broadcast on the Radio for almost thirty years, projecting his charismatic personality in interviews with émigrés who had succeeded in various fields. On occasion, I appeared at the microphone in his "Guest of the Week" series, discussing with him the various scholarly conferences on Soviet affairs I attended.[5]

After twenty months of oblique indications of the Soviet regime's antagonism to the Radio, the first overt reaction to our broadcasts occurred in December 1954, at the time of the Soviet Writers' Congress. The station had begun discussing the forthcoming meeting as early as July 4 with a broadcast entitled "Writers in Uniform" that reviewed the crushing of the arts under the dictatorship since the first Writers' Congress in 1934. Later in the year, the Radio reported that the 1954 Nobel Prize for Literature had been awarded to Ernest Hemingway, but added that the Swedish Academy had also considered two émigré Russian writers for the prestigious award: Boris Zaitsev and Mark Aldanov. The program made the point that these and other Russian writers abroad were more representative of Russian literature than works produced by Party fiat.

A regular feature of the broadcasts in the early years was a message to the Soviet armed forces. On the eve of the Writers' Congress, the Radio told them that the writers gathering in Moscow were merely "rubber-stamp speakers" who created "literary indoctrination courses." These sharp criticisms were supplemented by a series of messages from well-known émigré and American writers.[6] The gist of their statements was to emphasize their commitment to freedom of expression and to express their hope that writers in Russia would some day "again enrich us with their wisdom and genius," as Thornton Wilder asserted.

Upton Sinclair's pithy message declared that in his sixty years as a writer he had said what he pleased and that "no government authority has ever told me what to say." He added: "Can any of you Soviet writers say that?"

We asked for a statement from poet and publicist Max Eastman, whose radical politics had attracted him to the Bolshevik revolution. Eastman lived in Russia in the early 1920s, was close to Trotsky, and developed a lifelong hatred for Stalin. After he returned to the United States, he was among the most articulate critics of the Soviet regime.

I went to Eastman's apartment in Greenwich Village in downtown Manhattan to record his statement. He was tall and imposing, with a shock of white hair. (I could imagine him wrestling with Hemingway in the famous altercation they had in 1937 in the editorial office of Maxwell Perkins of Charles Scribner's Sons. The incident was given a *Rashomon*-like spin in that Eastman treated it differently in his memoirs from the way Hemingway's biographers handled it.) As I listened to Eastman contrast the plight of contemporary Russian writers with their nineteenth-century literary forebears, who despite czarist censorship produced "some of the greatest works the world has seen," I wondered how the Soviet officials would react to his and similar sentiments from the West.

Eastman concluded by telling the Soviet writers that they "seem to be in the position of the *katorzhniki* [exiled convicts] to whom, after the Decembrist revolution [in St. Petersburg in 1825], Pushkin addressed his beautiful poem *Message to Siberia."* He continued: "I think I can best express my feelings to the Congress of Soviet Writers by quoting Pushkin's matchless words." He was referring to a stirring sixteen-line poem the Russian poet sent in 1827 to one of the Decembrists by slipping it into the hands of the prisoner's wife as she left to rejoin her husband in exile. Pushkin counsels patience and courage in the face of adversity in the depths of the Siberian mines, holding out hope that the time would come when the heavy chains would fall and freedom would welcome the convicts.[7] Eastman recited Pushkin's classic in his own excellent translation into English. (He had learned Russian well and had married Elena Krylenko, the sister of the Soviet Commissar of Justice, equivalent to our Attorney General.) In the actual broadcast, his voice was faded into the background, and a Radio announcer read the Russian verses familiar to every educated Soviet citizen.

Just as Eastman captured the symbolism of Pushkin's message for contemporary Soviet writers, John Dos Passos focused on the relevance of nineteenth-century Russian literature today:

> While the classics of Russian literature remain on the shelves of their libraries, the peoples of the Soviet Union will never be able to be cut off entirely from the republic of humane letters. No matter how thoroughly the fanatics of the official Marxist dogma build their prison of terror and hate, the Russian classics will forever be opening windows into the real world. It is possible to hope that the writers of the Soviet Union, as the writers of West Germany did after the collapse of the Hitlerite nightmare, will someday emerge out of the long night of oppression. When they do, they will find friends to greet them.

The émigré writers who sent messages to the Writers' Congress offered their "inside" perspective. Alexandra Tolstoy said:

> Having learned of the Writers' Congress in Moscow, as a daughter of Leo Tolstoy I would like to share my thoughts with you. . . . No matter what Soviet propagandists tell you about censorship in [czarist] times, it was child's play compared with what we see now. What is done to literature in Soviet Russia cannot even be called censorship. It is the total enslavement of literary creation. True enough, even in my father's time, certain of his religious and philosophical writings were subject to censorship. Thus, "I Cannot Be Silent," an article by my father against the death penalty, was banned. But what happened? Hundreds of thou-

sands of copies of this article were distributed not only throughout Russia but throughout the world. . . . Not only was Tolstoy not arrested, he was not even exiled from Russia. Let some Soviet citizen write an article like that now—not against the Soviet government but solely against the death penalty. At the very least, he would be sent to a concentration camp!

Madame Tolstoy displayed an understanding of the pressures exerted on Soviet writers, whose "true feelings must be read between the lines" in order to separate them from the "blatant, vicious propaganda." She acknowledged that frequently, particularly during World War II, "we have been touched by sparks of genuine creation from Russian writers and poets." In the spirit of her father's religious fervor, she urged them to heed his advice and fulfill the will of God by serving and loving the people, and then concluded:

> Tolstoy said, "Literature, like a lens, should focus light to awaken the best in men." And Pushkin wrote, "When the word of God / Penetrates the inner ear, / The poet's soul will rouse itself / Like an eagle stirred from sleep."
>
> Eagles can be found in Russia today, but their wings are fettered. Yet there is an end to everything; there will also be an end to the Communist dictatorship. Our Russian writers and poets will spread their wings and carry Russian literature anew to the heights.

From Paris, Boris Zaitsev saluted his fellow writers and reminded them:

> In 1922, when I was president of the Moscow Writers' Union, such congresses had not been held. Much time has passed since then. Today you and we find ourselves in different worlds. You have a homeland, you have our great people, your youth and strength. But we have freedom! We write as we please. We Russian writers abroad may live modestly, but our freedom is not limited. Perhaps you live in riches and plenty, but you also live in servitude. From the bottom of my heart I wish that you at this Congress may make at least the first step toward freedom, for one cannot do without it in our craft. . . . And so, God grant that those of you who have been given talent may find the opportunity to cultivate it freely, without coercion.

This barrage of messages from writers in the West condemning censorship and calling for freedom of creativity must have infuriated the Soviet authorities and compelled them to counterattack openly. In his concluding speech at the Writers' Congress, Alexei Surkov, first secretary of the Union of Soviet Writers, supplied us with proof that we were getting through the jamming and getting under the skins of the Party bosses. As reported in the Soviet media, he declared: "The enemies of our country and our literature are not silent. On the occasion of our Congress, the White émigré, Boris Zaitsev, was dragged out of the literary trash basket to babble poisonous words of impotent malice over a White Guard microphone."[8] Surkov also assailed James T. Farrell and the American Committee for Cultural Freedom, an anti-Communist organization of three hundred writers, scientists, artists, and scholars headed by Farrell and including John Steinbeck, Robert Penn Warren, and Thomas Hart Benton.

In Munich and New York, we all felt gratified that the regime had finally lashed out against us, even if the name of the station was not openly uttered. We interpreted it as a sign that the Soviets could no longer remain passive in the face of this threatening competition from the Radio for the attention of their citizens. Clearly, Soviet writers must have been among our listeners if the Writers' Congress was used as the forum for discrediting the Radio. Note their attempt to dismiss Zaitsev—a productive Russian writer respected in the West—as a "White" émigré (that is, pro-monarchy) who was now "babbling" over a radio allegedly run by the "White Guard."

Surkov did not directly name the Radio. The first mention in Moscow's central press appeared on April 17, 1955, when *Izvestiya* wrote, "Radio 'Liberation' is an organ for the dissemination of filthy falsifications and black slander, invented by American intelligence and directed against the creative achievements of democratic peoples." This was not only an attack on us; it also seemed to be a thinly veiled threat aimed at the Soviet audience.

Thus began several decades of vituperation and distortions against the Radio in the Soviet media, and our dossier of these regime reactions grew thicker every year. However, we were not satisfied that the Kremlin had moved from jamming our signal, thereby indirectly acknowledging our effectiveness, to outright vilification. There was no doubt that we were infuriating the Soviet officials, and of course we were delighted. But they were not our principal intended audience. If our long-range mission was to drive a wedge between the regime and its subjects, to sow doubts about the Kremlin's claims to represent their best interests, and to offer positive democratic alternatives to a sterile ideology, we had to have a much clearer answer to the question of who our listeners were.

For almost two years the Radio had, as it were, shot its arrows into the air with only the jamming and harassment of our Munich émigrés serving as proof that at least the enemy was aware of us. After the Surkov speech, we could make some tentative conclusions. The establishment in Moscow had decided that enough people were aware of our existence to risk public attention. In addition to the writers, we made some general assumptions about the composition of our audience: shortwave listeners were more likely to be better educated, including intellectuals, skilled workers, students, even Party and government bureaucrats, all of them "seekers" of information and ideas outside the narrow spectrum of official censorship. The odds were that more men than women listened, since the latter were preoccupied with the many daily chores that their spouses disdained. More of them were likely to live in urban rather than rural farming areas, owning shortwave sets or relying on trusted friends to brief them confidentially on the latest broadcasts. The age range was uncertain but probably could be represented by a bell curve, with children and the elderly at the extremes.

To determine the composition of our audience more precisely, in our daily broadcasts we asked listeners to write letters to innocent-sounding addresses in West Berlin and other cities on the other side of the Iron Curtain. We urged the audience to make sure that their correspondence did not arouse the suspicion of the censors, and we launched the project only after we estimated that the volume of mail going back and forth to the Soviet Union after Stalin's death had increased to the extent that their letters might slip through undetected.

Not many letters came to us in the early years, but patterns emerged. Some letters clearly reflected the official propaganda line of the regime and may have been concocted by the KGB or simply written by indignant ideologists. A lathe worker from Tambov wrote: "You are traitors to the Russian people, and you have no business mourning over Russia. If you traitors intend to invade the land of the Soviets again, you'll get what you deserve. And this time don't expect any pity!"[9]

Other letters revealed a direct connection with the Committee for the Return to the Homeland, which was established in East Berlin late in 1955 to exhort émigrés over their own radio station. A certain Igor Sizov wrote: "You, my dear friends, cleared out of Russia and you're living it up all over the world. Better ask for permission to return to us. Maybe our government will take you back, and you can work honestly with our people."

Letters with an anti-Soviet tone were often unsigned, like one from Minsk that sent regards to Pylayev / Oktyabrev, the satirist. Others requested that we acknowledge receipt by broadcasting something they chose, such as a favorite song. A letter from Mogilev in Moldavia began by saying that "not one Soviet citizen believes your slander," but later, perhaps hoping that the censor was less attentive, he added: "Yes, there are those here who believe your slander." A correspondent from Lvov in the Ukraine wrote: "You should not be tempted to return to the motherland. Life here goes on as before and nothing has changed since you left." Letters of praise for the Radio's work were often worded cryptically: "Extremely grateful for your nice letters. Your relatives will be very happy to learn that you are young and strong enough to work hard and successfully for yourselves and for the common cause."

Through this feedback from thousands of letters received over the years, we were able to confirm the presence of a widespread audience inside the Soviet Union with various viewpoints about the content of our messages. In explaining our solicitation of letters in publicity releases, we said that we welcomed the dialogue, but added that the Radio "does not want or intend to provoke our listening friends to resort precipitously to anti-Soviet acts which would only doom them." We hoped to change their way of thinking gradually, to have them reevaluate their values and convictions so that "one fine day the Soviet government, deprived of its support and prospects, will itself die off."

From the mid-1950s on, the Radio sought to establish a bridge to our Soviet listeners over the heads of the authorities. Political and academic leaders in the West welcomed the opportunity to participate in the effort, and the Radio earned a reputation for credibility among its growing Soviet public by discussing imperfections in American society, and its distinctive profile was beginning to take shape.

Norman Thomas, who had been the American Socialist Party candidate for U.S. president six times, spoke frankly about the social injustices in the United States as well as abroad. After one of his interviews in our studio, he said to me with a broad grin, "You can't say that over the Voice of America!"

There was a contest in Moscow for the best joke.

First prize was three years in Siberia.

4 A BRIDGE OF IDEAS BETWEEN WEST AND EAST

The Radio's electronic bridge from the West carried not only news and feature programs but also special programs. Each focused on a central theme discussed by Western European experts and émigrés. The first of these series, pegged to the Soviet Writers' Congress, had proved successful in rallying writers in the West to call for freedom of artistic creativity. Our New York section created similar campaigns under Boris Shub's leadership, and as his deputy I was responsible for mounting them.

Among the vulnerabilities of the Soviet regime that we believed we could exploit were such themes as the need for education free of ideological compulsion and the right of workers to be free of the scourge of forced labor. In its official propaganda, the Soviet Union kept boasting that its system of free education was the best in the world, that its level of literacy was higher than in many capitalist countries, and that its workers enjoyed optimum working conditions with full employment and security provided by a solicitous government and benevolent Party, making it superfluous to go out on strike. The national anthem that the Soviet citizen sang proclaimed: "I know no other land like ours where a person breathes so freely."

The truth was that, despite the high quality of academic training, the nation's schools were strictly controlled by the authorities to ensure that the straitjacket of Marxist-Leninist teaching was imposed on all instruction. As for the workers—both workers in factories and workers on the collective and state farms—they were cruelly exploited by their bosses in the Kremlin and its far-flung bureaucrats in all corners of the land. The twin themes of freedom for students and workers seemed particularly appropriate for Radio Liberty. By offering the uncensored opinions of experts in the West, we hoped to encourage our listeners to think more critically about the realities of living in the Soviet Union.

A Free Voice at the Moscow University Bicentennial

We selected the two hundredth anniversary of Moscow State University (MGU), Russia's oldest and most famous *vuz* (institute of higher education), which fell in January 1955, as the springboard for broadcasts from American educators and scientists as well as émigré intellectuals.

The university had been founded on the initiative of Mikhail V. Lomonosov, the great scientist, scholar, and poet. His words "The sciences do not tolerate coercion" were inscribed in the university's charter. The university produced such writers as Lermontov, Turgenev, Herzen, and Chekhov, the historian Kliuchevsky, the surgeon Pirogov, the liberal statesman and historian Miliukov, and many others. It played an enormous role in the development of Russian culture and society and earned an international reputation as a research center in the natural and social sciences and in medicine.

On many occasions, liberalization of czarist policy came about as the result of discussion and political activity emanating from the university. In the pre-Communist era, it was a citadel of intellectual independence and political ferment. It educated leaders for the first parliament in Russia, the State Duma, for the institutions of municipal and provincial self-government (city dumas, rural zemstvos, professional associations, and so on), and for the ill-starred Constituent Assembly of 1918, which Lenin ordered to be dispersed by force of arms after his Bolshevik party failed to win a majority.

Under the Soviet regime, academic freedom was radically curtailed and contacts with the outside world were reduced to a minimum. The Soviet press and radio remained strangely silent on the 1955 anniversary of the university's founding, although observances were held in many parts of the free world. But this proud date was not lost to the Russian people; the Radio's messages called for a rebirth of academic greatness for the university and the early return of its scholars and scientists to the unfettered pursuit of knowledge and truth in the worldwide community of learning.

The Americans who responded to our invitation to broadcast included university presidents, professors of physics and chemistry, and a Nobel laureate in physiology and medicine.[1] Emigré scholars and scientists included Michael M. Novikoff, the last freely elected rector of Moscow University (February 1919–September 1920), two former faculty members of the university and several graduates, and former faculty members of St. Petersburg, Kiev, and Odessa universities.

Editors of two university student newspapers also participated: the *Harvard Crimson* and the *Columbia Spectator*. As a Columbia graduate, I was particularly pleased that mention was made in the message from Princeton's President Harold W. Dodds that both his university and my alma mater had recently celebrated their bicentenaries; Columbia's theme was "Man's Right to Knowledge and the Free Use Thereof." Dodds expressed his wish that Moscow University "may soon be restored to the freedom of its earlier years, and the doors of international intercommunication may once again be opened to its faculties and its students."[2]

Other university heads drew sharp contrasts between the current state of learning at Moscow University and in their own schools. At New York's City College, Marxist dogma was critically studied in precisely the same way as all other political frameworks; at Hunter (then an all-female school), tens of thousands of young women had attended for eighty-five years regardless of race, creed, color, or class. The professors who sent greetings emphasized respect for facts and reason as the only real authorities both in science and in politics, not men who impose their will by force. Professor George S. Counts of Columbia University's Teachers College expressed his confidence that "the day will dawn when the darkness engendered by the present all-embracing dictatorship will be only a dreadful memory." He added: "May your next anniversary be celebrated in an atmosphere of complete freedom for the human mind." If the current post-Soviet period of democracy survives its rigorous test in turn-of-the-century Russia, perhaps the 250th anniversary of Moscow State University in the year 2005 will fulfill Counts's wish.

The émigré contributors injected a special Russian feeling into their messages by striking a common chord of nostalgia for their school. Professor Novikoff, the erstwhile rector of Moscow University, who taught at several European universities and settled in the United States after leaving Russia, saluted his "dear, distant friends, professors, instructors and students" and noted that thirty-three years had elapsed since he was "forcibly torn from Moscow and exiled from my native land." But neither the long years nor the expanse of ocean had made his love for the university less ardent.

> We sometimes envy you, who live in our once golden-crowned Moscow. But at the same time we realize that to us, who are permeated with the spirit of freedom and independent thought, life would be intolerable where slave labor is used in concentration camps and where study at the universities is conducted along narrow Party directives. The old academic slogan "do not extinguish the spirit" has been abolished, and the Soviet scholar must be ever on the alert to avoid falling into one of the many forbidden deviations.
>
> True, large sums of money are sometimes placed at your disposal. But, as the Russian proverb has it, "tears flow even through gold." Luxurious buildings are being erected today for the university, but we might ask whether this is not done chiefly for the sake of advertisement and propaganda. Or perhaps to make possible even closer surveillance of your conduct.
>
> We are with you with all our hearts, and we feel confident that the day is not far off when your spiritual chains will fall to the ground and you shall once more join the international family of free scientists as full and equal members.

Mark Vishniak, a graduate of Moscow University, was the secretary of the All-Russian Constituent Assembly when it was dispersed by the Bolsheviks in 1918. He left for the West and lectured and wrote books on international law before becoming a contributing editor for *Time* for many years. In his message, he expressed the wish that the new graduates should be true Russian intellectuals, meaning that they should have "the courage to say 'no' to everything that reason and conscience condemn, even if there should as yet be insufficient strength to say 'yes' to that which seems true and just."

Vishniak was speaking more than a decade before Andrei Sakharov incarnated this image of the courageous Russian intellectual and thereafter became the beacon light of the Soviet dissident movement.

The *New York Times* printed an editorial on January 28, 1955, "Moscow Bicentenary," in which Radio Liberation was described as the bridge over which academic leaders in the West and former students and professors were reaching the university's present community. This comment, as well as other editorials concerning our broadcasts on significant Soviet anniversaries, came about as a result of my friendship with Harry Schwartz, a specialist in Soviet affairs on the editorial board of the newspaper. We met frequently for lunch, invariably at one of Manhattan's many midtown Chinese restaurants, where I kept Schwartz up-to-date about the Radio's programming and provided him with scripts in Russian, which he read fluently. My superiors at Amcomlib shared my pleasure that the most influential U.S. newspaper approved of us; it stood us in good stead several years later when we were threatened with extinction.

The Vorkuta Uprising

A cardinal principle of Radio programming policy was to expose the false claims of the Communist Party and the Soviet regime that they represented the proletariat, as well as to condemn their exploitation of the working class, especially through the use of forced labor. In July 1955, the Radio marked the second anniversary of the uprising of slave laborers in Vorkuta, a complex of concentration camps situated in the frozen wastes above the Arctic Circle. It was part of the vast network administered by the MVD (later KGB) known officially as the Chief Administration of Camps or, in Russian, *Glavnoye Upravleniye Lagerei*, abbreviated *GULag*, a name made infamous by Aleksandr Solzhenitsyn in the early 1970s in his monumental samizdat documentary *The Gulag Archipelago*.

With snow blanketing Vorkuta nearly ten months of the year, some 300,000 forced workers, the majority of them sentenced for real or suspected opposition to the Communist regime, endured incredible hardships scratching coal from forty pitheads to provide 6 percent of the Soviet Union's coal production. In July 1953, the long-smoldering unrest among the inmates flared into an open revolt, touched off by reports of the June 17 uprisings in East Germany. A strike of massive proportions quickly developed in one mine after another as slave laborers refused to enter the pits. Instead, they presented camp authorities with eleven demands for improved camp conditions. This organized defiance of the Bolshevik regime recalled the armed mutiny of the Kronstadt sailors in 1921.

Vorkuta's MVD officials frantically appealed to Moscow for instructions, then promised camp improvements—minor concessions that were rejected by the roused prisoners. The strike spread until it involved approximately 100,000 workers. Some MVD guards would not shoot when prisoners refused to return to the pits, and even aided in the revolt. As the number of participants in the strike steadily mounted, Moscow rushed in secret police reinforcements, but despite their bullets and organized terror the surging demonstration was subdued only weeks later, after several hundred inmates lay dead or wounded. Vorkuta was quiet once more, but word of the uprising spread throughout the Soviet Union and the free world until it became a symbol of active opposition to the Communist regime, which was compelled to make concessions to its slaves.

The turmoil among other gulag inmates in 1954 was reported to the West a year later, when a group of Austrian prisoners of war were repatriated from the Karaganda camp in Kazakhstan. Arriving in Vienna, they described the strike of five thousand inmates and their demands for revision of long sentences and discontinuance of the practice of chaining together prisoners on work detail. The revolt had been crushed by MVD tanks, cannons, and machine guns; some six hundred rebels were killed, and several hundred others wounded.

To keep alive the will to resist on the part of the gulag prisoners, and to communicate the West's concern for the plight of Soviet workers, the Radio observed the Vorkuta uprising anniversary with special broadcasts of hope, encouragement, and solidarity by prominent Americans, Europeans, and a former camp inmate. The participants included Eleanor Roosevelt; George Meany, president of the American Federation of Labor (AFL); Walter Reuther, president of the Congress of Industrial Organizations (CIO); and Norman Thomas.

The leitmotif of their statements was to salute Soviet slave laborers for their resistance to tyranny, to inform them that their struggle was supported abroad by world public opinion, and to encourage their belief that ultimately their cause would triumph. George Meany recalled that it was the AFL that had "initiated and pioneered the struggle against slave labor before the United Nations." Our Amcomlib board member, Isaac Don Levine, had provided Meany with a map of the gulag system, reconstructed from information brought out to the West by former inmates.

I interviewed Mrs. Roosevelt in her office at the United Nations and found her as warm and gracious in person as I had seen her on television and in newsreels. She spoke of the growing political consciousness in the outside world of what people inside the Soviet Union were trying to do and added: "I think that in the end their pressure, their belief, their effort to bring the opinion of the world to bear on the Soviet attitudes will bring results which will bring freedom to people even within the Soviet Union."

The full text of these messages was published by Amcomlib with an introduction by Howland Sargeant.[3] He also informed readers that, according to reports from released prisoners and escapees, the Radio was penetrating heavy jamming to reach Vorkuta and other forced-labor areas, as well as the Soviet occupation forces in Central and Eastern Europe and the major cities of the Soviet Union, employing eleven shortwave transmitters that broadcast in seventeen Soviet languages. He pointed out that thousands of workers in the Vorkuta area lived as "free" persons outside the camps and were permitted radios and newspapers, so that news of the outside world was relayed by them to the slaves with whom they worked side by side.

More than thirty years after the uprising, the miners of Vorkuta played an important part in the fall of the Soviet regime and the rise of Boris Yeltsin as a result of their use of the strike. Ironically, Yeltsin's popularity with Russia's miners plummeted in 1995, and early in 1996 they went on strike to protest working conditions, raising further doubts about the viability of his government.

The Dostoyevsky Anniversary

We at the Radio in New York and Munich were quick to exploit the Soviets' decision to observe the seventy-fifth anniversary of the death of Fyodor M. Dostoyevsky in February 1956 after years of silence about the author. As recently as 1952 (before Stalin's death), the anthology *Classics of Russian Literature* had omitted Dostoyevsky's name, for his deep faith in Christianity and hatred of socialism had made him anathema to the Communists. Now the new leaders wanted to benefit from the international fame of their native genius while continuing to deplore aspects of his world view.

The Soviets provided us with the ideological framework within which they would be treating Dostoyevsky. In the influential literary magazine *Novy Mir* in December 1955, a sixty-four-page article by V. Yermilov, leading with a quotation from Maxim Gorky, compared Dostoyevsky to Shakespeare in the force of his artistic expression. "He expressed with his creative work the infinity of suffering of degraded and abused mankind," but at the same time "he fought violently against any attempts to find real paths of struggle for the liberation of mankind from degradation and abuse." The article said of *The Possessed,* in which Dostoyevsky fulminates against socialism, that he was "consciously prepared in several instances to shun the requirements of art in the name of reactionary goals." In conclusion, the article stated:

> We Soviet people are proud of our hereditary idealistic connection with the great progressive Russian writers and thinkers, including our imme-diate predecessors, the brilliant revolutionary democrats. We are proud of our unbroken connection with all advanced progressive artists and thinkers of all times and peoples. And we cannot forget the obscurantist spite against the best democratic forces of his epoch which blinded Dos-toyevsky and was expressed in the most reactionary and tendentious of his works, nor can we forgive Dostoyevsky for it. Neither can we forget that in our time reactionary religionists and other obscurantists are try-ing to exploit his writings for their dark purposes.

This Soviet assessment of Dostoyevsky challenged us to offer our au-dience more than the parochial Marxist view. Weeks before the anniver-sary date (February 9), Boris Shub initiated a programming campaign that would consist of statements from major American and Russian émigré writers on the topic "What Dostoyevsky Means to Me?" As a first step, we sent letters to scores of writers in which we described the Radio as a dem-ocratic, anti-Communist station broadcasting to the peoples of the Soviet Union in seventeen languages. We explained that on various occasions the Radio carried messages from prominent Westerners to our Soviet lis-teners and that, in connection with the approaching anniversary of Dos-toyevsky's death, we planned to broadcast a series of statements by emi-nent writers, philosophers, psychologists, and artists. Our goal was to illustrate the variety of opinions in the Western world about the genius of Dostoyevsky—opinions that our audience would probably not get from their own media—that of Dostoyevsky the doubter, the believer, the prophet, the artist. We did not expect unanimity on the part of our con-tributors. The great value of these broadcasts lay precisely in the fact that each personal evaluation would be different from the others. We urged them to give us their personal, intimate impressions of Dostoyevsky from reading him, whether recently or many years ago.

The idea of paying homage to Dostoyevsky as a writer who inspired them, and at the same time of expressing their own credo of artistic creativity, struck a responsive chord among many of the people we approached. Statements, most of which we recorded, came from a veritable Who's Who of distinguished authors: W. H. Auden, Bennett Cerf, John Dos Passos, James T. Farrell, Granville Hicks, Sidney Kingsley, Joseph Wood Krutch, Arthur Miller, Isaac Bashevis Singer, and Lionel Trilling. Our Munich office received messages from Albert Camus, Boris Zaitsev, Salvador de Madariaga, Ignazio Silone, and Henri Troyat.

Upton Sinclair, whom Boris Shub knew personally—he had even immortalized Boris as a character in one of his Lanny Budd novels that dealt with postwar Berlin—turned us down this time. His short reply read:

> Wish I could oblige you, but I couldn't say anything about Dostoyevsky that would be of use. He is to me a psychopath, and no guide to anything. I admit his power, but so do I admit the power of a nightmare. I don't therefore seek or cultivate one. He piles horror on horror in *Karamazov* until I found it silly, and I so reviewed it long ago. Try again![4]

As the project gained momentum, Shub called me from Hollywood, where he had rushed with characteristic impulsiveness in hopes of enlisting the participation of movie stars and producers, especially Russian émigrés. He informed me that he had persuaded Anna Sten to play the role of Grushenka, the femme fatale of *The Brothers Karamazov*, in a short scene over the Radio. Sten had played the role in Russian, German (a famous film with Fritz Kortner), French, and English. Shub also spoke with a former colleague of Sergei Eisenstein's, Boris Ingster, who had worked with the great director on his film classic *The Battleship Potemkin*, accompanied him to the United States, and remained there after Eisenstein returned to the Soviet Union. Ultimately these and other projects involving Hollywood with the Radio never came to fruition. However, they exemplify Shub's "breeder reactor" brain, forever radiating ideas that could be harnessed for effective programming. He envisioned the response of the film capital's Russians as a possible prelude to future Radio productions.

I always suspected that Shub's antics did not please Howland Sargeant. He was on vacation during the Hollywood caper—which may have been why Shub decided to go there without asking Sargeant's permission, perhaps anticipating that Howland, then married to Myrna Loy, might not relish the notion of Boris rattling around the movie capital like a loose cannon. A few weeks before the Dostoyevsky anniversary date, Boris wrote me from the West Coast to express in vintage Shubian style his concept of the aim of our broadcasts:

> Radio Liberation today has little prestige as far as the audience in the Soviet Union is concerned. . . . The propaganda value for our Soviet audience in this galaxy of minds is this: the listener says to himself—"Aha, Radio Liberation is really something! Look at the kind of people who appear before this mike. These aren't simply paid émigré employees of an American operation or propagandists. These are people who have brains of their own, careers that amount to something, and they think Radio Liberation is worth the trouble to talk over. I know they do *because I have heard their voices.* So this Radio Liberation is a pretty interesting thing, no matter what crooked purposes those Americans (or émigrés, or White Guard bandits, or Mensheviks, or Fascists who run Radio Liberation) may have." "Say, Petya! (of the Central Committee or of the Kolkhoz or of the Brick House Workers). Did you hear the show RL put on for Dostoyevsky and what kind of Russians, Americans, Frenchmen, etc. appeared? One of them thinks Dostoyevsky is a second Christ, another thinks he's a psychopath." "Interesting," replies Petya. "Original!" says Mrs. Ivan Ivanovich or Mrs. Zhukov or the daughter of an MVD colonel in Vorkuta after she's heard RL's show. *That* is the purpose of the Dostoyevsky show. With the help of free (not cold war) minds (or employees of the station) to *begin* to convince the audience that RL is worth listening to.
>
> "The *True* Dostoyevsky" mentioned [by one of the New York RL bureaucrats in a telex to Munich] exists only in the immature mind. The beauty of Dostoyevsky is that he was so many contradictory things—so fair, so foul, so great, so mean, so enlightened, so bigoted, so hostile to arbitrary authority, so much in love with it. He incorporated all this and more, and only free voices speaking via a free station can say it.[5]

Arthur Miller's message deserves special mention. The Radio was not the only institution to ask the Pulitzer Prize–winning playwright to discuss Dostoyevsky. The Union of Soviet Writers in Moscow also invited him to make a public statement marking the anniversary, and even offered him a ten-day tour of the Soviet Union, all expenses paid, which Miller turned down. In addition, the American Committee for Cultural Freedom, which had contributed to our broadcasts for the Soviet Writers' Congress, also approached Miller with a similar request. Miller had recently come under fire as a "left-winger" and had been accused by the American Legion and the Catholic War Veterans of being connected with subversive organizations. Like other liberal American writers, he suffered from the fallout of the witch-hunting tactics of Senator Joseph McCarthy during the early 1950s. In fact, his later play, *The Crucible,* was inspired by that traumatic era.

Miller responded to all three organizations by sending them simultaneously a statement in which he said:

> I must confess to a very particular feeling of Dostoyevskian comedy in the arrival of these three invitations. Here I am, a writer who has only recently been deprived of his right to create a screenplay [on juvenile delinquency] in America; a writer who only a few years ago had his plays removed from the Soviet stages on the basis of his "cosmopolitanism," being asked to speak in celebration of an author who was exiled in his own time in Czarist Russia, whose works were forever being censored, and who until recently was suppressed by the Soviet Government.

Miller declared that he always felt that "the Soviet suppression of some of his works and the outright banning of others was a particularly indefensible act of cultural barbarianism." Commenting on the problem of the relationship between art and politics, he observed that "in neither the Soviet Union nor in the United States today could a man with [Dostoyevsky's] views have long survived without punitive condemnation, which in the Soviet Union could mean outright suppression if not worse, and in the United States an unofficial but, nevertheless, powerful process of social and economic ostracism." He concluded by declaring: "The attempt to draw the memory of this great and terrible man on to any political platform extant in the world today is vanity."

We sent Miller's statement to Munich along with the many other messages we received. At the same time, I got in touch with the American Committee for Cultural Freedom, which publicly challenged the Soviet regime to publicize Miller's statement. The *New York Times* devoted two columns to the story, quoting most of Miller's message. We were pleased by the publicity, especially since it illustrated that the Radio was not afraid to broadcast criticism of the United States along with condemnation of Soviet repression. This point was not lost on Harvey Breit in his Sunday *New York Times Book Review* column, "In and Out of Books." Although Breit alleged that Miller had fallen into the trap of equating American injustice with Soviet injustice, he called the playwright's statement "quite brilliant" and believed that Miller had put the Soviet Union "on the spot." Why?

Because, said Breit, Miller "refused the gambit of helping to create an anti-American, or rather pro-Soviet cause célèbre" by accepting their invitation to travel. (Breit guessed that the Soviets shrewdly anticipated that Miller might have passport difficulty with the American government.) Instead, "an invited potential guest of the stature of Mr. Miller has pulled the cat-bird seat out from under the Soviet writers and placed them on the hot seat. Radio Liberation has broadcast Mr. Miller's statement, in spite of his criticism of the U.S. It is asking that the Soviet Union broadcast the statement as well, in short, asking for equal time."[6]

After the series ended, we hoped that Amcomlib would publish a booklet containing the texts of the statements by contributors to the Dostoyevsky broadcasts, as it had previously done following our radio campaigns tied to other anniversaries. Everyone appreciated the tremendous public relations value for the Radio in making available to Western public opinion, including people in Washington, this evidence of the station's high-quality content and close ties with the intellectual elite of the United States and Western Europe. Alas, the booklet never got past the memo stage, perhaps because of the problems of selection, editing, and costs.

I have preserved what is undoubtedly the only extant collection of almost all the statements, which are a remarkable testimony of Dostoyevsky's impact on many of the leading literary masters of the twentieth century (see Appendix). One of the most interesting messages came from Isaac Bashevis Singer, whom I visited in his apartment on the Upper West Side of Manhattan. More than twenty years before he became world famous as the Nobel Prize laureate in literature, he recorded for us his thoughts on Dostoyevsky. The Radio broadcast the statement in the original Yiddish—one of the rare occasions Soviet listeners could hear that language coming out of their loudspeakers—and in Russian translation. Singer began:

> It is characteristic that all great writers in one way or another connect all the problems discussed in their works with the eternal questions: What is the aim of creation? What is the sense of suffering? Is there a Divine Justice? Wherein lies the supreme duty of man? The works of Dostoyevsky always discuss the fundamentals, the basic conceptions that preoccupy all religions and all philosophies. Dostoyevsky believes that human life is one crisis. The state of suspense in the works of Dostoyevsky is not coincidental, is not artificial, is not a literary whim. It is a direct consequence of Dostoyevsky's mood. In human life there is no

tranquillity since everything is always on the scales. Man is always compelled to choose between good and evil, between life and death. In this respect, Dostoyevsky is closer to Judaism than all the other writers, the Jewish included.

He concluded:

> There is much—or rather everything—that literature in general, and Yiddish literature in particular, can learn from Dostoyevsky. An amoral literature cannot exist. The serious reader has no more patience for the sweet chatter and tricks of the esthetes. Literature can exist only in the high temperatures under a high spiritual pressure, when all values are at stake, or suspended on a scale. Dostoyevsky was a gambler, not only in his personal life. He also gambled in his works, risking everything. He is always on the borderline between art and hack writing, between good and evil, between life and death. Dostoyevsky is the very opposite of a fatalist. The soul of his writing is freedom of choice.[7]

For me there was a sense of poetic justice in transmitting Singer's message. Only a few years earlier, toward the end of Stalin's era, twenty-four leading Yiddish writers, some of them world famous, had been arrested during a virulent anti-Semitic campaign that was to culminate in the mass expulsion of Jews to Siberia. Only Stalin's death in 1953 prevented it. Several years would pass before it was revealed that the writers had already been executed by the KGB.

The impetus for the ultimate exposé of Stalin's monstrous crimes against millions of his subjects began at the end of February 1956, when Nikita Khrushchev made a secret report to the Twentieth Congress of the Party. It was an earth-shaking event that was to have lasting consequences for the Soviet Union and the world Communist movement. Radio Liberation was quick to recognize the profound implications for the future of the Soviet regime and its citizens, and we proceeded to adjust our policy and programming to this seismic shift in the Soviet ideological fault line.

After a hard night's drinking, Igor brings
a new friend home to his shoddy apartment,
telling him about his talking clock.

The friend is fascinated. "Show me," he
says. The host bangs on the wall.

From the other side comes an angry
shout: "Don't you know it's two in the
morning, you son of a bitch?"

5 KHRUSHCHEV RELEASES THE ANTI-STALIN GENIE

Khrushchev's secret speech to a closed session of the Twentieth Party Congress on
February 24 and 25 marked a major turning point in Soviet history, on the eve of the
Radio's third anniversary in early 1956. For
six hours he tore off the mask of Joseph
Stalin as a benevolent and omniscient leader
and revealed—though not entirely—the
criminal activities of the *vozhd* (leader). As
Khrushchev later described in his memoirs,
"We exposed Stalin for his excesses, for his
arbitrary punishment of millions of honest
people, and for his one-man rule, which
violated the principle of collective leadership." This shocking and devastating condemnation of Stalin and his "cult of
personality" was not released inside the
Soviet Union. It was read to limited groups
of Soviet citizens, primarily Party members, but word of the sensational development soon became known in the outside
world, followed a few weeks later by the
actual text of the speech, which was leaked
to the West through the Polish Commu-

nists. The CIA got a copy, and the State Department released it on June 4, 1956.[1]

We at the Radio believed that we had a special obligation to disseminate the text as widely as possible to our Soviet audience and to provide the necessary commentary and perspective from experts in the West, especially émigré political scientists and historians. During three years of its broadcasts, the Radio had continuously repeated the accusations against Stalin and his regime that were now being admitted, at least in part, by his heirs. What grist for our mill!

John Gunther's encyclopedic one-volume survey, *Inside Russia Today*, was published in 1958 after four visits to the Soviet Union. As in his other bestsellers about various parts of the world, including his native America, Gunther displayed an extraordinary ability to distill the essence of a country's political, economic, and social character from his personal observations, enriched by voracious reading and investigative interviewing. In examining the Soviet Union, he was confronted with a police state that presented obstacles to a freewheeling journalist. All the more remarkable, therefore, that he produced an incisive analysis of Khrushchev's motivations in exposing Stalin that has largely weathered the test of time.

In one chapter, "De-Stalinization," he wrote that the current regime had to break with the past if the post-Stalin Soviet leaders hoped to enlist the cooperation of its citizens to build an efficient, modern industrial power rivaling and overtaking the United States. Therefore, Soviet society needed to relax the tyrant's Draconian methods, such as arbitrary arrests, forced labor, and terror. Perhaps the most perceptive of Gunther's judgments was that "profound emotional results may, in time, make themselves apparent within the Soviet Union" as a consequence of Khrushchev's revelations. "Perhaps in time a true public opinion may arise. If so, that will show the real and lasting importance of de-Stalinization, even if the leaders did not anticipate the results."[2]

In 1962, Gunther and his publisher engaged me to revise and update the first edition of *Inside Russia Today*. Although I made many changes that reflected the evolution of events in Russia and the world in the previous five to six years, I did not have to make any changes in his assessment of Khrushchev's secret speech. Indeed, his suggestion about the ultimate emergence of genuine public opinion as a result of the shock therapy initiated by Khrushchev was validated in the course of the next three decades. And Radio Liberty deserves some of the credit for contributing to that process.

During the spring of 1956, Howland Sargeant initiated discussions among the executives, émigré staff, and outside specialists concerning the implications of the speech. I was now manager of the program section, and I organized lunchtime chats with my writers in order to stimulate our thinking and contribute to the formulation of policy position papers that Sargeant distributed within Amcomlib. Sargeant expressed the hope that "by filtering ideas that all of us have through the basic assumptions of these papers, we can reach a better common understanding of our mission and of the bedrock of basic premises and goals on which each one of us stands."[3]

The Soviet regime, we concluded, was changing its tactics from Stalin's harsh methods to a more subtle approach, with emphasis on psychological warfare at home and abroad, given the unlikely prospect of a large-scale shooting war or Soviet military adventures. In such an atmosphere of ideological competition, radio would continue to be the most effective means of communication behind the Iron Curtain. But greater opportunities would open up for firsthand observation within the USSR and for contact with Soviet citizens who made temporary trips to the Free World. Less than three years later, I was one of the handful of Americans able to study Soviet life during a five-week visit to Moscow, Leningrad, and Kiev.

We emphasized the importance of avoiding polemics in the Radio's broadcasts, concentrating on providing facts and information, and welcoming the changes the regime made to improve the lot of the Soviet citizens. Our wise elder statesman Yuri Petrovich Denicke suggested to me that we say, in effect, "Da, no ne dostatochno"—Yes, but not enough. From the beginning of our existence, we were aware that a militant, provocative approach to programming was shortsighted and counterproductive and that radio per se could not hope to bring about the end of the Communist dictatorship, but that it could perform a valuable function in stimulating evolutionary change in the Soviet system along lines consistent with the legitimate aspirations of the peoples in the Soviet Union. Understandably, not all of our émigré staff agreed with this moderate approach and, as I mentioned earlier, glitches sometimes occurred, especially in the non-Slavic services, until American management's regular monitoring of those languages became possible.

Radio Liberation broadcast Khrushchev's speech and devoted a major portion of programming for many months thereafter to the analyses by pundits in the West, including Russian socialist émigrés like Boris Nicolaevsky, press editorials, and—perhaps most damaging to the Soviet image—the stunned reaction of Communists and fellow travelers in Western Europe and the United States as they confronted the destruction of the Stalin myth.

The most sensational reaction to Khrushchev's exposé that the Radio broadcast was a message from Natalia Sedova, the widow of Leon Trotsky, who had been assassinated in Mexico in 1940 on orders from the Kremlin. We succeeded in obtaining her statement with the help of Amcomlib trustee Isaac Don Levine, himself an expert on Soviet affairs. Levine was a legendary figure in U.S. journalism. A native of Russia, he had come to America as a young man and quickly established himself as a crack foreign correspondent, traveling to the new Soviet state and interviewing leaders there. He had also written a book about Trotsky's assassin. After a meeting with Boris Shub and me, Levine telephoned Daniel James, an American journalist and a former editor of the *New Leader,* who was living in Mexico City. James recorded Sedova's emotional message for us, and we relayed it to Munich. I passed along our translation to Harry Schwartz, and on July 9 the story made the front page of the *New York Times* under the headline "Mme. Trotsky Calls on Russians to Overthrow 'Stalinist' Regime," crediting the Radio as the broadcasting medium.

Cited below are excerpts from this historic document, arguably the only extant copy.[4] Speaking directly to Soviet citizens, who had been fed a distorted image of Trotsky as a traitor to the revolution and an agent of Western imperialism, Sedova's message was a 1,500-word *"j'accuse."* However, it was not an inflammatory exhortation to her audience that they now rise up against the Kremlin dictators, as the *Times* headline implied. Identifying herself as "Natalia Ivanovna Sedova, widow of Lev Davidovich Trotsky, speaking from Mexico City," she said:

> I am addressing myself to the workers and peasants, and in the first place, to the young people in Soviet Russia. The present rulers, Khrushchev, Bulganin, Mikoyan, and others, having inherited the Stalinist dictatorship, are conducting an intensive propaganda campaign so as to distract from themselves the powerful wave of dissatisfaction and hatred for the thieves of the proletarian revolution, a wave which has grown in your hearts. They are the same men who supported Stalin in all his bloody massacres, the aim of which was to frighten you with terror and thus to retain power in the hands of the Stalinist bureaucracy. The very method of the campaign through which these men hope to absolve themselves of responsibility for heinous crimes bears witness to the fact that the ruling clique is Stalin's faithful successor. . . .
>
> Just try and think—who are these direct heirs of the unbalanced

Stalin who declared themselves collective leaders of Soviet Russia? They admit to the entire world that for many decades not one among the collective leaders dared—for fear of his own life—to come out with a proposal of steps which would have saved the lives of millions of workers and peasants who were banished to concentration camps. These are the nonentities who dare to demand from Russian workers and peasants unimaginable sacrifices in the struggle for a great cause. How long will they hold on under the pressure of great events? All their lives they showed no interest in improving the lot of the toilers; they were interested only in holding on to power and to all the privileges that go with power. Besides, the training they received from Stalin makes the realization of a collective leadership unlikely even in the imperfect form they have in mind. How can they trust each other knowing full well that while Stalin was alive each one among them would have been happy to sacrifice all and everything just to hold on to his own power and position? Events unfold slowly, but it is unlikely that their leadership will last long.[5]

Sedova's prophecy came true a year later, in 1957, when Khrushchev broke up the collective leadership and removed many of his comrades-in-arms whom he labeled "anti-Party." Turning next to the falsification of the past, Sedova declared that she realized with bitterness that many of her young listeners were brought up completely in a Stalinist spirit, that they were taught history that was "thoroughly permeated with lies," and that "serious changes in the balance of social power will be required before you, young people, will be able to uncover historical truth."

Referring to the inquiry into the validity of the Soviet accusations against her husband, Sedova said:

> It is unlikely that the news of the famous commission that investigated the Moscow trials [in 1937–38], the chairman of which was the noted American philosopher, John Dewey, has reached you. This commission, after hearing the testimony of Trotsky and others, and carefully examining all the accusations, arrived at the conclusion that Trotsky and his son, Lev Lvovich Sedov, were innocent. The press throughout the world closely followed the work and verdict of the commission.
>
> From my distant exile where I have already spent so many years I find it difficult to estimate the number of people in Russia who would believe the accusations against Trotsky and others. Abroad no one believes any longer in the vile slander that Trotsky allegedly was linked with Fascists, foreign powers, espionage and the like. Russia's present rulers look into the future with some confidence. They know that during the reign of the Leader all the heroic figures of the proletarian revolution were

done away with. They believe that nowhere in the world are there any forces that might threaten them. Among themselves they have signed a temporary truce under the guise of collective leadership, since the only danger they see is discord among themselves. But they are wrong. Even a weak blow to the myth which they themselves created, even a partial unmasking of the falsehood of the regime on which their rule is based, cannot fail to sow doubts and discord among the new, growing generation. Idealism was always the characteristic and the strength of youth. I am convinced that the doubts will crush the hard convictions and that youth will not abandon its search for truth until it will find all the truth. Woe then unto the false leaders!

Trotsky's widow predicted that "the decayed Stalinist oligarchy" would not be saved by its attempt to assume the mantle of Lenin, and she concluded: "The task of overthrowing Stalinism is the task of the Russian workers and peasants. I send you my greetings and fiery confidence in your victory."

Natalia Sedova was seventy-four years old when her message was broadcast to the Soviet Union. She did not live to witness the final overthrow of Stalinism and would no doubt have been astounded to see it occur as part of an evolutionary process initiated by the Party leadership itself, rather than by a revolt of the masses. In fact, she probably would have been among those critics of Gorbachev who accused him of betraying Lenin and embarking on the capitalist road. Still, the passionate and fiercely partisan widow of Trotsky would surely have welcomed his long overdue restoration, in the era of glasnost and perestroika, from the *musorny yashchik istorii* (literally "the garbage can of history"), to which he had relegated his own opponents in October 1917.

It goes without saying that the Radio did not endorse Sedova's diatribe, although we agreed with a great deal of her criticism of the new rulers. In addition to her distinctly Trotskyite perspective, her immoderate tone and polemical arguments hardly conformed to the broadcasting policy we were urging our own writers to respect. But we were correct in using the message, because it did not express the opinion of a staff member, but instead demonstrated our role as enterprising communicators who were informing our Soviet audience of the various reactions abroad and at home to Khrushchev's speech.

Shock waves were felt in Eastern Europe, especially Poland and Hungary, among Communist parties throughout the rest of the world and among individual Communist intellectuals in the West who broke with the Party in their disillusionment. For years to come, the consequences of Stalin's dethronement would provide the Radio with effective programming that went beyond the carefully rationed disclosures of the Kremlin. Soviet citizens who had not been made privy to the speech when it was carefully disseminated within Party circles soon learned about it from Radio Liberation and other Western radios. It was not long before many of them were able to confirm the accuracy of the reports from abroad as the truth about the speech leaked out of the Party and spread within the Soviet Union.

The Radio made every effort to accelerate the erosion of faith in the infallibility of the Party after the devastating accusations by its leader concerning Stalin's criminal activities, which implied the complicity of his heirs and sowed doubts about their claim to represent the best interests of the people. Especially effective were the declarations of disenchanted Communists and fellow travelers. Early in 1957, Howard Fast, a famous American novelist and author of many popular books on political and social themes, broke with the U.S. Communist Party, which he had joined enthusiastically almost a decade and a half before. He was a hero in the eyes of the Soviet regime, which had awarded him the Stalin International Peace Prize in 1953, and among average Russian readers, who admired the fact that he took the side of downtrodden workers and oppressed black people in the unjust capitalist world outside. Fast had been among the best known and most widely read contemporary American authors in the Soviet Union. His renunciation made the front page of the *New York Times* on February 1. He defined his position by stating: "I am neither anti-Soviet nor anti-Communist, but I cannot work and write in the Communist movement."

It was "incredible" to him, Fast said, that Khrushchev had not ended his speech "with the promise of reforms needed to guarantee that Stalin's crimes will not be repeated, reforms such as an end to capital punishment, trial by jury, and habeas corpus. Without these reforms, one can make neither sense nor reason of the speech itself." Fast indicated that he had spent the months since the secret speech was made known to the West in struggling with the question of his future. He said that he admired Communist Party members as dedicated fighters for peace but that he personally felt that he could no longer submit to Communist discipline. In addition, incontrovertible evidence of official anti-Semitism in the Soviet Union influenced his decision.

Fast asserted that he had been a devoted Communist because of his belief in democracy, equalitarianism, and social justice. His anger at the

Khrushchev speech was particularly sharp because of his experience with the American judicial system: "I was tried and convicted in 1946 under circumstances that made a mockery of our pretensions of justice here," he said. "But while that was happening, I was consoled by the belief that in the Soviet Union a person would receive justice. I can no longer believe this." (Fast had served three months in jail on a charge of contempt of Congress arising from his refusal to cooperate with the House Un-American Affairs Committee.)

At an extraordinary meeting I attended, sponsored by the *New Leader* in 1957, many representatives of New York's liberal and social democrat elite heard Fast's confession of error with thinly disguised contempt, since most of them were longtime anti-Stalinists. During an acrimonious question-and-answer period, when Fast was being hectored by his critics, Bertram Wolfe interceded in his behalf by declaring that as a "member of the class of '29"—that is, having broken with Communism at that time—he would like those present to welcome, if belatedly, "a member of the class of '57." Wolfe understood clearly that however long it had taken Fast to see the light, his decision now would have considerable repercussions in the ideological struggle.

Radio Liberation gave heavy play to Fast's dramatic defection, which the Soviet media ignored for the next six months. Finally, in August, *Literaturnaya Gazeta,* the organ of the Soviet Writers' Union, went public by denouncing Fast as a "deserter under fire" and author of "anti-Soviet slander." Never one to remain silent, Fast replied a few days later by revealing that Communist diplomats from Eastern Europe with whom he was friendly in the United States had confidentially given him background information about Khrushchev's speech and about Khrushchev himself "even more monstrous than the document they supplemented," and that had helped him decide to break with the Communist Party. Apparently Moscow considered the August article insufficient to discredit Fast and needed an all-out indictment to destroy his reputation in the Communist world. In January 1958, *Literaturnaya Gazeta* devoted more than a page of a normally four-page newspaper to calling him a swindler, an opportunist, a savage, and a deserter, as well as a "militant Zionist" who was cheap, cowardly, dishonest, and indecent.

We were sure that if we could get Fast himself to reply directly to his critics over the Radio, it would shake up many Soviet listeners who admired him. He agreed to come to our New York studios to record his statement in English; we translated it into Russian using clips of his voice to establish his presence at the microphone. He struck back against the "maniacal castigation" of him and denounced it as a "contrived and shameless lie." He added that as far as he could remember not even Hitler had been so reviled in the Soviet press. "The sight of a great and powerful nation provoked to this disgraceful public display of bad taste and hooligan-like obscenity cannot be written off as official imperviousness to the obligations of civilized behavior." He suggested that the real meaning of the article was that other writers, "perhaps in Russia as well as in other places," had also been "critical of many of the practices" of the Soviet leadership. Then he addressed himself to his "many millions of readers in the Soviet Union, people who have cherished my work and have loved it," and told them that their newspaper was lying. "For many years this organ has been the craven and willing tool of the Party leaders in their war against free expression in the arts and in their war to subjugate independent thinking among all writers of Russia."[6]

The *Times* printed excerpts and informed its readers that Fast had recorded it for broadcast by Radio Liberation in Munich. We were delighted with the publicity, which helped our image in the United States as a champion of free speech and opponent of Soviet suppression of writers. More important, however, was the image the Radio projected to our audience inside the Soviet Union. A hero of Russia's literate masses was using our medium to reach them over the heads of their masters, and he said the same things that we had been telling them since we went on the air five years earlier.

Fast's remark that writers in Russia were also critical of the system was underscored at this juncture in the post-Stalin period by the appearance of a work that would soon win the first Nobel Prize for Literature ever to be awarded to a Soviet writer. Boris Pasternak, long a beloved Russian poet and novelist living in Moscow, was then unknown to most people in the West. His novel *Doctor Zhivago* told of his hero's hostile attitude toward the Bolshevik revolution and Soviet rule. Unable to publish it in the Soviet Union, Pasternak had smuggled it abroad. The Radio quickly obtained the Russian original from the Italian publisher Feltrinelli and proceeded to broadcast it in its entirety in daily installments. We even put it on the air at dictation speed, hoping that some listeners would dare to make copies and disseminate them clandestinely. When the Kremlin overreacted to the appearance of the work in the West and launched a vicious campaign attacking Pasternak, the Radio quoted articles and editorials by those who defended his right to speak the truth as he saw it.

I interviewed Howard Fast about the Pasternak case. He was, as usual, eloquent concerning the obligations of the writer to his craft, and damning in his indictment of the Soviet treatment of Pasternak. During the taping, someone from the newsroom informed us that Pasternak had just been denied permission to travel from Moscow to Stockholm in order to accept the Nobel Prize. This was Fast's spontaneous reaction:

> It's the most shocking and terrible thing of its kind that we have ever been treated to. We all know how much Boris Pasternak welcomed this prize, how he embraced the prize, how proud he was of receiving it, how grateful he was to receive it. We also have witnessed the filthy slanders directed against him, the evil threats, the dirty names that he was called—the whole exhibition of degenerate boorishness on the part of the paid and directed Soviet critics.
>
> Now Pasternak succumbs, he rejects the prize. How brave, how strong, can one old man of sixty-seven years be—alone, isolated, with no one with enough courage to stand up and speak for him and fight for him? It's no wonder that he rejected the prize. It's a sorrowful thing to see, a tragic thing to see. I don't think that anything that has happened in the Soviet Union in my lifetime was quite as disgraceful as this spectacle around Boris Pasternak. In the whole nation only he emerges with dignity. I don't know what more I could add to that. I could wonder how they got Boris Pasternak to reject it. Did they threaten him with execution?
>
> The incident itself is so shocking that it's very difficult to see any clear picture of this. The thing, the drama of Pasternak and the Nobel Prize, as it has been played out, has all the semblance of some horrible nightmare which might be shown to us as happening in another world and another planet. It's almost as if the Soviet Union has made a considerable decision to reveal the last bit of ignominious lack of dignity. There seems to be nothing left. I wonder how the Soviet writers feel about this.[7]

In addition to translating and broadcasting this emotional outburst, we released it to the press. The *New York Herald Tribune* printed excerpts in an editorial that they prefaced by mentioning the Radio and reminding their readers of Fast's background as a Communist and a favorite of the Russians who had been caused by the events of 1956 to see the "true nature of Soviet totalitarianism."

As for Pasternak, more than thirty years later, in Sergei Khrushchev's book about his father, he described how the Soviet leader had approved the campaign against the writer after his "ideologists" gave him a "tendentiously selected set of citations" from *Doctor Zhivago*. However, when he received a letter from Pasternak while the novelist was suffering considerable hounding and baiting, Khrushchev ordered: "Enough. He's admitted his mistakes. Stop it."[8] Ultimately, Khrushchev regretted his role in the affair. In his memoirs, he criticized the "decision to use police methods," which "left a bad aftertaste for a long time to come." He claimed he had proposed that the book be published and that Pasternak be permitted to go abroad at the government's expense to pick up his award, when the writer suddenly announced that he would not go. Khrushchev confessed that he had never read the book, but in hindsight he realized that he should have left it to the reader to judge. "Some might say it's too late for me to express regret that the book wasn't published. Yes, maybe it is too late. But better late than never."[9] *Doctor Zhivago* was finally allowed to be published in the Soviet Union in 1988, during Gorbachev's era—thirty years after it had appeared in the West and reached Soviet citizens of an earlier generation via RL.

The Bear Among the Lions

In the spring of 1956, our New York office played a modest role behind the scenes in the propaganda activities surrounding the forthcoming visit of Khrushchev and Bulganin to London. Bulganin, who was then de jure head of the Soviet delegation as chairman of the Council of Ministers—that is, prime minister—and Khrushchev, who was actually in charge as the Party's first secretary, went there in order to improve relations with Great Britain and its new Conservative government under Anthony Eden. Khrushchev describes the visit in his memoirs and recalls the dinner held for them by the British Labor Party's National Executive Committee and Shadow Cabinet. In contrast to the Conservatives, he felt more tension with the Laborites, who "considered themselves the representatives of the working people."[10]

The dinner took place at the House of Commons and was followed by toasts and speeches. Khrushchev delivered an hour-long tirade against the West and in defense of Stalin's prewar policies. His hosts were appalled and heckled him. Hugh Gaitskell, leader of the Labor Party, tried to calm the atmosphere, but then presented Khrushchev with a list of the names of several hundred socialists who were imprisoned in the Soviet Union and Eastern Europe, urging their release. He also expressed concern about the treatment of Russian Jews.

Khrushchev, infuriated, responded in crude language that there were no social democrats in the Soviet Union, that Moscow did not have any power to influence action in the satellites, and that talk of Soviet anti-Semitism was "nonsense." The evening ended in a shouting match, with George Brown in particular incurring the Soviet leader's wrath: "He was extremely hostile toward us. . . . Here we were, his guests, and he launched into a harangue against our policies!"[11]

The incident made headlines at the time, and even a few weeks later, after Khrushchev and Company had returned to Moscow, *Pravda* continued to fume about the meeting, accusing the *New Leader* of having cooked up the idea in New York. Actually, the magazine had participated in the preparation of the list for the Labor Party. In the United States, a group of prominent labor leaders put together a roster of 426 free trade unionists and social democrats who had vanished or were known to be in Communist jails, and issued an appeal for their posthumous exoneration or immediate release. The *New Leader*'s executive editor, S. M. Levitas, himself a Menshevik imprisoned by the Bolsheviks before escaping to the United States, supervised the translation of the appeal and arranged to send it to sixty top Soviet Party chiefs and editors.

Because of Boris Shub's close ties with the *New Leader,* where his brother, Anatole (Tony), was an editor from 1949 to 1958, we had been in on the project from the beginning. I do not recall whether it was Boris who came up with the scheme, but he certainly was active in its gestation. We helped distribute the appeal by sending a batch to Melvin Lasky, Tony's brother-in-law in Berlin, who was the editor of *Der Monat,* an American-sponsored, German-language anti-Communist magazine. Lasky handled the mailing of copies to key Communists in Eastern Germany.

Late one afternoon, after the office had closed, I found Boris still at work in his cubicle painstakingly licking German postage stamps and putting them on envelopes that were to be shipped to Lasky for mailing. He showed me that he was placing stamps with the portraits of Rosa Luxemburg and Karl Liebknecht side by side, and he gleefully anticipated the reaction of the orthodox Party faithful when they received letters with these anti-Lenin dissident German Communists staring at them!

The whole story of the Soviet leaders' visit to London was given full coverage in the Radio's Russian and non-Russian language services. In May 1956, we learned that Hugh Gaitskell was coming to the United States to address a convention of the International Ladies Garment Workers' Union in Atlantic City, New Jersey. A few of us from the Radio met the British labor leader at the airport and escorted him to Levitas, who accompanied him to the meeting. We decided to send one of our New York correspondents, Valerian Obolensky, to cover the proceedings and to interview Gaitskell. Regarding *Pravda's* charges that Levitas and others in the United States had prompted him to urge Khrushchev and Bulganin to liberate former trade union activists and social democrats who were in prisons and concentration camps of the Soviet Union and the "peoples' democracies" of Eastern Europe, Gaitskell said:

> Well, of course, it's complete nonsense that we were stirred up to asking for the release of social democrats by Wall Street, or indeed, if I may say so, by Mr. Levitas. We have frequently approached the Soviet government in the past, asking them to release social democrat prisoners. But up to now we haven't been very successful. These approaches have been made sometimes through the embassy in London, sometimes by letter. We also have our own lists of social democrats in prison which are very carefully compiled from good sources in London, not in New York. And it was this which led us to intervene, and nothing to do with the *New Leader*.[12]

Levitas was asked to comment on the claim in *Pravda's* attack that "the magazine *New Leader* carries out the dirtiest missions of Wall Street." He replied that it was a "cock and bull story." He added that the initiative he had taken in "the great work for the liberation of social democrats coincided with the initiative of the British Labor Party. Now that movement has taken on a worldwide significance."[13]

This was not the last time that Khrushchev expressed his irritation with Western representatives of the working class. In 1959, during his trip across the United States, he met Walter Reuther and other heads of the American labor movement and exhibited a similar lack of rapport with them; he got along much better at his meetings with American big-business tycoons. The Radio covered Khrushchev's coast-to-coast tour with frequent reports by our New York correspondent, Boris Orshansky, and by

Victor Frank, who had been flown in from Munich for this important assignment.

Reevaluating Radio Liberation's Role in the Late 1950s

A distillation of what Radio Liberation stood for after Khrushchev's speech and the revolution in Hungary it precipitated a few months later is contained in an informal talk given by Howland Sargeant as part of a course in "Propaganda and Public Opinion" at the New School in Manhattan on April 4, 1957.[14] Sargeant stated his concept of the reasons for communicating with peoples behind the Iron Curtain. First, "to show what it means to live as a free individual," and second, to challenge the totalitarian regime's efforts to convince their subjects to follow it blindly, even into a "thermonuclear frenzy," by providing them with "knowledge that would breed hesitation." He quoted the chairman of the Atomic Energy Commission, Gordon Dean, who had said that he had the "second most important job in the world" and had added that the "first and most important job is to pierce the Iron Curtain and bring home to the average Russian the true and peaceful intentions of us Americans." Sargeant liked that formulation so much that when the Radio released a brochure describing its work at that time, it was entitled "The Most Important Job in the World." It may have sounded pretentious to many Americans, but to us on the firing lines it seemed appropriate.

Sargeant analyzed the "lessons from Hungary." He said he thought that George Orwell's idea of 1984 had been exploded, because in spite of the indoctrination of Hungarians under a Communist dictatorship "with all the methods of terror, persuasion, inducement and thought control, you may still be highly resistant to the very thought of this ideology or for what it stands." He interpreted the impact of the revolt on the Soviet Union:

> I don't think the Soviet Union will ever be the same after Hungary. I don't know how long it will exist either within its present territorial borders or in essentially the form of dictatorship which it now represents. But I am convinced that the events of October and November 1956 represent something so fundamental that the Soviet Union can never reform and regroup as it was before these events. . . . I think certainly the events in Hungary and Poland have produced within the minds and hearts of many people in the Soviet Union—if it isn't a crisis of conscience—it is the brewer's yeast ferment of ideas and hard questions

and seeking for honest answers. I am suggesting that at the minimum, intellectual ferment is there which makes people more prone to pay attention to outside communication than at any time since the end of the war.

He described the Radio's role in stimulating that ferment, and he quoted from a written directive that has existed since the beginning of our broadcasting: "RL will not encourage any acts of premature overt violent resistance to the Soviet regime which could only result in fruitless sacrifice. It will make no promises which it cannot itself fulfill, and will never indicate that freedom and democracy will be achieved except through the will and endeavors of the peoples of the USSR themselves."

Sargeant pointed out that the Radio broadcast not only to Soviet citizens within the territorial borders of the Soviet Union, but also to Soviet troops, particularly those on occupation duty in the Eastern European countries. One of the most dramatic broadcasts to Soviet troops came at the height of their intervention in Hungary in November 1956. At a mass rally held at Madison Square Garden, Alexandra Tolstoy delivered a stirring message in Russian that the Radio transmitted "live" from the hall for instantaneous relay to listeners in Eastern Europe:

Soldiers, officers, and generals of the Soviet Army! Russian people and brothers! This is Alexandra Tolstoy, daughter of Leo Tolstoy, and president of the Tolstoy Foundation. Great events are taking place in the world. Poland and Hungary are fighting for freedom. Russian soldiers, where are you? With whom are you? Do you realize the invincible force which at all times the Russian army represented, the army which rid the Russian people of the Tatar yoke, which in 1812 drove the French out of Russia and vanquished the might of Hitler? On whose side are you? Are you with the heroic Hungarians, who have disdained terror, deprivation, suffering, martyrdom, and even death, and with their bare hands have fought against their enslavers, just as in the Second World War our Russian hero, General Vlasov, fought against the Kremlin hangmen? Or are you with the enemies and executioners of the Russian people who forced you to spill the blood of the Hungarian heroes who are fighting for their freedom and yours? Russian soldiers! Public opinion of the whole free world is following with revulsion the actions of the odious Kremlin hangmen, who, in order to save their own skins, have begun to rush about like wild animals, hoping to find salvation by spilling blood on the soil which has been consecrated by the heroism of the Hungarians.

Eternal memory to these heroic liberators. Cursed be the scoundrels, the Kremlin hangmen who have enslaved the Russian land and who are defaming the name of the Russians and the Russian army. The revolt of the Hungarians has been suppressed in torrents of blood, but the divine spirit of freedom and the love for one's fellow man and for truth lives on. It is impossible to suppress it with brute force, treachery, brutality, torture, even death. Russian soldiers! Can it really be that the desire to fight for truth and freedom, even if doing so entails sacrifice and suffering, has died in you? And if that spirit is alive, can it be that the realization of your legendary strength will not awaken in you? Can it be that you will not halt the bestial, traitorous massacre of our brothers, the Hungarian people? Can it be that you will not rise up as one for freedom against the evil that for almost forty years has infected our Russian homeland? For the freedom of Hungary and of all the enslaved nations of the world?[15]

Madame Tolstoy's heartfelt and provocative summons to the Russian army to "rise up" was, strictly speaking, a violation of the policy forbidding the Radio to encourage "any acts of premature overt violent resistance to the Soviet regime." However, it was one thing to restrain script writers, but not so easy to exercise censorship over a distinguished Russian émigré speaking at a rally where the audience was being whipped into a frenzy, and all the more so when the broadcast was being aired as she spoke! The problem of how to handle outside contributors to the program while conforming to the guidelines recurred from time to time throughout our history, and I was personally involved on more than one occasion.

Another ticklish part of Madame Tolstoy's address was her praise of General Vlasov. Andrei Vlasov was a famous Soviet commander who had surrendered to the invading Germans along with his besieged troops near Leningrad in July 1942. However, instead of sitting out the war in a prison camp, he made a deal with the Germans. They permitted him to head a special army of anti-Communist soldiers and officers made up of his fellow Soviet prisoners, who switched to the German side in the hope of defeating Stalin and liberating their homeland. Judging by the manifesto that articulated the goals of his "Russian Liberation Army," Vlasov envisioned that a democratic order would take the place of the vanquished Communist regime. Vlasov's army helped free Prague early in 1945, but he was captured by the Soviet army, brought back to Moscow, and hanged as a traitor.

For the Radio to praise Vlasov, therefore, was to fly in the face of Soviet propaganda's constant theme that he had served the Nazi cause. Moreover, some of the staff of the Radio in Munich were Vlasovites, former members of that controversial group. The American bosses who recruited cadres for the Radio justified their choice of such people on the basis of their proven hatred of the Soviet regime and minimized the damage the Soviets could inflict on the station by identifying the Radio as an outfit staffed by turncoats who fought against the motherland. Nevertheless, the hiring of former collaborators with the Nazis not only made the Radio vulnerable to Soviet attacks but also turned away some potential émigré contributors to our broadcasts and disturbed segments of the American public. In my many contacts with former Vlasovites on the Munich staff, I felt uncomfortable that Cold War politics had thrown me together with such strange bedfellows.

Madame Tolstoy's plea might have had a greater effect on the Soviet garrison troops when the Hungarian revolution first broke out. Those Russian soldiers displayed such sympathy for the local population that Moscow had to replace them with fresh troops drawn from non-Russian units in Central Asia. After the uprising was crushed, we received a message from a Hungarian: "This revolution hasn't been lost; it has only been prolonged. It started on its own and will continue without you, but if you stop broadcasting now you will abandon yourselves. It would mean that you were giving up what has become a vital part of your own fight which you in the West might still lose."

At this time in the late 1950s, Boris Shub and I had a long conversation with Archbishop John Shahovskoy of San Francisco. A Russian Orthodox priest, Shahovskoy regularly delivered sermons on the Russian service of the Voice of America. We discussed the repercussions of Khrushchev's anti-Stalin speech and asked the archbishop what he thought was likely to happen in the Soviet Union as a result of the forces the leader had unleashed. Without missing a beat he replied, "Everything." Reactions like that suggested to us that our listeners were more receptive than ever to positive alternatives they had not previously dared to think about consciously, and that we needed to study the audience scientifically in order to be able to encourage the formation of values favorable to a free system as effectively as possible. Intensive analysis of our technical power, as well as of the impact of our broadcasts on listeners in the Soviet establishment and among the population at large, began in the mid-1950s and developed into a major component of the Radio's operation.

Early Technical and Audience Research

Determining whether the Radio was getting through to the audience involved some extremely ingenious technical work in predicting shortwave propagation conditions, in picking the right frequency, and verifying the prediction. From monitors located as close to the edge of the target area as they could get, our engineers made recordings; the tape had both our program and the jamming on it, and indicated to us whether the receiving conditions corresponded with what we had predicted a month before. This technique of "check-point monitoring" near Soviet territory enabled us to extrapolate the probable audibility of the signal inside the Soviet Union; it became standard operating procedure on the part of the Radio engineers, who set up listening posts in places such as Trabzon (in Turkey) and in Berlin.

In addition, the U.S. Embassy in Moscow at times cooperated with us.[16] During trips that American diplomats were permitted to take to various republics of the Soviet Union, they would spot check the Radio's programs and include their findings in confidential reports to which staff members with the proper security clearance were given access. These classified documents were carefully controlled; for example, at Munich headquarters, where I worked from 1966 to 1970, I frequently went to a special room where one could pore over several of the latest reports from the Moscow embassy or from the State Department that dealt with Soviet foreign and domestic matters. In New York, I also had access to some documents from Washington.

The reaction of the regime to the Radio was an even better indication that we were getting through. Since 1954–55, Amcomlib and RL were increasingly attacked in the major newspapers of the Soviet Union, and over Radio Moscow, Radio Kiev, and others. The Committee for the Return to the Homeland, set up by the Soviets in 1955 with headquarters in East Berlin in order to urge the 2.5 million members of the emigration to return to the Soviet Union, regularly favored us with scathing indictments.

In March 1957, in the debate at the United Nations on a Soviet resolution charging aggression, we were honored by the Soviet delegate and the Ukrainian delegate and several other delegates, who openly expressed the view that we were indeed a very dangerous group of people. Dmitri Shepilov, then the foreign minister, made remarks about our work in an address to the Supreme Soviet that we took as a very considerable accolade.

The incessant jamming of Radio broadcasts from the first day of its existence attested to how much Soviet leaders feared us, and that fear persisted for thirty-five years. It would have been an advantage to permit these programs to be received without interference if that really could have served to confirm their condemnation of the Radio as a "subversive" network staffed by "traitors and fascist collaborators" attempting to overthrow the Soviet system. Actually, the broadcasts were more subversive because they told the unvarnished truth with remarkable restraint.

By the late 1950s, the Radio was reaching the Soviet Union from Europe and the Far East, from nine transmitters in Western Germany and four transmitters on Taiwan. An even more powerful transmitter station was soon established on the Costa Brava in Spain, largely due to Howland Sargeant's skillful negotiations with the Spanish authorities.[17]

Our newly established Audience Research Department was under the able direction of Dr. Max Ralis, a Russian-born social scientist who had been educated at Cornell University. I first met Max during my year in Munich with the Harvard Refugee Interview Project, where, as a consultant, he impressed us with his serious, scholarly approach to problems of Soviet politics and ideology. His father had been one of the original editors of *Pravda* several years before the October Revolution, when the staff still included non-Bolsheviks. Max was erudite, but he never quite mastered the English idiom. Some of us on the staff once made up a list of his malapropisms, including "That's the way the cookie bounces," "I had it on the tip of my thumbs," and "From my vintage point."

Ralis and his staff began collecting and studying the increasing flow of Soviet media attacks on the Radio. At the same time, they gradually assembled evidence of listener reactions, which came from such sources as letters sent to "accommodation addresses"—that is, innocent-sounding post office boxes and names of pseudonymous persons in several Western European cities, as well as interviews with Soviet visitors to the West, subtly and discreetly conducted by Russian-speaking men and women retained by Ralis. At the Brussels World's Fair of 1958, our representatives interviewed three hundred Soviet tourists and discovered that sixty-five were Radio Liberation listeners. Of course, such a small sample was insufficient for us to make any sweeping generalizations, but we welcomed such a response from members of a group of Soviet citizens who must have been carefully selected and well briefed before they were allowed to travel abroad. In time, the Audience Research Department expanded to encompass program evaluation, which was carried out by recently arrived émigrés and defectors.

In 1957, Max played host to Dr. Wilbur Schramm of Stanford University, one of America's outstanding specialists on communication research. Sargeant had invited him to go to Munich, examine our operation, and offer his insights and recommendations concerning the most effective means for the Radio (a) to determine the nature of our audience, given our inability to poll them inside the Soviet Union, and (b) to influence them with broadcasts that challenged basic assumptions and prejudices inculcated in them throughout Stalin's twenty-five years of brainwashing.

Schramm compared the Radio's attempts to ascertain the makeup of our audience to a fisherman who drops his line through a hole in the ice and tries without any bait to identify the fish that brushes against the line. In his written report to us, he confirmed many of the hypotheses on which we were already basing our programming policy, and reinforced our own intramural discussions.[18]

Schramm modestly called his report "considerably less than a treatise," but by applying his survey of the Radio to his previous twenty years in mass communication, he reached several conclusions of considerable significance for us. First, in order to get the attention of the listener, we had to make sure that the "promise of reward" was greater than the "threat of difficulty." In other words, realizing how difficult it was to catch our broadcasts through the jamming, we had to offer the audience enough incentive by selecting content that made it worth their while to choose us in preference to competing Western radios that at times were not blocked. Paradoxically, jamming was both a disadvantage and an advantage for us in that it discouraged sustained listening but also tempted the listener to make the effort in hope of receiving forbidden fruit.

Second, once we got the audience's attention our message had to jump another hurdle: it had to be "decoded." This the listeners could do only in terms of their own frame of reference. "A tribe that has never seen or heard of an airplane can only decode it as a noisy bird. A citizen of the Soviet Union who has never seen or studied a two-party system must have a very hard time comprehending what happens in an American presidential election." For us at the Radio, this meant that our émigrés were better able to understand the mind-set of their compatriots under Communist Party domination. But could our spokespeople be accepted as credible?

If what we told them could be supported by objective evidence, and if we were accurate in all matters relating to events within the Soviet Union, our credibility would overcome the natural suspiciousness of many listeners. Thus, when Khrushchev's speech, although delivered in secret, was leaked inside the country during the months that the Radio was informing them of the text, the station could be accepted more readily as a reliable source. Schramm noted that the Radio seemed to be quite realistic about our role as a catalyst for change and "is most careful about suggesting or expecting any particular action of its listeners in the Soviet Union." Our best hope was to plant facts that over the long run would attract listeners to trust us and be receptive to our guiding them in the direction of improving their social situation. We did not expect to convert any real Communists, although constantly providing information might gradually raise doubts even among them concerning the validity of their beliefs. We always admired and envied the BBC's reputation among Soviet listeners, but in time we won the confidence of a vast audience by scrupulously checking our facts.

Seeking sober appraisals of the Radio's limitations and opportunities characterized Howland Sargeant's modus operandi in the formative years of the station and throughout his twenty-one years as president. He encouraged us to maintain regular contact with State Department and USIA executives who dealt with Soviet affairs,[19] and he also kept in touch with high-level officials, such as Henry Loomis, director of the Voice of America from 1958 to 1965. Howland liked to quote Loomis's image of the combined VOA-RL broadcasts to the Soviet Union as two blades of a scissors working together to produce an effective cutting edge.

Sargeant urged us to pick the brains of American and European academic specialists as well as Soviet émigré scholars. During his first year on board, Howland took a few of us to Cambridge, Massachusetts, for a two-day seminar with Harvard and M.I.T. professors. Such outside expertise acted as a healthy corrective against any illusions some of us at the Radio may have cherished that the Soviet regime was on the verge of collapse. We came to realize early on that we were in for a long haul and that our best approach was to provide our audience with material that they could not obtain from their controlled media, particularly information about what was happening inside their country.

To that end, Munich made effective use of its system of monitoring internal Soviet radio broadcasts from several republics, which repeated material from the local provincial press. Whenever we caught items in one area that were not reported elsewhere and that revealed some problem or inconsistency or crack in the Soviet facade, we would "cross-report" them to other parts of the USSR. For example, Khrushchev made impromptu speeches in the provinces in which he would say something so outlandish that the censors had to cut it out of the text printed in the central Moscow press. This presented the Radio with ready-made program material: without commenting, we juxtaposed his original statement in his own voice with the passages deleted by *Pravda*. This kind of programming was calculated to sow skepticism about Khrushchev as a responsible leader and about the Soviet media as a reliable source.

The sophisticated monitoring network was not the only means of keeping abreast of internal Soviet developments. A research unit was created in the 1950s, first under the direction of Victor Zorza, a Polish émigré recruited from the BBC by Victor Frank. Zorza was eminently qualified by temperament and linguistic ability for the task of supervising the collection of thousands of clippings from the hundreds of issues of the Soviet press, central and provincial, that arrived in Munich. When I visited his office during my first trip to Radio headquarters, he showed me bin after bin of index cards, each classified according to subject, usually with a "cutting" (as the British call it) from a Soviet newspaper or the transcript of a monitoring report. From this primitive beginning, the Radio's famous "Red Archive," which served as an invaluable source for programmers as well as outside scholars and journalists, emerged. Zorza left the Radio in the mid-1950s to become one of British journalism's top Soviet specialists.

He was succeeded by Dr. Albert Boiter, an American scholar trained in the Russian language and in Soviet affairs who deserves great credit for expanding the Radio's Research Department and adapting it to the age of computers. Perhaps most important, in the 1970s, when the flood of samizdat writings poured out of the Soviet Union from dissidents of many stripes, Boiter and his staff, headed by Peter Dornan, one of the Radio's most conscientious and dedicated colleagues, collected, vetted, and organized thousands of these documents to be broadcast verbatim. At the same time, the materials were made available to Western governments, academicians, and the press, thereby focusing world public opinion on the ferment of opposition within the Soviet empire. In some cases, dissidents were protected from severe reprisals by the regime because of the publicity they received.

American Political Leaders Speak to the Soviet Public

In January 1958, the Radio commemorated the fortieth anniversary of the Russian Constituent Assembly, the first free parliament in Russian history elected by universal suffrage, which Lenin had ordered dispersed by force of arms on the very day it convened. Because the theme was an important event in Soviet history that the regime had distorted, we decided that in addition to commentary from émigrés we would solicit a series of messages from political figures in the United States.

Twelve senators and five representatives of both parties broadcast statements urging free elections in the Soviet Union. The group included Senators Lyndon Johnson, John F. Kennedy, Hubert Humphrey, Paul Douglas, William Knowland, and Clifford Case. Norman Thomas also spoke, along with several editors of newspapers and magazines. *Izvestiya* of January 23, 1958, struck back, and that morning Moscow Radio broadcast the full text of its editorial:

> It is not the custom to hold merry dances at the bier of a deceased person. Certain members of the Senate of the U.S.A., in spite of this rule adopted by all civilized peoples, had a merry time at a funeral banquet several days ago. This was the funeral banquet of the Russian Constituent Assembly, which died a peaceful death forty years ago. This unique anniversary was exploited for radio appeals to the Soviet people by several prominent Americans, and although the occasion was hardly suitable, the participants in the radio broadcasts made merry with all their might.

Izvestiya selected Senators Knowland and Johnson, and Norman Thomas, among others, for personal attacks. Such a quick and sharp reaction from the major organ of the Soviet government indicated that we had struck a vulnerable spot, and we wasted no time in obtaining and broadcasting several rebuttals. Thomas declared:

> Over this radio, I spoke to you briefly on the fortieth anniversary of the day when Lenin and Trotsky forcibly dissolved the Constituent Assembly which originally they had favored. Frankly I had doubted how many of you would ever hear what I, along with other Americans, said on that occasion. Imagine then my pleasure to learn from *Izvestiya*'s long diatribe against us that our remarks must have received your attention. To be sure, *Izvestiya* says that "Norman Thomas hysterically questioned his hypothetical Soviet listeners." Obviously, it would not have troubled to reply if all my listeners were hypothetical. And I am quite sure that those listeners, whatever their silent answers to my questions, would agree that neither the questions nor the manner of my asking them was hysterical. . . .

On questions of American policy our speakers represented different views. Many of them would challenge my socialism, but none my right to speak to you in a friendly fashion as an American and a Socialist. . . . My position and my party's on this and other matters critical of our Government was well known. Nevertheless the Federal Government has never kept me from speaking to you or my own countrymen, or denied me radio facilities to speak to you about peace and freedom.

I should not impose this personal statement on you except that it justifies my raising a question not only for you but for the editors of *Izvestiya* to consider: Is there any writer, speaker, labor leader or political figure in your own great country who has been on occasion as openly critical of your Government as I of mine, who has been allowed to speak and write in freedom in Russia, or been offered the facilities of Radio Moscow to speak to Russia in the name of peace and freedom for us all?[20]

William Knowland, the Senate's leading spokesman for the Republican administration of President Eisenhower, also answered the newspaper, and he expressed his conviction that "a freely elected parliament represents the *future* of the Soviet peoples rather than the *past.*" He added that because *Izvestiya* claimed the Soviet public was satisfied with the present political order, the Soviet government merely had to hold free elections "under conditions which would guarantee Soviet citizens freedom of choice at the polls between persons and groups of different viewpoints. The democratic world has enough confidence in the good judgment of the Soviet public to abide by the results of such an election."[21]

Similar confidence in Soviet citizens was expressed by Eleanor Roosevelt in her message pegged to the anniversary of the ill-fated Constituent Assembly. I visited her in her townhouse in Manhattan's East Sixties and was graciously received. As she scanned her text before the tape recording, she asked me in her high-pitched soprano, "Do you say short-lived, or short-līved?" I told her that I preferred the long "i." She smiled and said she would pronounce it that way. Her thoughts are still relevant for Russia in its difficult time of transition today:

This is Mrs. Franklin Delano Roosevelt. Just a few short months ago, I visited your country and traveled thousands of miles in many directions. I had the opportunity of meeting and talking with individuals in all walks of life: students, doctors, farmers, government officials. And there I confirmed at first hand what I've always known—that the people of your country want above all else peace, a lasting peace which will permit you to continue the remarkable work of rebuilding your nation after the devastating war in which our peoples fought together as allies.

In Russia, too, I saw that your people have reached a level of education and scientific achievement as high, and in some respects higher, than anywhere in the world. And I wondered why such a talented people still lack their own freely elected government, a government responsible to their will.

If a truly lasting peace is to come, it must come as the result of the people of both our countries exerting their will on their governments. That is why I am speaking to you on the fortieth anniversary of Russia's first freely elected parliament, the Constituent Assembly. Short-lived though it was, it still symbolizes today the democratic aspirations and strength of the Russian people. I know from meeting and talking with you that you are mature and wise enough to guide your own destiny through your freely elected government. And I am certain that the rebirth of Russian democracy will be a source of new strength and inspiration for democracy and personal freedom everywhere, including the United States.[22]

We were gratified by the willingness of prominent Western figures to reach Soviet citizens via the radio. It not only built up our stature as an influential medium in the West, but also provided our listeners with a view quite different from their domestic media's distorted picture of the Radio as a ragtag collection of renegades being manipulated by the American intelligence "organs."

In the late 1950s, despite the exacerbation of tension in East-West relations by the repression of the Hungarian revolution and Khrushchev's saber-rattling over Berlin, it was becoming increasingly possible for tourists, entertainers, and scholars to visit the Soviet Union. I seized the opportunity to travel there and experience for myself the reality of life in the Soviet police state.

A Soviet citizen comes home one day, looks around the apartment, and sees something is missing. Distraught, he rushes to the telephone and calls KGB headquarters:

"Comrade, I just lost my parrot, my pet parrot, and I want you to know that I don't share his opinions!"

6   LIBERATION TO LIBERTY

Before Stalin's death, travel to the Soviet Union by Westerners was restricted. However, by the late 1950s, cultural troupes like the "Ice Capades" and "Porgy and Bess" were welcomed in Moscow. In exchange, Russian artists like the Moiseyev dancers and Maya Plisetskaya, the exquisite ballerina, were allowed to perform in the United States. American scholars could now pursue their research in the Soviet Union, and some even spent an entire academic year at Moscow and Leningrad Universities.

In 1958, I defended my doctoral dissertation, "Children's Theater and Drama in Soviet Education," the phenomenon of nationwide professional children's theaters in the Soviet Union, and finally received my Ph.D.[1] But I had not been there; I had never seen a play performed. I needed to meet these adult playwrights, regisseurs, and actors who devoted their careers to performing for young people. Most of all, I needed to sit in the audience with the children and to talk with them and their teachers. The Social Science Research Council awarded me a $2,500 grant to travel to the Soviet Union, a generous amount in those days. It was the chance of a lifetime after years of studying Russia from a distance. Not only would I be meeting people in the children's theater world, but I would get a firsthand look at the Soviet Union.

Howland Sargeant encouraged me to make the trip, saying that it would not only enhance my career as a Soviet specialist but also contribute to the Radio's understanding of Soviet reality through the eyes of one of their executives. He proposed that I protect myself and Amcomlib by "resigning," although in fact I was taking a short leave of absence. Only a few staff members knew about my real plan. Since my friend Albert Parry of Colgate University frequently visited the New York office, the émigré staff put two and two together and got five. Everyone thought I had accepted a position at an American university as a professor of Russian literature. As Sargeant liked to say, they "jumped from an unwarranted assumption to a foregone conclusion." My colleagues said kind words at the farewell party and gave me an expensive leather attaché case.

I prepared for this first journey behind the Iron Curtain with some misgivings. After all, I worked at the notorious radio that had become a major target of the Kremlin's enmity. My name had already appeared in 1957 in an article in *Kommunist,* the leading ideological journal of the Communist Party. Was the trip worth the risk? Was I endangering myself? Was I an irresponsible husband and father to leave Gloria and two young children for what might be a hazardous adventure?

On the visa application, I identified my occupation as "graduate student"—period. I made no reference to the Radio. When I boarded the Aeroflot flight at Le Bourget airport in Paris for the three-and-a-half-hour nonstop flight to Moscow on March 27, 1959, I wondered whether the KGB had a dossier in their files and whether I would be the star or the heavy in a Russian "B" picture on international espionage. Two CIA agents had even come up from Washington to brief me before my departure. They met me secretly at the Commodore Hotel near Grand Central and gave me all sorts of useful advice, like putting a strand of hair in the suitcase zipper to determine whether my luggage had been searched, and taking precautions when speaking on the phone.

I need not have been so apprehensive. My thirty-three days there passed without serious incident, although on several occasions I was followed by KGB "tails" in cars and on foot. But so were other Americans who were in Moscow at that time, and I didn't take it personally. I was able to meet and talk with scores of Soviet citizens on many levels of society. My brief exposure to Soviet contemporary life, and my confidential conversations with a number of individuals, reinforced my feeling that the Radio was serving an important function in reaching people who were dissatisfied with the quality of their life under Soviet rule and eager to obtain uncensored information and broaden their horizons.

Some Impressions of My Trip

I was struck by glaring contradictions in the realities of everyday Soviet life. The metros in Moscow and Leningrad were showpieces, with sculptures and murals that resembled a museum rather than a subway. But when I went to the men's rooms in public buildings—even the elegant old Anichkov palace in Leningrad, which had been converted into a children's recreation center (renamed in Stalin's day as the A. A. Zhdanov Palace of Young Pioneers)—not only was there no toilet paper in the stalls (only sheets of Soviet newspapers impaled on a nail), but the conditions were far from sanitary. The same was true at the automatic soda-dispensing machines on the street; you had to take a dirty glass and give it a perfunctory spray before putting it under the spigot. (I resisted.)

My room at the "first class" Metropole Hotel opposite the Bolshoi Theater in Moscow was seedy, the rug was threadbare, and the walls were scarred with cracks, but this may have signified more than neglect. A *Life* photographer who occupied a nearby room told me the walls were bugged. In the bathroom, the washstand tilted toward me, and the tub lacked a plug. (Luckily, I had been forewarned and brought along a rubber stopper.)

In GUM, the main department store on Red Square, I saw suits and dresses of poor quality and style, and I overheard one couple complaining that "they advertise, but they don't have anything to offer." As for shortages of food, when I was walking on Gorky Street with Natalia Satz, the world-renowned children's theater producer and director, in the midst of our conversation she suddenly noticed a woman carrying a reticule filled with oranges. "Apelsiny!" she shouted, and dashed after the woman to find out where she could get some.

One of the most revealing conversations I had with Soviet citizens took place at a chance meeting with two young men in a restaurant in Moscow. They seemed genuine, unlike the unctuous types who offered to change money. Whenever a waiter approached us, they would stop talking and give me a nudge under the table. They said you couldn't trust the waiters, who reported everything. To escape the inhibiting atmosphere of the restaurant, we went for a long walk. The boys asked me to alter the circumstances of our meeting if I ever wrote about them in the West. They told me they hated the regime, but they steadfastly refused to say whether their hatred was typical of Soviet youth. "We can't speak for others, only for ourselves." Moreover, they said they were reluctant to be completely frank with me: "You'll have to guess from some of the things we say what life is really like here." Nevertheless, during our long stroll the boys became less cautious as they warmed up to the subject of the Party dictatorship. "The Party wants to do your thinking for you, and teaches you to react like a robot," one of them said. His friend added, "If the people could speak freely, the whole system would collapse."

Among the highlights of my trip was a visit with Ilya Ehrenburg in his apartment near downtown Moscow; his study was filled with original Picasso paintings and ceramics, gifts from the artist. He was one of the Russian intellectuals who returned to the Soviet Union several years after the revolution.[2] In Paris in 1921, he had written a political novel called *Julio Jurenito,* a brilliant satire on the West as well as on Soviet Communism. Once back in Russia, however, he became an important propagandist for the Stalin regime, and during World War II his voice had been among the loudest demanding vengeance on the Germans.

Ehrenburg survived the years of Stalin's persecution of the Jews—how he did so was a matter of some controversy—and in 1953–54 his novel *The Thaw* gave both name and sanction to the period of literary revival that followed Stalin's death. In an essay on Stendhal published in 1956, he argued that a novel must be like a mirror set in the middle of life's roads, capturing all its bumps and rocks as well as the smooth surfaces. A few years later, in an essay on Chekhov, he urged freedom for creative writers from political restraints and formulas imposed on literature.

I asked Ehrenburg for his opinion of *Doctor Zhivago.* He had read it, and although he had not joined in the public chorus of attacks on Pasternak at the time of the Nobel Prize award, he called it Pasternak's weakest work. He had only praise for the poetry at the end of the novel, especially "Hamlet" and "Winter Night," but he thought that the hero, Zhivago, was not a credible character. "The choice of a doctor was a poor one," Ehrenburg said. "A doctor is a humanitarian—as Chekhov was. But Zhivago experiences the revolution and the civil war without doing anything to help anybody. If he were a poet rather than a doctor, he would be credible."

Neverthless, he said he had favored the publication of the book in the Soviet Union, not feeling apprehensive about the consequences, because "the novel is alien to Soviet youth and will have no effect on them."

Ehrenburg denied that Soviet Jews were still being discriminated against. "Especially after the Twentieth Party Congress [1956], there was no such discrimination." I remarked that I had heard about the recent arrest of several Zionists; he answered that he was not interested in Zionists. Before I left for Moscow, Boris Shub had said that if I happened to meet Ehrenburg I should tell him that a friend of mine in New York thought he was a brave man. When I passed along the message, Ehrenburg smiled without commenting. I wondered what this complicated man was really thinking.

At the Moscow airport on my last day in the Soviet Union, I was surprised to find Ehrenburg a fellow passenger on the Air France flight to Paris. The plane was almost empty, and I went up to the first-class cabin, where I sat with him. I translated for him a London dispatch from that day's *International Herald Tribune,* which reported an interview with Soviet novelist Mikhail Sholokhov, who had told the British press that Pasternak was a writer little known in Russia and that his admirers were limited to a small circle of snobs. Ehrenburg said quietly that it was not true.

We talked about Mikhail Svetlov, a famous Soviet poet, whom I had also met while in Moscow. Svetlov was one of the most talented young writers of the early postrevolutionary years, but he had become disillusioned with the system and, after refusing to act as an informer for the secret police, retreated into alcoholism. However, he continued to write and eventually became a beloved professor at the Gorky Institute of Literature and Art. He was posthumously awarded the Lenin Prize in 1967.

Svetlov was famous for his heavy drinking as well as for his wit. He was already in his cups when he came over to the table at the Aragvi, a Georgian restaurant, where I was sitting with another American and a Soviet actor, a friend of Svetlov's. I was shocked to see in the flesh this unshaven, disheveled person whom I had known for years through his beautiful verse. When I quoted from his best-known poem, *Grenada,* he said wryly, "Ah, I see you know the classics." Later we drove him home, and as he said goodnight he remarked, "I like to associate with good and devoted people." I said that I was glad such a thing was possible today. His answer remained with me whenever I recalled my five weeks in the Soviet Union: "Today, yes. But what about yesterday and tomorrow?"

Upon my return home, I wrote a 20,000-word report titled "Thirty-three Days in the Soviet Union." Sargeant distributed it among friends in Washington and in the communications media, and he received many letters praising its insights and impressions. The British quarterly journal of Soviet and East European studies, *Survey,* edited by Walter Laqueur and Leopold Labedz, published part of it in the April–June 1961 issue.

After an absence of almost three months, I returned to work as policy coordinator in the New York Programming Division, a newly created position. I kept in frequent telephone contact with Robert L. Tuck at CIA headquarters, to apprise him of current programming. A few years later, Tuck was transferred to Munich to head the Russian service, among the few Radio staff members directly employed by the "Company," or "The Pickle Factory," as CIA employees often called the Agency.

The name of Radio Liberation was changed in May 1959.[3] After the uprisings in Poland and Hungary in 1956,[4] when the United States and its allies reacted passively to the Eastern Europeans' defiance of Soviet hegemony, Washington reevaluated the Eisenhower/Dulles policy of liberation, which in turn led to changes in the Radio's policy and the search for a new name. Staff members in Munich and New York were consulted, and they proposed many alternatives. Some thought the Radio should abandon any far-reaching purpose. "Radio International Information," "Radio Beacon," and similar neutral-sounding names were suggested. Others maintained that "Radio Liberty" was preferable: it did not carry the aggressive association of liberating the Soviet Union, which was misinterpreted by many listeners and exploited in regime propaganda attacks. "Liberty," on the other hand, resonated with the idealism of the French people against autocratic tyranny and was a positive association for Russians. The Russian word *svoboda* also means freedom—still an elusive goal for Soviet citizens, especially after the Khrushchev regime had ruthlessly suppressed the Hungarian revolution. If the Soviet media referred to us as *"Svoboda,"* it would constantly remind listeners of what they lacked. Indeed, once "Liberty" was adopted, the media were forced to preface it with "so-called" when they blasted us. Eventually the Radio confirmed from listeners' interviews and letters that there was general approval of the new name. The change took effect in the Radio's other languages, but the Turkic services kept "Azadlik," a form of "free" and usually translated as "liberty."

Another significant change took place in the evolution of Radio Liberty at the end of the 1950s, when our transmitter strength was increased exponentially. Howland Sargeant had labored tirelessly with the Spanish authorities to get their permission to establish a transmission site on the

Costa Brava north of Barcelona. Our engineers, led by the skilled and experienced Colonel S. Y. (Steve) McGiffert, who had worked with Sargeant at the Voice of America, recommended the shoreline of the province of Gerona as ideally suited for beaming powerful shortwave signals toward the ionosphere at the proper angle for them to bounce back earthward to the target. Situated on the Mediterranean, the transmitters gained additional power from the reflection of the water when the signal was sent skyward from huge "curtain" antennas. It took several years for the site on the Playa de Pals to achieve maximum effectiveness, but from its start in 1960 it gradually increased in strength to 1.5 million watts of power, with six 250-KW transmitters operating separately. During times of crisis, four could be linked together to send a megawatt signal. In the summer of 1963, Gloria and I visited Pals during an automobile trip in Spain en route to Munich for a few weeks of temporary duty. We saw the construction of Antenna Group D and were impressed by the sheer magnitude of the project and its potential impact on the audibility of broadcasts through the ever-present jamming.

In 1960, I was appointed director of the New York Programming Division, succeeding Eugene H. King, a commercial radio executive, who had occupied the position since 1957. The unit produced programs not only in Russian but also in several other Soviet languages, so that my responsibility extended beyond the Russian service, which I had managed before my trip to the Soviet Union.

When news of the death of Boris Pasternak was reported in May 1960, Isaac Don Levine happened to be visiting our office on one of his frequent trips from Washington. He, Boris Shub, and I brainstormed about what we could do to honor the writer in addition to the Radio's programming. Levine suggested that American writers express their sympathy by arranging for a floral wreath to be placed on Pasternak's grave at the funeral. I got in touch with the executive board of the American Center of International PEN, the writers' organization that included poets, essayists, and novelists, and they cabled the U.S. Embassy with their request. We learned later that their wreath was prominently displayed and appreciated by Pasternak's mourners, one of whom was Andrei Sinyavsky, who was himself to become famous within a few years (see Chapter 7).

In the fall of 1960, we produced a roundtable discussion of Pasternak in observance of the second anniversary of his Nobel Prize award and his recent death. My good friend Professor Marc Slonim, of Sarah Lawrence College, who was noted for his literary criticism and books on Russian literature, acted as moderator with a group of authors in an exploration of "the writer's need for courage." They included Joy Chute, then president of the American PEN Center (who wrote fiction under the name of B. J. Chute to conceal her female identity in the male-dominated publishing world); Herbert Gold, the young writer just starting his career as a novelist and author of short stories; Santha Rama Rau, originally from India; Ferencz Kormedy, a Hungarian-born novelist; and George Reavey, a British poet, critic, translator, and friend of Pasternak.

In my introduction to the program recorded in our New York studio,[5] I said that it was being sponsored by four literary organizations: the Authors League of America, the American PEN, the American Center of Writers in Exile of International PEN, and the Poetry Society of America. Their joint statement read:

> Thoreau once said, "We all do stand in the front ranks of the battle every moment of our lives. Where there is a brave man, there is the thickest of the fight, there, the post of honor." Boris Pasternak was such a man. He believed that a writer should dare to speak the truth as he saw it. It is to his memory that this program is dedicated.

The broadcast included messages from American writers who were unable to participate in the panel discussion—Langston Hughes, Saul Bellow, Elmer Rice, Ralph Ellison, and Howard Fast. Professor Slonim and the panelists spent a lively hour contributing a variety of observations. George Reavey's remarks were the most relevant for our Russian audience:

> What sometimes astonishes me about the Soviet scene is the number of writers who in the past thirty or forty years have, in one way or another, had their books banned, who have in some way or another tried to maintain or reaffirm the great nineteenth-century tradition of the writer as a man with a conscience and who owes public and ethical responsibility to the community. To mention a few: Andrei Bely; [Yevgeny] Zamyatin, the author of We; [Yuri] Olesha, the author of Envy; [Isaac] Babel, who was arrested in '37; the author of The Trial Begins, which has just been published in America [later revealed to be Andrei Sinyavsky using the pseudonym Abram Tertz]; and, of course, Pasternak.
>
> There are also many young Russian writers who in the past ten years have written works which have either gotten them into prison or very nearly so. In fact, the repeated ideological instructions which are issued

every now and again by the Party seem to me very often to point to the fact that there is a stirring beneath, a stirring against conformity. The Pasternak case, of course, has focused universal attention on the writer's predicament and his moral dilemma. Pasternak was certainly not a political writer. His interests were mainly aesthetic and moral. He was, however, a man of conscience, who, when obliged to speak, always spoke what he thought.

In fact, I have heard him speak on a platform, and his answers sometimes were so direct that the audience couldn't help laughing out loud, because the answer came as sort of an unexpected shock. What Pasternak has done in *Doctor Zhivago* has been to reassert and reaffirm, restate his moral, aesthetic, and religious view and also he has attacked various aspects, particularly those of hypocrisy, which again is a worm of universal corruption and is not the sole inhabitant of the Soviet Union. He attacks those aspects as well as those cheap, didactic slogans which are so current. Pasternak even in the middle twenties or thirties said what he meant. I want to quote a passage from a speech of his in 1936: "I shall not speak in the common language of these times which is common to us all. I shall not repeat what you have said, comrades, but shall dispute with you, and since you are the majority the dispute this time will be fatal and its issue will be in your favor; although I do not flatter myself here with any hopes, yet I have no choice. I am now living all this and I cannot do otherwise. We must not expect salvation by raising our efficiency, as has been said here. Art is unthinkable without risk and the self-sacrifice of soul. We must attain in practice the freedom and daring of the imagination."

It took almost thirty years, but when *Doctor Zhivago* was finally published in Gorbachev's era, Pasternak was finally vindicated—alas, posthumously, like so many other victims of the Soviet regime.

Our Munich colleagues appreciated programs like the Pasternak panel, which maintained the high standard previously set by Boris Shub. Boris worked for the Radio until 1961, when he was suddenly fired. His contempt for authority and his innovative, freewheeling style were probably too radical for the CIA sponsors. There always seemed to be a certain amount of tension between Howland Sargeant and Shub. I was present at the first meeting between them, when Reginald Townsend, vice-president of Amcomlib, brought Howland over to our loft of émigré writers in the diamond district. Boris had no sooner been introduced to Sargeant when he complained that Howland and his colleagues at the USIA had once rejected one of Boris's RIAS projects in Berlin. It was not the most felicitous beginning for their relationship. Several months later Boris told me that he and his wife, Libby, had gone to dinner with Howland and Myrna Loy, who was then Mrs. Sargeant. He and the boss sparred verbally, batting witticisms back and forth in an intellectual ping-pong match that possibly rankled the former Rhodes scholar and sowed more seeds of resentment toward his irrepressible colleague.

On the day Boris learned that his career at Radio Liberty was over, he and I walked the streets of midtown Manhattan. He wept openly as though he had lost a child—which in a sense he had. He later joined an American organization seeking to reduce Fidel Castro's influence in Latin America, and he was working there when he died unexpectedly on April 20, 1965, at the age of fifty-two, as the result of a bungled surgical procedure. The *Times* obituary rightly called him "one of the principal organizers of Radio Liberty" and a "pioneer in radio broadcasting to Communist countries." It described his childhood as the son of the socialist writer David Shub, who escaped from Siberia and arrived in New York in 1908. "As a boy, young Boris was surrounded by exiled revolutionaries, many of whom visited his father's home. Among them was Alexander Kerensky, the moderate former Prime Minister of the Russian provisional government."

In the long list of Shub's accomplishments as a writer and propagandist, the obit mentioned his collaboration with General Walter G. Krivitsky, a high-level Soviet intelligence officer who had defected in the late 1930s. The articles, which appeared in the *Saturday Evening Post,* included Krivitsky's prediction of the Stalin-Hitler pact of August 1939. "The Krivitsky disclosures about Soviet policy were credited with causing a wave of defections in the ranks of American Communists," wrote the *Times.* Also noted was Boris's role as the political director for RIAS, and the fact that "during the Soviet blockade of West Berlin, he helped organize a demonstration of 250,000 Berliners against the Soviet action."[6]

Shub will be remembered for the invaluable contribution he made to shaping the Radio's policy and programming in the 1950s, setting it on the course that eventually made it a catalyst in the erosion of the Soviet power. For me personally, his death was a tragic loss of an inspiring friend who taught me a great deal about propaganda in the best sense of that term. He often exasperated me, but he was always stimulating and thought-provoking, and we had a close rapport, even sharing the same birthday, July 24.

An eerie coincidence of historical anniversaries marked Shub's surgery and consequent death; his hero, Abraham Lincoln, had been shot one hundred years earlier (April 14); he died on Hitler's birthday (April 20), and was buried on Lenin's (April 22). Boris liked to quote the French revolutionary Saint-Just, "Revolutionaries can sleep in their graves"—meaning that time was too short to waste. It was his way of goading himself and others to stop wasting time and seize the day.

Satire on Radio Liberty

John F. Kennedy became president in 1961 and brought a fresh lifestyle to the White House. It was not long before a best-selling record album called "The First Family" appeared, in which Vaughn Meader impersonated the president with witty satirical monologues that made fun of Jack and Jacqueline, Bobby and Teddy, and even Caroline and little John-John. The Radio interviewed Meader because we wanted to make the point that in a democracy no one, including the leader of the nation, is exempt from criticism and even ridicule. Roscoe Drummond, the veteran political commentator of the *New York Herald Tribune,* devoted one of his columns to our broadcast, declaring:

> The Kremlin won't like this. The joys which Mr. Meader tells about in producing "The First Family" and seeing it zoom to a massive best seller could whet the appetite of the Soviet people to want their own humorists free enough to do something like it. The power and popularity of "The First Family" come because it pricks big balloons. It is a weapon of free people directed at government, not a weapon of government directed at the people.
>
> The Kremlin won't like this because satire in the Soviet Union, despite a very limited easing of repression, is allowed to be used only to point an accusing finger at Soviet citizens or minor officials whom the government wants to hold up to scorn. . . . There is no freedom to stick pins in Mr. Khrushchev's balloon—or even Mr. Mikoyan's. . . . Mr. Meader's counsel and challenge to Soviet satirists is that the only tolerable censor is good taste and that must come from self-censorship.[7]

The absence of freedom to ridicule leaders, and the many negative features of Soviet reality, led to the phenomenon of underground political jokes that circulated orally, even in Stalin's time, when a person risked his life if he were caught telling an *anekdot,* as the Russians call it. The Radio collected these examples of Soviet forbidden humor from debriefing new defectors and émigrés and broadcast many of them from time to time. I began to analyze them and later included them in my lectures, entertaining and informing scores of university students and faculty with these irreverent comments on Soviet reality. Some of my favorite *anekdoty* appear as epigraphs to each chapter in this book.

Further Unmasking of Stalin

Among the most significant events of 1961 that Radio Liberty treated in depth was the Twenty-Second Congress of the Communist Party. At that meeting, Khrushchev resumed his assault on Stalin, not in a secret speech but in a public disclosure of even more shocking crimes. In Roy and Zhores Medvedev's biography of Khrushchev, the dissident Soviet intellectuals stated that these revelations were "even more shattering and on a much wider scale" than those of 1956:

> Khrushchev told not about thousands of victims as he had at the Twentieth Congress, but about millions, with stunning details about Stalin's personally signing hundreds of death warrant *lists*. After this speech and subsequent open discussions of Stalin's cruel abuse of power, it was no longer possible to clothe his name with any vestige of honor as had been done after the Twentieth Congress because of pressure from the Chinese Communists and as a concession to Party conservatives. Stalin's name and place in history were irreversibly compromised.[8]

The embalmed body of Stalin, which lay beside Lenin, was removed from the mausoleum. (When I was in Moscow in 1959, I visited "the gruesome twosome," as the American Embassy staff called them.) Stalin was buried behind the tomb at the Kremlin wall in a small cemetery that held other Soviet leaders and famous foreign supporters. The new de-Stalinization campaign took the form of removing all portraits and monuments of the dictator and renaming geographical locales, most notably Stalingrad, which became Volgograd.

With cautious optimism, the Radio welcomed these signs that Khrushchev was continuing to defy the die-hard Stalinists in Mao Tse-tung's China, having earlier purged the Soviet Party of Molotov, Kaganovich, Malenkov, and Voroshilov—all accomplices in crimes against humanity under Stalin. The liberal trend was felt in the cultural world as well when the novel by Aleksandr Solzhenitsyn about Stalin's labor camps, *One Day in the Life of Ivan Denisovich*, was permitted to be published in 1962, along with

The largest transmitter site of Radio Liberty, situated on Spain's Costa Brava. (The other transmitters were in West Germany.) Six 250-kilowatt transmitters and "curtain" antennas beamed powerful signals into the Soviet Union, reinforced by reflection from the Mediterranean Sea. (Courtesy of RFE/RL)

Radio Liberty's headquarters in Munich from 1953 to 1967. Formerly the administration building of the Oberwiesenfeld airport, where in 1938 British Prime Minister Neville Chamberlain and French Prime Minister Edouard Daladier landed, en route to the historic conference with Adolf Hitler that doomed Czechoslovakia's independence. (Courtesy of James Critchlow)

Walter K. Scott, director of Radio Liberty from 1965 to 1975, with John Chancellor, Voice of America director, during his visit to Munich in 1969. (Courtesy of RFE/RL)

Howland Sargeant, President of
Amcomlib, later renamed
Radio Liberty Committee, from
1954 to 1975. (Photo by Tommy Weber,
courtesy of Dorothy Sargeant)

Boris Shub, head of the New York
Program Section (NYPS) of Radio
Liberation, later Radio Liberty.
The early role of NYPS was to
prepare scripts in Russian for
transmission to broadcasting
headquarters in Munich. Shub was
a leading architect of the Radio's
policy and programming during
the 1950s. (Photo by Blackstone Studios,
courtesy of Anatole Shub)

Voices of Radio Liberty. Clockwise from top left:

Vladimir Rudolph, Russian émigré writer and Radio Liberty commentator for thirty years. He wrote and broadcast as Vladimir Yurasov. (Courtesy of the Rudolph Family)

Aleksandr Galich, famous dissident bard who broadcast on Radio Liberty after he emigrated. (Courtesy of RFE/RL and Hermitage)

Eleanor Roosevelt. (Courtesy of RFE/RL and Ann Meuer)

The Rev. Martin Luther King Jr. (Courtesy of RFE/RL)

The author on Red Square during his first visit in 1959. (Author's collection)

The author with Mikhail Gorbachev at the celebration of Radio Liberty's fortieth anniversary in Moscow, 1993. (Courtesy of RFE/RL)

Russian poster attacking Radio Liberty and Radio Free Europe: "The mutts bark and revile us, but the winds carry off their howls." (Courtesy of Paul Goble)

The CIA hand controls a Zionist engaged in espionage, Radio Liberty and Radio Free Europe at the microphone, and a tourist carrying a book with a Russian Orthodox cross from which "anti-Sovietism" spills. (Courtesy of Evgeny Lein)

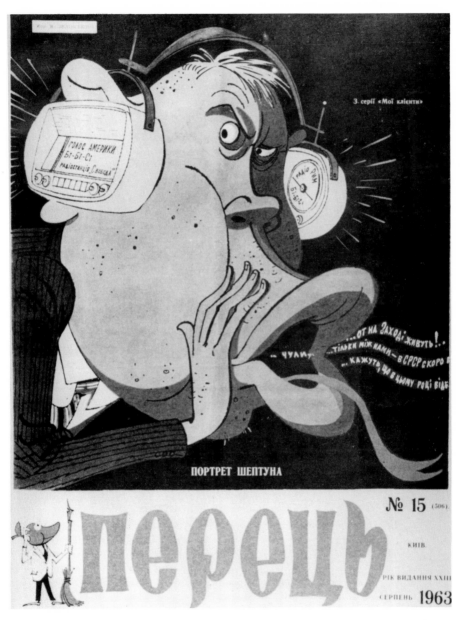

"Portrait of a Gossip" from Ukrainian satirical magazine *Perets* [Pepper], 1963. On the earphones are the names of Voice of America, BBC, Radio Liberty, and Radio Rome.

(Courtesy of RFE/RL)

Hillary Rodham Clinton at RFE/RL's new headquarters in Prague on July 4, 1996.
(Courtesy of RFE/RL)

millions of copies of other gulag memoirs. However, the Khrushchev leadership quickly realized that any wave of liberalism might be dangerous, that it could threaten the monopolistic position of Party bureaucracy and lead to other democratic innovations. By the end of 1962, Khrushchev demonstrated that he was opposed to modern trends in art by his vociferous reaction to an avant-garde exhibit in Moscow. Soon after, beginning in March 1963 at a meeting with prominent artists and writers, he retreated from the position he had taken during more liberal periods, and a recrudescence of tighter internal controls ensued.

The Pauling Affair

Radio Liberty deplored the new domestic hard line as it had previously inveighed against a foreign policy decision made by Khrushchev. A few months after President Kennedy took office, the Soviet Union suddenly resumed nuclear testing unilaterally. For three and a half years they had kept their promise not to resume testing unless the West started first. The world reacted with surprise and anxiety when the news broke on September 1, 1961. When I saw the text of the official Moscow statement in the *New York Times* that morning, I telephoned Linus Pauling at the California Institute of Technology. Dr. Pauling was already a Nobel Prize laureate in chemistry (he would later win the Peace Prize too) and was an honorary member of the Soviet Academy of Sciences. I was certain that he would condemn this abrupt unilateral abrogation of the agreement, and I hoped to persuade him to express his criticism on the air for Radio Liberty.

It was very early in the morning Pacific time, and Pauling had not yet seen the newspapers. After I read him the Soviet announcement, he was silent for a moment, then said quietly, "This is a step backward," and emphasized its implications for endangering world peace. I invited him to tape his reaction over the telephone, and he agreed, requesting that I call him back in fifteen minutes. He added that he would mention his connection with the Soviet Academy. The studio engineer got everything ready and Dr. Pauling spoke for a few minutes, identifying himself, in Russian, as a *pochyotny chlen* (honorary member) of the Academy. He expressed his shock and sorrow and urged the Soviet government to reconsider.

We broadcast his message, but the story did not end there. Six months later the United States, too, resumed nuclear testing, evidently fearful that the Soviets were getting ahead of us in the arms race. I again called Pauling to solicit his reaction, although I was aware that his reputation as a frequent critic of U.S. foreign policy and his image as a left-winger might raise some objections among our sponsors in Washington. However, if the Radio genuinely believed itself to be an independent medium of communication, we had an obligation to reflect opinion critical of U.S. government decisions as well. At first Pauling was reluctant, saying that it was one thing to condemn the Soviet government but another thing to condemn his own. I was surprised, because I thought that he would jump at the chance to rake Washington over the coals. I suggested that in view of his previous critique of the Soviet action we felt that we should offer him equal air time to discuss the American démarche. Convinced, he gave us a statement.

When our CIA overseers learned of the impending broadcast, they raised strenuous objections. Sargeant had always insisted that Radio Liberty must never waver from its policy of "telling it like it is," which in the long run contributed to our credibility, even if something negative about the United States reached the audience. He did not confront the CIA, but proposed that instead of censoring Pauling we balance the broadcast with a statement from another well-known American scientist who could defend the decision. This seemed to be a reasonable solution, and our New York office obtained a statement from atomic physicist Edward Teller.

But that decision still did not solve the problem. A flurry of exchanges ensued among staff in New York and Munich and among our CIA supervisors, who continued to oppose our quoting Pauling even when juxtaposed with Teller's remarks. They exerted considerable pressure on Munich to take the first version of the report off the air—which provoked Richard Bertrandias, then the Radio's director, to wire us from Munich:

> We truly fail to understand why it was necessary to pull it. Intrinsically, it is a natural for Radlib. Pauling, whom the Soviets have often used and who, for that reason, was lionized by us last year for damning the Soviet tests over Radlib, comes on Radlib again, again criticizes Soviet tests, and goes on to express his hope that the U.S. will not resume tests. Teller makes a nice pitch for freedom of discussion and shows effectively why he thinks Pauling is wrong. . . . All this raises serious questions in our minds here not only as to the integrity of the station but for our future handling of policy on such matters.[9]

Finally, after we solicited more statements from other scientists who defended the U.S. position, we were able to broadcast an approved version. Perhaps there were other instances of the CIA interfering directly in our programming until its connection with Radio Liberty was severed in 1971, but this one was undoubtedly the most disturbing. Not that there was a lack of surveillance of our daily activity. Throughout Sargeant's twenty-one years as president, his assistant, André Yedigaroff, was an agent of the CIA who had moved to New York to work with Howland. His job was to keep the Agency fully informed about the Radio's operation in Munich, New York, and elsewhere. Copies of memorandums, letters, telexes, and the like were routinely sent to Washington.

André Yedigaroff came from the Georgian aristocracy, his father had been a czarist guards officer, and his Russian was flawless. He lent a certain panache to our New York office. Once he invited some of us New York executives to lunch with his friend George Balanchine (born Balanchinadze, in Georgia). The famous choreographer regaled us with the account of his brush with Soviet bureaucrats—punctuated with Russian four-letter words—when they opposed his staging of Stravinsky's avant-garde *Agon* during a Moscow tour of his New York ballet company.

A debonair bachelor and expensive dresser, Yedigaroff carried on thinly concealed affairs with several of our secretaries. Later he married Lanna Saunders, an actress many years his junior and the daughter of our chief producer, Nicholas Saunders, a Russian-born actor on American television and on Broadway. For many years Nick combined his work for Radio Liberty with playing the role of Captain Barker, the foil of Phil Silvers on the television comedy series "Sergeant Bilko." Yedigaroff chain-smoked cigarettes, a habit that finally killed him, and he played bridge as often as he could—even during our lunch hour, when we had a game going almost every day (which we called "the oldest established, permanent floating bridge game in New York"). I first met him when he was still working in Washington, at a safe house where we debriefed a young Soviet named Yuri Rastvorov, who had defected in Japan. After the session, André took me to CIA headquarters, my first visit to the sanctum sanctorum.

The supervisor of Radio Free Europe and Radio Liberty at the CIA, Cord Meyer, was a sensitive and sophisticated intellectual who shared Sargeant's commitment to making the Radio the best possible surrogate voice for the silent Soviet peoples. The CIA's hands-off policy, though not observed 100 percent of the time, helped the Radio project an independent image that won the confidence of millions of its Soviet listeners, many of whom let us know that they considered it *svoi golos* (our own voice).

The programming policy staff in New York was strengthened in the early 1960s when a young woman, Catherine deBary Dupuy, joined us from the ideological section of the Voice of America, headed by Bertram Wolfe. Cathy had a scholarly mind and a flair for formulating policy and articulating it in cogent memorandums, and she made a major contribution to our strategic and tactical planning throughout the 1960s and 1970s. Howland Sargeant had great respect for her, and he relied on her insights and judgments until, tragically, she died of cancer.[10]

My program deputy in the New York Division from 1960 to 1966 was Valerian Obolensky, and Nika Thayer was my administrative assistant. Both came from the Russian prerevolutionary aristocracy; Obolensky was nicknamed "Zhuk" (Russian for "beetle") because of his dark eyebrows. Nika, the daughter of a czarist general, had come to the United States as a young girl.

The Cuban Missile Crisis

Radio Liberty faced a challenge during the last week of October 1962. At 2 A.M. in Moscow on Tuesday, October 23, President Kennedy began his speech exposing the presence of offensive Soviet missiles in Cuba and announcing a U.S. arms quarantine. Soviet citizens who tuned in at 4 A.M. heard a summary, and later that same day the full text, which was repeated every hour for the next twenty-four hours in seventeen languages. The Soviet media did not mention the speech until almost fourteen hours after it was delivered, and never reported the text in full. When Radio Moscow finally broke its silence, it said that Kennedy's speech was filled with "vulgar anti-Soviet attacks," called the quarantine an "act of piracy, a provocative action and an unheard-of violation of international law," and claimed that the USSR had been shipping arms to Cuba "for defensive purposes."

When the UN Security Council began its debate on October 24, our New York office relayed the stirring speeches of Ambassador Adlai Stevenson, in which the ambassador accused the Soviet Union of converting Cuba into a Soviet bridgehead in the Western Hemisphere, and the denials of the Soviet delegate, Valery Zorin. Radio Moscow, of course, ignored the dramatic demand by Stevenson that Zorin answer yes or no on the existence of offensive missile bases as he displayed aerial photos, declaring that he was prepared to wait "until hell freezes over" for an answer. TASS attacked "Stevenson's farce" in "bringing in faked CIA photos." As the tense superpower confrontation headed toward possible nuclear war, the Radio continued to give its audience a complete account of the news.

Finally, on October 27, the world learned of Khrushchev's letter to Kennedy offering the withdrawal of bases in Cuba if the United States would withdraw its bases in Turkey. Radio Liberty pointed out that this was tantamount to the Soviets actually admitting the existence of offensive bases in Cuba. Radio Moscow also reported the letter, the first official indication to Soviet citizens of the existence of the bases under the control of Soviet officers. When Khrushchev agreed to the dismantling of the missile bases and on-site verification by UN inspectors, the Soviet media began unfolding "plausible" explanations in order to present Khrushchev's backdown as a victory. We pointed out the confusion and contradiction in the Soviet press, as evidenced in the October 28 issue of *Izvestiya*, where a signed editorial on an inside page proclaimed:

> Measuring everything by its own cynical money-changer standards, there are those in the USA who speculate that in exchange for denying Cuba the ability to repel American aggression, one might "give up" some American base close to Soviet territory. . . . Such "proposals," if you can call them that, merely serve to betray the unclean conscience of the authors.

On the first page of the same issue of *Izvestiya,* however, Premier Khrushchev was quoted in his letter to President Kennedy: "Therefore I make this proposal: we agree to remove from Cuba those weapons which you consider offensive; the USA on its part would remove its comparable weapons from Turkey."

In the days after the crisis passed, we followed up with comments concerning the cost of the regime's recklessness for the citizens of the Soviet Union:

> For every missile that will now be dismantled and returned to the Soviet Union, enough money, material and labor had been expended to provide shoes for a quarter of a million people. The cost of every bomber or submarine sent to a foreign government would buy food for 50,000 to 100,000 children for a year.

We drew attention to the persistence of Stalinism in Soviet foreign policy:

> Khrushchev and other successors of Stalin, who in some ways have renounced Stalin's dogma, still are dogmatists and Stalinist in international affairs. They operate on the basis of the hopelessly obsolete, outdated formula about the increasing ferocity of the class struggle, and

this view is a terrible danger to the world, to the nation, to the people. The Cuban incident is precisely an example of this danger.

We quoted Lenin to demonstrate the regime's betrayal of avowed principles: "During the first days of the October Revolution, in November 1917, Lenin said, 'We are fighting against deceit by governments that speak of peace but in fact conduct predatory wars. We are against secret diplomacy and will act openly before the entire people.'" *Izvestiya*'s reaction to these comments was to condemn Radio Liberty in its November 5 issue for "lies, slander and the fanning of hatred for the Soviet Union."[11]

The resolution of the Cuban crisis did not end Radio Liberty's involvement with Cuba. In the months that followed, we prepared to beam Russian-language newscasts to Cuba every night in the hope that we would reach Soviet civilians and military personnel stationed there. By special arrangement with WBT, a 50,000-watt CBS affiliate in Charlotte, North Carolina, our New York division excerpted programs from our regular service to the Soviet Union and telephoned the tapes to WBT for relay into Cuba. The station's signal was reported to be clearly audible on the AM dial, and the broadcasts continued for several months and were then discontinued, presumably for budgetary reasons and because there was no significant feedback concerning the effectiveness of our message.

By 1963, the Radio was on a twenty-four-hour schedule with thirteen transmitters in West Germany and Spain and four on Taiwan. We beamed 210 transmitter hours daily on twenty-six shortwave frequencies in seventeen languages to the Soviet Union, reaching Soviet Siberia and the Far East. We identified ourselves as the most powerful free voice heard in the Soviet Union, working for the establishment of a democratic order on the territories of the Soviet Union, but leaving it to the citizens themselves to establish a genuinely representative government responsible to the will of the people. Although the station had become Radio Liberty in 1959, our parent organization was still known as the American Committee for Liberation (sans "Bolshevism") as late as February 1964, when it was finally changed to the Radio Liberty Committee. In a statement to the press, Howland Sargeant said the change was to "clarify for the public the mission and major role of the organization." Spencer Williams, director of press and public relations, who had been Moscow representative of the American-Russian Chamber of Commerce from 1930 to 1940, amplified the reasons for the change: "We consider that liberation is actually the task of the peoples of the Soviet Union themselves. It's not the task of foreigners to bring about liberation inside the Soviet Union. Our concept of liberation is restoration of a form of government responsive to the will of the people."

If there was still a vestige of hope on the part of some militant émigrés at Radio Liberty that their homeland could be liberated from outside, those of us in the American management made it clear that the Radio's image should be that of a "guest in the Soviet home." In our internal policy statements and releases for public consumption, we emphasized that the Radio "communicates with the Soviet listener as a guest who is intimately acquainted both with life inside the Soviet Union and beyond its frontiers," seeking to carry on a dialogue that "stimulates thought and gives cohesion to internal forces working toward freedom."

Letters from listeners frequently expressed approval of our approach—for example, a Moscow University professor wrote: "Radio Liberty is irreplaceable—the only station broadcasting from the West with a genuine Russian flavor." A Lithuanian student said that Radio Liberty's "strong point is that it is always in step with Soviet events. . . . It shows listeners the other side of the coin." A listener in Ufa, Bashkir Autonomous Republic, responding to a Tatar-Bashkir program, said: "I often get great satisfaction listening to you. There are many things which I would like to say, but I would like to sit with you and talk. Let us hear your voice more often."

Most significant of all, a retired Red Army officer and Communist Party functionary in Moscow admitted: "I can't think of any Radio Liberty program that I dislike. . . . I'm afraid I have been turned into a bad Communist by foreign radio listening."[12] Recalling Wilbur Schramm's advice in the 1950s that we should not expect to convert any real Communists, but by constantly providing information the Radio might gradually raise doubts even among them concerning the validity of their beliefs, we hoped that this Moscow official's reaction was shared by many of his comrades.

Why do KGB agents always travel in threes?

One of them can read, the second one can write, and the third one keeps his eye on the two intellectuals.

 7 PROGRAMS AND CONFERENCES IN THE 1960s

Before the Radio Liberty transmitters in Spain began operating in the early 1960s, the relative weakness of our signal and the strength of the Soviet jammers had inhibited the use of music on the air, except for the continuously repeated Grechaninov theme and melodious bridges between programs. One memorable exception in the 1950s was the appearance in our New York studio of Louis Armstrong, who announced in his gravel voice—in carefully rehearsed Russian—that he was speaking over Radio Liberty. Then he put his trumpet to his lips and played a popular Soviet tune called "Five Minutes" from a film hit, "Carnival Night." I don't know of any evidence that he received fan mail, but the program foreshadowed the tremendous popularity that American jazz musicians and the Beatles were to achieve among the Soviet masses.

In December 1962, after the brief period of liberalism following the Party Congress of 1961, the Khrushchev regime cracked down on the playing of jazz, attacking it as "decadent," as it had been called in Stalin's time.[1] It was an ideal opportunity for the Radio to fill the vacuum with a series of Russian programs on jazz. The Voice of America already had a jazz hour hosted by the popular and talented Willis Conover, who spoke in English over unjammed frequencies. We felt that our program would attract more listeners, especially youth, who would get into the habit of listening to Radio Liberty and absorb its more serious political and ideological fare.

Members of the Benny Goodman group had recently returned from a tour of the USSR with some original Soviet jazz compositions they had smuggled out. Joseph Valerio, a Radio Liberty producer in my New York division, had contacts in the jazz world and arranged for some of the Goodman group and other well-known performers to record the forbidden music from Russia in our studios, taking strict precautions to protect the identity of the Soviet composers. The noted jazz expert George T. Simon reported the unique "jam session" and the program series that evolved, which was inaugurated on June 30:

> Radio listeners who tune in Radio Liberty will hear the modern swinging sounds of eight American jazz musicians on a new show called THIS IS JAZZ. But they won't be playing the usual American fare. Instead they'll blow four jazz pieces composed by Russians which they recorded exclusively for Soviet consumption.
>
> The octet is headed by Bill Crow, bass, and alto saxophonist Phil Woods, members of the Benny Goodman band that toured the Soviet Union last year. Playing with them are two other Goodman alumni, tenor saxophonist Zoot Sims and pianist John Bunch, plus trumpeter Art Farmer (using mostly the fluegelhorn), trombonist Bob Brookmeyer, baritone saxophonist Nick Brignola and drummer Walter Perkins.
>
> The songs were sent in rough form to Crow and Woods who assigned them to Al Cohn, a top jazz arranger, to score for the octet. The tunes have modern jazz flavor, and the performances by these outstanding musicians compare favorably with the best jazz being recorded today.
>
> The entire project is a labor of love. The musicians aren't being paid, and their union has sanctioned this unusual move in the name of "international jazz coexistence."[2]

A recording of that historic jazz session was specially reproduced in a limited edition. Entitled "Jazz at Liberty," the liner cover carries a photograph of the Radio's transmitter site in Spain, along with Simon's review, and pictures of the famous jazz performers. It can now be revealed that one of the four songs written was by Gennadi Golshtein, a well-known composer and saxophonist. We chose it for the theme of "Eto Dzhaz" (This Is Jazz), a weekly half-hour program that included the best of modern American jazz and interviews with top performers. The program was produced in our New York studio by Boris Orshansky, who had a warm, relaxed style of delivery and was a natural for many types of shows and special events.

When Boris Shub was still in charge of the programming unit in the mid-1950s, he sent Orshansky up to Yankee Stadium to broadcast a game in Russian from the press box, by arrangement with the Yankee front office. Shub, a rabid Yankee fan, regarded baseball as a quintessentially democratic sport, a paradigm of a free society, where nine men act their individual roles of pitcher, catcher, and fielders but all work together for the common cause. By acquainting Russians with his beloved sport, he hoped, as always, to make a political point. He also appreciated the obvious publicity value for our radio in the United States, and we informed the press that a Russian would announce a game between the Chicago White Sox and the Yankees. Orshansky ad-libbed in Russian as he described Mickey Mantle at bat. He interspersed English words like "strike" and "error" in his narrative of the action on the playing field. The broadcast must have sounded strange to the Russian audience of the 1950s, but in the current post-Soviet era American players are teaching baseball to Russian youngsters, and today they even have a league of their own.

To further enrich our music programming, Joe Valerio invited the well-known composer Vernon Duke to broadcast over Radio Liberty. Duke, whose real name was Vladimir Dukelsky, told us that it was his friend George Gershwin who suggested the Americanized version of his name after Dukelsky had immigrated to the United States from Russia and launched his career as a composer of popular songs. He discussed in Russian his training in classical music and his transition to writing such memorable songs as "April in Paris." We all thought our listeners would like to hear that haunting song, so Duke translated "Yip" Harburg's lyrics and brought Nicolai Gedda of the Metropolitan Opera House to sing it (Gedda was part Russian). Duke had to make one change in the lyrics to preserve the stress on the word "April," which in Russian is *Aprel*, with the accent on the second syllable. He made it "Summer in Paris," which is "*Letom v Parizhe*." Gedda's rendition was poignant and evocative. He also sang an original song that Duke composed exclusively for Radio Liberty with lyrics by a good friend, the poet Ogden Nash. All three came to our office several times and enjoyed collaborating on that sentimental song, which expressed the joy one feels on returning home after wandering abroad for years.

Meetings and Conferences

Amcomlib's board of trustees held annual meetings in the posh Union Club on Park Avenue in Manhattan. I did not attend them in the early years, when I was still Boris Shub's deputy. After one such dinner in the mid-1950s, Boris told me that Allen Dulles, director of the CIA, had addressed the group and emphasized that the Radio had a great responsibility to make its message to the Soviet Union as effective as possible—or it would only be "a fart in a blanket." Boris and I privately joked that in such a case our acronym RADLIB would have to be changed to RADFIB.

At board dinners in the 1960s, I met old Moscow hands, CIA executives, and other representatives of the American intellectual and political power elite. Richard Helms, who later became a CIA director, told us a political anecdote at one dinner to illustrate the cultural and ethnic differences among the various nations in our sphere of interest. If a husband were to return home unexpectedly and discover his wife in bed with another man, the scenario would vary according to the nationality of the principals. Thus, an irate Russian's rage would be answered by his wife, who shields her lover with her body as she shouts, "Shoot *me,* Ivan, not him!" On the other hand, a Chinese would slowly approach the bed and coolly tell his wife, "Ming Toy, I am giving you serious warning number 457," a reference to the Communist Chinese habit of issuing "serious warnings" when foreign aircraft came too close to their border or penetrated their territory.

The trustees complimented Radio Liberty on its progress and assured us that moral and fiscal support from Washington was dependable and ongoing. These were the years before 1971, when only a few senators and congressmen knew about the connection between the U.S. government and the Radios. In that year, Senator Clifford Case of New Jersey blew our cover. For many months thereafter, the foes of Radio Liberty and Radio Free Europe in Congress, led by Senator J. William Fulbright of Arkansas, chairman of the Foreign Relations Committee, fought to eliminate the Radios. (See Chapter 9.)

My only meeting with Allen Dulles occurred in early 1962, when I represented the Radio at a Princeton University conference devoted to the role of American information, public and private, in the Cold War. The distinguished guests included Dulles, recently retired from the CIA; George Gallup, director of the American Institute of Public Opinion; Professor Frederick Barghoorn, Yale's expert on Soviet politics and ideology (who was arrested by the KGB a year later on trumped-up charges and released from the Lubyanka prison, thanks to the personal intercession of President Kennedy); George Allen, director of the USIA; and Lewis Galantière, Counselor for the Free Europe Committee.

When I learned that Galantière was scheduled to speak about the role of Radio Free Europe, it seemed to me a glaring omission not to mention Radio Liberty. I asked the organizer of the conference, John Whitton, for the opportunity to say a few words, and he invited me to follow Galantière with a brief description of Radio Liberty. The text of my talk appeared a year later in a book entitled *Propaganda and the Cold War*.

Describing our special function as an "internal" voice (we had not yet used the word "surrogate"), I pointed out that Radio Liberty's émigré staff members share "a common heritage and know from firsthand experience the fundamental interests and aspirations of their brothers in the homeland." Noting that the increase in transmitter power since we started broadcasting helped to overcome the jamming, I said:

Evidence that we are heard inside the Soviet Union comes from hundreds of interviews with Soviet tourists and members of delegations in the West, from conversations with Soviet citizens held by Western tourists, students, and guides, and perhaps most important, from letters that slip through the net of Soviet censorship and reach Radio Liberty's mail drops in the free world. The great majority of this audience mail is favorable and encourages RL in the conviction that its basic premise is sound, namely, that in all walks of Soviet life people are thirsty for information and ideas denied them by the official media, that in the current era of ferment after de-Stalinization they seek a deeper understanding of their own society.

Youth in particular is skeptical, often disillusioned, and searching for greater perspective. For example, we received a letter not long ago from a sixteen-year-old in the Moscow area who asked us to put on a regular program which he would like us to call "Russia Yesterday, Today, and Tomorrow." We have responded to the young man's request and are attempting to give him and others like him an insight into the heritage of Russia's liberal thinkers—men like Alexander Herzen, whose ideals of personal and political liberty have great relevance today, and for the Russian future. The same is true, of course, for our approach to the Ukrainian, the Georgian, and the other nationalities.

R. H. S. Crossman [the British MP and expert in propaganda] once said that the first step in the erosion of a totalitarian dictatorship is the development of individuals who think independently. This is Radio Liberty's goal as it strives to break the monopoly over communications which the Soviet regime tries to impose on its subjects. In time, we believe, through an *evolutionary* rather than a revolutionary process, the Soviet people may not only *think* about how to fulfill their deep desire for peace, a more abundant life, and greater freedom of self-expression—they may begin to *act*.[3]

In 1969, a long diatribe against Radio Liberty, Radio Free Europe, and the Voice of America entitled "Filth on the Air" appeared in the Moscow periodical *Komsomolets*. Among the false accusations against several of Radio Liberty's émigré writers and American staff members was the following:

> Some time ago at a symposium in Princeton University in the USA on the theme of "Propaganda and the Cold War," a speech was made by one of the specialists of "psychological warfare," Dzhini Sossin [*sic*], head of the New York bureau of Radio "Liberty." In explaining the operation of the radio station, Sossin spoke out for the dissemination of false and provocative rumors with the aim of sowing discord among separate socialist states as well as among various social, ethnic, and age groups in each of these states.[4]

From time to time other Soviet articles referred to that Princeton speech, which may have irked the authorities because I wrote that the Soviet people were becoming active in their search for change. Another conference in which I took part also led to an attack that appeared in *Neva*, the leading journal of literary criticism in Leningrad, which published a short piece in 1956 written by G. Aleksandrovich. He said:

> In November 1962 a secret conference was held in the State Department of the USA on problems of "psychological warfare," in which leading collaborators with the propaganda and intelligence services participated. In addition, the conference also invited representatives of reactionary émigré circles, which, in the opinion of Washington, made up an important detachment of subversive propaganda. The participants

in the conference decided to create an operational-coordinating bureau to lead "psychological warfare" against the socialist countries. This bureau is under the National Security Council. The staff of the bureau was kept secret, but it became known later in the press that the leading role is played by representatives of the CIA and USIA. In the process of planning "psychological operations," they are employing the services of about sixty so-called "scholarly research institutes," called on to gather and systematize relevant information.

One of the participants in the conference, the director of the New York bureau of Radio "Liberty," Dzhini Sosin, set forth in his speech with cynical frankness a program of subversive measures against the peoples of the socialist countries. It is curious that in that program the item about broadcasting "works of underground literature" (such as the libelous anti-Soviet writings of Tertz-Sinyavsky, Arzhak-Daniel and Tarsis) symbolically was placed side by side with the item concerning the dissemination among Soviet citizens of lying and provocative rumors.[5]

Thomas Sorensen, then an executive of the USIA, was present at Princeton. He was one of three talented brothers, including Theodore, who was John F. Kennedy's speechwriter and confidant, and Robert, who had been a consultant to Radio Free Europe. When Tom saw me chatting with Allen Dulles during one of the coffee breaks, he sidled up to me later and with mock horror whispered, "Gene, your cover is showing." That evening, Professor Hadley Cantril of the Princeton faculty invited a few people from the conference to his home for a nightcap. Cantril was a psychologist who specialized in "transactional psychology," a branch of the discipline that investigated and shed light on the perceptions of human beings, their responses to verbal and visual stimuli, and their preconceived attitudes and prejudices based on their cultural background.[6] Hadley was a friend of Howland Sargeant, who loved to tap the brains of academic specialists in hope of improving the Radio's broadcasts. We often consulted Cantril in order to gain a better appreciation of the psychological barriers we needed to overcome to reach a Soviet audience from abroad.

Four of us met that evening in Cantril's house: the host, myself, Allen Dulles, and Louis Fischer, the renowned American expert on Russia. I was struck by Dulles's deference toward Fischer. Here was America's legendary spymaster modestly acting like a student at the knees of a revered professor as he questioned Fischer about Stalin's personality and policies, which Fischer was well qualified to analyze as a result of his years of experience inside Stalin's Russia.

When Fischer's *Life of Lenin* was published in 1964, I invited him to our microphone for a broadcast that soon stimulated letters from the Soviet Union, including a request for a copy of the book, and another disputing some of Fischer's interpretations of Lenin. Fischer responded in another talk and in effect conducted a dialogue with his listeners in the Soviet Union. Lewis Nichols of the *New York Times Book Review* described the unusual exchange in his column "In and Out of Books," which was illustrated with an amusing drawing of a young Soviet sitting at his desk near Lenin's portrait and bust and writing a letter while listening to his radio.[7]

In addition to my responsibility for the production of radio programs for Munich, I frequently made public appearances. In November 1961, the City of New York inaugurated a television station over an ultra-high-frequency station, WUHF. The first day's program was a potpourri of interviews and discussions on theater, music, and politics. In his review, Jack Gould, television critic for the *New York Times,* praised the premiere as "an attractive TV version of WNYC radio." He wrote:

> The evening's final feature was a first-class panel discussion of Soviet policy conducted by Dr. Gene Sosin of Radio Liberty. The participants—Hal Lehrman, Charles Malamuth, Valerian Obolensky and Christopher Emmet—had the time, two hours, to dig into the complexities of Communist behavior. The speakers offered an admirable amount of specific factual detail to back up their views and also effectively complemented each other. The common purpose was to provide a comprehensive analysis, not to win an argument.[8]

Hal Lehrman was a veteran newspaperman; Charles Malamuth was a well-known Russian expert, having served as a programming and policy adviser to both the Voice of America and Radio Liberty in their Munich offices; Christopher Emmet was active with the International Rescue Committee. We welcomed such a favorable review inasmuch as Radio Liberty was still rarely mentioned in the media.

The U.S. Army War College in Carlisle, Pennsylvania, invited me in 1962 and 1963 to join their "strategy seminars" along with other specialists on Russia, such as Professor Albert Parry of Colgate. At one point a colonel came up to me and said: "You know, we have the deterrent against Soviet aggression, and God forbid that we ever have to use it. But you have a powerful deterrent that you're using every day." I never forgot those perceptive words, for he expressed precisely one of the raisons d'être of our broadcasts—namely, to discourage the Kremlin leaders from risking war with the United States by keeping them in doubt about their citizens' behavior in a crisis. Our constant flood of information thwarted the regime's attempts to sow hatred against the West and to brainwash the public to obey orders blindly. Someone else at another point in Radio Liberty's history declared that we were worth several military divisions.

The Radio Changes Directors

At this time, Howland Sargeant appointed Lewis Shollenberger, the Washington head of special events and news operations of the American Broadcasting Company, as the director of Radio Liberty in Munich. He succeeded Richard Bertrandias, who had served there since 1956, having worked for the CIA's radio operations in the Far East. Dick had been an able administrator during our evolution from "Liberation" to "Liberty."

Unfortunately, it soon became clear that Shollenberger lacked the international background and decisiveness of leadership that the position demanded; he kept referring to his job as a "learning experience." Although in New York I was less affected by the day-to-day mismanagement of the operation, I gradually became aware (sometimes in urgent overseas telephone calls from my American colleagues) of gripes and resentment against Shollenberger's modus operandi, which also impinged on the New York division's effectiveness. During a trip to Munich in the spring of 1964, I witnessed the confusion and plunging morale of the staff.

Back in New York, I continued to get complaints from Europe and told Sargeant in some detail what was going on in Munich, urging him to do something. Howland listened quietly and thanked me for my candor, saying: "It's very important for the general to know what's really happening on the front lines." He took immediate action by arranging for an independent survey of the situation by a Washington official. Within a short time, Howland fired Shollenberger, carefully softening the blow with the proper diplomatic language in which he was so skilled.

Walter K. (Ken) Scott, a career foreign service officer, was named director of Radio Liberty. He had recently served in Lagos, Nigeria, as the deputy chief of mission and had been U.S. consul general in Munich in the 1950s. His wife, Irene, was a charming German woman, and they had many friends in Bavarian intellectual and social circles as well as among U.S. civilian and military representatives there. Ken took over as director in 1965 and remained for ten years, overseeing the difficult transition of the Radio from its CIA sponsorship to its unpredictable future when it merged with Radio Free Europe under the supervision of a newly created Board for International Broadcasting. I came to know and respect Scott as a result of close association with him when I worked in Munich from 1966 to 1970 as his senior adviser and deputy (see Chapter 8).

Munich was a familiar city, because Gloria and I had lived there during 1950–51 when we were with the Harvard Project. I had made several trips to Radio Liberty in the 1950s, and in the summer of 1962 we took our children, Don, age ten, and Debbie, age eight, for a delightful trip to several countries in Western Europe, ending up in Munich, where I spent several weeks working with Dick Bertrandias and the Munich programmers. It turned out to be good training for the four-year assignment later in the 1960s.

Khrushchev's Era Ends

Rumors of the sudden and stunning ouster of Nikita Khrushchev reached our office on October 14, 1964, after Munich's daytime staff had already left work. I got a call from Leo Gruliow, editor of the *Current Digest of the Soviet Press,* an invaluable periodical for Western scholars and journalists who either did not read Russian or, if they did, simply had no time to pore over the many newspapers that the *Digest* excerpted. Leo was a frequent consultant to Radio Liberty concerning programming and policy in the 1960s before he moved to Moscow for several years as head of the *Christian Science Monitor*'s bureau.

Leo's tip, relayed from his sources in Moscow, who noticed suspicious goings-on, was soon officially confirmed. Obolensky and I went to work preparing the Radio's editorial comment on this momentous event. We decided to raise some basic questions about what the new regime would do to ensure peace and fulfill the needs and aspirations of Soviet citizens. We felt that the Radio's most useful approach was to present the audience with a checklist of criteria to use in evaluating whether Khrushchev's successor was acting in the best interests of the people:

> Will the threat of nuclear war be diminished? Will the policy of peaceful coexistence be continued? Will the efforts further to relax international tension be continued? Will disarmament efforts be continued? Will the promises to raise the standard of living and to improve agriculture be fulfilled? Or, on the contrary, will the armaments race weigh down

the country's economy? Will the primary objective of the new leadership be the solution of the country's basic political, economic, and social goals? What will be the new regime's attitude toward people's private and spiritual lives? Will civil rights and the dignity of the individual be respected? Will the problems of clothing, food, and shelter be finally resolved?

Will the ordinary citizen be able to express himself more freely and exert a greater influence on the government in reaching decisions made in the name of the people? Will all the people be given greater access to truthful information about both the outside world and actual conditions within the country? Will the contacts and cultural exchange with all peoples be continued in the future? Will open and frank discussions of the events of recent history, which are still hidden from the people, be permitted? Will the public be able openly to discuss the real problems of our time? In other words, will the process of de-Stalinization that was begun under Khrushchev be continued, accelerated, and brought to its logical conclusion?[9]

At such a crucial moment, Sargeant understandably asked to see the final draft of the text. We telexed the editorial to Munich in time for the early morning broadcast, Moscow time. Radio Liberty continued with emergency programming for the next few days, including a "political obituary" of Khrushchev and special correspondents' reports from major Western European capitals with reactions to the startling event.

It did not take long for the new Brezhnev regime to show its ugly face. Within the next year, Andrei Sinyavsky (pseud. Abram Tertz) and Yuli Daniel (pseud. Nikolai Arzhak) were arrested and tried for writing "treasonable" fiction, in which their characters expressed anti-Soviet sentiments. At their trial in February 1966, the fact that the Radio had broadcast their works was used against them by the prosecutor. The judge, hardly an objective participant, read a transcript of a monitored Radio Liberty program in which the reading of a story by Daniel was allegedly preceded by "anti-Soviet attacks." When Sinyavsky attempted to defend his writing, the judge responded: "Only the court can decide whether your works are anti-Soviet, and the reactions [in the West] merely prove how and by whom they are being used. Look at Radio Liberty, which devoted three broadcasts to *Lyubimov.* Do you suppose they did that for no good reason?"[10]

The Radio also broadcast Sinyavsky / Tertz's powerful *Sud Idyot* (The Trial Begins), read by Victor Frank in installments over eight and a half hours. Sinyavsky was sentenced to seven years, and Daniel to five years, in the gulag.[11] For the first time in Soviet history, writers had been convicted on the basis of their published works. As British expert Max Hayward remarked, "Many Soviet writers have been imprisoned, banished, executed, or driven into silence, but never after a trial in which the principal evidence against them was their literary work." The Sinyavsky-Daniel affair caused consternation among the intelligentsia and other segments of the population and led to their deepening disillusionment, and in some cases to outright dissident protests.

Faced with a neo-Stalinist reactionary regime under Brezhnev, Radio Liberty turned to academic, media, and government experts on the Soviet Union for advice on how to adapt the programming. In the fall of 1965, Sargeant asked me to organize a two-day conference at New York University. Professor George Gordon, a specialist on communications, cooperated, and the first day began with a keynote address by Ithiel de Sola Pool of M.I.T., followed by a discussion period with invited guests from the media and academic community.

Professor Pool was director of the so-called "Comcom" Project on Communist communications at M.I.T.'s Center for International Studies. Max Ralis and his deputy, Gene Parta, supplied Pool with information gleaned from about two thousand Soviets traveling abroad. Based on this and other sources, and with the help of a Harvard mathematician, Pool attempted a computer simulation of the internal communication system of the Soviet Union and formulated hypotheses concerning the impact of Western media on the Soviet population. His speech, which drew on the research of the Comcom project, was prophetic:

> . . . But if the winds of free Western thought did not penetrate into the Soviet Union, the abatement of the revolution would have been slower and less liberal in quality. *Most of the things of a positive character that are happening in the Soviet Union today are explainable only in terms of the influence of the West, for which the most important single channel is radio.* [Italics added.] It does seem possible to predict with high probability that in the long run Russia will achieve a more modern type of society with a more normal form of social coordination that relies more heavily on freer mass media instead of Party control, and is generally more pluralistic. The main reason for predicting this is indeed the growth of mass media that bring information from abroad and the fact that Soviet society is essentially an imitative one. In the long run those who are talking to the Soviet Union are not talking to deaf ears. Their voices will be heard and will make a great deal of difference.[12]

We at Radio Liberty frequently quoted from Pool's talk, especially the italicized sentence.

The dinner speaker was Zbigniew Brzezinski, then a Columbia professor. As master of ceremonies, I warmed up the audience with some of the latest underground jokes from the Soviet Union, and handled the lively question-and-answer period after Zbig's talk. We spent the second day in a private colloquium at which Sargeant moderated a roundtable with some of the top Western experts on the Soviet Union from universities, newspapers, and the government, who exchanged ideas with several Radio executives from Munich and New York and offered their suggestions for fine-tuning the content of our broadcasts. This highly qualified panel included Richard Davies, William Griffith, Leo Gruliow, Max Hayward, Daniel Lerner, Richard Pipes, Ithiel de Sola Pool, Richard Rowson, Colette and Marshall Shulman, Michel Tatu, and Vladimir Treml.

The group reached a consensus on several positions that basically confirmed the Radio's own approach to policy and programming: Radio Liberty should exercise great caution in formulating specific long-range goals concerning the development of Soviet society, and the goals that are formulated should be very general, based on ascertaining present-day trends in Soviet society that are desirable to encourage. The Radio must be a stimulus for fresh ideas, rather than the mirror of official American opinion; it must be scrupulously objective in its news reporting of events both internal and external to the Soviet Union. To maintain credibility as an objective source, the Radio should not hesitate occasionally to take positions that on specific issues may differ from those of the U.S. government. Throughout its programming, the Radio should be as "un-American" and "un-original" as possible—"un-American" in the sense that an American image damages the station's credibility from the viewpoint of the Soviet listener, and "un-original" in that its programming would be more credible if the Radio could draw on reliable sources other than the station itself.

Radio Liberty should strive to put forth the image of a compatriot who is speaking to internal events in the Soviet Union as someone on the scene would speak if that person had the right to express a difference of opinion; the Radio should present itself as a constructive opposition. The participants generally agreed that the image defined for itself by the Radio as a "guest in the living room" was a correct approach. Both the tone and the content of programming should be positive rather than negative; it should avoid provocative and objectionable terminology and must not be patronizing in tone.

Although the Radio should not present a detailed platform for future Soviet development, it need not avoid speculation on the future in its broadcasts. Indeed, this will be necessary in reaching a society as future-oriented as the Soviet Union. In sum, the programming should make the station a "constructive catalyst" in internal Soviet debate. Through a "freewheeling," objective transmission of ideas, Radio Liberty should seek to create an almost international body of opinion among the leaders of the intellectual community in the Soviet Union. The intelligentsia, in both its scientific-technical and creative components, should be the Radio's primary audience, insofar as any group is designated foremost.

Several panelists stated that Radio Liberty's neutral approach to the nationality question was even more conservative than the Soviet constitution, which guarantees to the various national groups in the Soviet Union the right to their own state. These participants believed that the nationality question would become more acute in future years and that the Radio should be more forthright in its handling of the problem. They recognized that appealing to aspirations of the national minorities without being branded as a "separatist" station in Russian areas presented a dilemma that would not be easily resolved. They considered, however, that keeping alive interest and pride in the various national cultures and languages was a service Radio Liberty should continue to perform.[13]

At one point during the discussion, Sargeant asked me to say a few words about Radio Liberty's treatment of Russian émigré literature:

SOSIN: This is one area where Radio Liberty can play a unique role. We've been talking about the way we can project the richness and vitality of Western literature into an area where it still is denied in a broad spectrum. But let us not forget the wealth of Russian, and to some extent non-Russian, émigré literature in the West. Particularly Russian émigré literature. I'm thinking of Bunin—the Bunin that is still not available—and others of the older writers. I'm thinking of some of the critics, and the younger writers whom you find in the pages of *Novy Zhurnal*. And I'm thinking of them not only as keepers of the flame, of the traditional values and faithfulness to the word-as-such that they've preserved while Soviet Russian has degenerated into "newspeak." I'm referring to the evolution of attitudes within the Soviet Union that has led Soviet citizens, particularly youth, who may once have considered émigrés as traitors to the homeland, to appreciate now the fact that the émigré has not simply quit once he went abroad, but has maintained the continuity of the humanitarian Russian tradition, the humanistic values, the literary values, which some day are going to be replenished at home in some kind of new variant that inevitably has to take into consideration fifty-odd years of Soviet history.

HAYWARD: I think that's an admirable point. Because we were, at the beginning of the discussion this morning, trying to define Radio Liberty in specific terms—what distinguishes it from other stations broadcasting in Russian. I think that is one particular thing where Radio Liberty clearly can make a special contribution.

But regarding the broader cultural scene, projecting the Western cultural scene to Russia, you'll probably be duplicating a lot that is being done by the VOA and the BBC who are not jammed, and therefore are able to give longer and more complex treatment of the Western cultural trends. So I am in favor of projection back to Russia of émigré things, and also early Soviet things, which I'm sure you meant to include. . . . I had one startling example of the way this kind of thing gets through. I think I can mention now a deputy of the Supreme Soviet and that great writer of the Russian land, Pyotr Panfyorov, who when he visited England—it must have been about 1959—showed an acquaintance with the poetry of Elagin [Ivan Elagin, a noted émigré poet living and teaching in the United States] that he heard on Radio Liberty and was very enthusiastic about it.[14]

Long before he became national security adviser in the Carter administration, Zbigniew Brzezinski was a consistent supporter of Radio Free Europe and Radio Liberty.[15] However, he did not always agree with some of our broadcasting policies. This became evident in early 1966, when our CIA sponsors asked him to join three other citizens in the private sector for a confidential evaluation of both radios. The four experts, dubbed the "Clover Group," consisted of John Hayes, a commercial radio executive (later ambassador to Switzerland and chairman of the merged RFE/RL board); William Griffith, a professor at M.I.T., who had been a policy executive at Radio Free Europe; Richard Salant, a CBS news director; and Brzezinski. They spent a day with us in New York before going to Munich for intensive talks and observation of the activities at headquarters.

Ken Scott reported in detail the thrust of their questions and comments in a memo to Sargeant. Professors Brzezinski and Griffith criticized Radio Liberty's nationality policy, which they felt was too passive; they argued for adopting a more militant line in the non-Russian broadcasts, which would stimulate anti-Russian antagonism. As they said: "Your [RL's] job is not looking out for their [the Soviet listeners'] interests; it is to promote U.S. interest and it is in the U.S. interest to weaken the Soviet regime." This position ran counter to the Radio's fundamental policy of nonpredetermination, whereby we offered no ready-made prescription for the future configuration of the present Soviet Union, but instead left it to the various nationalities to decide for themselves. We always considered that it would be irresponsible and counterproductive for RL émigrés to encourage listeners inside the Soviet Union to take action against the regime and the Russian majority.

John Hayes appreciated the answer he received to his question "What do you want for your audiences?" The reply came from Trude Gunther, manager of the non-Slavic desks (a sensitive position for a woman superior in rank to her Muslim writers): "I want them to have a chance to preserve their national and cultural heritage and not to be swallowed up by the Russification policy of the regime." One of Hayes's favorite questions, frequently repeated when he spoke with staffers in Munich, was "When can RL go off the air?" The answers varied from "When the USSR ceases to be an expansionist power" to "When a similar radio station can operate legally inside the USSR." Robert Kelley commented that we might not be able to count on continued American support if the Soviet system became modified to the point where it was no longer an expansionist threat to the United States.[16]

By 1966, I had been working for fourteen years in New York, but I had not been at the center of Radio Liberty's operation in Munich for more than a few weeks. I requested a tour of duty at Radio headquarters. Howland Sargeant welcomed the proposal, and he and Ken Scott created a special position for me in Munich as senior adviser to the director. I would assist Scott, who was not a Soviet specialist, but I would not be responsible for the day-to-day operation of the Radio. My family and I arrived in Munich in September 1966, and I spent four stimulating years in the city where I had first come to know Soviet émigrés.

By the time I completed my assignment abroad, the world witnessed the invasion of Czechoslovakia by Soviet and Warsaw Pact tanks and troops. The deepening disillusionment of Soviet intellectuals led to defections to the West and, even more important, the emergence inside the country of voices of protest from such dissenters as Sakharov and Solzhenitsyn. They gave further impetus to the domestic opposition, and, by sending their writing abroad, succeeded in spreading their message throughout their own land, thanks to Radio Liberty's unique role as the people's radio.

What is the definition of a Russian string trio?

A Russian string quartet just returned from a trip abroad.

 # THE MUNICH YEARS, 1966–1970

Ominous developments in the international arena took place during my four years at the Munich headquarters of Radio Liberty. The late 1960s witnessed the tightening of the screws internally by the new Brezhnev regime, beginning with the arrest of dissident writers Sinyavsky and Daniel. The Six-Day War of June 1967 in the Middle East provoked Soviet vituperation against Israel, accompanied by thinly veiled anti-Semitic attacks on Soviet Jews for daring to express solidarity with their spiritual brethren. Most important, the invasion of Czechoslovakia in August 1968, carried out by members of the Warsaw Pact led by Soviet tanks, dealt a blow to the hopes of Soviet citizens that it might be possible to achieve "socialism with a human face." The Kremlin would hardly allow any liberalization at home after crushing Dubček's attempts in Prague.

A few days after the invasion, a handful of courageous intellectuals, including Pavel Litvinov, grandson of Stalin's foreign minister, staged a demonstration of protest on Red Square. They were swiftly arrested, imprisoned, tried, and exiled to Siberia. This event gave great impetus to the growing dissident movement. When Radio Liberty received evidence of popular support for Litvinov and his fellow protesters, we shared it with our audience.[1]

In the summer of 1968, the Radio beamed back into the Soviet Union the full text of academician Andrei D. Sakharov's samizdat essay, "Thoughts on Progress, Peaceful Coexistence, and Intellectual Freedom," a seminal work that had long-range repercussions among thinking Soviet citizens.

The success of the 1965 Radio Liberty–New York University conference had encouraged us to continue exchanging ideas with academicians during the Brezhnev era. The topic chosen for the second meeting in March 1967 was "Communication with Soviet Youth." Professor Philip E. Mosely of Columbia University and Professor Alfred Rieber of the University of Pennsylvania were the principal panelists, along with journalists and other scholars. From the Munich end we had a radio-telephone linkup that enabled the audience in the NYU auditorium to hear three of us in the Munich studio: Victor Ryser, Morris Diakowsky, and myself.

There was a striking coincidence that week: Stalin's daughter, Svetlana Alliluyeva, defected from the Soviet Union to India. The New Yorkers were particularly curious about how the Radio handled the breaking event. We told them that we had immediately informed our audience of the news and were following up with details as they became available—the Radio's standard operating procedure for informing the Soviet public about what the official media were ignoring or distorting.

A few weeks later, Svetlana arrived in New York, where she gave a press conference. Later, when her first book, *Twenty Letters to a Friend,* was published, she came to our New York studios and recorded two chapters; the rest was read by a freelance announcer who was the daughter of Fyodor Chaliapin, renowned Russian basso. We considered it quite a coup for Radio Liberty to attract the daughter of Joseph Stalin to reach her compatriots with her revelations. At the press conference, she confirmed the consternation that the Sinyavsky and Daniel affair created among Soviet intellectuals, including their demands for the writers' exoneration and release. One letter, signed by sixty-two Soviet writers led by Kornei Chukovsky and Ilya Ehrenburg, was addressed directly to the Twenty-Third Congress of the Communist Party. That protest, along with others that were mailed to Soviet newspapers but were not published at home, reached the Western press, and the Radio beamed them into the Soviet Union.

An especially noteworthy statement came from Aleksandr Ginzburg, a young dissident who served time in the gulag as a political prisoner and who was now editing and distributing his underground publication, *Syntax,* considered the first samizdat journal. He gained fame as a leading fighter for human rights, and he served another prison sentence before emigrating to the West. His letter, addressed to Premier Kosygin, cited Article 19 of the 1948 UN Declaration of Human Rights (calling for freedom of information regardless of frontiers) as guaranteeing the right of Sinyavsky and Daniel to act as they did. He admitted that he listened to foreign radio broadcasts because details of the case had not been published at home. Ginzburg declared, "I love my country and do not wish the usual uncontrolled actions of the KGB to blemish its reputation. I love Russian literature and do not wish for another two of its representatives to be sent to chop down trees under armed guard. I respect Andrei Sinyavsky—a remarkable critic and prose writer."[2] Despite these protests, Sinyavsky served six years in a prison camp near Potma, three hundred miles east of Moscow. He was allowed to leave for the West in 1973 and settled near Paris, where he taught Russian literature at the Sorbonne, resumed his writing, and often broadcast over Radio Liberty before his death in 1997.

In July 1967, I flew with my family from Munich to Israel for an exciting first visit. We were among the first Americans permitted to arrive after the Six-Day War, during which the U.S. government had banned all travel. My RL press pass enabled Gloria and me to enter the newly occupied territories of the West Bank and Gaza. We joined in celebrating the return of Mount Scopus to Israel after nineteen years at an unforgettable concert in the amphitheater of Hebrew University high above Jerusalem overlooking the Dead Sea. David Ben Gurion, Levi Eshkol, and other leaders sat near us as we thrilled to the music of Mahler's Resurrection symphony, conducted by Leonard Bernstein, with our friend Jennie Tourel, the famous soprano, as soloist. Our children spent most of the summer in a camp in Ashkelon, and toured the country from the Golan Heights to Eilat and the eastern edge of the Sinai. I shared my impressions and experiences with my Munich colleagues, who, along with the rest of the world, had closely followed the events in the Middle East.

Because of our friendship with Sulamith Nardi, assistant to Zalman Shazar, president of Israel, we were invited to meet privately with him for afternoon tea in his official residence in Jerusalem. We conversed in Russian and in English with our cordial, unpretentious host, who was interested in Radio Liberty. Years ago he emigrated from Russia to Palestine. His original name was Rubashov, and I asked him whether he had ever met Arthur Koestler, whose hero in his novel *Darkness at Noon* is called "Rubashov." Shazar said no, but he had heard that the author speculated about what might have become of a revolutionary socialist like himself if he had joined Lenin's party and remained in Soviet Russia. (In the novel, Rubashov, a loyal Bolshevik to the end, is arrested in Stalin's purges and executed.)

In Jerusalem, Gloria and I taped an exclusive interview for RL with Mayor Teddy Kollek, the dynamic Vienna-born politician who remained in that office for the next twenty-five years. A longer-range contribution to the Radio was our meeting with a young woman who had come from Riga, Latvia, to settle in Israel. The Russian service in Munich had asked us to evaluate her as a possible addition to the staff. Molly Gordin turned out to be a charming and vivacious person who we were certain would be a welcome addition to Radio Liberty. We recommended her highly and she was hired. During the next twenty-five years, Molly became well known among Soviet listeners as Inna Svetlova; her programs were among the Radio's most popular, and she regularly received a large amount of fan mail. She told me that in 1992, when she could at last visit Moscow, her greatest thrill came when she was standing in line in front of a food store and chatting. Another woman shopper recognized her voice and shouted in delight, "You're Inna Svetlova!"

As Ken Scott's senior adviser, I rarely interfered directly in day-to-day programming matters, although members of various language desks often visited my office confidentially to complain about the bureaucratic behavior of some of their American bosses. However, I regularly attended the daily news meetings of the Russian service, when the priority items for broadcast were chosen. On the morning of April 5, 1968, we learned that Martin Luther King Jr. had been assassinated in Memphis, Tennessee, and at the daily news meeting I suggested a rebroadcast of our exclusive interview with Dr. King recorded by Ronny Ronalds a few years earlier. King's role as a leading fighter for civil rights had obvious relevance for our audience. The programming executives told me, however, that the Russian desk editors had erased the tape with their approval—not accidentally, but as part of a shortsighted decision on someone's part to erase "outdated" programs that were taking up too much space in the archives. I condemned this flagrant example of bureaucratic incompetence and urged that henceforth the languages services take greater care to preserve tapes, especially those with indisputable historical value, such as the King interview.

While on two months' home leave in the summer of 1968, I visited

Washington and dropped into CIA headquarters, primarily to pay my respects to my old "skipper," CIA Deputy Director Admiral Rufus Taylor. (I served in Naval Intelligence in World War II under then Commander Taylor, an expert in Japanese and cryptography.) He received me warmly and complimented Radio Liberty on its work. I also met with a small group of CIA specialists on the Soviet Union, and because it was the height of Dubček's "spring" in Czechoslovakia, we discussed the chances of a Soviet invasion. No one present thought it was possible. In fact, the only person I know who predicted it was Professor Albert Parry, then a resident scholar in Munich with Radio Liberty. Albert had sent the *New York Times Magazine* a long article justifying his conviction that Brezhnev had no other recourse than to crush the seeds of democracy that were sprouting in Czechoslovakia, lest they spread to the Soviet Union. The *Times* hesitated to print it, but when all hell broke loose on Wednesday, August 21, and Soviet tanks advanced on Prague, they called Parry and urgently requested him to update the piece. It appeared on Sunday, September 1, and reinforced Parry's reputation as an astute analyst of Soviet politics. He appeared frequently at the Radio's microphone, speaking authoritatively in his native Russian.

At the very hour when the Warsaw Pact armies prepared to cross the border, Gloria and I were visiting a CIA safe house in Greenwich, Connecticut, to meet Arkady and Natasha Belinkov, who had recently defected from the Soviet Union. Arkady Viktorovich Belinkov was born in 1921 in Moscow and studied at the Gorky Literary Institute and Moscow University. He was arrested in 1944 for his dissident literary activity, in particular for his unpublished work, a blasphemous anti-Soviet novel, and was sentenced to death after a twenty-two-month investigation, during which he was subjected to various forms of torture. He was reprieved, but he suffered in prisons and labor camps, where he endured hunger and cold. Undaunted, he managed to write two more unpublished novels, for which he was resentenced. Released in 1956 during Khrushchev's thaw, Belinkov was allowed to teach at the Literary Institute in Moscow. After his defection, as his health further deteriorated he wrote at a feverish pace to expose the Soviet regime's suppression of the intelligentsia.

A few months after we met, the Belinkovs came to Munich, where they contributed to Radio Liberty programs and broadcast planning. In December 1969, Arkady was the star panelist at a conference on Soviet censorship held in London under the sponsorship of the Munich Institute for the Study of the USSR. I represented the Radio at the sessions. Belinkov arrived in a wheelchair, his leg in a cast. The week before, while driving on the *autostrada* in Italy, he had been run off the road. His car crashed and the other car disappeared. He was certain the accident was deliberate. He was taken to a provincial hospital, where the doctors put his leg in a cast, but Arkady was in pain when he arrived in London. Gloria took one look at the foot, which was beginning to turn blue, and insisted that we get medical help immediately. Laura Rowe, of the Radio's London bureau, called a Harley Street orthopedist who removed and replaced the cast, telling us that the leg would have turned gangrenous without prompt attention. Although Arkady recovered, unfortunately his poor health finally caught up with him after the cruel years he spent in the gulag, and he died in New Haven, Connecticut, in May 1970 after open-heart surgery.[3]

At the December 1969 London conference,[4] moderator Max Hayward introduced Belinkov as the most qualified person to launch a discussion of Soviet censorship. Hayward called Arkady's book on the writer Yuri Tynyanov, which had been published in the Soviet Union, "both a penetrating study in its own right and a brilliant piece of Aesopian art; there can be few literary critics in the Soviet Union who would have cared to run the risk of making the daring statements we find on many of its 635 pages."

Natasha Belinkova, who also took part in the conference, was a first-class critic and editor in her own right. Having studied at Moscow University, she worked for the journals *Novy Mir* and *Moskva*. In addition, she was a staff member of the Sociological Department of the Moscow Radio and Television Committee and was able to see the high value placed on the work of foreign radio broadcasts among the Soviet intelligentsia. After her arrival in the West she told us:

> I well remember the efforts made by my friends to hear, despite the difficulty, the unfettered word filtering through jamming. My invalid husband would spend hours sitting tensely before the radio, operating the volume and tuning controls with both hands. We saved our money, and even went without necessities, in order to buy the most sensitive receiver; all of us had homemade schedules of broadcasts by the BBC, VOA, and Liberty. People bought (illegally, of course) special adapters for Soviet-made receivers in order to increase the range of frequencies. We would report to each other immediately on what we heard, and set up a timetable to take turns listening. I happen to know that recently this timetable has been operating throughout the night when the jammers are ineffective. The technique of listening has been perfected; broadcasts are being recorded on tape recorders. The broadcasts that

are most prized by listeners get transcribed on the typewriter and become part of samizdat.[5]

Natasha was a staunch supporter of Radio Liberty and often advised us. In 1970, when she was still living in New Haven after Arkady's death, she wrote me in order to follow up on a long talk we had together about Solzhenitsyn when he won the Nobel Prize in literature. We were apprehensive about devoting too much air time to this event, lest we harm Solzhenitsyn by providing ammunition for his enemies to link him with our "traitorous voice." Natasha emphasized the importance of our informing the Soviet public about Western press reaction to the award, reporting on articles and books dealing with the author, and providing data about the circulation of his books abroad in various languages—all designed to make use of world public opinion, which, in her words, was "the great moral bulwark of opposition to Soviet government policy." Recognition of Solzhenitsyn as a world figure, she said, "would tie the hands of criminal elements in the USSR and strengthen Soviet opposition elements for the fray."

As the wife of an equally uncompromising fighter against the Soviet regime, Natasha Belinkova was quite aware of the calculated risks that Solzhenitsyn had taken "from the moment when he wrote his first line back in the camp and entered into conflict with his state." "It was his aim," she said, " to confront the stifling and inhuman policy of the Soviet state, at least in the field of literature. His goal was not self-preservation but victory. In consenting to accept the Nobel Prize, he issued a new challenge to his government. Our silence in the West may help to preserve him, but it will not give him victory." She fully understood, too, "the degree of responsibility I am assuming in suggesting that radio broadcasts to the Soviet Union adopt an active rather than a passive position in connection with the award of the Nobel Prize to Solzhenitsyn. If necessary, I authorize you to use my letter as an argument."[6]

Although Belinkova's advice may seem obvious today in light of later confirmation from dissidents that the West's attention helped rather than hurt them, at that time we were cautious in our treatment. She and others qualified to know the best method of aiding Solzhenitsyn encouraged Radio Liberty to adopt a proactive role in broadcasting everything possible about him, including the serialization of his works. The cumulative impact of the West's campaign to raise Solzhenitsyn to his deserved position of prominence as a major literary figure must have played a part in the regime's decision in 1974 not to arrest him and send him to the gulag, but to get rid of his annoying presence by forcibly throwing him out of the country.

Professor Marc Slonim was also concerned about Solzhenitsyn. In the fall of 1968, he called me from Geneva, where he and his wife, Tanya, had moved after Marc retired from Sarah Lawrence College in Westchester. He wanted to enlist my help in connection with Solzhenitsyn's fiftieth birthday in December. Because Aleksandr Isayevich was already in deep trouble with the Brezhnev regime as a result of his samizdat writings, Slonim believed that if writers in the West sent him telegrams of congratulations it would boost his morale and also make the authorities aware that his fellow craftsmen abroad supported him. From Munich, I contacted friends at PEN and individual writers who had previously contributed to Radio Liberty programs, while Slonim approached his friends among writers and publishers. The result was a barrage of telegrams, some addressed to Solzhenitsyn in care of *Literaturnaya Gazeta* and *Izvestiya* in Moscow, others sent directly to his residence in nearby Ryazan. It is surprising that he received all or most of them, and he later expressed gratitude for the moving displaying of solidarity. I never found out whether he learned of the Radio's participation in organizing the birthday greetings.

Another major participant in the London censorship conference was Leonid Vladimirovich Finkelstein, born in Ukraine in 1924. In 1947, as a student in the senior class at the Moscow Institute of Aviation, he was arrested and spent five and a half years in the gulag. After Stalin's death, he was released and rehabilitated, completed his studies, and graduated as an automobile engineer. He began writing articles on popular science and became a full-time journalist and author of four books on science published in the Soviet Union. In June 1966, during a visit to London with a group of Soviet writers and journalists, he applied for political asylum. Using the pen name "Leonid Vladimirov," he continued writing books in the West while working as an editor and commentator for Radio Liberty and later the BBC.

Alexei Yakushev was another defector at the conference. He had received a Ph.D. from Moscow University, where he taught philosophy until 1966, when he was appointed research professor at the Institute of Philosophy and Sociology of the Polish Academy of Arts and Sciences in Warsaw. He arrived in the West in 1969 and served as an adviser to Max Ralis in the Radio's Audience Research Department before moving in 1970 to Sydney, Australia, and later settled in the United States. In the 1970s and 1980s, he lectured on various U.S. campuses, and for many years he has taught Russian at the Army Language School in Monterey, California. Like other defectors during the late 1960s, he confirmed for us the vital service that we were giving Soviet citizens and offered valuable counsel on how to make our message even more effective.

Another panelist, Anatoli Kuznetsov, was born in 1929 in Kiev and began writing at the age of fourteen, recording what he saw of the German occupation. In 1946 he won his first literary competition for a series of short stories. He also wrote film scripts and three novels, and his books in print in the Soviet Union reached a circulation of about seven million and were translated into more than thirty languages. While in London in 1969, he defected and settled in England, where he changed his name to "A. Anatoli" in order to show that he had broken with his past as a Soviet writer and had renounced the Soviet editions of his works. In 1970 he reissued *Babi Yar,* his "document in the form of a novel," which described the massacre by German invaders of Kiev's Jewish population in September 1941. (Kuznetsov was half Russian, half Ukrainian.) The original manuscript had been emasculated by the Soviet censors when it was published in Moscow in 1966, with half the text cut out and the sense of the book distorted. (The principal culprit among the censors was the notorious hard-line writer Boris Polevoy, chief editor of the magazine *Yunost,* where *Babi Yar* first appeared.)

Anatoli had succeeded in smuggling out films of his complete uncensored text, which Jonathan Cape published with the restored passages shown in bold type. On the thirtieth anniversary of the tragedy in September 1971, Anatoli read the relevant passages over Radio Liberty, alternating with a staff announcer in order to highlight the erstwhile forbidden segments. Soviet listeners heard facts about the Nazi atrocities that the censors had not permitted, in conformity with the regime's policy of muting the martyrdom of the Jewish population during the German occupation.

The censorship conference provided Radio Liberty with valuable background material for broadcasts. A transcript published by the Munich Institute is fascinating reading because it reveals in detail the strictures imposed by the regime over Soviet writers and critics. As Albert Parry, who also participated, said during his remarks in London, "In Russia a telephone pole is a pine tree that has been edited."

A young Muscovite named Andrei Amalrik, who is credited with being the first dissident to establish regular contacts with the West through his friendship with foreign correspondents, was the subject of controversy at the Radio in late 1969. Most of the human rights documents of the 1960s—transcripts of trials, as well as political and artistic literature—were sent abroad because of his efforts. He considered his most important success to be the transfer of Sakharov's famous essay in 1968. His own samizdat work *Will the Soviet Union Survive Until 1984?* triggered his arrest in 1969.

When the text became available to Radio Liberty, the émigré staff members heatedly debated the authenticity of the document. Some writers and editors suspected Amalrik of being a KGB agent. To establish the trustworthiness of the author and his work, I sought the advice of Max Hayward, Peter Reddaway, Martin Dewhirst, Victor Zorza, Leo Labedz, and other Western specialists in London. They all responded unequivocally that Amalrik was a genuine dissident, and they indignantly rejected the accusations circulating in the West. Such rumors, they declared, could be inspired by the KGB to discredit Amalrik and prevent his work from being taken seriously. They could understand Radio Liberty's caution in using a document that contained Russophobic passages that might embarrass us unless we dissociated ourselves in the broadcasts. But under no circumstances did they feel that the Radio should cast any suspicion on him in our commentaries.

Victor Frank, senior staff commentator in Munich, also spoke with Soviet area specialists in London for the conference, including Professor Karel van het Reve of the University of Leyden, a former Dutch correspondent in Moscow who became secretary of the Alexander Herzen Foundation in Amsterdam, the publisher of samizdat works by Russian dissidents. He told Frank that he knew Amalrik intimately in Moscow between 1967 and 1968, had published the essay after it was brought to Amsterdam by a fellow foreign journalist in Moscow who got it from Amalrik, and had assured Frank that Amalrik's work was a "godsend for RL." In a memorandum to Bob Tuck, director of the Program Operations Division, Frank wrote:

> The time has now come for a firm operational decision in this matter. We have fully ventilated the problem, and the discussion proved very useful at the beginning, but by now the arguments have become repetitive and sterile. I was greatly distressed to learn, on my return from London, that RL has still failed to use Amalrik's pamphlet for its own purposes—the more so, since both the Russian service of the BBC and the VOA are doing so. I urge you most emphatically to arrange for the transmission of the full text. As suggested by the Policy Adviser, a roundtable discussion may follow the broadcast of the text.[7]

Radio Liberty broadcast the work in six installments—with appropriate caveats and disclaimers at key points in the transmission—in its series

"Documents from the USSR," a program intended (though not openly stated) for listeners with tape recorders, so that such documents could get back into samizdat circulation. Roundtable discussions explored such topics as the reason for the great interest in the West created by Amalrik's thesis concerning inevitable war between the Soviet Union and China and the end of the Soviet regime.

Amalrik's reliability was soon confirmed by his arrest, although some of our Russian colleagues refused even then to believe that it was not a KGB trick. When he was released from the gulag and permitted to leave the country, we became better acquainted with this remarkable young man. The day after he was flown to Amsterdam, our Munich correspondent, Yuri Melnikov, taped a long interview with him that was aired in three daily installments.

Amalrik ranged widely over the Soviet scene, offering incisive views on the nature of the regime and its attitude toward dissidents. "As for me," he said, "the authorities had a choice since they considered me a bothersome person who stirred up trouble inside the country; they could either put me in prison or simply destroy me, or else they could shove me out of the country." Putting him in the gulag brought no results; it only attracted more attention to him and publicized his book. After Amalrik's release, the authorities decided that in order to "save face in the West, to show that détente exists within the Soviet Union, too, and that no cruelties are practiced," they got rid of him and hoped that after the initial fuss over him abroad died down his influence would wane. But he told Radio Liberty: "I hope that I will be useful in explaining the situation there, and that in this way my seeming defeat—the departure from Russia—will turn into a victory for our cause. How realistic my plans are, only the future will show." The following dialogue took place:

MELNIKOV: You began to act according to the principle "live not by lies," even before Solzhenitsyn coined the phrase. But this utopia can only become a reality if many people accept it at the same time; then the risk becomes less for the individual person. Suppose, for example, that instead of only a handful of scholars of the caliber of Sakharov, Shafarevich, and Orlov, the whole Academy of Sciences had risen to their full height. The question arises: Why doesn't something like this happen? Must we give up hope for such an eventuality?

AMALRIK: Well, you see, even if everyone else begins to live not by lies, the Academy of Sciences will live by lies. . . . In general, the academic community, from a moral point of view, is a bad milieu. And besides, they are a Soviet generation of scholars. These are people who went through a very vicious process of selection in order to climb up the academic ladder; they were forced to do extremely bad things, from a moral point of view, and this formed their character. Andrei Dmitrievich Sakharov is an amazing exception. . . .

Now, need there be a lot of such people? In order to have a healthy society it's not necessary that there be a lot of saintly people. It is enough that there are several, because every kind of life is always a certain compromise between the moral conditions that one lives in and pragmatically tangible conditions. The main thing is to achieve a balance and to have examples—famous examples of people who live according to high moral standards. The fact that we have several such people changes the atmosphere a great deal, and also stirs other people to be guided by higher moral principles. And this is very significant.[8]

Amalrik continued to fight for freedom in his homeland until his untimely death a few years later in an auto accident on a dark, rain-swept road in Spain en route to Madrid to attend an international conference on human rights. As far as I know, there was no evidence of foul play.[9]

During my years in Munich, a sailor named Oleg Tumanov arrived after having defected earlier from the Soviet Union by jumping ship. He was a good-looking young blond, a typical Slavic type from "central casting," and he quickly established himself as a competent newswriter. In fact, he rose to the position of Russian news editor in the 1980s, but then suddenly disappeared, surfacing in Moscow at a press conference. There he revealed that he was a spy for the KGB who had been planted at Radio Liberty. The whole story appears in his book *Tumanov: Confessions of a KGB Agent*, published in 1993 with many inaccuracies about the Radio and its employees.[10] Some people doubt his claim to have been an agent from the outset; they say he was an authentic defector who was "turned." Oleg Kalugin, a KGB general who became disillusioned with the system and joined the Russian democrats in the late 1980s, alleges that he was personally responsible for the recruitment of Tumanov. In his autobiography, which appeared in 1994, Kalugin writes that the KGB opened Tumanov's letters to his family soon after he had defected and learned that he was unhappy in the West. As a result, a KGB agent met him in Vienna and encouraged him to seek employment with Radio Liberty, where he could be useful to his motherland and vindicate himself. According to Kalugin, Tumanov was the best of several agents he had planted in the Munich station, and was an accomplice in arranging for the bombing of the office in 1981, for which

Kalugin takes credit. I would not be surprised to learn that there were spies in the New York bureau too. If I had been in charge of the KGB, I certainly would have made every effort to infiltrate the radio station that represented the greatest danger to the Soviet regime's manipulation of information. Kalugin confirms that our broadcasts "drove the Soviets crazy."[11]

The Institute for the Study of the USSR in Munich, subsidized by the Radio Liberty Committee, often held scholarly conferences like the London meeting on censorship. Another symposium in 1969 dealt with religion in the Soviet Union, and I presented a paper on Judaism.[12] My thesis was that the future for Soviet Jews was bleak and that their only hope for preserving their identity was to emigrate. Thanks to pressure from the West, combined with the Brezhnev regime's self-interest, tens of thousands of Jews were permitted to leave for Israel in the 1970s and 1980s, providing the Radio with a fresh source of talent for its staff and programming. Conflicts soon arose between some older staff members who were Russian anti-Semites and their newly arrived Jewish colleagues (see Chapter 11).

After four years in Munich, Gloria and I felt it was time to come home. We did not want to become expatriates. We could easily have stayed on and enjoyed the perquisites, such as housing and the overseas pay scale, but that would mean separating our family. Donald was already a freshman at the University of Michigan, and Debbie would soon finish high school. Our parents were getting on in years, and we wanted to be closer. Another factor in our decision was that, as Jews, we still had misgivings about continuing to live in Germany, with memories of the Holocaust, although no members of our family had been victims. Whenever we met people our age, we asked ourselves where they had been under Hitler. We were constantly amazed at the paradox of attending first-rate concerts, where we sat with cultured German lovers of classical music, but aware that a few miles north of Munich lay Dachau, the scene of unspeakable horrors perhaps approved by many of these same people less than twenty-five years earlier.

It had been a pleasure to work closely with Ken Scott, who exercised his authority with good humor and subtlety. He and Howland Sargeant created a position for me in New York as the Radio's liaison with the American academic community in order to expand our contacts and enrich the broadcasts. We sailed home on the *France* in the summer of 1970 and prepared to adjust to life—and liberty—in the United States. It was not long, however, before Radio Liberty faced its most serious threat—and not from Moscow but from Washington.

What is the difference between
Capitalism and Communism?
Under Capitalism there is exploitation
of man by man, but under Communism it's
the other way around.

9 RADIO LIBERTY'S COVER IS BLOWN

My newly created position as director of broadcast planning focused on long-range preparation of program series, with special emphasis on attracting American academicians to broadcast over Radio Liberty. My immediate superior was technically still Ken Scott in Munich, but in New York I worked closely with Howland Sargeant and Zhuk Obolensky, who had succeeded me as director of the programming division.

At this time, our executive staff was strengthened when Sargeant appointed John Scott as vice-president of the Radio Liberty Committee. Scott (no relation to Ken Scott) was an expert on the Soviet Union who had worked there as a young man in the 1930s to help build Stalin's industry in the Ural city of Magnitogorsk. He rationalized the sacrifices the Soviet people made as being necessary for the young nation's growth and defense, but he was appalled by the cruelty of the regime and the political purges carried out in the name of socialism. He returned to the United

States with a Russian wife, wrote a memorable book about his experiences, *Behind the Urals*, and worked closely for years with Henry R. Luce, publisher of *Time*. In the 1960s, John and I had recorded for Radio Liberty an interview he had with his old friend Earl Browder, general secretary of the U.S. Communist Party from 1930 until 1945, when Stalin expelled him as a "right revisionist."

A few months after my return to New York, Jim Critchlow, John Scott, and I were debriefing an American professor of mathematics who had just come back from a trip to Moscow. As usual, we did not mention our government sponsorship. However, later in the day (a Saturday) word came to us from Washington that the full story of the CIA's connection with Radio Liberty and Radio Free Europe was about to break on Monday. On Sunday, Critchlow and I, who were neighbors in Westchester, met for a long talk and discussed the potential damage that Radio Liberty might incur. We agreed that it would be a disaster if the cause for which we had worked so long fell victim to adverse public opinion, and we resolved to do everything we could to help the Radio survive.

On January 25, 1971, the truth about the secret subsidy of Radio Liberty by Congress via the CIA was revealed to the American public. Senator Clifford Case of New Jersey demanded the end of the connection with the CIA. He was supported by Senator J. William Fulbright of Arkansas, chairman of the Committee on Foreign Relations. Case was willing for Radio Free Europe and Radio Liberty to continue operating if they could be openly and directly funded by Congress, but Fulbright was unalterably opposed to the stations, believing they were irritants and meddlers that obstructed the path to improved Soviet-American relations, and declaring that they were "outworn relics of the Cold War." He was determined to use the unmasking of the Radios as clandestine CIA assets to discredit the validity of their communicating with the peoples of Eastern Europe and the Soviet Union.

Actually, references in the U.S. media to the CIA connection with Radio Free Europe and Radio Liberty had appeared as far back as 1967, but the focus was primarily on RFE. In March, a CBS documentary, "In the Pay of the CIA: An American Dilemma," emphasized for the first time on coast-to-coast television that Radio Free Europe was not merely a private undertaking supported by public subscription, as the "plugs" on radio, television, and the newspapers maintained, but was an arm of the CIA. Radio Liberty was barely mentioned. Dr. Frank Stanton, president of CBS and also chairman of both the executive committee of the Radio Free Europe Fund and the U.S. Advisory Commission on Information, said after the program that he believed funds for Radio Free Europe, whether governmental or private, should be publicly identified.

Jack Gould, the television critic for the *New York Times,* wrote a long review of the documentary in a column entitled "A New Twist for Espionage." He concentrated almost exclusively on Radio Free Europe, pointing out that "not just in the last few days or months, but for at least fifteen years, it has been common knowledge in world broadcasting circles that Radio Free Europe was a creature of the CIA." Gould devoted only one sentence to Radio Liberty as a similar CIA "device." He concluded: "The CIA withdrawal from broadcasting would have the virtue of enabling the United States propaganda effort to be judged on content alone and not on other motives that might jeopardize concern for reportorial truth as an end in itself. Being understood by the rest of the world remains too important a consideration to be cast under the dark shadow of extra-curricular espionage."[1]

Shortly after the election of Richard Nixon in 1968, Rowland Evans and Robert Novak, writing in their regular *Washington Post* column, called the clandestine financing of Radio Free Europe "one of the many loose ends left by the lame duck Johnson Administration for President-elect Nixon to tie up." Again Radio Liberty was mentioned in passing as the recipient of a more modest CIA subsidy.

Evans and Novak stated that after the CIA's subsidies of the National Students Association and other supposedly private organizations had been exposed (by *Ramparts* magazine in 1967), President Johnson named Under Secretary of State Nicholas Katzenbach to head a special committee to study the problem and forestall a wide-ranging congressional investigation of all clandestine financing by the CIA. It was then that the Radios "came under high-level official scrutiny for the first time."

> At one point in the committee's closed-door deliberations, Katzenbach seemed inclined to end Radio Free Europe's subsidy along with all the others—raising apprehensions among highly responsible students of Communist Europe both inside and outside the State Department.
>
> They pointed out to Katzenbach that in the dozen years since the tragedy of the 1956 Hungarian revolution, Radio Free Europe had halted all appeals for violent overthrow of Communist rule and instead advocated peaceful liberalization of Red regimes. . . . Consequently, although Katzenbach's report a year ago recommended an end to all secret subsidies, he has permitted continued financing of Radio Free Europe and

Radio Liberty from CIA funds, with one change in the direction of credibility: A demand that Radio Free Europe cease its misleading appeals for money on U.S. television.[2]

The columnists predicted that the subsidy would surely continue under the Nixon administration, either by the CIA or "as a regular congressional appropriation." The radios were left undisturbed for two more years, probably because of more urgent problems like the Vietnam War and the social turmoil it was causing in the United States.

Readers of the "Outlook" section of the *Washington Post* would not have been startled by Case's revelations, because a long article by John M. Goshko from Munich several weeks earlier, on November 22, 1970, had described the current operations of the Radios and declared: "From the available facts, there seems no doubt that the CIA played a big role in creating Radio Free Europe and continues to be its principal bankroller . . . (a similar kind of financial relationship also appears to exist with Radio Liberty)." The dispatch gave high marks to the professionalism and objectivity of Radio Free Europe (apparently Goshko did not spend any time at Radio Liberty) and concluded that the CIA did not seem to control or even influence its broadcast policies: "Those who work for RFE insist without exception that they have never seen any pressure to follow a 'government line' or to soften news or commentary that might be at variance with U.S. policies or interests. Nor are these disclaimers as disingenuous or self-serving as they might seem to a skeptical outsider. To go inside Radio Free Europe and observe its workings is to discover a remarkable degree of independence and respect for conflicting opinions." Had the *Washington Post* correspondent investigated Radio Liberty, he would have come away with the same conviction, although the CIA's pressure to censor Linus Pauling's broadcast of 1962 was unfortunate and unjustifiable.

Pravda was quick to exploit Case's revelation. In an article on February 9, 1971, entitled "The Anatomy of a Dirty Business: Caught in the Act," the writers inveighed against the "lie factory," where subversive activity and espionage against the Soviet Union was being carried out by the CIA. This hampered the lessening of tensions in Europe, *Pravda* argued, and the improvement of mutual understanding and trust among peoples of European countries. Therefore, the existence of Radio Free Europe and Radio Liberty on the territory of West Germany could not be considered the "private" affair of the United States and the Federal Republic.

Senator Case told CBS News that he objected to "this particular instance of covert activity" on the basis of his "increasing concern about giving credibility to the general idea that seems to be growing in the United States that everything is phony." He added:

> We ought not to have the government engaging in a very substantial degree in something that has to have shades pulled on it. . . . Anything of that nature [that is, financing of RFE and RL] it seems to me ought to be a matter—it's not an emergency any longer—clearly a matter of open activity by our government. And I just hope that that's what we're going to decide.[3]

Case introduced a bill in the Senate "to bring Radio Free Europe and Radio Liberty under the authorization and appropriation process of the Congress." This was in contrast to the expenditure over the past twenty years of several hundred million dollars from secret CIA budgets to pay almost totally for the costs of the two radio stations. "In the last fiscal year alone, over $30 million was provided by the CIA as a direct Government subsidy; yet at no time was Congress asked or permitted to carry out its traditional constitutional role of approving the expenditure." Fulbright's committee noted that the Voice of America's annual budget at that time was $41 million for its *worldwide* operations (their emphasis).

Hearings began in the Fulbright Committee in May with Martin J. Hillenbrand, assistant secretary of state for European affairs, among those testifying. Hillenbrand presented a substitute bill, preferred by the administration, that would establish a nongovernmental, private, nonprofit corporation called the American Council for Private International Communication. The corporation would channel government funds to Radio Free Europe and Radio Liberty, but also make it possible for other private broadcasters or information media reaching abroad to be eligible for financing. Before making any further decisions concerning the long-term future funding of the Radios, the Fulbright Committee requested that both the Library of Congress and the General Accounting Office submit in-depth background studies. In July, Case's bill was adopted with minor changes as stopgap legislation "designed primarily to bring into the open the Government's role in financing" both radios, and $35 million (a modest increase) was authorized for the following fiscal year.

Fulbright's hand can be clearly detected in the July 30 report of his committee, which deplored the fact that the American people and their elected representatives had been "deceived" by five administrations since Truman's. "Indeed, as one of the witnesses who testified during the Committee's hearings of May 24 reminded the Members, 'we had been led to believe that Radio Free Europe was financed by dimes from school children and voluntary gifts from concerned citizens anxious to keep truth alive behind the Iron Curtain.'" The new bill was intended, he declared,

> to terminate this deception; it is intended to let the people know what they are paying for and how much. This assumes, of course, that both Radio Free Europe and Radio Liberty perform useful broadcast services and, although the Committee is divided in its thinking on this point, a majority of the Members believe that the Radios should be given the benefit of the doubt—a serious doubt indeed in view of the public's repeated reluctance to provide through private contributions the amount of financial support the Radios say they need. But in adopting [the bill], the Committee indicated its unwillingness to give the Radios the benefit of the doubt beyond the current fiscal year or to give them the kind of organizational and financial flexibility contained in . . . the Administration-approved bill.[4]

The committee expressed its hope that the studies it had requested would "provide the kind of analysis that will permit the Committee to make a more informed judgment as to whether or not these radio stations are in the public interest."

Senator Claiborne Pell's views were appended in the same report. He praised Radio Free Europe for having improved since the 1956 Hungarian revolution, having learned to be less strident and more objective and to "plug directly into the present thought processes of its radio audiences." However, he gave Radio Liberty short shrift:

> There is a difference, though, when it comes to Radio Liberty. This is a program that I believe is more questionable as its basic objective is the removal of an indigenous, stable and apparently permanent regime. I think we would have done better to concentrate in this legislation only on Radio Free Europe. Nevertheless, if the two programs must be treated together, I would prefer to see them both remain than to see Radio Free Europe dropped.[5]

Pell made the same mistake that other Western politicians and many "experts" on the Soviet Union made in those days by failing to understand that the Soviet regime was not as strong as it appeared to be, and therefore they were inclined to accept the status quo.

The Library of Congress studies requested by the Senate Foreign Relations Committee were undertaken by James R. Price for Radio Free Europe and by Dr. Joseph G. Whelan for Radio Liberty. Whelan had received a Ph.D. with honors in history from the University of Rochester, where he taught before joining the government and working for twenty years at the Library of Congress. His analysis of Radio Liberty origins, structure, policy, programming, and effectiveness made up fifty pages in the *Congressional Record* of March 6, 1972. In the small type used for printed matter inserted into the *Record,* it came to almost 100,000 words, not counting the appendixes. This was, and is perhaps to this day, the most thorough exploration of the Radio ever made.[6]

The report had been submitted to the Foreign Relations Committee on January 14, but its public appearance was delayed for several weeks. Fulbright's introductory remarks explained that he was calling for the insertion of both RFE and RL reports, "in view of the controversy surrounding these reports and the allegations that I and members of the committee staff have tried to suppress this information or alter its presentation."

Evidence that Senator Fulbright was doing just that is in the *Congressional Record* of February 28, which carried a speech by Congressman Robert Steele of Connecticut accusing Fulbright of leading the effort aimed "at killing these vitally needed radio stations" by suppressing the "expert findings" of two Library of Congress senior analysts that were "highly favorable to the radios." Steele commented that when Fulbright commissioned the studies in May 1971, "his remarks at the time leave little doubt that he expected them to put the Radios in a bad light. The manuscripts of the reports were delivered to . . . the Committee staff in mid-January, and as far as I can find out they have just been sitting there ever since then, seen only by a handful of outsiders." Quoting passages from the reports praising Radio Liberty and Radio Free Europe that had been published in the *New York Times* and by syndicated columnists Evans and Novak, Steele demanded that copies be made available to the House Committee on Foreign Affairs and that "the Congress of the United States keep Radio Free Europe and Radio Liberty alive until we and the public can have ample time to study these findings." Congressman Steele was referring to the *Times* lead editorial of February 21 entitled "Saving Free Voices."

I have noticed that in recent years the *Times* has been described as one of the few newspapers then opposed to Radio Free Europe and Radio Liberty, but that is far from the truth, because the *Times* editors had declared:

> For a generation now, Radio Free Europe and Radio Liberty have contributed enormously to enlarging the marketplace of ideas in Eastern

Europe and the Soviet Union. A Library of Congress study of these stations, made at the request of the Senate Foreign Relations Committee, has paid high tribute to these organizations' contributions to liberalization of the Soviet world.

But now both these stations are threatened with extinction tomorrow unless House and Senate conferees end a Congressional stalemate. This situation arose because each chamber voted a different bill authorizing the continuation of these broadcasts.

If the deadlock kills Radio Free Europe and Radio Liberty, the chief gainers will be the Soviet bloc's hard-liners who hate the two radio stations as allies of the liberal and progressive elements in the Communist world. Moreover, the demise of these broadcasts because of the inability of House and Senate conferees to agree would hardly project a flattering view of the American legislative system, nor would it add to American prestige for Europeans to see an important political question decided by a mere technical stratagem.

We believe the work of these two stations has a lasting validity and importance, but even those of a different view must realize that the existence of these organizations provides potential bargaining counters for President Nixon's Moscow visit next May. At the least, all concerned should be able to agree that a final decision on the future of Radio Free Europe and Radio Liberty cannot be made until Mr. Nixon has returned from the Kremlin, and Congress can take a hard look at the post-Moscow situation of American foreign policy.[7]

Such support from the most influential newspaper in the United States boosted our morale and gave us ammunition in our conflict with Fulbright. So did Whelan's fnal chapter, "Some General Observations on RL," which concludes: "There seems to be little doubt that RL is what it claims to be, namely, a surrogate 'Home Service' to the Soviet people. In this role, it tries to establish a dialogue directly with the Soviet people, fill the gaps created by Soviet censorship, remove the distortions of Soviet propaganda, and act as an 'echo chamber,' broadcasting back to the Soviet people the thoughts and ideals of their own 'loyal opposition.'"

In contrast to Fulbright, the report saw the Radio as "assuming the stance of a 'patriotic' Soviet communicator," acting on the democratic principle of a free press and "identifying itself with what it believes to be the best interests of the Soviet peoples, [speaking] in their behalf, and hoping that in the long run this effort will contribute to those forces seeking to bring about a democratic transformation of Soviet society. For RL's ultimate goal is the peaceful democratization of the Soviet Union; and it holds to the belief that the best assurance of peace with Russia is through the diminution of Soviet totalitarianism and the growth of democracy."

Fulbright excerpted the above paragraph in order to exploit it as an argument *against* continuing Radio Liberty. In his introduction of March 6, he made a specious connection with President Nixon's recent trip to China by quoting from the two governments' joint communiqué of February 27:

> The United States supports individual freedom and social progress for all the peoples of the world, free of outside pressure or intervention, and the United States believes that the effort to reduce tensions is served by improving communications between countries that have different ideologies so as to lessen the risks of confrontation through accident, miscalculation or misunderstanding. Countries should treat each other with mutual respect and be willing to compete peacefully, letting performance be the ultimate judge. No country should claim infallibility and each country should be prepared to re-examine its own attitudes for the common good.

For Fulbright those sentiments were opposed to the objectives of Radio Free Europe and Radio Liberty:

> If after one short week we can reach the kind of understanding with the People's Republic of China that would foreclose a "Radio Free China" aimed at reforming the Peking government, then I find it incomprehensible after these years of direct contact with the Soviet Union that we must continue to support a "Radio Liberty" whose objective is the "diminution of Soviet totalitarianism." I regret that the Library's reports do not come to grips with this kind of issue.[8]

Fulbright's animosity toward Radio Liberty ran counter to the fundamental goals of U.S. foreign policy. This is confirmed by the history of the last quarter-century, during which the world witnessed the gradual diminution and final collapse of Soviet totalitarianism. As for China, despite improved relations between our two countries in the late 1990s, the U.S. government considered it important enough to create Radio Free Asia, modeled after Radio Free Europe/Radio Liberty, with the aim of diminishing Chinese Communist control and advocating human rights.

A more rational approach to the future of Radio Free Europe and Radio Liberty was expressed by Senator Charles Percy in a Senate speech delivered on February 22, 1972. While acknowledging that Senator Fulbright was "quite correct" to ask whether the two stations were playing a useful role and whether their operations were compatible with the objectives of U.S. foreign policy, Percy asserted: "It would be unwise to discard assets which are of great value and cannot be easily reconstructed if abandoned at this time." Furthermore, he said,

> I believe we should avoid subordinating the two radio stations to the Department of State. These two stations have built their reputations as independent broadcasters largely because they have not had to reflect on a daily basis the requirements of the diplomatic position of the United States. They are not another Voice of America, and we should not treat them as official broadcasters representing American foreign policy.
>
> So long as Radio Free Europe and Radio Liberty maintain programs of objective news and responsible commentary, I believe they should be supported. They serve to show the peoples who do not have the benefit of a free press that we are concerned about them and their opinion. They serve to keep alive in many countries the hope that freedom may some day be attained.[9]

In order to flesh out his Library of Congress study of Radio Liberty with firsthand observation and interviews, Whelan visited Munich and New York. He expressed his feeling of humility, having assumed the responsibility of digesting in so short a time the mass of excellent material provided by our staff and turning in an objective report that would do justice to the Radio. Impressed by our mission, he said that Senator Fulbright of all people ought to appreciate the work of Radio Liberty in offering Soviet citizens a diversity of views. He realized that the senator was probably expecting a report that would confirm his allegations that the Radio is a "Cold War operation," but he himself was convinced from his briefing that our function as an independent spokesman was in the best long-range interests of the United States, and he regretted that we were not sufficiently understood and appreciated in Washington.

Whelan told us that Radio Liberty needed to cope with the image among those people that we fomented hostility and were a barrier to détente. We replied that no détente could be meaningful so long as the Soviet leadership enjoyed a monopoly of control over information, and that our function was to enable Soviet listeners to have access to the facts, similar to the way the *New York Times* published the Pentagon papers. In his report, he quoted from my speech at the 1962 Princeton conference on propaganda, in which I described the Radio's educational function in a long-range evolutionary process toward democracy. He used the quotation to support his contention that Radio Liberty rejects "the politics of confrontation" and directs its energies "toward developing rational thought among its listeners," on the assumption that "the Soviet citizen has within himself the natural capability of eventually shaping his country's destiny."

Summarizing his positive and negative evaluations of Radio Liberty, Whelan said first that the Radio had "established what appears to an outside observer to be an impressive organization," with a professional staff and extraordinary research facilities, as well as programming, which "tested by time and two decades of association with the Soviet audience, appears to be practical, yet imaginative and purposeful." Its politics "are attuned to the most refined thinking in the Western community of Soviet specialists from which it draws for counsel in programming and policy formation." Its audience research "attempts to make the most of a virtually impossible task," and its broadcasting facilities "would seem to rank among the best in the world of foreign radio broadcasters." Its philosophical orientation, "reformist, idealistic, and pacifistic, is in the tradition of American Jeffersonian-Wilsonian democratic liberalism."

On the negative side, Whelan listed (1) an aging staff and difficulties in recruitment; (2) failure to give more attention to the non-Russian nationalities; and (3) an inactive Board of Trustees. He rightly noted that "to play its role effectively as a 'Home Service,'" Radio Liberty required a staff that is "immersed in the Soviet environment, with knowledge, habits, and linguistic abilities attuned to a new generation." With so many senior staff members from the older emigration, he predicted that the problem would become progressively acute in the next few years, especially in the Russian service. Actually, the attrition of the older employees was soon compensated by the phenomenon of the "third emigration," when masses of Soviet émigrés were allowed to leave in the 1970s and 1980s, providing Radio Liberty with a fresh supply of younger employees and freelancers intimately familiar with current Soviet reality. However, as already mentioned, because many of them were Jews, regardless of their predominantly Russian rather than Jewish acculturation, their ethnic origin was often resented by the more conservative Russians at the Radio and later caused considerable friction between the two generations.

The infusion of young blood for the national minority staffs was seen by Whelan as less of a problem because personnel resources existed in Turkey to draw on. He criticized the Radio for its favoritism shown to the Russian programming, even though he acknowledged that "it is within this group where now and perhaps in the distant future resides the power and authority for shaping the country's future destiny; that historically it is the Great Russian who has held the commanding heights in Russia; and that, therefore, it makes sense to allocate the greater resources of the organization into the Russian service." Nevertheless, he continued,

> The nationalities seem to have a legitimate point of view, deserving attention. One of the most powerful forces in the modern world is nationalism, and though the Soviets deny its relevance in the Soviet setting, still they have been powerless to deny its penetration of the Soviet environment. A dramatic example in recent years has been the growing self-awareness among Soviet Jews that has been generated by a new anti-Semitic campaign initiated by the Soviet leadership.

For Whelan, the increasing prominence of the developing areas such as India and Pakistan, and the reentry of China upon the world stage,

> reinforce an argument made with RL in the mid-1960s, namely, that Soviet Russia's nationalities, especially the non-Slavic, have gained another measure of importance owing to their unique relationships with these areas, and should be treated accordingly. Samizdat records the growing concerns of the nationalities, making them a force to be reckoned with. This new energy, combined with that emerging in Russia proper and channeled within the constructive purposes as defined in RL policy, could prove to be an asset that may not now be fully appreciated.

The third negative feature, the passivity and ineffectiveness of the Board of Trustees, was contrasted to the active role played by the board of Radio Free Europe and interpreted as deference to Radio Liberty's president. "Apparently, the strength of Mr. Sargeant as an administrator has compensated for any organizational deficiencies that might have resulted. If RL is to continue, particularly under the various proposals now under discussion, then this Board must be strengthened considerably and its role as an active participant in the organization's functions more sharply defined."

Fulbright churlishly leveled further criticisms at the Whelan report, which he dismissed along with the Radio Free Europe report as "two rather dreary commentaries on two very bureaucratic organizations whose common goal is to liberalize the governments of Eastern Europe and the Soviet Union by broadcasting 'balanced news' to the peoples of these countries."

The people, in turn, according to the theory, then "pressure their respective governments for democratic reforms, and this, in turn, serves to create conditions for world peace. . . . Such a theory, I believe, is based on nothing more than an arrogant belief that people around the world will act like we want them to act if we only tell them how."[10]

Either the senator was disingenuous or he missed the essence of the Radios' mission, which, far from foisting alien ideas on their audience, gave listeners the opportunity to hear their own compatriots—many of them inside their borders as well as abroad. And instead of quoting any of the strong letters of support for Radio Free Europe and Radio Liberty that were flowing into his and his colleagues' offices, he chose one hostile letter from a veteran foreign service officer who requested anonymity. That "expert" declared that the need for the Radios, if there ever was such, no longer existed and that they were merely being perpetuated so that the staff could keep their jobs.

The energies and talents of many of the American executives on the staff of both radios were now harnessed in the struggle for survival. In New York, Sargeant was helped particularly by his dynamic duo, Information Director Jim Critchlow and his assistant, Gretchen Brainerd. My focus was primarily on the academic front, rallying our friends in the universities to lend their support by writing to Fulbright or others on his committee. Among those who responded to my appeal was Philip E. Mosely, my former professor and mentor at the Columbia Russian Institute. Mosely had been active in government work during and after World War II and was one of the Americans responsible for arranging the quadripartite division of Berlin into the U.S., British, French, and Soviet zones. During the Cold War, he was a frequent consultant to the State Department, which relied on his fluency in Russian and his experience in negotiating with Moscow. In 1971 he was still at Columbia as Adlai E. Stevenson Professor of International Relations, director of the European Institute, and associate dean of the Faculty of International Affairs. Phil sent me a copy of his long letter to Fulbright in June, in which he expressed his "deep dismay" at the threat to Radio Liberty in view of its "modest but essential role" in molding public opinion, helping Soviet citizens to "an awareness of rights that they can and should claim under the laws of their own country," and transmitting "a wide range of information on which the individual can base his own judgment," thus "supporting freedom of individual thought and a sense of shared needs and desires." He cautioned Fulbright that eliminating Radio Liberty would go far to strengthen the efforts of the Soviet leadership to maintain a monopoly of control over the flow of information, and would also signal large numbers of Soviet citizens that the West had abandoned the values it represented. Finally, he asserted: "Since the 1970s will be crucial for the evolution of Soviet society and its ability to influence the regime toward recognizing basic human values, . . . this is a particularly disastrous time to consider the abolition of Radio Liberty."[11]

Mosely told Fulbright that his opinion was "based upon a substantial sampling of Radio Liberty programs." His remark about the 1970s as a crucial time is especially noteworthy in the light of the subsequent flowering of samizdat and the dissident movement in the détente period, which gained even greater momentum as the decade progressed. If the Radio had gone under as a result of Senator Fulbright's misguided motives, Soviet intellectuals would have lost a major ally in their opposition to Brezhnev's suppression of human and civil rights—rights he so piously endorsed in Helsinki in August 1975. The indispensability of Radio Liberty was later acknowledged by leading participants in the dissident movement, most notably Ludmilla Alexeyeva (who emigrated to the United States in 1977) in her encyclopedic book, *Soviet Dissent,* and in her autobiography, *The Thaw Generation.*[12]

Despite Senator Fulbright's myopic view of the role of Radio Free Europe and Radio Liberty as a vital component of American foreign policy, he made a lasting contribution to international understanding through the scholarships he established in his name that enabled many Americans to study overseas, thereby broadening their own horizons while representing the best in American values abroad.

Professor Richard Pipes of Harvard, a staunch supporter of Radio Free Europe and Radio Liberty throughout the Cold War (as an academician and in the 1980s as a member of President Ronald Reagan's National Security Council), wrote to Fulbright in August 1971 that, although he shared some of Fulbright's sentiments about the manner employed to finance the Radios in the past, "I would hope that in debating the future of these two institutions this issue would not be confused with the transcending issue of their functions." He declared that neither he nor any Soviet or Eastern European experts with whom he was acquainted both in the United States and the United Kingdom

> has the slightest doubt about the importance of radio broadcasts to that part of the world which is under Communist control. For many people living under these conditions, radio information coming from abroad is

literally a constitutional weapon which exercises a check on the over-whelming demands made by the state. This check, in turn, is a stabiliz-ing force internally, for it compels the Communist governments to jus-tify themselves before their subjects and to exercise some prudence in their international dealings.

Pipes concluded: "If Radio Free Europe and Radio Liberty can be as-sured of proper and overt financial support, then I take it your main ob-jection to them would fall away. That is why, once again, I should like to urge you to exercise your prestige and influence to assure their undis-turbed function."[13]

A pleiad of American and British scholars with equally impressive cre-dentials articulated similar sentiments.[14] Foy Kohler, a professor at the School for Advanced International Studies of the University of Miami, for-merly director of the Voice of America and ambassador to the Soviet Union, argued that the Radios contributed to long-range stability in U.S.-Soviet relations by working for "evolutionary progress in the target countries."

Kohler praised the quality of the programs, which "in their level of professionalism compare favorably with commercial media in the United States and Western Europe." He concluded:

> None of us can be certain how the systems of the USSR and Eastern Europe will evolve; whether they will develop into more cooperative members of the international community, or whether they will remain locked on a dogmatic, authoritarian course. I think we will not know the answer soon. I do not wish to convey the impression that the Radios by themselves will change the history of the Soviet Union or of Eastern Europe. I do believe that the Radios have a real and beneficial influence on internal events there and that to maintain this influence is in the in-terest both of these peoples and of ourselves.[15]

Kohler's prescient words are relevant today, almost thirty years later, when it is still not clear whether the post-Soviet democratic states will "develop into more cooperative members of the international community."

At a convention of the American Association for the Advancement of Slavic Studies (AAASS) held in Dallas, Texas, in March 1972, I enlisted the help of Professor Richard Burks of Wayne State University, who had held an important policy post at Radio Free Europe before entering the aca-demic world. He quickly drafted and circulated petitions among our col-leagues in the field and succeeded in obtaining almost one hundred signatures from professors in several different disciplines at universities all over the United States. Burks sent the documents to each of the sixteen members of the Senate Committee on Foreign Relations. The signers identified themselves by name and academic position and informed the senators that they wanted to convey their "deep-felt conviction" about the importance of Radio Free Europe and Radio Liberty in providing a "substitute free press" to its listeners. They praised the "research effort of the two radios, upon which much of their broadcasting is based, [which is] generally recognized by scholars in the West as wide-ranging, thorough and objective," emphasizing that

> with the gradual development of détente in the relations between East and West, and because the two transmitters have detached themselves from cold war propaganda in good time, adopting a constructive attitude to the problems of the internal evolution of these countries, the influence of RFE and RL in Eastern Europe is now at a maximum. If their work is not interrupted, these transmitters will play a major role in promoting the evolution of societies with which the peoples of the area and we in the West will be prepared to live.[16]

Jim Critchlow used his contacts with the U.S. press to good advantage by providing writers and editors with background information on Radio Liberty's unique activity. With only a handful of exceptions, the newspapers backed RFE/RL and called for our continued support by Congress despite the end of the CIA connection.

In August 1972, President Richard Nixon appointed Milton S. Eisenhower, president emeritus of Johns Hopkins University, to head a commission of distinguished citizens to study RFE/RL's operations in depth and to report on their findings. The commission included Edward W. Barrett, dean of the Columbia School of Journalism and a former assistant secretary of state for public affairs; Edmund A. Gullion, dean of the Fletcher School of Law and Diplomacy at Tufts University; John A. Gronouski, former postmaster general, former ambassador to Poland, and dean of the Lyndon B. Johnson School of Public Affairs at the University of Texas; and John P. Roche, professor of politics at Brandeis University.

Roche was also a syndicated columnist. Before he was invited to join the Eisenhower commission, he had spent a day with Jim and me in the New York office. After asking us for a sandwich, a typewriter, and an empty room, he wrote a column defending the Radios and criticizing Fulbright that appeared in several newspapers in February and March 1972. We at

Radio Liberty and Radio Free Europe could not have asked for stronger support from a prominent shaper of U.S. public opinion:

One of the most bizarre—and terrifying—scenes in Aleksandr Solzhenitsyn's masterpiece, *The First Circle*, describes a visit to a Soviet prison by a distinguished American, a woman with high political connections. A group of prisoners are put through a special drill for her benefit, dressed decently, put in a clean cell with an ikon, and told by the police that if they don't perform, zap! They did go through with the charade and the American visitor left with a high opinion of Soviet justice.

What made this sort of thing possible, of course, was the total isolation from the world outside. Once caught up in the toils of Joseph Stalin's terror apparatus, it was every man for himself with no hope of succor, no hope that outsiders would even learn of the situation. Part of Solzhenitsyn's power comes from his description of how some human beings resisted atomization and persisted in acts of decency.

The prerequisite for running an efficient tyranny—as Aristotle pointed out more than 2,000 years ago—is to destroy this human sense of solidarity, and to convince each victim that he is alone in the face of overwhelming power, that no one cares. This had become more difficult with modern techniques of communication. It is hard to jam all incoming radio messages, and the spread of the transistor radio and of tape recorders has launched a whole new era in underground communications. Through Radio Liberty and Radio Free Europe the United States has for almost a generation brought to the peoples of the Soviet Union and Eastern Europe the message that they are not alone.

To take but one example, a Soviet Jew signed a petition attacking the appalling Leningrad trials [in 1970, of would-be hijackers of an airplane to take them to Israel]. Thirty years ago he would have dropped this pebble down a bottomless well, but now, the next morning at 2:30, Radio Liberty was on the air with the text of the petition and the names of the signatories. This man, now in Israel, recalls the sense of triumph as he heard the broadcast: "They [the KGB] can take us now, but our testimony will stand in history."

Radio Liberty and Radio Free Europe have reunited these peoples with history. And in the view of Sen. J. W. Fulbright that is a capital offense. Just about the time this column is printed, these radios—formerly subsidized by the CIA—will go broke unless emergency action is taken.

Both houses of Congress have approved their continuation with overt funding, and there is overpowering consensus that they have done a splendid and non-provocative job in a very delicate area, but Fulbright singlehandedly has been blocking a compromise between House and Senate versions of their appropriation.

Fulbright refused to call a meeting of the House and Senate conferees, obviously hoping that in this back-handed fashion he can quietly destroy what he has called these "cold war relics." It's a clever move: if he can stall, key personnel will have to find other jobs and the expertise built up over a generation will dribble away. He must not be permitted to get away with it.

No one who reads this column will suffer from the illusion that I believe the United States is perfect, but we Americans have been fortunate. We have never had to rise at 2:30 and turn on a radio to learn that we are still members of the human race, that we are still part of history. We can not allow Fulbright to deprive our brothers of this priceless link with humanity.[17]

Roche and his fellow members of the Eisenhower Commission studied RFE/RL for six months, including many formal and informal interviews, a firsthand examination of the Munich operation, and lengthy sessions among themselves to arrive at a consensus. The report submitted to the White House in February 1973 concluded that the broadcasts had "not deterred but rather contributed to the search for long-term détente." It recommended preserving the Radios as private American corporations with continued financial support from Congress, which would transmit its appropriations to a newly created Board for International Broadcasting (BIB). That arrangement was adopted, and by 1975 the two Radios were merged as RFE/RL Inc., although the two separate boards continued until 1982, when the BIB took over direct supervision.

The purposes of both radios were reaffirmed in the BIB Act of 1973, in which the U.S. Congress declared:

That it is the policy of the United States to promote the right of freedom of opinion and expression, including the freedom to seek, receive, and impart information and ideas through any media and regardless of frontiers, in accordance with Article 19 of the Universal Declaration of Human Rights;

That open communication of information and ideas among the peoples of the world contributes to international peace and stability, and that the promotion of such communication is in the interest of the United States;

That Radio Free Europe and Radio Liberty have demonstrated their effectiveness in furthering the open communication of information and ideas in Eastern Europe and the USSR;

That the continuation of Radio Free Europe and Radio Liberty as independent broadcast media, operating in a manner *not inconsistent with the broad foreign policy objectives of the United States* [italics added] and in accordance with high professional standards, is in the national interest.[18]

The wording of the italicized passage was essential for RFE/RL to preserve its integrity as a medium capable of operating more flexibly rather than as a mere mouthpiece of the U.S. government.

During the interim period, when the precise structure of the new corporation was being worked out, the State Department acted as a caretaker of the operations. By 1975, the BIB was formed, appointed by the president of the United States, with five members of the majority party and four members of the minority party. The first chairman was David M. Abshire, a well-known figure in Washington politics and then head of the Georgetown University Center for Strategic Studies. Sig Mickelson, a longtime CBS executive, became the first president of the merged entity in 1976. His book, *America's Other Voice*, published in 1983, gives a detailed account of the transition.

Howland Sargeant retired in June 1975.[19] He sent handwritten personal notes to scores of staff members in New York, Munich, and other installations. Each one of them focused on that person's contribution to Radio Liberty, and Sargeant took care to avoid repeating himself, mentioning the uniqueness of each addressee's work. After his death in 1984, Dorothy Sargeant, his widow, invited me to go through Howland's papers. I found carbon copies of these letters, evidence of his compulsive habit of saving everything. (Dorothy told me that he had even kept notes from his mother since boyhood.) Howland's message to me read:

Dear Gene,

You are one of the early pioneers of RL, with a rich variety of experience here and abroad in the maturing of RL. You have been a great colleague to work with, and I have enjoyed it tremendously. Your small unit is developing exciting programs, of high quality and distinction. Keep it up!

Dorothy and I are happy to have enjoyed the friendship over so many years now with you and Gloria, and to have had a few glimpses of the growing up of your fine children along the way. Your verses written for our recent luncheon have given all of my family much pleasure, and it seems typical of our relationship that you found time to compose them in the midst of many pressing other obligations. With warmest good wishes, and profound thanks—Howie.[20]

Shortly after the merger of Radio Free Europe and Radio Liberty, the new management conducted a sweeping reevaluation of the executive staff of both radios, and several heads rolled in what is now called down-sizing. My own position was preserved, and I continued my activity in policy and programming, which Radio Liberty was obliged to fine-tune in light of the growing effect the dissident movement was having on Soviet public opinion.

Did you hear the one about Brezhnev being found floating in the river with a knife in his back?
No, but I love the way it begins!

10 THE TRANSITION PERIOD, 1971–1975

As Radio Liberty was in transition from its CIA sponsorship to an uncertain future, Soviet society itself was experiencing significant changes. The early 1970s witnessed the acceleration of the dissident movement that had gained momentum after the repression of Sinyavsky and Daniel and the invasion of Czechoslovakia. Howland Sargeant, always sensitive to the need for reexamining Radio Liberty's policy and programming assumptions, took the lead in urging the staff in Munich and New York to maximize contacts with Western scholars. They could help us assess the potential value for RL of the samizdat writings by Soviet intellectuals that were spreading exponentially.

Taking this new phenomenon in Soviet society into account, Radio Liberty sponsored a panel discussion in London on "The Future of Samizdat: Significance and Prospects" in April 1971. Albert Boiter, director of research in Munich, chaired the conference at which the only other radio representative was Edward Van Der Rhoer, the Radio's policy director. None of us in New York attended, although our suggestions were welcomed and included in the discussion. One American expert, Abraham Brumberg, editor of the prestigious USIA magazine *Problems of Communism*, and several distinguished British scholars and journalists participated. These academicians were among the staunch defenders of Radio Liberty against Senator Fulbright later in the same year: Michael Bourdeaux, Martin Dewhirst, Max Hayward, Peter Reddaway, and Leonard Schapiro. In addition, David Floyd, Soviet affairs specialist of the *Daily Telegraph*, and Leopold Labedz, editor of the British journal *Survey*, took part.

Boiter was only slightly exaggerating when he introduced the gathering as a "summit meeting" of Western samizdat experts.[1] The purpose of the discussion was to take a retrospective look at more than five years' experience as "observers of the phenomenon of visible dissent in Soviet society we call samizdat." Two questions were posed as the framework for the day-long colloquy: What is likely to happen to samizdat over the next two to five years? What is the proper role of Radio Liberty—or of any foreign radio station or publication—in regard to samizdat?

The consensus was that samizdat was enormously important for its insights into how Soviet intellectuals really think; that it represented the continuation of an old Russian tradition; and that it would probably continue to grow in spite of regime attempts to inhibit it, unless the Brezhnev regime resorted to mass terror, which seemed unlikely in the absence of another Stalin. Indeed, it was observed that samizdat had been almost legitimized in recent years by casual references to it in the controlled press, implying a reluctant acceptance of samizdat by the regime as inevitable in an environment where fear had diminished. Moreover, the support of Soviet physicists and mathematicians helped further embolden the movement.

The experts approved highly of the increased emphasis on broadcasting samizdat texts and our commentaries between the time that the first few programs began in 1969 and the first quarter of 1971, when one-sixth of the Russian language service (an average of fifty-eight hours a week) now dealt with samizdat. The function of Radio Liberty was variously described as a valuable "forum," an "echo chamber," and a "sounding board" for Soviet citizens to express themselves and exchange information. Professor Schapiro called the Radio the "*Kolokol* [Bell] of the present age," an allusion to the famous mid-nineteenth-century émigré magazine edited abroad by Alexander Herzen, who reproduced the views of dissidents in czarist Russia and sent them back for wider dissemination. Schapiro's image of the samizdat movement as "hydra-headed" was endorsed by others. Max Hayward recalled an anonymous document, "A Voice from Russia," that emerged back in 1959 and that declared: "You may think in the West that we Russians have totally lost our ability to think and to react in any other way than that which appears from the official press, but don't forget that this is the country of Pushkin, of the Decembrists. . . . These are slow processes, but remember that we are hydra-headed; they will cut off our heads but some of us will always come up again."

During the 1960s and early 1970s, samizdat had already become more sophisticated and complex in its political, cultural, ethnic, religious, and philosophical content. The experts generally agreed that Radio Liberty should reflect the wide range of themes becoming available in the uncensored writings. We should be scrupulously objective in selecting and commenting, without imposing our own censorship and bias, even when the views of the samizdat writer who is a right-wing chauvinist or even fascist might conflict with those of the Radio or the responsible editor. "It is a hundred times more important to demonstrate to these people [that is, the listeners] what objective liberal reporting is than it is to pursue any particular opinion." However, documents should be given greater prominence if they had "practical utility," dealing with specific current facts and specific abuses of civil and human rights. Soviet citizens should be apprised of their own laws in order to buttress their demand for justice. Radio Liberty should broadcast "again and again" the advice of Aleksandr Yesenin-Volpin, a well-known dissident and pioneer in judicial education, concerning the way people should conduct themselves when being interrogated. "It is wonderful, practical information. It tells what you legally can do and what you cannot do." (Volpin was the son of the beloved Russian poet Sergei Yesenin, who committed suicide in 1925. He emigrated to the United States in the 1970s and often visited our New York office.)

The importance of verifying the authenticity of samizdat documents was also stressed by the participants. One of the best tests, according to Peter Reddaway, was the appearance of documents in the *Chronicle of Current Events,* the major reliable medium of information on the human rights movement. The *Chronicle* was born in Moscow in 1968, and within the next ten years it had earned the praise of Andrei Sakharov as the greatest achievement of the movement. Radio Liberty made sure that each issue reaching the West (sixty-three of them by 1983) was made available to its radio audience.

The final portion of the London conference explored how Radio Liberty could share its valuable collection of samizdat with interested people in the West. Many useful suggestions were adopted by Boiter and his deputy, Peter Dornan. They and their staff in Munich deserve special credit for making Radio Liberty the chief repository of thousands of samizdat materials that were vetted, registered, systematically cataloged, bound in volumes, and made available not only for integration into the Radio program but also to the vast community of Western scholars, journalists, and government specialists. This helped overcome the negative image that the revelation of our CIA connection produced among some segments of American public opinion. Indeed, the message of support that one hundred American scholars sent to Senator Fulbright in 1972 was a by-product of their enhanced respect for the Radio.

Joseph Whelan's study of Radio Liberty for the Library of Congress correctly emphasized the importance of samizdat and the Radio's involvement as "the principal source for disseminating samizdat throughout the Soviet Union." He added: "And it does so without risk to the individual. As a recent newcomer from the Soviet Union said, 'If one listens over the radio . . . there are no documents that could cause trouble.'" Whelan quoted from the transcript of the London conference to demonstrate how Radio Liberty sought guidance from Western Sovietologists, and he noted that one of the direct results of the meeting was the formulation of a broadcast directive on the use of samizdat documents, which he reproduced in an appendix.

The main caveats were that Radio Liberty would not knowingly broadcast a fabrication; that it would not knowingly broadcast genuine works, or versions of them, distributed in the West by agencies of the regime with the intention of harming the authors; that it would relay the direct verbatim text whenever possible, and always dissociate the author from Radio Liberty's use of his text, separating the Radio's comment from the document itself; and that it would not endanger an author whose position seemed precarious.

A few months after this London "summit" meeting, the first conference on samizdat in North America was held under the auspices of McMaster University in Hamilton, Ontario. As the representative from the Radio, I participated and conveyed my impressions to Boiter and Van Der Rhoer. Whelan summarized my message to Munich:

> [Sosin] indicated that the conference acknowledged that dissent and samizdat are a fact of current Soviet life worth taking seriously. Those

academicians present agreed that it would have been unthinkable to call such a conference even a few years ago and anticipate the convening of another one in the near future. Stress was placed on foreign radio broadcasts as a major factor in amplifying voices of dissent, encouraging this or that group to emulate others more bold and acting as a partial restraint on regime repression. Respect was evident for RL research on samizdat combined with urgent requests from many participants that RL provide them with material.[2]

Khrushchev's Death

Early in 1971, in anticipation of the ultimate death of Nikita Khrushchev, we solicited statements for our radio "morgue" from such specialists as Professor Robert V. Daniels, of the University of Vermont, and Harrison Salisbury, editor of the Op-Ed page of the *New York Times* and a former Pulitzer Prize–winning correspondent in Moscow at the time of Stalin's death. It wasn't long before Radio Liberty used them when Khrushchev died in September. To supplement the statements already on file, I asked Isaac Don Levine for his evaluation. With his typical flair for placing events in historical perspective, Don came through with the following, which he wrote and recorded in Russian:

> Historians of our epoch will never forget that Nikita Sergeyevich Khrushchev opened a window to Europe and America for the progressive generation of peoples of the Soviet Union. After a thirty-year reign of the Genghis Khan of our time, Nikita Sergeyevich—this son of peasant and working class Russia—dared to rip off the mask of the demigod which Stalin wore while enthroned in the Kremlin, and reveal to the entire world the true features of the bloodiest tyrant in history.
>
> Nobody can forget that it was Khrushchev who showed thinking Soviet citizens Stalin's colossal errors and crimes which brought Russia back to the era of the Tatar yoke, and the Soviet state to the brink of destruction. We are indebted to Khrushchev for reviving the half-dead corpse into which Stalin, with the help of his *oprichniki* [ancient Russian hatchet men] the Zhdanovs and Yezhovs, had transformed the great culture of creative Russia. It was precisely this self-taught Khrushchev who gave us Solzhenitsyn and the whole pleiad of new cultural pioneers and champions of free thought who are the harbingers of an imminent free Russia. The curtain that today's rulers of the Soviet Union have drawn around the open grave of Khrushchev at Novodevichy Cemetery only serves to underline his merits for the whole culture of mankind.

All civilized peoples, who have evaluated and measured Khrushchev's biography with extensive obituaries have spoken about the thaw and respite of his era, have witnessed themselves what obscurantists stand today at the helm of a great country. Even the autocratic [czarist] government would not have ventured to exhibit such behavior. It has caused a great loss of prestige for the Kremlin dictatorship, tantamount to the defeat on the international arena which it suffered three years ago when it invented the Brezhnev doctrine in order to justify the Soviet army's intervention in the internal affairs of Czechoslovakia. Comrades Brezhnev, Kosygin, and Podgorny displayed themselves before the progressive and avant-garde masses of the outside world in such a vulgar, indecent light that they ought to postpone for several months their forthcoming tours of Europe and Canada.

Thus, lying in his casket, Khrushchev has won, thanks to the unprecedented behavior of his political enemies. It is now becoming clearer than ever for friends of the Russian people and for Communist and socialist parties of the free world, that the embryonic reforms of Khrushchev cannot be stifled by the petty imitators of Stalin. They are trying to close the little window opened by Khrushchev and to stop the flow of fresh air into closed-off Russia. But in the depths of underground Russia the roots are growing and promising to bring the long-suffering people a real and lasting spring, when self-rule on the basis of a democratic constitution of free elections will become the achievement of the whole population of the Soviet Union, and when the humane traditions of Tolstoy, Turgenev, and Gorky will rise again and lead Russia to the forefront of civilized humanity.[3]

Bertram Wolfe, who was most famous for his biography of Lenin, Trotsky, and Stalin, *Three Who Made a Revolution,* provided an equally incisive analysis of the late leader's significance in Soviet history, along with sharp criticism of his successors. Unfortunately, the programming executives in Munich spiked the broadcast of the two statements on the grounds that they violated policy. It seemed to me at the time, and I have not altered my opinion today, that this was a case of overkill. True, the statements contained passages that violated Radio Liberty's policy of avoiding invective against the current Soviet leaders, but why drown the baby with the bath water? Judicious editing could have toned down the texts and still preserved the insights of these two Western experts. Actually, when one looks at the Soviet regime of the 1970s from the vantage point of the 1990s, everything Levine and Wolfe said about Brezhnev et al. has been validated by history—and candidly admitted by the post-Soviet leadership.

In fairness to the Munich editors, however, I should add that when I was stationed there in the late 1960s I reluctantly agreed to the emasculation of an emotional tribute by Arkady Belinkov on the death of his friend, a fellow dissident named Alexei Kosterin. Belinkov branded the Brezhnev regime "a band of criminals who killed Kosterin." But in this case we simply cut out what was considered too offensive to the Kremlin in the days of détente and saved the rest.

It should not be inferred that the Radio's taboo against insulting the Soviet leaders was accompanied by a softening of our attacks on the dictatorship and its evils. If the Voice of America was not jammed during most of the détente period of the 1970s, it was in turn careful to tone down its criticism in order to prevent the resumption of interference. In contrast, Radio Liberty's function as the surrogate voice of the Soviet peoples required that we stick to our basic principles and goals despite the vagaries of East-West relations. Thus, it was no surprise that Radio Liberty never for one minute enjoyed unjammed airtime from 1953 to 1988, despite the evolution of programming policy from "liberation" to "liberty."

Coverage of Watergate

The biggest news story in the United States in the early 1970s was the Watergate scandal. One would suppose that Soviet media would have a field day gloating over the exposure of corruption in high places in Washington. However, an attack on the Nixon administration was not in the best interests of the regime's much-needed détente with the United States. Consequently, Soviet media sought to conceal the extent of President Richard Nixon's involvement and the threat of his impeachment. Even at the time of his resignation in August 1974, Radio Moscow told the Soviet public that Nixon was the victim of partisan politics, the economic situation in America, and the malicious propaganda of our mass media. Then they shifted their focus to President Gerald Ford's statements on the continuity of foreign policy.

Adhering to the standards of objective journalism, unlike the Soviet treatment of these events, Radio Liberty news contained both the charges against Nixon and his aides, and their replies. With a programming staff of former Soviet citizens, we were uniquely able to draw analogies to the operations of the Soviet government in a way that would answer the listeners' questions and meet their interests. The judicial proceedings, Watergate hearings in the Senate, House impeachment hearings, as well as reports on U.S. media coverage offered opportunities for meaningful explanation of the American system. We gave step-by-step reports on the week of Nixon's resignation and the inauguration of the new president. Soviet listeners also heard reviews of the world press expressing admiration for the vitality of American democracy.

Aleksandr Solzhenitsyn

On February 12, 1972, the *New York Times* published on the Op-Ed page a prose poem by Aleksandr Solzhenitsyn dedicated to his late friend, Aleksandr Tvardovsky, once editor of the liberal monthly *Novy Mir.* Solzhenitsyn's shattering chronicle of conditions in the gulag, *One Day in the Life of Ivan Denisovich,* appeared in that magazine ten years earlier, thanks to Tvardovsky's courage and recognition of the author's genius. However, that was during one of the relatively tolerant periods of Khrushchev's era. Tvardovsky was removed from his position after Brezhnev and his hard-liners came to power. In Solzhenitsyn's lament for his friend who had died two months earlier, he inveighed against the "flabby crowd" in the leadership of the Writers' Union who took away from Tvardovsky "his offspring, his passion, his journal" and "hunted him down with unholy shrieks and cries," thus hastening his death.

The Nobel laureate rejected the notion that those who had destroyed *Novy Mir* and its editor had won. He declared: "You need to be deaf and blind to the last century of Russia's history to regard this as a victory and not an irreparable blunder! Madmen! When the voices of the young resound, keen-edged, how you will miss this patient critic, whose gentle admonitory voice was heeded by all."[4] About a month after Solzhenitsyn's message was published, and broadcast over Radio Liberty, he was attacked in a letter to the *New York Times* written by Y. Smelyakov, a well-known Soviet poet and a member of the board of the Writers' Union. Radio Liberty's Russian program of March 13 carried the full text of Smelyakov's letter.

Solzhenitsyn rebutted Smelyakov's attack during a four-hour conversation with Hedrick Smith and Robert Kaiser, the Moscow correspondents of the *Times* and the *Washington Post.* The American journalists asked him how he learned about the letter. He replied that he heard it on Radio Liberty. "If we ever hear anything about events in this country, it's through them."[5] We were overjoyed to get this testimonial to our effectiveness from such a distinguished person, particularly at a time when Senator Fulbright was trying to destroy us.

In January 1974, Radio Liberty began serializing Solzhenitsyn's *Gulag Archipelago* in daily half-hour installments. Unlike other works by dissident writers, the book did not circulate in samizdat form in the Soviet Union before its publication in Paris at the end of 1973. The entire 260,000–word chronicle of Stalinist brutality and duplicity was read over the course of three months.[6] (The Voice of America limited its broadcasts to excerpts and comments in the U.S. press.) A few days after these broadcasts began, five prominent Soviet dissidents signed a statement of support for Solzhenitsyn, quoting passages from the book. Because they did not have access to it inside Russia, they must have heard it on Western shortwave media. The five intellectuals were Andrei Sakharov; Professor Igor Shafarevich, a mathematician at Moscow University; Vladimir Voinovich, a novelist and playwright; Vladimir Maximov, a novelist; and Aleksandr Galich, the famous dissident balladeer. The signatories called on "honest people" everywhere to resist attempts to prosecute the author of *Gulag Archipelago*.

Aleksandr Galich

I first became aware of Aleksandr Galich and his underground songs of protest while I was in Munich in the late 1960s, but it wasn't until I returned to New York that I began seriously to analyze his lyrics. After 1970 he became increasingly active as a dissident and joined with Solzhenitsyn and Sakharov in openly criticizing the Brezhnev regime's arbitrary treatment of its citizens. He was expelled from the Union of Soviet Writers and the Union of Cinematographers in December 1971. His situation became precarious and, in addition, he had a bad heart.

In an article on the *New York Times* Op-Ed page, I described Galich's plight, calling attention to this major talent among Soviet writers who also fought for human rights side by side with the better-known Russian intellectuals. My translation of his song "The Gold Prospectors' Little Waltz," a mordant criticism of those who remain silent in the face of injustice, was quoted in full. It was one of Galich's most powerful statements, and it helped him earn the admiration and affection of countless Soviet citizens who committed to memory his sardonic advice to those who would get ahead in Soviet society: Silence is golden, so "just keep mum / and rich you'll become."[7]

As a result of mounting public opinion in the West, Galich was finally permitted to emigrate in 1974. He first chose Norway, but soon he was invited to Frankfurt, Germany, by NTS (National Labor Union), a right-wing Russian émigré group that published his forbidden songs in their *Posev* publishing house. Soon afterward he joined Radio Liberty in Munich and quickly projected his charismatic personality over the microphone. He delighted his admiring public back home with his weekly program of witty commentary interspersed with old and new poems set to his own music and played on his guitar. In one of his first broadcasts, he sang the "Gold Prospectors' Little Waltz" and urged his listeners: "Friends and unknown persons in the East and West—do not be silent!"

David Abshire, chairman of the Board for International Broadcasting, asked me to invite Galich to visit the United States on an all-expense-paid trip in the spring of 1975. He would spend some time in New York giving concerts for Russian émigrés, after which I would escort him to Washington, where Abshire had arranged for him to meet important government people to talk about human rights. I obtained a visa for Galich and met him at the airport. Two of his oldest friends from Moscow, Victor and Galya Kabachnik, who both worked for the Radio in New York, were with me. Galich dedicated one of his ballads, "Song of Exodus," to them when they emigrated in 1971, calling it "my sorrowful goodbye present." It was a joyous reunion for them at the airport, and the ride into Manhattan was punctuated by the newcomer's excitement at seeing the legendary New York skyscrapers.

Within a day of his arrival Galich was invited to be a special guest at an AFL-CIO banquet. The labor union was in the forefront of the campaign for workers' rights in the Soviet Union and was aware of Galich's activity as a dissident. I acted as his interpreter and explained the meaning of the "guitar poetry" he sang for the assembled members. Galich was a warm, outgoing person who loved life and was fascinated by America. He and I were soon on *ty*, meaning that we addressed one another using the familiar pronoun like the French *tu*, and I informally called him "Sasha" instead of the polite use of his name and patronymic, "Aleksandr Arkadyevich."

Rather than fly to Washington, Sasha preferred taking the train. It would give him a chance to relax and see something of the countryside. Gloria and I boarded the Metroliner with him at Pennsylvania Station. A few minutes after we started, while we were in the tunnel under the Hudson River, the electricity suddenly conked out. We sat silently in the darkness for a few moments, until Sasha's voice rang out in Russian: *"Zapadnaya tekhnologiya!"* (Western technology) he proclaimed in a mocking tone. Years later, in 1989, when I made a speech at a celebration of Galich in Moscow, I told that story to an appreciative audience that was long familiar with Sasha's ironic sense of humor.

In Washington, Galich met with members of Congress and the State Department. His visit coincided with an exchange of cultural delegations between the United States and the Soviet Union in the spirit of détente that was in progress. Fully aware of the kind of people that made up a Soviet delegation, Galich inquired of the State Department representatives, "How is it that you send your writers on trips to the Soviet Union but you let KGB generals come over here in exchange?" The Americans were either too startled or too embarrassed to reply.

The rest of Sasha's visit in the capital and back in New York was filled with standing-room-only concerts for the émigré communities. Colette Shulman, who had known Sasha in Moscow when she was a foreign correspondent, arranged a special concert for students and faculty at the Columbia Russian Institute. Mikhail Baryshnikov, the ballet dancer, came to hear his dear friend and stood unobtrusively at the rear of the crowded room.

Galich returned to his work at Radio Liberty in Munich, making good use of his experiences in America for his weekly radio chats, one of which included generous praise for my translations of his songs. He also continued to give concerts in Europe, and in the fall of 1975 he made his first trip to Israel, where his agent had set up several appearances in Tel Aviv and other cities. By a happy coincidence, Gloria and I were in Jerusalem on the day he was due to arrive from Europe, so we rushed to Ben Gurion airport to surprise him as he came through customs. He looked at us in amazement and said "No problem!"—a reference to our watchword during the Washington trip, when he discovered that everything was easy for him to get, even a bottle of whiskey at midnight in the hotel.

Galich was visibly moved by his visit to Israel. Born "Ginzburg," he changed his name as a young actor in Stanislavsky's theater company. Although he later converted to Russian Orthodoxy, he always felt connected to his Jewish roots. Sasha's premiere concert in the Mann Auditorium in Tel Aviv was filled to overflowing with former Soviet citizens who demanded encore after encore. He had worried that many of the Jewish émigrés would resent him for having converted, but to the contrary, the audience was not only entertained by his satirical ditties about Soviet life but also affected by his more serious songs about the Holocaust, anti-Semitism, and the Six-Day War.

As we took Galich around the city in our rented car, Gloria and he sang Yiddish folksongs he remembered from his childhood. We accompanied him to a reunion with old friends who had recently emigrated from Moscow: Zhenya and Janna Levich, the son and daughter-in-law of Benjamin Levich, an internationally respected Soviet physicist who was then still a "refusenik," forbidden to leave the Soviet Union. They went with us to visit Natalia Mikhoels, the daughter of Solomon Mikhoels, the great Yiddish actor and director of Moscow's State Jewish Theater, who was world famous for his interpretation of King Lear and who had been murdered in 1948 on Stalin's orders.[8] Radio Liberty later broadcast several programs about Mikhoels when we inaugurated a special series for Soviet Jewish listeners. The program featured a rare recording in Yiddish with Mikhoels as Tevye the Milkman in Sholom Aleichem's famous story, which became *Fiddler on the Roof* on American stage and screen.[9]

Gloria and I were warmly welcomed into their circle, and we got a glimpse of the spirit of Russia's intelligentsia as we enjoyed their songs and quips. It was clear that their joie de vivre as émigrés was tinged with nostalgia for Moscow, a feeling that Sasha expressed so poignantly in his song "When I Return." Actually, Galich had composed the song before he left Moscow, because, he explained in one broadcast, "One of the most widespread illnesses of the emigration is nostalgia, so I decided to 'de-nostalgize' myself in order not to worry about it once I left."

That was the last time we saw Galich. He moved from Munich to Paris, and continued his talks on Radio Liberty until he died suddenly in December 1977. His wife, Anya, found him almost lifeless lying near the radio, his hands badly charred. Evidently he had electrocuted himself trying to set up a new stereo system without knowing enough about the electric current. Suspecting foul play, the police investigated but were satisfied that his death was an accident. Anya later described it: "Sasha had dreamed for a long time of having a special Grundig system. When the workers delivered it, they said a technician would come tomorrow to set it up. I went out to shop, but Sasha started to put it together and the current shot through him. When I returned he had lost consciousness but was still alive. I rushed to the telephone, but by the time the doctors arrived, Sasha had died in my arms."[10]

Predictably, the Soviet press blamed the CIA, and many opponents of the regime both at home and in the West blamed the KGB, concluding that Galich's Radio Liberty broadcasts had provoked their retaliation. To this day, when I discuss Galich's death with émigrés from the former Soviet Union, they suspect that it was not an accident. Even Andrei Sakharov declared in his memoirs that he was never 100 percent certain. He cited as evidence a letter Sasha's mother had received almost a year before his death, which she had brought to Sakharov in an agitated state. Inside the envelope was a page from a calendar with a typewritten message: "It has been decided to kill your son, Aleksandr." He tried to calm her down, pointing out that if they really meant to kill him they would not give any warning. But Sakharov wrote, "The KGB really does engage in that sort of cunning operation, so it is entirely possible."[11]

An extraordinary human being was gone, although his rich repertoire of sixty songs lives on. I analyzed some of these underground songs in my chapter in *Dissent in the USSR*, published in 1975. Sasha's weekly program had been one of the most popular programs of the Radio's Russian service. His friend Julian Panich, a director at Radio Liberty and himself a well-known Soviet actor before he emigrated, compiled a book immortalizing his broadcasts in print: *Aleksandr Galich at the Microphone*.

In 1990, while on a trip to France, Gloria and I made a pilgrimage to Galich's grave in the Russian Orthodox cemetery in Ste. Geneviève des Bois, south of Paris, where famous Russian writers like Ivan Bunin and Viktor Nekrasov, and ballet dancer Rudolf Nureyev, are also buried. We stood at Sasha's grave and said Kaddish, the Hebrew prayer for the dead that exalts God, and we wondered whether the prayer had ever been spoken in that cemetery before. We were sure that Sasha would have been pleased, because he was proud of his Judeo-Christian heritage.

Further Insights from Academicians

In the fall of 1973, Abraham Brumberg organized an important international symposium on East-West affairs in Salzburg, Austria, and invited me to attend as an observer for the Radio, along with Ronny Ronalds, executive director of Radio Liberty. Abe assembled a group of specialists on the Soviet Union, and for good measure he chose Edward Albee, the playwright, who was concerned about the repression of Soviet writers. In describing the broad spectrum of ideas and information that the Radio offered our audience, I remarked that we aimed to show the regime that "there are more things in heaven and earth than are dreamt of in your Marxist-Leninist philosophy." Two of the academic participants, Allen Kassof, of Princeton and the director of IREX (International Research and Exchanges Board), and Loren Graham of M.I.T., asked me afterward to give them some examples of our broadcast content. I proposed that they select a recent date at random, and on my return to New York sent them transcripts of that day's program. It was an effective way of persuading skeptical scholars who may otherwise have continued to regard Radio Liberty as an abrasive Cold War instrument.

After the symposium ended, I escorted several of the participants to Munich on a chartered bus to attend our own conference at Radio Liberty. As we approached the Austrian-Bavarian border, I gathered all the passports, and when we stopped at the customs building I went inside to hand them over for checking. The tragic murder of Israeli athletes during the 1972 Olympics in Munich was still fresh in everyone's memory, and the customs official who flipped through the passports asked me in German: *"Keine Araber?"* "No Arabs aboard," I assured him. My fellow passengers, including such definitely non-Arab professors as Friedberg, Schapiro, Dallin, and Pipes, appreciated the irony.

The topic for the one-day meeting chaired by Ronalds was "Radio Liberty in a Period of Détente."[12] Al Boiter and I also represented the Radio. Guest experts were Richard Loewenthal, the eminent West German professor of international relations from Berlin; Klaus Mehnert, another well-known specialist from Aachen; Renato Mieli, a journalist from Milan; Karel van het Reve, the publisher of samizdat from Amsterdam; Per Hegge from Oslo, who had been the Moscow correspondent of *Aftenposten;* François Bondy, from Zurich's *Die Weltwoche;* old friends from Great Britain, Leonard Schapiro and Martin Dewhirst; and American academicians Alex Dallin from Stanford, Maurice Friedberg, then of Indiana and later of Illinois, and Dick Pipes of Harvard.

Ronalds posed the fundamental problem: "Perhaps some of you may agree with our critics that Radio Liberty no longer serves a useful purpose in the present era of détente, that it stands in the way of improved relations between East and West or that it duplicates efforts of other Western broadcasters. Whatever you think, we want you to be perfectly frank." The experts generally agreed that Radio Liberty broadcasts, especially those concerning internal developments, contribute to an enlightened Soviet public opinion; an ignorant or uninformed Soviet public, totally dependent for its news on Soviet media, is a public that can be manipulated far more easily than one that is enlightened. Thus, the Radio contributes to world peace and stability. A sine qua non of Radio Liberty's mission was broadcasting samizdat, the experts stressed, regardless of the Soviet regime's attitude toward the station. As Loewenthal put it: "It's in the nature of its existence as an organ of Russian dissent and not just an organ of a foreign government that it will be singled out as particularly hostile and dangerous."

They unanimously endorsed the importance of broadcasts in non-Russian languages of the Soviet Union as well, but bearing in mind the sensitivity of the Russians, it was important not to identify Radio Liberty with a separatist approach, which risked throwing some of the less alienated or establishment intelligentsia into the arms of the regime, a regime that was becoming more jingoist. We assured the visitors that from the time the Radio went on the air it had observed a policy of "non-predetermination"—that is, it recognized that only the people within the Soviet Union could decide what any future political structure of the area might be. Moreover, it was always our policy not to broadcast programs that would tend to set one people against another.

The group discussed the continued jamming of Radio Liberty during the détente period, when the Soviet Union stopped interfering with the broadcasts of the official Western stations. They believed it showed the authorities' apprehensiveness about the Radio's concentration on Soviet life; while the Soviet leaders theoretically recognized the right of other countries to express their own points of view, permitting unjammed broadcasts by the Radio would imply a recognition of the right to dissent in the Soviet Union. The authorities objected more to Radio Free Europe and to Radio Liberty because they feared the Radios' potential force in the formation of a collective opposition; hence it was a major interest in their fight against ideological subversion to get rid of these stations. The group concurred that the Soviets had undoubtedly timed the cessation of jamming of the Voice of America with the Radio Liberty and Radio Free Europe appropriations coming up before the U.S. Congress, in order to undercut support for the two stations.

Although the name of Radio Liberty had been changed from Radio Liberation more than a decade earlier, we wondered how they regarded it. They agreed that it would be counterproductive to change the name, not only because it had been established as a "trademark" but also because such a move would be bad politically. "To go away from Liberation made sense because it expressed the fact that you are not pursuing an active policy in that sense. But you don't run away from Liberty. What's the point of having a station for Russia unless it's called Liberty."

Those of us responsible for keeping Radio Liberty on course welcomed the opportunity to test our hypotheses periodically with knowledgeable scholars on both sides of the Atlantic. Their insights were valuable in confirming existing policy and programming or encouraging us to make corrections or additions.

Programming for Soviet Jews

Special broadcasts for Soviet Jews had been considered as far back as the mid-1950s. There had been objections that the Jewish audience was fluent in Russian and would not understand Yiddish, except perhaps in the Baltic and certain large cities of Russia and the Ukraine. Broadcasting to them in Russian was also opposed, because Russian and Ukrainian anti-Semitism had never died out under the Soviet regime and it was believed that Radio Liberty might antagonize some of its Slavic listeners by openly reaching out to Jews. To be sure, on rare occasions in the early years of the Radio, Jewish festivals were observed in special programs. In December 1960, the story of Chanukah, which commemorates the Jewish struggle for religious freedom against tyranny, was broadcast in Russian, Ukrainian, Tatar, Belorussian, and Georgian in order to inspire hope among listeners of various backgrounds. But we had kept such programs to a minimum lest we give Soviet propaganda organs additional ammunition.

By the early 1970s, however, it was clear that, despite the pitfalls, a program for Soviet Jewish listeners was needed. The Library of Congress report stated that as a result of the Six-Day War in the Middle East, Soviet Jews' consciousness and pride in their cultural and religious roots had grown to such an extent that Radio Liberty was obligated to respond. More and more Soviet Jews were being denied their civil and human rights by Brezhnev's anti-Semitic regime, which was thinly disguised as anti-Zionist but blatantly discriminatory against Jews in the Soviet Union who sought equal treatment in gaining access to first-class institutions of higher education and in their choice of careers. Since many Soviet Russian intellectuals were championing the right of Jews to freely express their age-old identity, how could Radio Liberty remain silent?

We initiated a weekly half-hour program under my direction and in close cooperation with Maurice Friedberg, one of the Radio's most frequently consulted academic éminences grises. It was produced in Russian, but often used Yiddish for emotional effect through interviews with famous stage and screen artists like Ida Kaminska. On Jewish holidays we broadcast Hebrew prayers and songs, restoring to Soviet Jews the rich tradition from which they had been almost completely cut off by the double barrier of an atheistic and hostile regime. Those responsible for the weekly programs from New York were Slava Tsukerman, a former Moscow film director who made a successful avant-garde movie after he came to New York; Jacob Dreyer, an economist who went on to assume an important post in the Treasury Department under President Carter; and later Arkady Lvov, a gifted novelist from Odessa, who produced the program for more than a decade until it was terminated in the early 1990s.

The movement of Soviet Jews demanding emigration during the 1970s was supported vociferously by public opinion abroad, especially by American Jewry. Radio Liberty covered all the important "Solidarity Sunday" demonstrations in New York sponsored by the Coalition for Soviet Jewry. Prominent local and federal government officials were always present. We frequently interviewed Avital Shcharansky, the courageous wife of the leading Jewish refusenik, Anatoli Shcharansky, who was imprisoned in the gulag. She told the Soviet listening public and the eavesdropping authorities about her tireless efforts abroad on behalf of her husband. (He was released in 1986 after eight years and joined her in Israel, where he changed his name to Natan Sharansky, headed a party of fellow émigrés in the Knesset, and became a cabinet minister in Benjamin Netanyahu's government.)

In Munich, the Jewish program was enriched by interviews from Israel and Western European cities that reflected Jewish life. Reaction from Jewish listeners was positive. Aside from this special program, Radio Liberty broadcast thousands of pages of samizdat petitions by Jews in the Soviet Union who demanded their rights, especially after the Helsinki Accords of 1975.[13]

At the Conference on Security and Cooperation in Europe held in Helsinki, the Soviet Union expected to benefit by trading recognition of human rights for the West's acceptance of the political status quo in Communist-controlled Eastern Europe. However, by joining with President Gerald Ford and other heads of state in signing the Final Act of the conference, which endorsed the principle of "human rights and fundamental freedoms," Leonid Brezhnev in effect provided Soviet dissidents with a powerful weapon in pursuit of their goals. It was not long before unofficial citizen groups were organized in Moscow and other major cities of the

Soviet Union to monitor the regime's adherence to the obligations imposed on it by this unprecedented document.

For the next decade—the final ten years of "stagnation" of Soviet society under Brezhnev and his short-lived successors, Yuri Andropov and Konstantin Chernenko—the Helsinki monitors inside the Soviet Union and their counterparts in the West kept pressing the Kremlin to adhere to the "spirit of Helsinki." Radio Liberty's program schedule became increasingly devoted to broadcasting the documents emanating from the various groups inside and to informing the public about the regime's arrests of dissenters who dared to demand that the regime honor its promises. At the same time, we communicated the reaction of rights organizations abroad like the U.S. Helsinki Watch and Amnesty International. The Russian desk in Munich, in particular Viktor Fedoseyev, mounted special programs on human rights that analyzed and commented on the movement that would ultimately play an important part in the evolution of Soviet society into the era of glasnost and perestroika under Mikhail S. Gorbachev.

What is the transitional stage between
Socialism and Communism?
Alcoholism.

⓫ ☗ FROM STAGNATION TO GLASNOST
AND PERESTROIKA, 1976–1985

The act of Congress creating the Board
for International Broadcasting was signed
into law on October 19, 1973; the BIB was
formally constituted on April 30, 1974, and
began its oversight. The corporate merger
of Free Europe Inc. and Radio Liberty
Committee Inc. into RFE/RL Inc. was con-
summated on October 1, 1976. The new
corporation was chartered under the laws
of the State of Delaware as a nonprofit,
educational organization. Headquarters
moved from New York City to Washington,
and the staff of the combined radios was
cut almost in half. Sig Mickelson, formerly
president of CBS News, became the first
president of RFE/RL. In Munich, RL personnel moved into Radio Free Europe's
enlarged building in the Englischer Garten
at an annual rent savings of $650,000. RL
had been situated in the Bogenhausen section across the Isar River since 1967, when
it had to move from the old airport building
in Oberwiesenfeld to make room for the
site of the 1972 Olympics.

By the fall of 1976, a total of 1,099 employees were working together, coexisting for the first time under one roof. Although Radio Free Europe's target area did not coincide with Radio Liberty's, many of the RFE senior staff, especially the Americans, had always regarded Radio Liberty as superfluous, condescendingly referring to it as "Radio Hole-in-the-Head." They did not take seriously a radio aimed at the Soviet population, who were not controlled by foreign troops or a foreign master—unlike the captive nations of Eastern Europe, whose peoples resented the presence of Kremlin-appointed gauleiters and Soviet tanks on their native soil. In other words, the RFE loyalists saw little chance for fundamental change ever to take place inside the Soviet Union; their hopes rested on the Czechs, the Poles, the Hungarians, and others who would ultimately free Europe from Communist hegemony.

Even after the RFE/RL merger, the hostility between the two groups was reflected in the adolescent makeshift signs that divided the separate newsrooms. Walking from the RFE area to Radio Liberty one read: "You are leaving Free Europe," and on the opposite side a sign proclaimed "Liberty ends here." Shades of Berlin's Checkpoint Charlie! Within a short time, however, the two news services, correspondents, and bureaus in Europe and the United States were consolidated, the rivalry simmered down, and the unified radio worked more smoothly, although it was never totally free of tension.

The complex merger process involved adjusting the different accounting procedures, pay scales, benefits programs, and recruiting concepts. Only program production and the research departments of RFE and RL remained as separate operational divisions of the parent corporation.

Meanwhile, on August 1, 1975, the Final Act of the Conference on Security and Cooperation in Europe, held in Helsinki, Finland, raised expectations for a freer flow of information. Leonid Brezhnev and President Gerald Ford were among the thirty-five signatories. With respect to international broadcasting, the Final Act declared: "The participating states note the expansion of information broadcast by radio, and express the hope for the continuation of this process so as to meet the interest of mutual understanding among peoples and the aims set forth by this conference." This expression of hope implied the need to end interference with international broadcasts. However, the Soviet government continued to act against the "spirit of Helsinki" by intensifying jamming of all Radio Liberty broadcasts to the Soviet Union.

For the first time in the Cold War, the Soviet leader himself publicly attacked Radio Liberty along with Radio Free Europe. On June 29, 1976, addressing a conference of European Communist parties, Leonid Brezhnev declared: "On the territory of some European countries, well-known subversive radio stations, which usurped for themselves the name of 'Liberty' and 'Free Europe,' are carrying out their activity. Their very existence poisons the international atmosphere. It is a direct challenge to both the spirit and the letter of the agreements reached in Helsinki. The Soviet Union energetically calls for the cessation of the activity of these weapons of psychological war."[1]

The Federal Republic of Germany, the host government of RFE/RL, responded with a formal declaration in the Bundestag by the minister of state of the Foreign Office: "The Federal Government sees in the activities of the radio stations Radio Free Europe and Radio Liberty neither a violation of the goals and principles of the Charter of the United Nations, which include the strengthening of human rights and basic freedoms, nor a violation of the final document of Helsinki in which the participants of the conference made it their goal to facilitate the freer and more comprehensive dissemination of all sorts of information."[2]

Nevertheless, the unrelenting campaign against the Radios waged by the Soviet Union and its Eastern European colonies achieved some success at the winter Olympic games in Innsbruck, Austria. RFE/RL sports reporters were refused accreditation by the Olympic Committee as the result of Soviet initiative, despite the firm position taken by the West German government, as well as the United States, other governments, and such bodies as the North Atlantic Assembly. The Radios managed to keep listeners informed through broadcasts from outside the Olympic grounds, and by the time the summer games opened in Montreal, the committee permitted complete coverage.

The Nixon, Ford, and Carter administrations in turn voiced their strong support of the Radios and condemned the continued jamming. Soon after he became president in 1977, Jimmy Carter observed in his report to Congress of March 22, 1977, "International broadcasting is a key element of United States foreign policy," and declared: "Our most crucial audiences for international broadcasting are in the Soviet Union and Eastern Europe." He requested that Congress finance eleven additional 250-KW transmitters for the Radios to supplement the nine already in operation. Radio Liberty was broadcasting in sixteen of the languages spoken in the Soviet Union, including a twenty-four-hour Russian service. Shortly before the merger with Radio Free Europe, Radio Liberty inaugurated weekly broadcasts in the three Baltic languages: Lithuanian, Latvian, and Estonian. By September 1975, all three services were broadcasting daily.

During the first year of its existence, the BIB developed a "Mission Statement" that endured well into the Gorbachev era as the fundamental policy position for the Radios. The document stated the Radios' mission:

> . . . to encourage a constructive dialogue with the peoples of Eastern Europe and the Soviet Union by enhancing their knowledge of developments in the world at large and in their own countries. In openly communicating information and ideas to peoples restricted by censorship, RFE and RL help to maintain an informed public opinion in the USSR and Eastern Europe. . . . They seek to create neither "American radio" in the narrow national sense, nor "exile radio" in the sense of organized political opposition, but international radio. It is international in the breadth of its coverage, its freedom from national or sectarian bias, its dedication to the open communication of accurate information and a broad range of democratic ideas. At the same time, it is "local" in the sense that broadcast content is focused on the interests of the audiences.[3]

A vivid example of Radio Liberty's coverage of "local" events was its reporting of the "Moscow Group for Monitoring Compliance with the Helsinki Agreement," also called the Helsinki Watch Group, founded in May 1976. Similar groups were formed on the Moscow model by activists in the Ukraine, Lithuania, Armenia, and Georgia. The members were dissident intellectuals who had taken seriously the Soviet regime's professed commitment to a free flow of information and had begun to check on the actual adherence to the promise of greater respect for human and civil rights. Violations were documented in detail, and when Radio Liberty received copies they were promptly aired, along with reports of arrests and harassment of the dissidents by their government.

On the international scene in 1976, an important phenomenon known as "Eurocommunism" was gaining momentum as a counterweight to the Soviet model. Major Western European Communist parties challenged the monopoly claimed by the Soviet leadership and criticized the Kremlin's repressive policies, while developing an ideological rationale that diverged from the Soviet mandate. Radio Liberty broadcast the results of the Pan-European Conference of Communist Parties, held in East Berlin in June 1976, at which independent-minded Italian, French, and Spanish Communist leaders expressed their points of view. (It was there that Brezhnev attacked Radio Liberty.) The final conference document represented a setback for Moscow's effort to assert itself as the unquestioned leader of European Communism. Our Soviet listeners heard the full texts of the unorthodox statements of the Western European Communists that were censored by their domestic media.

When the Nobel Peace Prize award to Academician Andrei Sakharov was announced, Radio Liberty was the first to interview his wife, Elena Bonner, who had been undergoing medical treatment in Italy. On December 10, 1975, she went to Oslo to deliver the acceptance speech for Sakharov, because the Soviet authorities had not permitted him to attend the ceremony. The Russian service broadcast the event live, and her husband and children heard her in Moscow.

As a gesture to the West during the détente period of the 1970s, the Soviet regime had stopped its jamming of the VOA, the BBC, and other foreign radios in September 1973, but maintained its interference with the signals of Radio Free Europe and Radio Liberty. This situation lasted until August 1980, when the Polish workers' Solidarity movement, under the leadership of Lech Walesa, frightened the Kremlin into resuming all jamming. ABC television sent an interviewer to my office on the day the news broke, and I explained that the Soviet regime had to inhibit its citizens from hearing the facts about this proletarian defiance of the Polish Communist authorities, lest the contagion spread to their own workers.

Despite the severe jamming Radio Liberty broadcasts were subjected to during those seven years, the "core" audience remained remarkably stable. Audience research survey data for 1977–79 showed that Radio Liberty listenership averaged 7.6 million people a week, far below the unjammed Voice of America (23.9 million), and short of the BBC (10.2 million), and Deutsche Welle (8.7 million). The computer simulation project that M.I.T. conducted for many years used several thousand interviews, mainly with Soviet citizens traveling in Western Europe. The composition of the audience for Radio Liberty's Russian-language broadcasts was estimated at 78 percent urban, 71 percent male, 86 percent under the age of fifty, 21 percent with a university education, and an additional 34 percent who had completed secondary education.

Program Evaluations

During the first few years of oversight by the Board for International Broadcasting, the BIB relied on its own members and staff for evaluations of specific language-service programs, and on periodic assessments from U.S. missions in the audience area. In 1979, it called on two American academic experts on the Soviet Union to provide independent evaluations of Russian programming. Robert V. (Bill) Daniels of the University of Vermont examined one full week of broadcasts, and Maurice Friedberg of the University of Illinois separately examined a second week. (Friedberg also broadcast frequently on Soviet culture over the Voice of America and Radio Liberty. After the Soviet Union collapsed, he made frequent visits to Russia, where he appeared on television and gave public lectures. In the fall of 1995, he told me that he had just returned from Yekaterinburg, formerly Sverdlovsk, in the Urals, where he lectured to university students. He was introduced to the young audience as a person whom their parents knew because of his broadcasts on the Voice of America and Radio Liberty.)

Both specialists found the Russian service product satisfactory and in many respects excellent. However, both raised serious questions about the coverage of Soviet dissent, non-Russian nationalities, and the overall tone of the broadcasts. Friedberg rated coverage of Soviet dissent as "probably the best of any radio station in the world" but wondered "whether RL is not overdoing a good thing." He urged greater selectivity in broadcasting samizdat documents, and he expressed disappointment that, apart from the weekly cultural program in the Russian service for Jewish listeners, there was no regular Russian program dealing with the other national minorities. He found the tone of some programs to be "very hostile," often because of heavy irony, and recommended that immediate attention be paid to this serious problem. Friedberg also found many Radio Liberty staff members "ignorant of the West," and even of Western books dealing with Russia and the Soviet Union, with the result that "reportage of events may be quite good, but the analysis that accompanies it is all too weak."[4]

Bill Daniels found Radio Liberty's coverage of internal Soviet politics, history, and ideology to be weak or usually neglected, but at the same time he found an overemphasis on dissidence. As a result, "the overall impact of programming is to give RL the appearance of being an émigré organ beamed at other potential émigrés." Like Friedberg, he found that "affairs of the non-Russian nationalities, apart from questions of active dissidents and Jewish emigration, are omitted altogether." Daniels stressed the need to broaden the Radio's audience by addressing programs not only to "outsiders" in Soviet society but also to "loyal" Soviet citizens, and specifically "to the frame of reference and potential curiosity of the Soviet officialdom, the higher the better."[5]

The BIB got similar reactions from academic experts who evaluated Estonian and Tajik broadcasts. Professor Tonu Parming, of the University of Maryland, offered constructive suggestions for improving the Estonian broadcasts—for example, greater use of published material by Western scholars on Estonia and of interviews with Western visitors to Soviet Estonia. Further, he said, "greater restraint should be exercised to avoid overly propagandistic pieces, whether super-positive about the West or super-negative about the USSR." Dr. Eden Naby, of the Center for Middle Eastern Studies of Harvard University, noted serious flaws in the Tajik broadcasts. She found that "the body of material, its accuracy, impartiality, sources, and verifiability are open to question" and that the tone of broadcasts was occasionally "snide." Her review of Azeri broadcasts resulted in a positive evaluation, but she called for better information sources and greater analytical depth.

The first major evaluation of Radio Liberty's Ukrainian service was conducted by the eminent Canadian political scientist and Slavist Professor Bohdan Bociurkiw of Carleton University, whose overall impression was positive. He found the great majority of broadcasts satisfactory, some excellent, and rated the literary standards, language, and pronunciations "comparable with and sometimes superior to Soviet Ukrainian media." However, he found that coverage of domestic politics (apart from culture and dissent) was the most neglected area, with poor coverage of topics outside the Soviet Union another weak point. Among Bociurkiw's recommendations were that "better use should be made of RL research experts" and that "the circle of outside contributors be expanded."

The new Board for International Broadcasting concluded that "management's paramount challenge was to improve the professional quality of broadcasts to the Soviet Union." In 1978 the BIB welcomed the formation of a program committee of the RFE / RL board of directors to investigate and evaluate programming problems. The committee, chaired by Professor George Hoffman of the University of Texas, devoted its first on-the-scene inquiry in Munich to the Russian service and made a number of valuable recommendations, including increased American supervision; measures to improve the speed and quality of news and news features through more effective use of central news and research materials; acquisition of the Associated Press service; an accelerated program of English-language training for the Radio staff in order to eliminate double-processing of news from English to Russian to nationality languages; and greater interaction with academic specialists on the Soviet Union.

In 1981, Professors Daniels and Friedberg were asked to update their 1979 report by analyzing two days of Russian programs. In addition, Peter Reddaway of the London School of Economics and Political Science evaluated a one-week sample. Each of them singled out individual programs for praise and found Radio Liberty's performance to be generally satisfactory, with no major violations of policy. However, all three agreed on the need to make better use of the Radio's own Soviet area research (consistently held in high esteem by Western scholars) and greater use of outside specialists on the air. They also urged eliminating the "hostile tone" in some broadcasts, which might alienate portions of the audience. In reviewing certain new historical and ideological programming, Daniels observed: "Unfortunately the treatment of this material tends to be tendentious and even overtly monarchist, thereby playing into the stereotype of Soviet denunciations of RL."

Intramural Conflict

In the late 1970s, a serious problem arose and persisted into the early 1980s. Radio Liberty had been without a director since May 1977, when Ronalds left to join the Voice of America in Washington. With this lack of supervision, some of the émigré writers and editors who held bigoted views were able to insinuate their prejudices into programs on historical and religious themes, particularly in Munich's Russian and Ukrainian programs. In November 1980, in response to various allegations emanating mainly from employees in Munich, the BIB assigned James Critchlow, who had left RL a few years earlier and was now the Board's planning and research officer, to investigate the situation by monitoring actual broadcasts and studying tapes and scripts. Unlike the academic consultants, Critchlow was not to make a general assessment of quality but to determine whether policy violations were occurring. He documented a small but alarming incidence of "serious policy violations, including antidemocratic, anti-Western, anti-Polish, and anti-Catholic references, as well as material potentially offensive to non-Russian nationalities of the USSR." A program devoted to Konstantin Pobedonostsev (1827–1907)—principal adviser to Czars Alexander III and Nicholas II, and notorious in Russian history as an anti-Semite and foe of democracy—praised him as a "great conservative thinker."[6]

Jewish staff members in Munich protested against this and other evidence of anti-Semitic sentiments creeping into the broadcasts. On the other hand, the Russian nationalists on the staff had alleged for years that the service was losing its "Russian spirit." One of Radio Liberty's oldest employees, Victoria Semyonova-Monditch, an announcer, protested an assertion made in 1976 by the deputy chief editor that "our broadcasts are not made for the Russian people but for the Soviet people in the Russian language." The fact that the remark was made by Vladimir Matusevich, a Soviet Jew who had recently emigrated, did not contribute to harmonious relations in the Russian service. Monditch was so upset that she sent a memorandum to members of the U.S. Congress and the Board for International Broadcasting. The Russian émigré press supported her contentions. Matusevich called himself a "victim of the anti-Semites" and told then Director Ronalds: "You have created a situation in which organizers of a chauvinistic and anti-Semitic campaign are celebrating victory." The contretemps came to be known as "the October Revolution of 1976." Although a talented writer and an attractive radio personality, Matusevich was abrasive and undiplomatic in his relations with his colleagues. Despite clashes with colleagues, he later became the chief editor of the Russian service.

The situation did not improve even after the appointment of George Bailey as director of Radio Liberty in 1982. Bailey was a Russian-speaking American journalist with impressive credentials in the magazine and newspaper world. His political orientation leaned more toward Solzhenitsyn's conservative, authoritarian approach than toward the Soviet dissident democrats. In Paris, he helped found a Russian émigré magazine, *Kontinent*, with a noted right-wing writer, Vladimir Maximov, as editor. Bailey's laissez-faire attitude toward the nationalist views of certain staff members of the Russian and Ukrainian services led to the broadcast of programs that caused further resentment and protests from Jewish staff members, who sent some of the allegedly anti-Semitic scripts to scholars and newspaper columnists in the United States.

Shortly after assuming office in 1981, President Ronald Reagan appointed a fellow conservative, Frank Shakespeare, as BIB chairman. In the spring of 1984, Shakespeare received a letter from Senator Charles H. Percy, chairman of the Committee on Foreign Relations, who enclosed a copy of a report from B'nai B'rith International concerning "incidents of insensitivity to Jews and democratic ideas in Radio Liberty broadcasts." Percy was particularly troubled about the information contained in the report that reflected adversely on the "quality, effectiveness and professional integrity" of the Radio "within the context of the broad foreign policy objectives of the United States."[7]

The cover letter to Percy from Gerald Kraft, president of B'nai B'rith, urged an investigation of the "repugnant programming" described in the attached report by Dr. William Korey, his director of policy research. Korey, a well-known Russian-speaking scholar, writer on Soviet Jewish affairs, and expert on international human rights issues, cited several recent Radio Liberty programs that violated the RL policy guidelines. One of them was the above-mentioned complimentary reference to the obscurantist czarist official, Pobedonostsev.

Another was a Ukrainian program broadcast after the BIB had adopted a resolution in 1981 instructing the management of Radio Liberty to tighten policy controls. The broadcast in January 1984 quoted from the memoirs of Mykola Kovalevsky, the minister of agriculture in the pre-Soviet, anti-Bolshevik government of Ukraine in 1919. Korey wrote:

> In the selection of the memoirs which were broadcast, and thereby given an indirect endorsement, Kovalevsky makes incendiary and provocative comments that justify the massive pogroms against Jews in the Ukraine, even if he ultimately deplored them. Blame for pogroms was placed on "the radicalism and fanaticism of part of the Jewish youth which considered it a duty to support the Bolshevik advance into the Ukraine not only passively but actively." The "terrible pogrom" was declared a consequence of "the aggressiveness of volunteer Jewish detachments" which made it difficult "to restrain the indignation of the Cossacks," some of whom "saw in every Jew his enemy."

As an experienced analyst of Soviet anti-Semitic propaganda, Korey drew an analogy between this "American broadcast justifying pogroms against Jews" and Soviet books by "the notorious anti-Semitic writer, Vladimir Begun, and the most vitriolic anti-Semitic writer, Lev Korneyev," whose book was hailed by *Izvestiya* as "rich in factual material." Korey said: "It should be emphasized that anti-Semitic violence in the Ukraine during 1918–20, whether encouraged or conducted or tolerated by the pro-czarist armies, had the most tragic and traumatic impact upon Jews since the pogroms of the mid-17th century." He continued:

> In this connection, we are shocked that in Radio Liberty's historical series, favorable broadcasts have been made of such White Russian czarist generals as Baron Peter Wrangel. He was glorified in program broadcasts on September 14–15, 1983. It was under the aegis of such military leaders that numerous pogroms took place even if the commanding generals may not have been necessarily or directly responsible for them. At the very least,

such broadcasts indicate an extraordinary insensitivity to Jewish concerns and to democratic and human rights considerations generally.

Korey condemned the sympathetic portrait of General Andrei Vlasov, acknowledging: "There may, of course, be varying interpretations of Vlasov's motivations." However, he criticized Radio Liberty for permitting a special program "which is presented in an uncritical and sympathetic manner" about a collaborator with the Nazis, who was, moreover, "widely regarded in the USSR as the most notorious traitor of World War II."

Korey drew attention to antidemocratic programming as well as anti-Semitic content. He cited a Russian broadcast in December 1982 of a speech by Solzhenitsyn in Taiwan, which accused the West of demanding that Taiwan establish "democracy bordering on chaos, on state treason, on the right to freely destroy one's own country, the way Western countries allow it at home." A broadcast in June 1983 cited Solzhenitsyn's friend Maximov, who contended that Soviet émigrés in the West "had the opportunity to become convinced that democracy in its traditional meaning has slowly but steadily begun to outlive itself." Korey concluded his report to the president of B'nai B'rith: "Details on these matters have been presented in the Staff Report by Geryld B. Christianson to the Senate Committee on Foreign Relations. The new material, included in our research report, supplements Mr. Christianson's findings and underscores the need for public airing. American democracy can more effectively penetrate the Iron Curtain only when our message is consistent with the highest ideals and respect for pluralism that characterizes our nation."[8]

During this time, I followed the developments in Munich with great concern and frequently received copies of memorandums circulated by Jewish staff members, as well as confidential exchanges within the BIB. Korey and I were friends and colleagues, both graduates of Columbia's Russian Institute, and frequently lunched together. At his request, I provided him with transcripts of Radio Liberty programs. As a Jew and an executive of the Radio, I felt a double responsibility to help put an end to these egregious lapses and hoped that Korey's contacts with Washington and the media would carry greater weight than any indignant memorandums I might write to Munich.

From the perspective of the 1990s, these violations of program policy and the tensions between opposing factions in Munich seem relatively insignificant compared with the majority of effective broadcasts that we communicated to our audience, and the positive influence Radio Liberty ultimately exerted on the attitudes of Soviet citizens. But at the time, they poisoned the atmosphere and brought into the open the hostilities lurking beneath the surface among the émigrés. In retrospect, it is interesting to note that the conflicts at the station resemble the present-day antagonisms between the ultranationalists and the democrats in post-Soviet Russia. Indeed, the centuries-old conflict in Russia between the liberal Westernizers and the conservative Slavophiles seems never-ending.

The Munich tempest in the samovar boiled over and onto the pages of the American press. After a decade during which the publicity surrounding the revelation of the CIA connection to Radio Free Europe and Radio Liberty had subsided, the American media once again took note of what was going on in the area of international radio broadcasting financed by U.S. taxpayers, this time focusing on the program content. In November 1983, for example, *Newsweek* carried a feature titled "A Superpower War of Words" that described the current operations of the Voice of America, Radio Free Europe, and Radio Liberty.

> The United States may be losing the propaganda war on at least one front. Critics charge that under the Reagan administration [the three Radios] no longer report the news objectively, and have become little more than forums for extremist Eastern European émigrés or strident voices from the White House. Perhaps the most extreme shift has occurred at RL in Munich, where several staffers have either resigned or been fired after protesting the station's new programming policies. Critics charge that station director George Bailey has given right-wing extremist Soviet and Eastern European émigrés free rein—often with embarrassing results. In addition to its blatantly anti-communist reports, the station has broadcast some anti-Semitic and anti-Catholic commentaries and others that criticized Western-style pluralism and democracy.[9]

Former U.S. Senator James L. Buckley, RFE/RL's president (successor to Glenn W. Ferguson, who served after Sig Mickelson from 1978 to 1982), sent *Newsweek* (December 5, 1983) a swift denial. Buckley expressed his astonishment at the "recklessness" of the article in alluding to "unnamed critics and unsupported charges about our programs." He added: "These accusations were printed without any attempt to check them against an ample record or to assess the tone and content of our broadcasts from readily available tapes. Fortunately for our more than fifty million listeners, an article such as yours would never survive the safeguards we insist upon to assure the truth of what we broadcast."[10]

Newsweek explained in a footnote to Buckley's letter that the BIB itself had commissioned an official report (Critchlow's) in 1981 and had made public the existence of these problems. The magazine noted that, shortly after the investigation, President Reagan had appointed Frank Shakespeare, the new BIB chairman, to supervise the stations more effectively. "A number of former employees of RFE/RL and independent listeners have contended that anti-Semitic commentaries and news reports slanted against Israel were still being broadcast at RL." *Newsweek* conceded, however, that it had "overstated the case in saying flatly that such broadcasts have occurred, without specifying that these were allegations." Despite Buckley's attempt to gloss over the matter, policy violations had indeed occurred in the period of relaxed control over the right-wing émigrés, and they did not cease immediately. As late as 1985, editorials in the American press were still criticizing Radio Liberty's broadcasts along with some aired by the Voice of America.

A *New Republic* editorial titled "Taking Radio Liberties" singled out a program based on a passage from Solzhenitsyn's *August 1914* about Dmitri Bogrov, a Jewish anarchist who assassinated Pyotr Stolypin, Czar Nicholas II's prime minister, in 1911. The program included descriptions of Bogrov—none of which Solzhenitsyn himself had used—as a "cosmopolitan" with "nothing Russian either in his blood or his character" and a "degenerate of homeless radicalism." The script writer repeated words once leveled at the assassin by his enemies—a "serpent" with "vulgar" Satanic qualities—and he described Stolypin as a "Slavic knight." Bogrov's act was a "shot at the Russian nation itself," and it set in motion events leading to the Bolshevik Revolution. And finally, the program quoted a passage from the fraudulent *Protocols of the Elders of Zion* that likened the Jews to a serpent that "devours" other peoples. The same editorial explained that this "bizarre" analysis was "startlingly evocative of the anti-Semitic tradition of Pan-Slavism, which historically has depicted Jews as an alien race bent on the destruction of Holy Russia and the Slavic race."

The magazine also referred to Radio Liberty's having broadcast without critical comment Solzhenitsyn's speech in Taiwan, in which he said that Western democracy was "bordering on chaos, on state treason, on the right to freely destroy one's own country." The reason for these lapses, according to *The New Republic,* seemed to be that

> Radio Liberty has fallen under the influence of Russian émigré zealots whose views are not exactly those of the United States. In 1982 the Rea-

gan administration appointed an émigré [*sic*] named George Bailey (a close associate of Solzhenitsyn's) as director of Radio Liberty. In the name of promoting "creativity" among émigré broadcasters, he all but dismantled RL's strict procedures for controlling broadcast content, and got rid of American supervisors who monitored RL broadcast editors. He also installed a group of Russian émigré broadcasters who share Solzhenitsyn's particular Russian nationalist views.[11]

These charges were indignantly refuted in a long letter from Frank Shakespeare and Ben Wattenberg of the BIB that *The New Republic* printed two weeks later. Calling the editorial "flagrantly inaccurate, misleading, and irresponsible," the writers addressed the criticisms point by point:

You claim Radio Liberty announcers made anti-Semitic characterizations in an August 19 [1984] broadcast. In fact, these characterizations were describing passages from Solzhenitsyn's *August 1914* to determine whether they were anti-Semitic. (The scriptwriter's conclusion is that they were not.)

You claim our announcers quoted a passage from the *Protocols of the Elders of Zion*. You neglected to mention that the announcers described the Protocols in the broadcast as a "vile anti-Semitic forgery."

You describe George Bailey, the director of Radio Liberty, as an "émigré." Mr. Bailey is an American. He is the former Executive Editor of Max Ascoli's distinguished publication, *The Reporter*.

You claim that Bailey got rid of American superiors who monitored Radio Liberty broadcast editors. But Bailey has not initiated any changes in the monitoring of the Russian service of RL—and that is where the program was aired.

You claim Bailey installed broadcasters who are "Russian nationalists," a movement which, you simplistically maintain, contains a strong element of anti-Semitism. But many of Bailey's key appointments have been Jews. These include the director of the Russian News Service, Edward Kuznetsov, a Russian Jewish dissident hero, recruited directly from Israel.

You claim "Reaganites" run Radio Liberty. The Board of Radio Liberty is bipartisan by statute and includes such distinguished Americans as Lane Kirkland and James Michener, surely not Reaganites.

Shakespeare and Wattenberg also noted that "Jewish-oriented broadcasting constitutes a sizable block of our programming" and that a weekly program called "Democracy in Action," which extolled democratic virtues, had recently been introduced. They insisted that "stringent controls" had been put into effect to prevent "any possible anti-Semitic statement," but they emphasized: "Our job is to run a free, pluralistic radio station, broadcasting to people who are denied access to a variety of news about their own history and circumstance. Our board intends to honor that mandate by airing a spectrum of responsible views, some of which at times we are, singly or collectively, not necessarily in agreement with. That's what good democratic journalism is all about."

Finally, the BIB supervisors declared that the 5,000 hours of original programming produced each year in fifteen languages of the Soviet Union were checked "more carefully than any other station in the world." Despite such control, they acknowledged that "some of our programs, alas, are not as clear, as accurate, as interesting, as wise, as moderate, as we would like. Some can be misinterpreted or misconstrued. The program in question may indeed have been one such." In a concluding thrust, Shakespeare and Wattenberg called the editorial a "pretty good example of just how bad—very bad—well-intentioned journalism can sometimes get. It could never have passed muster on Radio Liberty."[12]

The editors of The New Republic appended their reply to the Radio Liberty letter, arguing that "our 'irresponsible' view of the broadcast in question is not very different from that of RFE/RL's president, James Buckley." They cited a memo from Buckley to Bailey on August 30, 1984, eleven days after the broadcast on Solzhenitsyn's novel, in which he told Bailey that he was "appalled that despite meetings we had . . . in which we underscored in every possible way the need to pay attention to sensibilities [where the subject of Judaism and Jews was concerned] we find ourselves (again) over a weekend and with many people on vacation, with a script loaded with all the wrong words." Buckley added that it was "depressingly clear that there appears to be a certain Russian mind-set that makes it impossible for too many of our editors (including a number of Jews) to be aware that a given script might even conceivably bruise anyone's sensitivity." The New Republic wondered "why would the current management have added 'stringent controls' if it didn't think there was a problem?" The only apology the magazine made was for their misidentification of George Bailey.[13]

Other newspapers weighed in with their comments; perhaps the most balanced appraisal of the problem appeared in the Washington Post's editorial, "Trouble in the Air":

The difficulty seems to lie in the re-creation, in sectors of the heavily émigré staffs at the two stations, of some of the ethnic and political tensions of their native land. That the older senior ranks tend to come from the mostly Russian emigration of the Cold War years, while newer staff members come from the Jewish emigration of the 1970s, has created a strange and volatile political chemistry—one that American-born radio executives may sometimes find difficult to assay and control.

This is the context in which a dispute arose over whether there was a hint of anti-Semitism in a new passage of a Solzhenitsyn novel broadcast on the Russian service of the Voice of America. . . . As with similar charges that have been made about some programs aired by Radio Liberty, the issue requires a very fine sorting out of the broadcaster's message and the listener's perception. *In radio, with its emphasis on verbal and cultural inflection, the possibilities of mixed signals are considerable.* [Italics added.]

A number of congressmen are concerned about the matter, and the General Accounting Office has been looking into Radio Liberty. This is unpleasant but necessary. The Voice of America, speaking for the American government and people, and Radio Liberty, which seeks to provide its listeners with the native material their governments censor, are important instruments of American foreign policy. Most of their work is beyond cavil. The stations, however, are very delicately constructed and balanced enterprises. It would be intolerable if either station harbored any trace of the prejudice, which is rampant, under official sponsorship, on Soviet soil.[14]

The italicized sentence expresses my chief concern with certain programs that reached the airwaves at that time. Even if no Russian or Ukrainian writers may have deliberately sought to include anti-Semitic content—and I have no doubt that a few of them did—it was, to say the least, inappropriate under conditions of jamming to choose potentially incendiary topics such as the Jewish origin of an assassin of a Russian hero or the *Protocols of the Elders of Zion*.

The conservative pundit William F. Buckley Jr. wrote a column for the Op-Ed page of the *Washington Post* in which he called "preposterous" the charge that the leadership of RFE/RL "has been insensitive to shards of anti-Semitism that have burst into broadcasts beamed to the Soviet Union." He pointed out that Frank Shakespeare "has a long public career unblemished by the least insinuation of bigotry. The vice-chairman is Ben Wattenberg, a distinguished Democratic anti-Communist, who is Jewish."

Furthermore, "the president is James L. Buckley, who, if only because he is my brother, is *eo ipso* without original sin." Pointing to the broadcast of the passage from Solzhenitsyn's book concerning the assassin of Stolypin, William Buckley asked: "Is it flirting with anti-Semitism to mention that Bogrov was Jewish?"[15] Yes, Mr. Buckley, if the adjectives that described him could fuel the prejudices of many listeners.

The spotlight of the American mainstream media on Radio Liberty's broadcast of the controversial excerpt from Solzhenitsyn's *August 1914* provoked a heated clash among scholars concerning whether Solzhenitsyn was an anti-Semite. A long article in the *New York Times* discussing the pros and cons quoted Solzhenitsyn's own denunciation of the charges, along with supportive statements from Elie Wiesel and a majority of academic experts in Soviet affairs.[16] But the problem for Radio Liberty was not Solzhenitsyn; it was the use of his writing on the air, which might be misinterpreted when beamed into the Soviet Union.

"60 Minutes"

During this time of charges and countercharges concerning the content of some Radio Liberty broadcasts, another threat to the station's reputation arose in the form of an investigation by the top-rated CBS-TV program, "60 Minutes." In the spring of 1982, CBS informed RFE/RL's New York Programming Center that Mike Wallace wanted to bring his camera crew to our office. They were interested in pursuing information published in a new book, *The Belarus Secret,* by John Loftus, a Boston attorney and former employee of the U.S. Department of Justice Office of Special Investigations.

Loftus had uncovered evidence during his work in Washington that Radio Liberty hired former Soviet citizens who collaborated with the Nazis during the German occupation of Belorussia in World War II. Anthony Adamovich, a writer for Radio Liberty, was included in Loftus's list. New York Director William Kratch consented to the interview and asked me to join him in front of the camera when Wallace appeared to tape the segment. I called Howland Sargeant for advice, inasmuch as he had been president of Radio Liberty from 1954 to 1975. He confirmed that several members of the Radio's staff in Munich and New York had been collaborators, but that they had been cleared by the proper authorities in the U.S. government before we hired them. In other words, their wartime association with the Nazi occupation was forgiven because the Nazi invaders had offered them the choice of collaborating or being shot. In the case of Adamovich, he had been an editor of a Belorussian newspaper in Minsk and was forced to cooperate with the Germans by continuing his activities under their supervision.

Mike Wallace interviewed Kratch and me for about ten minutes, throwing in a question about the Radio's former clandestine association with the CIA, as if that cast a shadow on all of our activities. I explained that it was Radio policy to employ former Soviet citizens who combined expertise in journalism with personal knowledge of our target area, always making sure, however, that they had a clean bill of health from American counterintelligence. Wallace then acknowledged, "You people are not to blame." But when the show was aired on May 16, 1982, his spontaneous comment had been left on the cutting-room floor at CBS.

To make matters worse, he interviewed Adamovich, an elderly man in poor health, who wilted under Wallace's notorious prosecutorial technique. The telecast produced a negative image of Radio Liberty's hiring policy and tarnished the generally good reputation we had painstakingly built since our struggle with Fulbright and other opponents in Washington. Congresswoman Elizabeth Holzman vented her indignation against Radio Liberty's misuse of American taxpayers' money by allegedly consorting with war criminals.

On the day following the "60 Minutes" telecast, Barry Farber called me. His popular late-night radio talk show emanated from WMCA in New York and was syndicated in about thirty-five cities throughout the United States, and I had been his guest several times in the 1960s. In 1964 I had broadcast to him a special report from Berlin on May Day, in which I described the stirring speech in front of the Reichstag delivered by Mayor Willy Brandt. Farber invited me to debate Ira Rosen, the producer of the "60 Minutes" segment, directly on the air. The next night, Rosen and I arrived at midnight at the WMCA studios, where for two hours Farber moderated a lively and at times acrimonious exchange of views. After I played the tape for my colleagues in the New York office and sent a copy to the BIB in Washington, the consensus was that I had vigorously defended Radio Liberty's position and made many telling points about our unique role in the arena of Cold War politics. But the audience of such a top-rated television show as "60 Minutes" was far greater than listeners to my rebuttal on a radio talk show with limited distribution.

In September 1982, CBS scheduled a repeat of the program, and I sent a strongly worded telegram to Don Hewitt, chief producer of "60 Minutes," Ira Rosen, and Mike Wallace. At the end of the telecast on the following Sunday, Wallace read the part of my message stating that we hired émigré staff members and freelancers only after they had been cleared by the proper U.S. authorities. Happily, there were no further repercussions. Perhaps the issue was too remote and esoteric for the American public to get exercised about it in the 1980s. The Soviet press gleefully reported the CBS program, but it did not damage Radio Liberty. Our popularity grew tremendously after Gorbachev came to power in 1985 and ultimately divulged previously censored information about many aspects of Soviet reality that Radio Liberty had consistently exposed for three decades, thereby confirming our trustworthiness and reliability.

During the last decade of the Brezhnev regime and his successors, Yuri Andropov and Konstantin Chernenko, Radio Liberty intensified its broadcasts of samizdat documents and Western advocacy of human rights for Soviet citizens. Current news, as always, occupied a large part of each day's program, along with excerpts from the columnists and editorial writers of American and Western European newspapers, and a rich diet of feature programs. What especially distinguished Radio Liberty was its unwavering emphasis on the articulate minority of dissenters among Russians, Ukrainians, and other nationalities within the Soviet Union who at great personal risk dared to voice their protests and spell out their demands on behalf of the silent majority.

Other Forbidden Fruit

Underground political jokes called *anekdoty* continued the long tradition of satire against authority in Russia going back to czarist times. Censorship was much stricter and punishment was more severe in the Soviet era, especially under Stalin, with sentences of twenty-five years in the gulag and often death awaiting the person caught telling an antigovernment joke. These *anekdoty* expressed the public's pervading cynicism and disenchantment with the empty slogans of Soviet propaganda. We leavened our programs with witty barbs aimed at the Party, the KGB, the poor quality of everyday Soviet life, and other aspects of reality. By identifying itself with its audience as partners in ridiculing the hated system, Radio Liberty contributed to its image as their surrogate voice.

Magnitizdat, the recording on tape of uncensored material, especially songs of dissent, assumed an important place in the lively counterculture that flourished in the Soviet Union during the Brezhnev era. In the early 1970s, Radio Liberty started gathering tapes brought to the West by émigrés and beamed the songs back to the Soviet listeners. The three most popular "guitar poets" were Bulat Okudzhava, Aleksandr Galich, and Vladimir Vysotsky, although other poet-bards emerged, among them Yuli Kim (half-Russian, half-Korean), Mikhail Nozhkin, Novella Matveyeva, Mikhail Ancharov, Yuri Vizbor, Anatoly Ivanov, and Yevgeny Kliachkin.

After the *New York Times* published my article about Galich in 1972, with my translation of his famous song about silence, I was asked to write a chapter for a scholarly book, *Dissent in the USSR*, edited by Professor Rudolf Tökés of the University of Connecticut. This analysis of the lyrics of songs by the three giants of *magnitizdat* was the first study of its kind by an American specialist. After Johns Hopkins University Press published it in 1975, I was frequently invited to lecture on campuses throughout the United States. I discussed and played tape-recorded songs for student and faculty groups and distributed copies of the lyrics. The texts were both in Russian and in English translation (mostly my own and those of Misha Allen, a Lithuanian émigré in Toronto who was an expert on Vysotsky). The students enjoyed hearing colloquial Russian and kept the texts for future study. The lectures added to their understanding of the current Soviet scene as reflected in the bards' unflattering mirror. In these lectures, I always described Radio Liberty's mission and illustrated examples of our programming such as *magnitizdat* and *anekdoty*. Many of the students and their professors came away with a clearer appreciation of how the Radio broke through Soviet censorship with heretical ideas from inside its own society. My "showing the flag" helped build goodwill toward Radio Liberty.

Many academicians were now more willing to appear at the Radio Liberty microphone to be interviewed by Boris Shragin, a former dissident from Moscow. Gloria and I met Boris and his wife, Natasha Sadomskaya, a well-known anthropologist, the day after they arrived in the United States in the summer of 1974. They had come to Westchester to visit their old friends, Pavel and Maya Litvinov, who had emigrated from Moscow a few months earlier. We established a close rapport and kept in close touch over the years, especially after the Shragins settled in New York, where Natasha taught at Queens College and Columbia University, and Boris joined Radio Liberty as a regular freelancer. Shragin was never hired as a staff member because he was bitterly opposed to Solzhenitsyn's right-wing Russian politics, thereby making enemies among émigrés in Munich who influenced their American bosses.

Shragin's weekly analyses of Soviet affairs by Western experts, as well as his program, "Democracy in Action," consistently received high praise from émigré panelists selected to audition our broadcasts for quality control. Moreover, positive reactions to his programs came to us from inside the Soviet Union. While we were still working together in the early 1980s, Shragin asked me to suggest a musical introduction to his series on democracy. I proposed a theme from one of Beethoven's *Leonora* overtures that also appears in his opera *Fidelio*, with a trumpet proclaiming the theme of liberty. Long after I retired and tuned in to Radio Liberty, I would hear that emblematic passage. When Boris died of lung cancer in 1990, I spoke briefly at his funeral, not only for myself and my wife but also for all those Americans who had been touched by this warm and erudite human being who was realistic about the attraction to authoritarianism in Russia but never willing to give up fighting for reforms.

During the decade between the merger with Radio Free Europe and the arrival of Gorbachev, détente between the United States and the Soviet Union became increasingly strained as the Kremlin flouted the Helsinki accords and continued its repression of human rights. The most flagrant example was Andrei Sakharov's exile to Gorky, where he, and later his wife, were kept in virtual house arrest from January 1980 until Gorbachev brought them back to Moscow in 1986. The Soviet invasion of Afghanistan (which Sakharov vigorously condemned) further exacerbated relations between the two superpowers. These events were given major coverage by Radio Liberty, which spoke out against the regime's contempt for humanitarian values and the national sovereignty of its neighbors. In addition to regular news reports concerning the growing fiasco of the military campaign in Afghanistan, Radio Liberty correspondents went to Pakistan to interview resistance leaders and defectors from the Soviet army who had surrendered to the partisans, and depicted the terrible truth of a misconceived aggression that was costing the lives of thousands of young men and severely draining the Soviet economy—topics kept from the public by the heavily censored official media.

Andrei Sakharov

The great dissident scientist Andrei Sakharov occupied a major place in Radio Liberty's programming from the mid-1970s to the mid-1980s. During that period, we reported the protests of leading intellectuals and human rights organizations in the West through interviews with writers such as Arthur Miller and William Styron, and publisher Robert Bernstein, chairman of Helsinki Watch in New York. When Sakharov expressed his views in 1983 on arms-control issues in a letter to physicist friends in the United States, we broadcast the entire text and followed it with an exclusive interview with one of the physicists to whom it had been addressed, Dr. Sidney Drell, deputy director of Stanford University's Linear Accelerator Center. Both programs were rebroadcast several times in an effort to improve Soviet listeners' understanding of these life-and-death issues.

Until August 1984, Elena Bonner had been permitted to travel from Gorky to Moscow, where she informed the outside world through Western correspondents about the conditions of their exile, and in turn the Soviet public heard the details from foreign radio broadcasts. However, the regime cut off that contact when she was tried for "anti-Soviet agitation and propaganda" and sentenced to five years' exile—not in the gulag, but in Gorky with her husband. As a result, information was meager concerning Sakharov's health, which was deteriorating because of debilitating hunger strikes and increased stress on his heart.

Radio Liberty also covered the "Sakharov hearings" held in 1975, 1977, 1979, and 1983 in Copenhagen, Rome, Washington, and Lisbon. These international tribunals—at which former Soviet dissidents, now émigrés, gave a panel of distinguished Western scholars and public figures their personal testimony of Kremlin repressions—originated in response to a petition smuggled abroad in 1974. The "Moscow Appeal" signed by Sakharov, Elena Bonner, and two dozen other prominent dissenters, some of whom had not yet emigrated, included V. Maximov, M. Agursky, B. Shragin, P. Litvinov, Y. Orlov, S. Kovalyov, and L. Bogoraz. Their samizdat document was given to foreign correspondents on February 13, the same day that Aleksandr Solzhenitsyn was expelled from the Soviet Union. They demanded the publication of his *Gulag Archipelago,* as well as archives that would present a full picture of the activities of the secret police since the Bolshevik revolution. Finally, they called for "an international public tribunal for investigating crimes committed [by the regime]."

The authorities reacted swiftly by arresting and imprisoning some of the signatories, and exiling others to the West. O. F. Andersen of Denmark is credited with creating the international hearings, at which a jury of outstanding statesmen from several countries would collect the facts about the current status of human rights in the Soviet Union, inform the world about their objective analysis, and condemn Soviet violation if it had occurred. The witnesses appearing before the jury were exclusively individuals who had recently left the Soviet Union and spoke about their own life and experiences there.

The impact of the hearings reverberated not only in the Western press but also in the Soviet press, which expressed its displeasure at the public exposure of the real situation in the Soviet Union concerning the persecution of heretical thinkers, the use of psychiatric hospitals for political ends, and the violation of religious and ethnic freedoms. Sakharov's official representative abroad was Yefrem Yankelevich, his son-in-law, who had been active in the human rights movement before his emigration to the United States in 1977 and who took part in three of the sessions. Yankelevich asserted at the fourth session, held in Lisbon in October 1983, that the hearings were "a great event for those who are learning about them in the Soviet Union from broadcasts on Western radios." Sakharov followed the reports of the hearings with great interest. The Radio's audience research established that the Soviet public became increasingly sympathetic as we made them aware of the physicist's role as "the conscience of our people."

Among the regular feature programs initiated during the mid-1970s was "Documents and People," produced by Viktor Fedoseyev, which remained on the air almost two decades. It countered the Soviet media's attempt to calumniate the dissidents by presenting their authentic samizdat writings, from Sakharov and other individual fighters for human rights to such groups as Baptists, Crimean Tatars, Jewish refuseniks, and Lithuanian Catholics. "Eastern European Meridians," produced by Yefim Fishtein, introduced Soviet listeners to the reform movement in Poland and Czechoslovakia; they heard for the first time such names as Lech Walesa, Solidarity, and Charter 77. Yuri Melnikov's program "From the Other Shore" offered excerpts from the works of Solzhenitsyn, Shalamov, Sinyavsky, Daniel, Nadezhda Mandelshtam, Yevgeniya Ginzburg, and Lidia Chukovskaya. Melnikov (the pseudonym of Yuri von Schlippe on Radio Liberty) discussed every interesting Russian book that came out in the West or any significant article that appeared in Russian émigré periodicals. When he covered Solzhenitsyn's first press conference in the West in 1974, the writer recognized his voice and complimented Yuri on his reading of *Cancer Ward*.

In the late 1970s and early 1980s, many of the prominent Soviet dissidents who arrived in the West appeared frequently at Radio Liberty's microphones. They included elite members of the intelligentsia (writers, theater directors, artists, lawyers, scholars), such as Vasily Aksyonov, Ludmilla Alexeyeva, Sergei Dovlatov, Anatoli Gladilin, Dina Kaminskaya and her husband Konstantin Simis, Jonas Jurasas, Lev Kopelev, Anatoli Kuznetsov, Yuri Lyubimov, Vladimir Maximov, Ernst Neizvestny, Viktor Nekrasov, Aleksandr Nekrich, Mark Popovsky, Mstislav Rostropovich and his wife Galina Vishnevskaya, Ayshe Seytmuratova, Boris Shragin, Andrei Sinyavsky, Georgi Vladimov, and Vladimir Voinovich. Some of them became regular commentators; all of them enriched the Russian program with their insights on contemporary Soviet reality.

An exceptional figure among the contributors to Radio Liberty was Pyotr Grigorenko, a Ukrainian and former general who had been a professor at the Frunze Military Academy, holder of countless medals and honors, and a convinced Communist. As far back as 1961 he had spoken out in criticism of the policies of the Party and government. He was demoted and transferred to an obscure post in Soviet Asia, but his persistent dissidence led to his expulsion from the Party and dishonorable discharge from the army. He became a leading member of the Helsinki Watch monitoring groups, first in Ukraine and later in Moscow, focusing his activity on the violation of the rights of Crimean Tatars. After being incarcerated in a psychiatric hospital—a favorite punishment for dissenters during Brezhnev's era—Grigorenko was exiled and came to New York. It was a privilege to meet this dignified and courageous person and his equally impressive wife, Zinaida Mikhailovna, when they visited our studios for frequent interviews.[17]

Radio Liberty's ability to keep in tune with its audience was immeasurably strengthened by the contribution of these and lesser known members of the "third emigration," men and women of the post-Stalin generation who brought a fresh perspective on Soviet life that was lacking among the older staff members who had emigrated earlier. The non-Russian language services also benefited from the infusion of talent from their respective areas.

Since the 1950s, when two members of the Munich staff were murdered, most likely by KGB agents, and an attempt had been made to poison RFE employees in the company cafeteria, no violence had been committed against personnel or property until 1981. The night of February 21, a bomb exploded at the headquarters in the Englischer Garten. Four employees were seriously injured, and property damage exceeded $2 million. Who planted the bomb remained a mystery for many years, until a dissident KGB general, Oleg Kalugin, claimed that he and his department of dirty tricks had been the instigators. However, Richard Cummings, head of security for RFE/RL in Munich—who carefully researched the subject, including top secret documents of the former East German intelligence service known as Stasi—made a strong case against Kalugin's claims by accusing the notorious international terrorist Carlos.[18]

One of the most dramatic incidents of the early 1980s was the shooting down of Korean Airlines Flight 7 over Soviet territory in September 1983. On the morning that Secretary of State George Shultz disclosed that the KAL passenger plane had been blown up by a Soviet fighter plane with 269 aboard, it was mid-afternoon in Munich, but within the hour Radio Liberty was reporting details of the event in its newscasts. By evening, the Russian service was also providing feature coverage in two programs— "Events and People" and "Radio Journal on the Soviet Union"—with voiced cuts of Shultz's speech, analysis of the initial misleading statement by TASS, discussion of the previous (1978) Soviet attack on a Korean aircraft, and worldwide reaction. While the Kremlin was still denying that the Boeing 747 had been shot down, the Russian service aired the tapes of the doomed airliner's last minutes. Later, after the Kremlin admitted the deed but claimed that the plane was flying without lights, Radio Liberty aired the tape of the interceptor pilot's report that he could see its lights. These and all subsequent Soviet efforts to obscure the case were exposed in numerous special broadcasts with careful comparisons of Soviet official statements with known facts.

The death of Leonid Brezhnev in November 1982 offered another striking demonstration of the way Radio Liberty filled the information gap created by rigid Soviet media practices. Radio Moscow announced his death at 11 A.M. Moscow time. The Radio's Russian service flashed the news immediately and within ten minutes began broadcasting a half-hour obituary, while Radio Moscow was playing only solemn music. Immediately afterward, the Russian service was ready with the first of five programs devoted to Brezhnev's role in the development of the Soviet Union and the potential impact of his death after eighteen years in power. Radio Moscow was still playing music, interrupted only by its broadcast of the official obituary. Radio Liberty followed up with special programs on the problems of succession, human rights, and nationality policies, augmented by reports on international reactions and evaluations filed by its correspondents in Europe and the United States. Thus, Soviet listeners had a continuous flow of news, analysis, and opinion while Moscow remained silent.

We covered Yuri Andropov's accession to power by emphasizing that he was head of the KGB for many years. He died soon after and was succeeded by Konstantin Chernenko, who also died in office. Soviet leaders were dying so quickly one after the other between 1982 and 1984–85 that an underground *anekdot* then circulating told of the fellow who tries to get into Chernenko's funeral at the Moscow House of Unions and is challenged by the guard at the entrance: "Where's your pass?" He replies: "Pass, hell! I have a series subscription."

In March 1985, Mikhail Gorbachev succeeded Chernenko as general secretary of the Communist Party. To take charge of the media and propaganda, he selected Alexander Yakovlev, who had recently served for ten years as the Soviet ambassador to Canada. Yakovlev's exposure to the West had started much earlier, when he came to Columbia University in 1958 as one of the first three Soviet graduate students in the United States under the exchange agreement concluded during the Eisenhower administration. Like Gorbachev, Yakovlev was convinced that reform of the Soviet system was long overdue, and the two men worked closely together to achieve glasnost and perestroika.

At about the same time, RFE/RL also changed leaders. James Buckley was succeeded by E. Eugene Pell, a former NBC News correspondent in Moscow who was director of the Voice of America. Malcolm S. (Steve) Forbes Jr., head of Forbes Inc. and deputy editor-in-chief of *Forbes* magazine, took over from Frank Shakespeare as chairman of the Board for International Broadcasting. Forbes became better known in 1996 when he ran for the Republican presidential nomination.

After more than three decades that spanned the period from the inauguration of our broadcasts at the time of Stalin's death to the arrival of Gorbachev, I retired from Radio Liberty in August 1985. But my involvement with the Radio was far from over. If the new regime created exciting opportunities for Radio Liberty to spread our influence, it also offered me the chance to travel to the Soviet Union for the first time since Khrushchev's era and to witness the changes that were taking place.

During the campaign against alcoholism, Volodya tells his friend Ivan that Gorbachev was against drinking because he probably was a teetotaler.

Ivan replies, "It could be worse. He could be celibate."

12 THE SOVIET ERA DRAWS TO A CLOSE

The new era of Gorbachev proclaimed the watchwords *glasnost* and *perestroika*— "openness" and "restructuring of society." But in practice, *glasnost* meant "highly selective candor," as an American professor noted. After almost seven decades of censorship, old habits were not quickly changed. The first impetus came after the horrendous nuclear disaster at Chernobyl in the Ukrainian SSR on April 26, 1986. The official Soviet media suppressed the news for several days, but Soviet citizens heard of the catastrophe from Western radios. Our audience research reported that Radio Liberty listenership shot up dramatically during the weeks following the tragedy. We learned from audience reports that "at a time when the Soviet media hardly broadcast anything at all about it and merely claimed that the situation was under control, Radio Liberty devoted a great many broadcasts to Chernobyl."

The unique value of RFE/RL was demonstrated countless times since the founding of the Radios, but never more forcefully than during the Chernobyl event. The radioactive fallout within and outside the Soviet Union was a direct threat to the health and lives of millions, but the Gorbachev regime reacted, like its predecessors, by keeping silent during the first crucial days and, even after admitting the fact, distorting the truth and minimizing the extent of the tragedy.

The Ukrainian service increased its broadcasts to cover all aspects of the story, discussing safety precautions and medical instruction concerning radiation. The Estonian service broadcast a major program on Estonians who were forced to work in the Chernobyl area to "clean up" the disaster. Technically, the Estonian service was now under Radio Free Europe. After almost a decade of broadcasting on Radio Liberty, it had been transferred in 1984, together with the Lithuanian and Latvian services, conforming to the long-standing U.S. policy of nonrecognition of the Soviet annexation of these countries. Radio Liberty continued to broadcast in Russian and in eleven languages of other Soviet nationalities.

Radio Free Afghanistan (RFA), a new service of Radio Liberty, went on the air on October 1, 1985. The result of legislative initiative by Senator Gordon Humphrey of New Hampshire, it was the first expansion of RFE/RL's broadcast area in more than thirty years. Operations commenced with twice-weekly broadcasts of thirty minutes in Dari, a principal language of Afghanistan. Soon the broadcasts were on the air one hour a day, five days a week, and another language, Pashtu, was added. Even before Radio Free Afghanistan began broadcasting, however, the war in Afghanistan was a major theme of Radio Liberty coverage. The Russian service sent correspondent Giovanni Bensi from Munich to Pakistan twice to interview Afghan refugees and resistance leaders. The service also featured interviews with four Soviet soldiers who surrendered to the partisans and described their experiences in the unpopular war that Soviet propaganda sought unsuccessfully to justify.

To Russia with Love—and Trepidation

Immediately after I retired in 1985 and was no longer connected with Radio Liberty, I couldn't wait to go back to the Soviet Union for the first time since 1959. But Paul Cook, a veteran State Department expert on Russia who had served in our embassy during part of the Cold War years, cautioned me against going at that time. After so many years with the Radio,

I was still "too hot"—meaning that I might be vulnerable to harassment or worse by the Soviet authorities.

A year later, Gloria and I did go there with a small group (nine of us, including Gloria's sister and her son) on an American tour. I was still reluctant to call attention to myself by arranging an individual trip. The travel agency eliminated Kiev from the itinerary because of Chernobyl and assured us that we would not go anywhere near the fallout area. It was Gloria's first trip to the Soviet Union. Twice before she had been given the chance to go—once in the early 1960s as one of the first American teachers of Russian (all expenses paid), and later with a group from the Munich Institute for the Study of the USSR—but both times Radio Liberty management refused to give her permission to go, because as the wife of a senior executive she might be compromised, be at risk personally, and embarrass the Radio.

At last, we left for Leningrad in October 1986. I took along a small Sony shortwave receiver and the current broadcast schedule. On our first night in Leningrad, I stood near the hotel window and held the set close to my ear as I fidgeted with the dial. I was thrilled to hear our musical signal and Lev Roitman's Munich roundtable from inside the Soviet Union. During our three-week tour of Leningrad, Tbilisi, Odessa, and Moscow, Radio Liberty was audible everywhere despite the jamming.

The most glaring example of the persistence of censorship that we observed was in the literary museum in Odessa. The exhibits in each room were tastefully and imaginatively mounted, using stark black and white punctuated by streaks of red; they displayed the memorabilia of famous writers of the nineteenth and twentieth centuries who were associated with this vibrant city, either as native sons or as temporary residents. We stopped to look at the section devoted to Isaac Babel, one of Odessa's great writers, who achieved world renown for his tales of the city's underworld and his experiences with the Red Army during the early postrevolutionary years. Photographs, documents, and even his eyeglasses were on the wall, but not one word about his fate as a victim of Stalin's purges. I protested vehemently to the guide, who gave me some lame excuse. My sister-in-law nudged me and was certain we would be hauled up before the KGB. Our fellow American travelers were embarrassed by my outburst, and one of them complained, "Why don't you leave that to the Voice of America?" I didn't tell him of my long association with Radio Liberty, but I felt I could not remain silent about this example of Soviet contempt for historical truth that the Radio had exposed since it started broadcasting and that was still evident in Gorbachev's era.

Glasnost Slowly Takes Hold

After the Chernobyl tragedy and the worldwide political fallout caused by Gorbachev's omissions and distortions, Gorbachev's information policy gradually became more honest. Alcoholism, poor health care, petty corruption, domestic airplane crashes, and other subjects were no longer taboo, and works by previously banned writers appeared. By 1988 the media were more lively, timely, and informative. The content as well as the technical presentation of Radio Liberty broadcasts had to be adapted to these changes if the competition for the attention of the listener was to continue to be effective. Various modes of radio programming, such as "live" interviews, group discussions, more sophisticated use of musical segments, and "billboards" (highlighting of upcoming programs) were introduced. Other improvements included more cross-reporting of events in one area to audiences in another part of the Soviet Union; more programs for specific groups (youth, workers, women); more topical shows dealing with science, medicine, sports, music, history, religion; better utilization on the air of material in the widely praised Radio's research papers, especially about Gorbachev's policies, economic reforms, and problems of nationalities; and a centrally prepared Western press review representing different opinions on significant issues. These programs not only informed Soviet citizens but also contributed to the further expansion of glasnost, because they put the Soviet media under greater pressure to treat more subjects frankly if their vaunted openness was to be more than a hypocritical policy.

Interviews with dissidents who had been repressed by the Brezhnev regime, such as the Jewish refusenik Anatoly Shcharansky and Russian physicist Yuri Orlov, continued to lend weight to the station's critique of Soviet reality. After his release from the gulag and arrival in the West in 1986, Shcharansky testified to the vital role played by Radio Liberty in enabling Soviet dissidents to survive and work effectively by keeping them in the forefront of public consciousness.

Joseph Brodsky

When Joseph Brodsky received the Nobel Prize in literature in 1987, the Swedish Academy said that, for Brodsky, "poetry is a divine gift." At first the Soviet media were silent, but word leaked through Radio Liberty and other foreign shortwave broadcasts, and they finally had to acknowledge the award.

We had covered Brodsky's career and conflicts with the Soviet regime as far back as the mid-1960s. Brodsky was born in Leningrad in 1940, and at age fifteen he dropped out of school and became a laborer, writing poetry whenever he could. The authorities did not like his poems, and he was tried for being a "militant parasite" and sentenced in 1964 to five years' hard labor in Arkhangelsk in the far north of Russia, just south of the Arctic Circle. His sentence created an international furor, and protests on his behalf came from leading American and Western European writers and public figures, as well as influential Soviet intellectuals. He was released after serving only eighteen months.

In 1972 he was deported from the Soviet Union, already enjoying a worldwide reputation as Russia's greatest living poet. I met him soon afterward in Ann Arbor at Gloria's alma mater, the University of Michigan, where we were visiting Donald and Debbie, who were students there. Carl and Ellendea Proffer, publishers of Ardis books and staunch supporters of Soviet dissident writers, had arranged for Brodsky to become poet-in-residence at the university. Brodsky arrived in the West with a negative image of Radio Liberty, in part because the Radio hired former Vlasovites, members of the Soviet military who had joined the Germans to fight the Soviet Union. He invited Gloria and me to his tiny, cluttered dormitory room, where he consented to record his first interview for Radio Liberty about his impressions of America.

Brodsky had just received a letter from the Soviet Union, and we asked to see the envelope. Gloria carefully tore it open at the seam and showed him a tiny numerical imprint. According to an émigré friend in New York, it was the censor's mark, something Brodsky had never seen before. When we came back the next day, cigarette butts were all over the floor. Brodsky was sitting on the bed surrounded by countless envelopes; he looked tired and disheveled. He had spent the night searching for that telltale number and suspected that his correspondence was being monitored.

A few years after the Nobel Prize award, Brodsky was appointed poet laureate of the United States—the first foreign-born poet to receive this honor. Before his untimely death from a heart attack in 1996, he did several broadcasts for Radio Liberty, sharing his new poetry with his many admiring compatriots.[1]

Professional Code

The Board for International Broadcasting approved a new "Professional Code" for the Radios in 1987. Basically, there was nothing new in its emphasis: accuracy and reliability of information as essential to RFE/RL's credibility; the need to carefully evaluate samizdat or other documents originating in Eastern Europe and the Soviet Union; avoiding a "stridently polemical tone" in discussing the actions and personalities of government and party officials in the target area; avoiding material that could be construed as "inflammatory, as incitement to violent actions, or as irredentist"; refraining from encouraging defection; avoiding any suggestion that "might lead audiences to believe that, in the event of civil disorder or international crisis, the West might intervene militarily in any part of the broadcast area." However, the last paragraph of the new code was a direct reaction to the brouhaha that had erupted among the Radio Liberty émigrés in Munich during the late 1970s and early 1980s:

> Scrupulous care shall be taken to avoid religious, ethnic, class-based, or cultural slurs upon any persons or groups in our broadcast audience. Whenever historical enmities are discussed, they shall be treated sensitively and fairly, and in a way transcending any one-sidedness.
>
> Legitimate aspirations of groups, religious bodies, nations or nationalities shall never be expressed in a form derogatory of other groups, religious bodies, nations or nationalities. Anti-Semitic, anti-Catholic, and any other anti-religious locutions shall be scrupulously avoided. RFE/RL professionals shall represent a public model of tolerance and of respect for pluralistic diversity and the human rights of all persons.[2]

To ensure that broadcasts adhered to the code, all language services were subjected to regular and comprehensive reviews, both in-house and through BIB-sponsored analyses by prominent scholars and journalists. To gain a better sense of how listeners reacted to programming, Soviet Area Audience and Opinion Research (SAAOR) now under the direction of R. Eugene Parta, who succeeded Max Ralis in 1981, organized a focus group of recent émigrés. They listened to several hours of specific Russian-language series and commented on the sound, content, language, and tone, offering recommendations on how to make the programs more appealing to Soviet listeners. This quality control has continued during the 1990s, but today's panelists are no longer émigrés; instead, they reside in several cities of the former Soviet Union, where they listen to Radio Liberty broadcasts at home and comment on the technical quality as well as the content (see Chapter 14).

As programming was adapting to the new conditions in the Soviet

Union, plans were initiated to strengthen Radio Liberty's voice. In June 1987, the United States and Israel signed a historic agreement to construct a U.S. shortwave relay station in Israel. A joint project of the Board for International Broadcasting and the United States Information Agency, the relay station was to consist of sixteen 500–KW transmitters, enabling the VOA and RFE/RL to penetrate massive Soviet jamming and send a much stronger signal into the heartland of European Russia and the Central Asian republics of the USSR, where the Muslim population was growing at a rate more than four times as fast as the Soviet Union's ethnic Russian population. Situated deep in the Negev desert, this was to be the first new site for RFE/RL in thirty years. After the Soviet Union halted its jamming of BBC and Voice of America broadcasts in 1987, the Radios considered it imperative to expand their facilities, although the construction would have taken several years to complete. However, Israeli ecologists vigorously opposed the project, citing dangers to the environment. Ultimately it was abandoned after the end of the Cold War.

Between 1980 and 1987, the broadcasts of the BBC and the VOA had been jammed because of the rise of the Solidarity movement in Poland. Soviet leaders feared that Western broadcasts might spread the "germ" to the Soviet Union. Several of the jamming transmitters that had been aimed at these two broadcasters were now redirected at Radio Free Europe and Radio Liberty, indicating that the Gorbachev regime and its East European allies were unwilling to tolerate a surrogate domestic station. Even before the suspension of Soviet jamming against the BBC and the Voice of America, RFE/RL had been the target of more than 70 percent of all Soviet jamming. Soviet spokespersons made it clear that the regime had no intention of ever suspending jamming against the two stations, even if and when it decided to ease up on other broadcasters still being jammed, such as Deutsche Welle and Kol Israel.

RFE/RL's continuing access to its broadcast frequencies was considered an absolute imperative and was made possible by international arrangements under the authority of the International Telecommunications Union (ITU). In 1987, a session of the "World Administrative Radio Conference for the Planning of the High Frequency Bands Allocated to the Broadcasting Service," known as WARC, was held under ITU auspices. RFE/RL's U.S. director of engineering, Stanley Leinwoll, played a key role in obtaining adequate shortwave frequencies for the Radios in the face of increasing spectrum congestion.

Gorbachev's reformist policies stimulated an increase in the number of nonofficial documents circulating within the Soviet Union and reaching the West. Samizdat still remained the only avenue for Soviet citizens who wanted to discuss human rights, the aftereffects of Chernobyl, ecology, and so on, to reach their own people.

The Radio Liberty samizdat section collected, verified, and published more than 6,000 documents beginning in the early 1970s. Between 1,500 and 2,000 pages of documents were issued in the 1980s, providing rich programming material for the edification of Soviet listeners, such as Sakharov's talks at the Moscow forum, "For a Nuclear-Free World, for the Survival of Mankind"; documents relating to the demonstration of Crimean Tatars in Moscow; and open letters written by noted Russian and Ukrainian fighters for human rights.

SAAOR's task of conducting audience research for Radio Liberty was always more difficult than for Radio Free Europe. Fewer Soviet citizens traveled in the West than East Europeans, and travelers were generally in groups and under surveillance. Many of them were apprehensive about answering questions by strangers, especially when asked to fill out questionnaires. Soviet travelers tended to be atypical, less representative of the population as a whole than their East European counterparts. On the other hand, the travelers included wide representation from the groups that Radio Liberty was most interested in reaching, particularly urban, educated adults.

During the détente period of the 1970s, when greater numbers of Soviet travelers came to the West, SAAOR began to systematize its data-collection methods. Interviews were entrusted to independent survey research institutes, and a standard questionnaire was developed. But Soviet travelers were wary, so the interviewer carried on a general discussion of the media, not focusing on Radio Liberty but dealing with the broader subject of Western broadcasting to the Soviet Union. The interviewer himself filled out the questionnaire immediately after the meeting.

Over the years, the techniques became more refined and scientific. By late 1987, a computerized database of more than 35,000 interviews had been compiled, and about 5,000 interviews with Soviet travelers were being conducted annually. As mentioned earlier, the material was analyzed with highly sophisticated procedures developed at M.I.T. and Harvard in the early 1970s. The resultant computer-simulation model of the Soviet population allowed SAAOR to develop estimates of the size and composition of listeners to Western radios. SAAOR further improved its methodology by defining and concentrating on the core audience of urban, educated adults, who accounted for approximately one-quarter of the total adult population of the Soviet Union. This was the subset of the population most heavily represented in SAAOR samples, and one that research had shown to be most interested in international radio broadcasts. Examining listening trends specifically in that core audience increased the reliability of the figures, with fewer fluctuations caused by listening behavior among the different strata of the population, where the sample was relatively weak and the referent populations were large (for example, elderly, uneducated rural women).

SAAOR's findings indicated that Radio Liberty broadcasts (including the three Baltic services under the Radio until 1984) gained listeners among the core audience during the period 1982–86, both in absolute numbers and relative to the other major Western broadcasters. In terms of demographics, these increases were most noticeable in two groups: women, and listeners over thirty years of age. It was estimated in 1988 that the Radio reached roughly 9.5 million listeners on an average day, about 19.5 million listeners during an average week, and about 22 million listeners in the course of an average month. Nevertheless, it was not until after 1988 that Radio Liberty began to draw ahead of the VOA, the BBC, and other Western stations.

BIB Chairman Steve Forbes visited Moscow in September 1988 to participate in U.S.-Soviet talks on international information policy. Charles Z. Wick, director of the USIA, headed the U.S. delegation, and Valentine Fain, head of the Novosti press agency, chaired the Soviet delegation. Forbes raised the issue of Soviet jamming, characterizing it as a violation of international law and a contradiction of the spirit of glasnost.

Jamming of Radio Liberty ceased abruptly a few weeks later, after more than thirty-five years. On Tuesday, November 29, technical monitors at Munich headquarters reported that after 21:00 CET all Radio Liberty broadcasts in languages of the Soviet Union were heard "loud and clear." Forbes hailed the Soviet action as a "welcome and positive development" and added: "By ending this practice, which violates a number of international agreements to which the USSR is a signatory, Mr. Gorbachev has sent a strong signal of his commitment to glasnost." Engineers at the VOA and the BBC estimated that the Soviet Union had spent between $500 million and $1 billion annually for jamming—more than the combined annual operating budgets of the VOA, RFE/RL, the BBC, and Deutsche Welle.

In addition to the cessation of jamming, another interesting dividend of glasnost was that Western public opinion researchers were granted permission to conduct surveys among Soviet citizens inside the country. With the cooperation of the Moscow-based Institute of Sociological Research,

CBS and the *New York Times* polled Muscovites, asking whether they had noticed any changes in their lives in the Gorbachev era. Approximately half the respondents noted positive changes, while the other half felt that there had been no changes; a few answered in the negative. The survey offered Radio Liberty's SAAOR an excellent opportunity to test the validity of its own audience research among Soviet travelers, because the results were almost identical. Comparison between the Radio's polling and a survey made in Lithuania by the official newspaper *Sovetskaya Litva,* concerning radio listening habits among students in Vilnius, also revealed similarity in data that reassured SAAOR of its accuracy.

With significant changes in the Soviet media taking place during glasnost and perestroika, Radio Liberty began to focus more attention on its domestic Soviet competition. The Soviet central press served as a forum for the discussion of reform proposals, and the press was no longer monolithic even in the national republics. Consequently, foreign radio was no longer the sole source for alternative viewpoints on Soviet issues. Television was now the principal source of information for Soviet citizens, and livelier and more interesting broadcasts made them more attractive. Radio Liberty monitored Moscow television in Munich and provided prompt analysis for the programmers.

Clearly, glasnost still had its limits in 1988, as was evident from the official media's treatment of the conflict between Armenia and Azerbaijan in Nagorno-Karabakh, the Armenian enclave inside Azerbaijan; the withdrawal of Soviet troops from Afghanistan after almost nine years of an unpopular war; and the twentieth anniversary of the Soviet invasion of Czechoslovakia. Radio Liberty filled in the gaps with appropriate emphasis on these neglected topics.

At the time of the earthquake in Armenia in December, the liberal weekly *Moscow News* praised "the Munich station [for offering] its channels to listeners in the area searching for their relatives." The newspaper added: "We heard on a foreign band what we should have heard on our own." The non-Slavic language services devoted a large part of their airtime to the struggle in the Caucasus. A series of programs entitled "From the Prague Spring to the Moscow Summer," which focused on the impact of the invasion on the Soviet human rights movement and the significance of the Dubček reforms for Gorbachev's Soviet Union, was especially noteworthy in the Russian service. The Ukrainian service, in particular, commemorated the millennium of Christianity, which began for the Slavs in Kievan Rus'.

Monumental changes took place in Eastern Europe and the Soviet Union in 1989: the "velvet revolution" in Czechoslovakia, and the emergence of a non-Communist government there as well as in Poland and Hungary; the dismantling of the Berlin Wall; and the first contested Soviet elections in seven decades. For the first time, RFE/RL language service correspondents could travel to Poland and the USSR to report on major political developments. At the same time, the Russian service relied on an extensive network of freelance contributors inside the Soviet Union for live coverage of the elections to the Congress of People's Deputies, and Radio Liberty announced the winners before the official media announcements.

Many of the Soviet freelancers were prominent independent journalists, and they contributed to the daily programming. The popular writer Anatoly Strelyany filed a series of radio sketches about the impact of perestroika on life in the Soviet hinterlands. The Russian service provided a forum for a wide range of opinion from Soviet political leaders like Boris Yeltsin, who was then emerging as an outspoken opponent of Gorbachev; economist Nikolai Shmelev; Yuri Lyubimov, director of the avant-garde Taganka Theater; writers Andrei Voznesensky and Anatoly Rybakov; former prosecutors Telman Gdlyan and Nikolai Ivanov; and leading scientists and deputies of the Supreme Soviet Andrei Sakharov and Roald Sagdeev.

"Aspects," a new weekend show on the Russian service, brought together the most important stories of the week and also discussed the many letters Radio Liberty received from listeners in the Soviet Union. "At the Newspaper Kiosk" presented excerpts from a wide range of provincial and small-circulation newspapers not available to the average Soviet reader. The literary program "Ex Libris" presented works by young Soviet writers who had not received much attention at home. Latvia's newspaper *Sovetskaya Molodyozh* (Soviet Youth) noted that a short novel by Sergei Kaledin, *The Construction Battalion*, was a "work of genius" that was finally published only because it had first been broadcast on "Ex Libris." A controversial screenplay by Aleksandr Kabakov, *Nevozvrashchenets* (The Defector), was also dramatized on the air. The author later indicated in a Radio interview that he was pleased with the radio play. The popular Soviet television show *Vzglyad* (Viewpoint) acknowledged the importance of this special program.

The Ukrainian service, the largest of the non-Russian services, highlighted miners' strikes in the Donbass and the formation of the Ukrainian Popular Movement for Restructuring (Rukh). Relying on extensive telephone contacts, the Munich staff obtained a list of demands put forward by the strike leaders, including independent trade unions. Two Ukrainian people's deputies were interviewed, one of them an economist, the other representing his constituency in the Donbass. Many programs were devoted to Rukh and its inaugural congress. The Ukrainian service pulled off a journalistic coup by interviewing a liberal people's deputy after he was jeered at an anti-Rukh meeting organized by the Kiev Party authorities. He was able to tell Ukrainians what he had been prevented from saying at an open meeting in Kiev.

Three members of the Munich staff, including Radio Liberty's senior research analyst, Elizabeth Teague, went to Moscow to attend a conference on "The Soviet Union in the 1990s: Perestroika and Global Opportunities for East-West Economic Cooperation." Teague and another colleague were told on their arrival that their visas had been issued "by mistake" and that they would have to leave the next day. Finally, they were permitted to attend the conference, where Teague found people "bemused and amazed" to see Radio Liberty representatives. She was impressed that ordinary Soviet people were now taking a lively interest in political developments. The trio reported that although a great deal of information was available from Soviet sources, no one said "We don't need Radio Liberty now." They added that in times of crisis (for example, when Boris Yeltsin was removed as first secretary of the Moscow Party Committee in February 1988), Radio Liberty's coverage was preferred to that of the domestic media. They were told that it would be good if the Radio had a correspondent to travel around the country, "someone who could get feedback from the people." Keith Bush, Radio Liberty's director of research and a widely known specialist on the Soviet economy, also succeeded in visiting the Soviet Union after having been initially refused.

Another "first" occurred in the summer of 1989, when the Soviet magazine *Sobesednik* (Interlocutor) printed an interview with Vladimir Matusevich, head of Radio Liberty's Russian service. In August, Fatima Salkazanova, of our Paris bureau, received a visa to Moscow after weeks of frustrating red tape and spent two weeks filing telephone reports from the capital. Arriving there after more than twenty years' absence, Ms. Salkazanova was greeted warmly and openly. She had no difficulty telephoning the Munich news desk during most of her stay, unlike a previous correspondent from Munich who had come in 1988 but was not allowed to report. But she did have other difficulties: the KGB followed her constantly; her address book disappeared for two days; and she was called into the Foreign Ministry where an official complained about the "inflammatory" content of her reporting. It is surprising that after the meeting other members of the Foreign Ministry greeted her openly in their canteen. "We listen to your programs," they said. "Even if we don't agree with everything, there is no reason we can't have a correct relationship." Ms. Salkazanova came away convinced that Radio Liberty had underestimated its popularity in the Soviet Union.

I made my second postretirement trip to the Soviet Union in May and June of 1989, with a grant from IREX to study Soviet citizens' attitudes toward Vladimir Vysotsky. This time, Gloria and I arranged our own itinerary and traveled alone for six weeks in five Soviet republics and twelve cities by plane, train, and rented car. The atmosphere was markedly different from our 1986 trip, in that people on all levels of society were more willing to speak with us. But I was still careful not to identify myself as a former RL staff member, because the KGB was as vigilant as ever, despite perestroika. Everywhere I went, I asked about Vysotsky. Mentioning the beloved balladeer permitted me to establish instant rapport with taxi drivers, chambermaids, flight attendants, train conductors, fellow theatergoers, and members of the cultural intelligentsia, all of whom unanimously confirmed that the late guitar-poet was enshrined in their hearts as their unofficial national hero. Hundreds of his songs, filled with both pathos and trenchant satirical comments, unerringly depicted Soviet reality. Radio Liberty had devoted many programs to him and his songs.[3]

I monitored our Russian broadcasts everywhere I went, day and night, and kept a detailed log of the programs and audibility for my former colleagues in Munich, whom we visited after we left the Soviet Union. It was not difficult to catch Radio Liberty on several frequencies without any jamming in Moscow, Leningrad, Odessa, Kiev, the Ukrainian countryside, as well as the Baltic cities of Vilnius, Riga, and Tallinn. I especially enjoyed a program I heard during a bumpy train ride from Riga to Tallinn in the middle of the night: Boris Shragin broadcasting his weekly program from New York in the series "The Soviet Union in the Eyes of Western Scholars." He reflected the expertise and perspective of American and Western European Sovietologists on the rapidly unfolding events.[4] (On the same train, the conductor played a tape of Vysotsky's irreverent songs that was piped into every compartment!)

From my talks with Soviet citizens, I learned that they still depended on Western radio broadcasts to supplement their knowledge of what was going on in their country. I spoke with a factory foreman from Mariupol, Ukraine, who had heard Radio Liberty's report about soldiers brutally killing Georgians who were demonstrating in Tbilisi earlier that year. He told me that he shared the news with his co-workers, who were at first skeptical, but after the Soviet press finally admitted the tragedy, they looked up to him for citing a reliable source from abroad.

Our visit that spring coincided with the opening of the new democratic parliament in Moscow. We were astounded by the reaction of ordinary Soviet citizens everywhere to this event. They were glued to their televisions and radios; in the hotels, staff members gathered at sets placed in the lobby and near the elevators on each floor, totally neglecting their duties; in taxis, the Radio was invariably tuned into the sessions, and the driver could hear democracy in action as liberals and conservatives hurled invective at one another and disputed fearlessly about crucial issues. It must have been both shocking and exhilarating for citizens fed up with decades of mendacity and banality of Party slogans and government proclamations.

Before we left Moscow for the West, Gloria and I were invited for lunch at Spaso House, the residence of U.S. Ambassador Jack Matlock. I had known Jack for many years, since his graduation from Columbia's Russian Institute. During his long service as an expert on the Soviet Union, a diplomat, and a member of the National Security Council under Reagan, he was always a strong supporter of Radio Liberty. Jack listened with great interest to our account of driving on the back roads in Ukraine, and he was particularly grateful for our impressions of the three Baltic Soviet republics, where he could not visit in an official capacity because the United States did not recognize Lithuania, Latvia, and Estonia as part of the Soviet Union. It was a pleasure to wind up our exciting six-week tour at a small lunch with him, his wife Rebecca, a talented photographer, and two other couples.

Inevitably, the subject of perestroika came up during our conversation. One of the guests, the Philippines ambassador, told a joke circulating in Moscow: A young man returns from his job in the capital to visit his elderly mother in his native village. She asks him, "Sonny, just what is this perestroika?" He replies: "Watch, Mama, and I'll show you." He takes two coal scuttles, fills one with coal and leaves the other empty. Then he lifts the full scuttle high over his head and pours the coal into the empty one. "That's perestroika," he tells her. "I don't see any difference," she says. He answers: "But Mama, the NOISE, the NOISE!"

While we were in Odessa, a city long famous for its comedians and satirists, we had heard similar commentary on the state of the Soviet Union under Gorbachev. A local balladeer wrote new verses to a popular song about Odessa that was the quintessential expression of the ordinary citizen's frustration with the snail's pace of economic reforms. Describing the governor of the city in the early nineteenth century, the Duc de Richelieu, whose statue stands atop the famous "Potemkin steps" leading down to the port, the poet says:

> And Papa Duke stands on his pedestal
> With outstretched arm, but he is offered nothing.
> He waits for fishing barges filled with mullet;
> He's a statue—he can afford to wait.

The Soviet and Western media announced the sensational news that Solzhenitsyn's *Gulag Archipelago* was to be published in the USSR in July 1989, and everyone expected that the publication would be followed by the rehabilitation and return of the writer from exile. It would be difficult to find a more appropriate theme for Radio Liberty, which had championed Solzhenitsyn and devoted more air time to his censored works than any other Western broadcaster. However, for two weeks this news was not mentioned in any segment of the Russian program. It was not until August 5 that "Over the Barriers" reported Solzhenitsyn's June 18 interview with *Time,* a week after the interview had already been published in the Soviet press. In contrast to his earlier influence with conservative staff members in Munich, Solzhenitsyn now frequently accused Radio Liberty of losing contact with the Russian population and their interests owing to the Radio's "principled alienation from Russian national consciousness." If the Russian service delayed broadcasting such important news out of resentment for the writer, it was an unfortunate breach of Radio Liberty's own vaunted policy of glasnost.

Despite Solzhenitsyn's criticism, Radio Liberty must have been fulfilling its mission, for by 1990 the Russian service had become the preeminent Western broadcaster to the Soviet Union. Many listeners considered it their "own" station, and several thousand well-wishers even gathered that summer at Moscow's Luzhniki sports complex for an officially sanctioned night of tribute to the Radio. Throughout the year, as all segments of the Soviet leadership openly acknowledged the severity of the crisis afflicting the USSR, listeners turned increasingly to Radio Liberty for independent, indepth analysis.

The radio provided discussions with Western economics specialists, including Nobel Laureate Milton Friedman, who analyzed the roots of

Soviet difficulties and suggested possible solutions. Radio Liberty also gave firsthand accounts of recent economic programs in Eastern Europe and examined their applicability to the Soviet Union. A program about basic business practices in the West featured interviews with Russian émigrés who spoke about setting up private businesses in Western cities. The Russian service also responded to the increasingly serious nationality problems in the Soviet Union by examining ethnic problems around the world in which Western experts analyzed how other societies cope with the complexities of a multiethnic population.

The New York Programming Center inaugurated a twice-weekly program called "Broadway 1775" (its address in Manhattan), one of the favorite shows among listeners. They enjoyed the reports of various aspects of American life, interviews with Soviet visitors, and discussions of political issues of interest to the Soviet audience. Boris Paramonov's radio essays on ethical themes became increasingly popular.

In Moscow, Radio Liberty's freelance correspondents conducted interviews with major figures inside and outside the Soviet establishment. Two days after Gorbachev met in the Kremlin with twenty radical and progressive public figures, three of the more prominent participants discussed this meeting on the air, giving Radio Liberty's audience a unique insight into Gorbachev's personality and the Soviet leadership's decision-making process. Radio Liberty interviewed former KGB Major General Oleg Kalugin, who spoke about secret police excesses one week before the rest of the world press caught up with the story. It also received exclusive rights to broadcast the memoirs of rising Soviet politician Boris Yeltsin, who broke with Gorbachev, embraced democracy, won the support of the masses, and became president of the Russian Federation in 1991. Yeltsin's popularity may have been given an additional boost toward the presidency by a dramatic broadcast on Radio Liberty. On January 13, 1991, Yeltsin, then chairman of the RSFSR presidium, flew to Tallinn shortly after Soviet troops had used force against Lithuanian citizens in Vilnius with extensive loss of life. He was determined to support the Baltic peoples' drive for independence and to prevent further bloodshed by Russian soldiers under Gorbachev's command. Yeltsin issued an appeal to Russians in the armed forces not to obey orders to attack civilians in the Baltic states, because such violence "will bring about crises in Russia itself and harm Russians living in other republics."

The Estonian foreign minister, Lennart Meri, arranged for Yeltsin's eloquent message to be transmitted by telephone via Stockholm and Helsinki to RFE/RL in Munich, where the chief of the Estonian service, Toomas Ilves, rushed it to Radio Liberty's language desks for broadcast into the Soviet Union. Ilves told me that he cannot be certain whether Gorbachev was inhibited in further use of force by the widespread dissemination of the appeal, but that it may have contributed to the rise in Yeltsin's popularity that led to his election as president of the Russian Soviet Federated Socialist Republic (RSFSR) in June 1991.[5] Ilves, the American-born son of Estonian émigré parents, later left RFE/RL and gave up his American citizenship to accept the appointment as Estonia's ambassador to the United States after the nation's independence. In November 1996, he became foreign minister under President Meri.

On an almost daily basis, Radio Liberty talked with prominent political, economic, or cultural personages by telephone inside the Soviet Union or in Munich and the other studios abroad. Top-echelon members of the Supreme Soviet, ministers of state, policy advisers to the Soviet leadership and government, and popular front leaders from the non-Russian republics all presented their views to their citizens at home.

In a development that would have been unthinkable in previous years, the Soviet media now frequently carried favorable references to Radio Liberty programming. Noteworthy was a forty-minute program about the station on the liberal Leningrad television show "Fifth Wheel." Some of the best publicity for the Radio came from unofficial newspapers, which published the broadcast schedule along with extraordinary tributes. The paper *Samara* in Kuibyshev printed one person's praise: "Sometimes my friends call RL 'the second all-Union radio.' But if one considers the efficiency and accuracy of Radio Liberty's broadcasts, then there is good reason to consider this station the first all-Union radio."[6]

There were also radical changes in the non-Russian language services. The telephone became a vital tool for programmers, with almost all nationalities' services maintaining regular contact with their listeners. They also obtained broadcast material from an increasing flow of Soviet travelers to the West who now freely gave interviews. Directors and other members of the Munich staff visited their broadcast areas, where they met ordinary listeners, officials, scholars, writers, and other prominent individuals.

The Ukrainian service was present inside the republic to cover the spectacular human chain linking Kiev and L'viv, hundreds of miles away, organized by democratic forces to commemorate anniversaries of Ukrainian independence and unification. The director of the Munich service, Bohdan Nahaylo, went for three weeks to Ukraine, where he gave numerous television, radio, and newspaper interviews. Papers carried pictures and displayed RFE/RL logos, and many Ukrainian actors, singers, and musicians visited Radio Liberty in Munich and broadcast concerts and plays by some of the country's finest artists.

Similar breakthroughs occurred in relations with the other non-Russian areas of the Soviet Union. A Georgian literary weekly printed excerpts from Radio Liberty programs services; the noted Kirghiz writer Chingiz Aytmatov broadcast over Radio Liberty and praised its work. The greatest challenge for the Azerbaijani service was to provide dispassionate coverage of the Soviet army's intervention in the ethnic and territorial conflict with Armenia. When these broadcasts violated the RFE/RL Professional Code, management took corrective action to ensure the required journalistic objectivity in treating this sensitive issue.

In June 1991, in an article in the Leningrad newspaper *Chas Pik* (Rush Hour), the head of the Center for the Study and Forecasting of Social Processes released data showing that 800,000 Leningraders listened to Radio Liberty "with various degrees of regularity," and that 240,000 listened "at least every other day." The writer declared:

> Once upon a time our solicitous ideological guardians decided that: "You'll never hear the era of Liberty" and set up a bacchanalian, roaring-howling accompaniment . . . to all sorts of "foreign voices," and above all to Radio Liberty which stubbornly attempted to disturb the communist sterility of our political consciousness. This was at a time when the "Ministry of Truth" carefully presented us with the one and same correct text in all the newspaper and radio and television programs . . . which affirmed the direct opposite to what we saw and heard in the reality around us.
>
> Radio Liberty is no longer jammed. Nowadays Julian Panich broadcasts from the Lenkom stage and Anatoly Strelyany and Igor Klyamkin [Radio Liberty freelance stringers living in the Soviet Union] communicate with their compatriots from their Moscow apartments with the aid of this same Radio Liberty. Even Colonel Viktor Alksnis [a hard-line deputy of the Supreme Soviet] shares his views with us direct from the Kremlin through this very same radio station.[7]

After eighteen years in the West, where he was a leading personality in Radio Liberty's Russian service, Julian Panich returned in triumph to Leningrad in January 1991. Formerly a well-known Soviet stage and screen actor and director, Panich appeared as master of ceremonies in two of Leningrad's theaters before packed houses. The production, "Three Lives," was mounted by an organization of Leningrad's performing artists specifically to portray three periods in his own life as an artist in the Soviet Union for forty years, abroad at Radio Liberty for eighteen, and now the object of affectionate public recognition in his native city.

Radio Liberty's musical signal and standard opening announcement introduced the program, and Panich began with homage to Aleksandr Galich, including taped broadcasts of the late balladeer's poems and songs. Actors then performed segments from Panich's radio productions for Radio Liberty. To round out the evening, an interviewer from the popular Soviet television show "600 Seconds" questioned Panich and members of the audience about the Radio's broadcasts. A show of hands revealed that Radio Liberty and the Leningrad television tied more or less each time for number of listeners. Panich was also interviewed on a nationally televised program, where he brought greetings from his colleagues in Munich and spoke of the Radio's work. When he returned to Munich, he said: "I have been in the theater all my life, and these days in Leningrad represented the crowning achievement of my career."

Another startling sign of the changing atmosphere was a letter sent to the RFE/RL Research Institute on June 19, 1991, from the chairman of the KGB, V. Kryuchkov. He welcomed their publication of a book of Soviet biographies by Radio Liberty's Aleksandr Rahr.

> I am delighted to realize that the new political thinking born in the USSR is gradually winning adherents on the other side of the ocean also; your book bears clear witness to this. The very fact of its appearance speaks of the unflagging interest throughout the world in events taking place in the USSR.
>
> I am deeply convinced that a closer acquaintance with the main biographical facts about personalities who earlier were less well known to the world public, and with their political views on the fundamental questions of today, should give an opportunity both to professional politicians, and to all those who are interested in the processes taking place in our country, to appreciate more clearly the aims and problems of perestroika in the USSR.
>
> I can assure you that we will continue to be open to all contacts of mutual interest.[8]

Exactly two months after this profession of willingness to establish contacts, Kryuchkov was among the ringleaders of the infamous uprising against Gorbachev. A cabal of "Reds" and "Browns"—die-hard Communists and ultranationalists—threatened to scuttle the reforms and turn back the clock.

> *Dear Moscow Radio:* You keep broadcasting that we don't have any food shortages in our country, but my refrigerator is always empty. What should I do?
>
> *Dear Comrade:* Plug the radio into the refrigerator.

 FROM GORBACHEV TO YELTSIN

In August 1991, Gorbachev prepared to sign a treaty that would decentralize economic and political authority from Moscow to the fifteen republics. The cumulative impact of glasnost had escalated open dissension, no longer confined to intellectuals but spreading to the proletariat. Miners' strikes in Siberia and other parts of the Soviet Union were the principal factors in Gorbachev's decision to negotiate with the republics for a new Union Treaty to be signed on August 20, leading to a loose confederation of independent states. This was the last straw for the KGB-military-industrial coalition of hard-liners that opposed his policies. On August 19, a "State Committee for the State of Emergency" seized power.

Radio Liberty's role during this historic crisis was its "finest hour," to quote from Winston Churchill's unforgettable wartime phrase. The leaders of the coup—or *putch,* as the Russians call it, borrowing from the German *Putsch*—frantically tried to stanch the flow of information inside the country, as the rest of the world anxiously followed the ominous events in Moscow via satellite television. Domestic television broadcast folk-dancing and concert music interspersed with terse statements from the self-proclaimed emergency committee. In order to find out what was happening in their own country, Soviet citizens tuned into shortwave broadcasts from the West.

When TASS broke the news of the putsch at 4:29 A.M. Munich time on August 19, the Central Newsroom quickly notified key personnel. Staff members who heard the news on local German radio stations rushed to work early. By 6:00 A.M. a live Radio Liberty newscast included reports of the coup; by 7:45 the Russian service was on the air with special live programming. Radio Liberty had direct access to most of the main participants. An extensive network of stringers, five of whom were in Moscow, reported the story. Two were in the "White House," the Russian parliament building, throughout the ordeal; they were given an open telephone line to Munich. Another stringer reported the movements of the coup leaders. The fourth forwarded information from the Soviet media to Radio Liberty editors in Munich, while the fifth covered workers' reactions, including the activities of several miners' strike committees. The Moscow stringers knew they were in potential danger, but they did not flinch. On Tuesday night, August 20, Mikhail Sokolov telephoned Munich with an urgent and emotional eyewitness report from his eleventh-floor vantage point in the White House that tanks were moving on the building: "Proshchaite [Farewell]. I'm afraid this is my last report," he said, and then abruptly terminated the broadcast. "But the telephone line was kept open. Mr. Sokolov later came back on the air to report that the tanks were turning back."[1]

Throughout the following days, the Munich editors maintained contact with stringers in the Russian Soviet Federated Socialist Republic (RSFSR) inside and outside Moscow and in other republics and beamed exclusive stories on the fast-breaking events.

Nikolai Vorontsov, USSR Minister of Environment and an RSFSR parliamentarian, gave a minute-by-minute account of the crucial August 19 extraordinary session of USSR cabinet ministers at which the coup was hatched.

Sergei Stankevich, RSFSR State Secretary, gave a detailed account of the arrest of Gorbachev.

General Konstatin Kobets, defense minister, reported on the military situation in the capital, including troop movements, in the first two days of the coup.

Another RSFSR parliamentarian gave a detailed account of the arrests of former KGB Chief Kryuchkov and former Defense Minister Yazov.

Valery Stepanyenko, RSFSR prosecutor general, discussed the progress of the ongoing investigation of the coup and the role of the KGB.

When Boris Yeltsin courageously defied the plotters with his speech on top of a tank, Radio Liberty informed the entire nation, describing the resistance of the Moscow crowds and the passive behavior of the troops. CNN and NBC also covered the coup in Moscow and announced several times that nearly everyone was listening to Radio Liberty.

Scott Shane, the *Baltimore Sun*'s Moscow correspondent from 1988 to 1991, emphasized the impact of Radio Liberty during the coup. When the Radio "reported the first and only casualties—three young men killed while trying to block tanks they believed were headed for the White House, Andrei Mironov was listening in his apartment. 'I felt ashamed to be inside while people were dying,' he said later. He left the building and began heading around the Garden Ring toward the American Embassy, where the bloodshed was reported. To his surprise he found dozens of young people headed in the same direction, having heard the news the same way." Shane quoted Leonid Ionin, a political commentator who wrote a few weeks later in the liberal *Nezavisimaya Gazeta:*

> Radio Liberty and the BBC defeated the KGB and the CPSU. . . . If the high-level plotters had . . . seized the newspapers, radio stations, television, cut off the telephones and isolated the White House from Moscow, and Moscow from the rest of the Soviet Union and the world—they would likely have succeeded. Any other way they were doomed.[2]

Iain Elliott, Radio Liberty's associate director, happened to be in Moscow at that time and wrote a vivid eyewitness report. He described how he stood in the rain on Monday afternoon, August 19, and "watched the indignant crowds on Kalinin Bridge and the Smolensk embankment building barricades and thrusting leaflets into the hands of young, confused tank crewmen. . . . At five o'clock a familiar sound caught my attention: the news from Radio Liberty emerged loud and clear from the center of a large cluster of umbrellas at the end of the bridge."[3] Later he summed up:

> Everyone I talked to, on the barricades, at the White House, or in newspaper offices and institutes, had warm words for Radio Liberty and for the work of our freelance correspondents in particular. Sergei Markov, a young politics professor at Moscow University, told me how he had recorded from a broadcast Yeltsin's first decree opposing the junta. Markov cycled through the rain to the local soviet at Dubna and had the satisfaction of watching the executive committee put Yeltsin's instructions immediately into effect after they had listened to the recording. Markov, who is leader of the Russian Social Democratic Party, spent the long night of August 20–21 in the White House with Radio Liberty providing a steady stream of information from Russia and abroad.[4]

When Soviet President Gorbachev returned to Moscow from house arrest in the Crimea, he told the world at his press conference:

> The most difficult aspect of the situation was the lack of information. Everything was cut off except the television on which statements by the State Committee for the Emergency alternated with feature films and orchestral concerts. But the security officers from the bodyguard, very smart boys, found some old radio receivers in the service areas, fixed up aerials and started to pick up foreign broadcasts. The best reception was from the BBC and Radio Liberty.[5]

The Russian Federation President Yeltsin moved quickly to demonstrate his gratitude:

> During the coup, during these 3–4 days, Radio Liberty was one of the very few channels through which it was possible to send messages to the whole world and, most important, to the whole of Russia, because virtually every family in Russia listens to Radio Liberty. . . . I think that by its work and its objectivity, Radio Liberty deserves that [the Russian government] establish direct contact and invite the management of Radio Liberty to visit us . . . [and] I can assure you that we will accredit you.

On August 27, Yeltsin issued a decree permitting Radio Liberty to open a permanent bureau in Moscow. The decree (Russian, *ukaz*) read as follows:

> In connection with a request by the administration of the independent radio station "Liberty"/"Free Europe," which is financed by the Congress of the USA, and taking into account its role in objectively informing the citizens of the RSFSR and the world public at large about the course of the democratic processes in Russia, the events in the country and the world, and the activities of the legal leadership of the RSFSR during the coup d'état in the USSR, I decree:
>
> 1. To allow the administration of the independent radio station "Liberty"/ "Free Europe" to open a permanent bureau in the city of Moscow with offices for correspondents on the territory of the RSFSR.
> 2. For the RSFSR Ministry of Foreign Affairs to grant official accreditation to correspondents [of RFE/RL] and to provide them with the possibility of carrying out their journalistic activities on the territory of the RSFSR unimpeded.
> 3. For the mayor of the city of Moscow to assign office space for the [RFE/RL] bureau in the city of Moscow.
> 4. For the Ministry of the Press and Mass Information, and the RSFSR Ministry of Communications, Information and Space to provide the [RFE/RL] bureau with the necessary channels of communication.
> 5. This Decree takes effect from the moment of its signing.[6]

It was unprecedented for a news organization to receive accreditation through a decree from a head of state. Gene Pell, the president of RFE/RL, noted: "It is especially gratifying that it is this particular head of state at this moment in his country's history. It is a great honor that President Yeltsin has chosen this way of recognizing the Radios' role in the last weeks, and through the years, in bringing free information to his people."[7]

The Moscow bureau opened in January 1992, a few short blocks from Mayakovsky Square in downtown Moscow, on the third floor of a renovated old residence with a courtyard. A small up-to-date studio, staffed by local talent, linked the office with other cities of the former Soviet Union. When I visited there a year later, I told some of the young staff members how differently Radio Liberty was regarded in the old days of the Cold War. They presented me with a tape recently made in their studio by Mikhail Zhvanetsky, one of Russia's favorite standup comedians, who pleaded for continued U.S. support of the Radio in a hilarious open letter to "Dear Bill."

In the days following the defeat of the right-wing rebels, tributes in the press to RFE/RL's broadcasts appeared in the press of many countries of the West and in Eastern Europe as well. *Večernik*, a Prague daily, wrote: "We had our ears glued also to Radio Free Europe. . . . With their help we could take part in what was going on not only in the Soviet Union but in the whole world. Therefore thanks, colleagues."[8] The director of the international service, All-Russian State TV and Radio Company, Sergei Timofeyev, signed a statement on August 22 thanking Radio Liberty for its "efficient coverage of the tragic events of August 19–21 in the USSR" and declaring: "Millions of Soviet people deprived of the possibility of receiving information through Russian media have listened to your free voice. It strengthened their faith and their determination to combat dictatorship. We believe in further fruitful cooperation with your radio station."[9]

The Communist system and the Soviet empire collapsed at the end of 1991. The opportunity to pursue democratic reforms and a market economy finally emerged after decades of Marxist-Leninist *Gleichschaltung*. But the economy of the entire country was in shambles; independent institutions were still in their incipient stages of development, and national passions threatened to exacerbate deeply rooted interethnic tensions.

Since its birth in 1953, Radio Liberty operated on the assumption that the Soviet regime could not last forever because it was fundamentally antithetical to the hopes and aspirations of its subjects. Yet, like almost everyone in the world of Soviet studies, my friends and I were astounded that the end came so suddenly and with so little bloodshed. The precipitating event that led to the demise of the Soviet Union was the attempted putsch in August, which was clumsily launched and quickly bungled by the hardliners, headed by Yanayev, Pugo, and Kryuchkov. They failed miserably in their move to end Gorbachev's perestroika and return the country to the status quo ante, when the Party and KGB controlled the commanding heights and stifled dissent.

Elena Bonner's introduction to a documentary paperback that Radio Liberty published several months later describes her reaction to the role of the Radio:

> Before me lies a manuscript. Like every book it needs an introduction. This is therefore mine. I did not want to read the ms. But after the first page, I stole a glance at the clock (it was past midnight, twenty to one in the morning) and I realized that I could not tear myself from it until I had finished the last page. It isn't a detective story, nor a novel, nor a tale, . . . but just a record of what was broadcast over the airwaves of Radio Liberty during the August days.

19 August. It was 7:45 A.M. there (in Munich) 9:45 here (in Moscow). Judging from the sound of their voices they were dismayed—Fatima Salkazanova, Wladimir Matusevich and Mikhail Kartashev [RL's military expert]. Like us here in Moscow. After we had been stupefied during the first hours (the telephone routed us about 7 A.M.), my daughter [Tanya Yankelevich] went to the bakery. She returned on the verge of tears: "It's a coup d'état, and there's a colossal line for vodka. They're selling it there without ration coupons!" By "they" she meant the GKChP [the Emergency Committee of coup leaders]. By "there" she meant our local wine store on Chkalov St. and along with it the whole country, the whole wide world. . . . She went to the kitchen and nodded at the radio receiver. "What about Liberty? What are they saying?" "The same as we are. They're on our side."

And now this manuscript. A diary, or rather an hour-by-hour and minute-by-minute chronological account of what we did and who we were during those three days when our freedom hung by a thread, when our [domestic] radio was cut off, when our TV was one long "Swan Lake" with the intermissions taken up by Yanayev and his trembling hands. And what our fellow-workers at "Liberty" did—in Munich and here in Moscow. Rereading it I'm convinced that the putsch wasn't child's play. And without "Liberty" it would have been incomparably more difficult for the nation to survive it.[10]

Bonner spent most of the August coup inside the White House supporting Yeltsin. She saw with her own eyes the heroic performance of the Radio Liberty correspondents who were with her. Later she told them: "Boys, during these days you were on the barricades with us."

RFE/RL's in-house monthly, *Shortwaves,* carried Bonner's article about her years as a devoted listener. She first heard Radio Liberty at the time Stalin died in 1953, and it "occupied a special place for us" because "from the very beginning it was quite different from other Western stations—different not only because of its content (which was far closer to our everyday life), but different also in terms of its use of language, a language incomparably more up-to-date than that used by other stations." For Bonner this made Radio Liberty "somehow more trustworthy. As if those people in Munich had eaten our not always well-baked bread, stood in line at the store, or been hospitalized—not in a proper ward (no spaces available), but along with us in the drafty corridor."

In 1956, Bonner said, she began to listen to Radio Liberty regularly after "we obtained our first receiver (an unwieldy 'Vostok') seemingly in anticipation of the events in Hungary. At night its dials were lit up brightly. It seemed as if the whole world would come into that dark room along with the lighted dials and crackling of shortwave broadcasts." Radio receivers became "an absolutely essential object" for the intelligentsia, and later "this boom would spread to other segments of the population. Our own mass enlightenment and education had begun."

In spite of the difficulty, they listened to Radio Liberty along with other foreign stations in the larger cities. "But in the provinces [where audibility was better] listeners clearly preferred Radio Liberty to other foreign broadcasters." She did not remember exactly when Senator Fulbright "found the Radios unneeded, and when he proposed that they no longer be financed. It would have been one of America's greatest historical mistakes if the U.S. Congress had listened to him. And I hope that this lesson has not been forgotten." Turning to the present period [1991], Bonner said:

> It would seem that one might be able to make do without Radio Liberty now that the Berlin Wall has fallen, now that our own newspapers take battle with those who cling to power, when our own magazines are full of samizdat and Russian literature reprints from abroad. But in listening every evening to Radio Liberty, I am convinced over and over again that, apparently, things here are better seen and heard in Munich. And, by the way, I notice the same thing reading *Russkaya Mysl'* weekly [the popular émigré newspaper published in Paris]: In Paris, it seems that the view is better than in Moscow, and the field of vision is wider. And in those busy days in August, Radio Liberty, like its famous namesake in the Delacroix painting, was not only figuratively, but literally, on the barricades with us.
>
> When I learned that Radio Liberty and Radio Free Europe had been nominated for the Nobel Peace Prize [by the Estonian foreign minister in the autumn of 1991], I was overjoyed at how natural and right this nomination was. And I was struck that I had not thought of this earlier. Hearing every day the words "We conduct our broadcasts with the goal of distributing information," I know that daily they protect our right to receive and distribute information (the Universal Declaration of Human Rights) and protect peace on earth. And I know of no other mass media organization that has done more than RFE/RL to help create the Europe in which we live today—a Europe not divided into two opposing camps.
>
> And yet today's new conditions will require doing no less than has already been done. Our country has by no means become a democratic society, where freedom of speech is guaranteed, where wide-ranging and correct information is accessible to the people. In Georgia, Moldavia, Turkmenia and Tajikistan, people can learn the truth about their own

countries only from Radio Liberty. And even we Muscovites learn more about what is happening in the former Soviet republics than from central Soviet TV or from the Russian [domestic] news. Aside from this, it is quite possible that central Soviet TV will soon cease to exist. The newly created states will no longer want to subsidize it. And then Radio Liberty will become the main channel of information, of ties, between the peoples of the former USSR.

Now, after a hot Moscow summer, Radio Liberty has been invited to open a studio in Moscow. Let me greet our new Moscow neighbor, a most worthy candidate for the Nobel Peace Prize. And I hope that we shall tread the long path towards democracy and peace together with Radio Liberty. That sweet word "Liberty."[11]

Less than one month after the abortive coup, Soviet television dedicated a day to Radio Liberty. On September 14 the popular news program *"Vremya"* (Time) introduced the moderator, Mark Deich, as a "Moscow correspondent of the Radio Liberty program 'V Strane I Mire' (In the Country and the World)." Because *"Vremya"* had for years mirrored the views of the top Soviet leadership, the audience must have understood Deich's appearance as signaling official recognition of Radio Liberty. Later the same evening, Russian television marked the anniversary of an independent Moscow weekly magazine, where Soviet celebrities praised Radio Liberty coverage of the August events, reinforcing the impression created by *"Vremya."*

The Russians were not alone in expressing their appreciation for Radio Liberty's work. In Kiev, a stringer reported the appearance of stickers saying "Thank you, Radio Liberty." On September 29, sixteen members of the "democratic organizations and movements" of Turkmenistan sent a message to the U.S. Congress and to RFE/RL informing them that in the present atmosphere of continuing censorship and severe control over the media by the "Communist-totalitarian regime, the single champion of democracy for Turkmenistan has been Radio Liberty." The statesmen urged that the scale of broadcasts be increased "to help in our cause of establishing a civilized governmental system on Turkmen soil." They added that the democratic organizations nominated the editorial staff of Radio Liberty for a prestigious national award—"the highest honor our republic can bestow," to confirm the "high manner in which we evaluate the efforts of Radio Liberty towards the establishment of democracy and overall human values in Turkmenistan."[12]

Radio Liberty's former Soviet audience research department was now known as "RFE/RL Research Institute's Media and Opinion Research Department" (MOR). Under Gene Parta's direction, it conducted surveys in nine Soviet cities and seven of the former Soviet republics to measure the extent of listening to Radio Liberty during the coup. MOR communicated by telephone, fax, and personal delivery between Munich and cities where good working relationships had already been established with survey research groups. Data indicated that Western radio was preferred to the domestic media and that Radio Liberty was listened to more frequently than the Voice of America or the BBC. Many who tuned in regarded the broadcasts as a source of moral support during the tense days of the crisis.

As 1991 drew to a close, Ukraine and several other Soviet republics declared their independence. Radio Liberty was the first communications medium outside the republic to announce Ukraine's proclamation on August 24. The actual *"coup de grâce,"* as Jack Matlock described it, was administered against the USSR early in December at a secret meeting in a hunting lodge in Belovezhskaya Pushcha (Bison Forest), Belarus. Yeltsin, together with Leonid Kravchuk, the newly elected president of Ukraine, and Stanislav Shushkevich, chief of state of Belarus, signed the Agreement on Creating a Commonwealth of Independent States. On December 26 the Soviet Union ceased to exist.[13]

Was there any reason for Radio Liberty to continue to operate in the new era of freedom in Russia and the former Soviet republics? Ostensibly, the principal goal for which the Radio had striven since the early 1950s had been attained. The totalitarian grip of the one-party dictatorship had been dissolved, surprisingly, with a minimum of violence (although the shedding of blood in Lithuania in 1991 was a tragic exception).

Those in the West who believed that democracy and economic prosperity would somehow follow quickly were naive. Reality set in abruptly in 1992 with evidence that volatile and dangerous times lay ahead for the newly independent nations. Ethnic hatreds that had been kept under control by the Soviet power now erupted into open warfare in Moldova (formerly Moldavia), the Caucasus, and Central Asia. Manifestations of both extreme nationalism and neo-Communism appeared in Russia and other countries as a consequence of the frustratingly slow pace of transition from a command to a market economy, threatening to subvert the reform program and the fledgling democratic institutions.

A "Task Force on U.S. Government International Broadcasting" appointed by President George Bush submitted its recommendations after an intensive six-month study of the VOA, RFE/RL, and other American information media in December 1991. The bipartisan group of eleven distinguished Americans, headed by John Hughes and including Richard Allen and Stuart Eizenstat, concluded that the broadcasts of Radio Free Europe and Radio Liberty had shown themselves to be a "unique tool of incalculable worth in promoting democracy" and that they had important missions to fulfill in the years to come. However, the task force considered that their role was evolving from a pure "surrogate" mission to an "alternative" mission. In contrast to serving as a domestic service based abroad that provided ideas and information forbidden by the controlled media, Radio Liberty would assist the local media, now striving to become trusted, independent sources but still hampered by residual political controls or old habits of self-censorship, by the legacy of popular distrust, and a lack of resources—factors preventing them from functioning effectively as a stabilizing and sustaining force for democracy in the critical transition period.[14]

The Board for International Broadcasting welcomed the endorsement of the task force and in its annual report for 1992 described how the Radios were adjusting to the new challenge:

Through its focus on domestic and regional affairs, alternative programming supplements the local media and encourages its development through competition and cooperation. RFE/RL programming meets these goals by:

Providing a moderate, alternative non-partisan perspective on domestic and regional affairs, and a counterweight to voices of extremism;

Offering a platform through which moderate, responsible voices representing majority and minority communities can explore solutions to the problems of interethnic and national tensions that beset all countries of the region;

Promoting the development of market economies by examining the difficulties facing its audience countries, sharing the experience of other nations, and by analyzing the strengths and weaknesses of current efforts for reform and transformation;

Providing practical examples and lessons from Western societies and cultures that convey the challenges and rewards of democracy in ways that relate specifically to RFE/RL broadcast countries;

Explaining the purpose and activities of multilateral organizations such as the European Economic Community, the Council of Europe, the

Commission on Security and Cooperation in Europe (CSCE), and others that play crucial roles in integrating the newly free nations of Europe and the Atlantic community.[15]

The BIB cited other reasons for the Radio to maintain its presence as an alternative broadcaster:

> According to reports by academic specialists and U.S. government officials, many obstacles remain after the lifting of [USSR] state censorship: the lack of an economic base to sustain print and electronic media; shortages of trained journalists; state control of radio television, and the distribution of newsprint; the tradition of partisanship in the media that blurs the line between reportage and commentary; and the constant threat of intervention by State authorities in the working of the media.
>
> With time, Western help, and the onset of economic recovery, many of these problems will abate, and commercially viable, professional media should begin to flourish. In the interim [RL] is helping in important ways to compensate for the weaknesses of today's media.[16]

In contrast to the old days, when there was no way that Radio Liberty could send correspondents to travel inside the Soviet Union, it was now possible to obtain firsthand accounts of major events unfolding in various parts of the country. Two Radio broadcasters dodged bullets and risked their lives in army helicopters to record interviews with officers, soldiers, and townspeople whose lives were being ravaged by the ethnic warfare in Nagorno-Karabakh, North and South Ossetia, and Chechnya. The outcome of these and other conflicts were of central importance to people throughout the former Soviet Union. Audience surveys showed that they perceived the split location of Radio Liberty—partly abroad and partly in the home country—as providing an "arm's-length" distance from the daily political fray and, at the same time, on-the-spot familiarity with the domestic scene.

Radio Liberty was virtually the sole source of comprehensive and unbiased news in the troubled areas. The newly independent state of Moldova asked the Radio to provide local FM transmitters with Russian programming (and Radio Free Europe to provide Romanian programming) in order to counter the often biased views heard from Moscow and Bucharest.

One of the Radio's important new functions was to interview leading political figures from Yeltsin on down to inform the public about the intentions, plans, and philosophy of key policymakers and members of parliamentary opposition groups. A special interview with Mikhail Gorbachev on the first anniversary of the August 1991 coup had a unique format. Radio Liberty invited its listeners to call in questions to an answering machine in Moscow. Within three days, the Russian service received 8,000 calls, ranging from eulogies to profanities. Twenty-five representative questions were chosen, cut, arranged in sequence, and presented to the former Soviet president. Many of the questions were plaintive and emotional: "Why did you wait so long to tell people about the Chernobyl nuclear accident?" and "Why did you give out money to Communist parties abroad when people did not have enough to eat at home?" Gorbachev's responses were frank, heartfelt, and even emotional.[17]

Another series of programs focused on Western humanitarian aid to Russia. One Radio Liberty journalist, Irina Khenkin, accompanied a German group bringing donated clothing to the city of Yekaterinburg in the Urals. Flying aboard the giant Antonov cargo plane, she interviewed the participants in the mission and later described how 140 tons of warm winter clothing were distributed. So successful were the programs that Naina Yeltsin, the president's wife, invited Ms. Khenkin and a colleague to her Moscow office. In the midst of thanking them, Mrs. Yeltsin stopped in midsentence and said, "Wait, I know you! I know that voice very well. You are Irina Kanevskaya [Ms. Khenkin's radio name]. Now the voice and the face come together!"[18]

During 1992, the Russian service introduced a "live-exchange" program called "Kontakty," a call-in program for Russian listeners to discuss their concerns about life, the social situation, and living standards. Taking advantage of new opportunities for travel in Russia, the editor went to outlying towns and to specific institutions, such as medical clinics and factories, and declared: "We need to get to the heart of Russia—to find out what the actual wants and needs of our listeners are. These are the people who really need us."

A View of Radio Liberty from Moscow

Sonya Berezhkova, a senior editor on Radio Moscow's programming staff and a Ph.D. candidate in the journalism faculty of Moscow State University, chose Radio Liberty as her dissertation topic. She wrote a conscientious study that reflects scholarly objectivity and great perceptiveness. She traveled to Munich several times and met with programmers and with

Gene Parta and his audience research specialists. She and I started corresponding in 1992 and shared information that proved valuable in our separate investigations of the Radio's history and influence.

I asked whether she could find someone who heard the Radio's broadcasts in the early days, and she found a certain Nikolai Alekseyevich Golyadkin, who caught a broadcast in the spring of 1953, when he was fourteen years old and lived in Saratov Oblast. By chance, while his brother was tuning in his shortwave set, they picked up a program called "Enemies of the People Are Sitting in the Kremlin." Golyadkin told Berezhkova that he had been frightened by the title. He wouldn't have been so afraid if the program had been called "In the Kremlin They Don't Think About the People," or something else less provocative. He was sure that he heard it in the spring of 1953 and that it was over RL. It certainly sounds like one of the early broadcasts, judging from that aggressive title.[19]

Berezhkova also informed me that Radio Moscow had a monitoring service that started in 1964. A colleague in that department told her that in the mid-1970s the chief editor of the information section proposed, "just for fun," that a monetary prize be awarded to anyone who could find a lie in the broadcasts of foreign radio stations. A large file labeled "Lies," which still existed as late as 1993, remained largely empty, and although they did manage to pick out two texts containing factual errors (incorrect figures), no lies were detected. Berezhkova and I met during my 1993 trip to Moscow, and she subsequently sent me interesting materials. Her article, "The Iron Curtain Was Not Soundproof," pegged to the fortieth anniversary of Radio Liberty's Russian service, appeared in the *Vestnik* (Bulletin) of Moscow University, a scholarly magazine. She recounted accurately the evolution of Radio Liberty as a product of the Cold War that was first picked up by shortwave enthusiasts and now was heard by more than 30 million listeners all over the former USSR. "It is difficult to imagine the complex process of perestroika in the former Soviet Union without the alternative information which this radio station offered listeners."[20]

Another of her articles in Radio Moscow's *Bulletin of Foreign Broadcasting* treated the Radio Liberty Russian broadcasts for 1991 in depth, declaring that the Radio certainly maintained its position as one of the leading international stations beaming into the Soviet Union. "[RL] is undoubtedly not only the largest in size but also the most interesting of Russian foreign stations. Its mission and status are unique. For almost forty years RL has attempted to fill the internal vacuum in the USSR, and in recent times it is becoming a model for domestic media of mass information."[21]

Berezhkova contrasted Radio Liberty with the Voice of America, noting that despite financial support from the U.S. Congress, "its broadcasts are more candid in shedding light on events in the USSR and Eastern European countries than the VOA." An example of the contribution of RFE/RL was the nomination of the Radios for the Nobel Peace Prize in April 1991 by Lennart Meri, then Estonia's foreign affairs minister. Addressing the Prize committee, he said: "My brother Estonians and I wish to give due credit to RFE and Radio Liberty and to the people of the U.S. for their forty years of work in the cause of aid to us in preparation to restore our democracy. We wish to support them in order that they may continue this important work in the future." Vaclav Havel, Lech Walesa, Josef Antall, premier of Hungary, and Zhelyu Zhelev, president of Bulgaria, joined in this proposal. In a talk with the staff of the Radios in Munich, Meri said: "RFE/RL is especially valuable in that they supported the living democratic thought and preserved the cultural and historical memory of our people—that which the Communists attempted to destroy."[22] Berezhkova commented on the proposal:

[It] was endorsed by many leaders of Eastern European countries, but the stations did not receive the prize . . . [which went to Burmese dissident Daw Aung San Suu Kyi], but L. Meri's nomination got wide publicity and appeared in many of the newspapers and magazines in our country and Eastern Europe.

That was especially important for the fate of the stations, inasmuch as, following the victory of the democratic revolutions in Eastern Europe and the end of the "cold war," many American experts were inclined to think that RFE/RL should soon be shut down or merged with the VOA since its mission had been fulfilled.[23]

Berezhkova cited Walter Laqueur's *Washington Post* article in the summer of 1991, in which the eminent scholar and political scientist argued that it was premature to make such a move, for "the price that may have to be paid for such a mistake might be very high."[24]

Less than a month later, the attempted coup proved his point about the importance of Radio Liberty. Berezhkova commented that it would be a mistake to ascribe the opening of the Radio's Moscow bureau exclusively to its performance in August. "Talks about a bureau began several years ago, first with M. Gorbachev and later with B. Yeltsin."

Despite her praise for Radio Liberty's analysis of Russian events, especially on economic and political subjects with such successful programs as "Barometer: Law, State, Politics," "After the Empire," and "Our History and Yours," Berezhkova concluded that foreign stations were losing their popularity as a result of the competition from Radio Russia, Ekho Moskvy (Echo of Moscow), Baltic, Europe Plus, and other new stations of the former Soviet empire, which now "can speak about that which they formerly kept silent." She quoted the head of Radio Liberty's Russian service, Vladimir Matusevich, who told *Nezavisimaya gazeta:* "When some have their mouths shut and others have a gag in it, that's not competition. But now it will be a competition of professionalism, honesty, and talent."[25]

If Radio Liberty is to keep its listeners, Berezhkova wrote, it must seek a new form and style, and above all attract a young audience. She felt, however, that the majority of the editors in Munich and the bureaus were almost ready for pensions and had been there so long that they were reluctant to make changes.

The major contribution to recent programming, she said, was the hiring of young stringers during the period of perestroika. "It is fair to say that the turning point in the Radio's history was not in 1985 [when Gorbachev came to power] but on November 29, 1988 [when jamming was lifted]. From that moment on, the gradual 'rehabilitation' of RL in the USSR began and cardinal changes in its mode of work were noticeable." Berezhkova said that literally a few days after the end of jamming the first "legal" Moscow correspondent appeared, Dmitri Volchek. After him came Andrei Babitsky, Mark Deich, Karen Agamirov, Mikhail and Maxim Sokolov, Vugar Khalilov, and others in St. Petersburg, Kiev, Riga, Tallinn, and Tbilisi. Where previously Radio Liberty had depended on accredited Western journalists for information from within the Soviet Union, especially the BBC, the *New York Times,* and the *Baltimore Sun,* now the stringers made the programs more effective and timely.

"In the past two and a half years, about 100 stringers have appeared in our country. Those whom RL especially rely on are invited to Munich to learn 'the Western style of work.'" This approach, Berezhkova added, enabled Radio Liberty to scoop other media; for example, the stringer in Tbilisi landed the first interview with Tengis Sigua, the prime minister of Georgia.[26]

As of early 1992, the standard program schedule of Radio Liberty's Russian service consisted of ten minutes of news followed by fifty minutes of features. Original programs made up nine hours out of twenty-four and were repeated several times, especially the popular shows "Over the Barriers," the "Roundtable" of RL commentators, "Broadway 1775," and "Paris Meetings."

Berezhkova remarked that it was understandable that Radio Liberty writers and reporters who had not been in Russia for many years and finally succeeded in traveling there for a short time made errors of judgment. She criticized Vadim Belotserkovsky for suggesting in the Munich program "Man and Society" that more drastic measures be taken to achieve reforms than the gradual approach from above:

> It's very easy from a "nice distance" to propose something else, but the radio commentator should consider the possible consequences of such a risky appeal, especially in this complicated situation. Naturally, it's not a matter of the personality of this or that commentator, it goes more deeply. Other colleagues at the station are more cautious, but it is also difficult for them to work when they have been cut off from the country to which they are broadcasting. What was earlier a plus for RL has now become an obvious minus.[27]

She regretted as well the disappearance (through death and for other reasons) of well-known writers who had broadcast regularly over Radio Liberty. Among the audience's favorites was the late Sergei Dovlatov, a member of the New York staff until 1990, who once said: "Finding myself in the emigration, I worked out a genre of my own. Since I didn't know American life, and had a poor knowledge of the American press, and didn't keep abreast of American art, I introduced a [memoir] genre."

One of the most successful recent new programs, according to Berezhkova, was produced by Julian Panich, who called it a "radio film" because he selected background music to underscore subtly the atmosphere of the script (a technique that could be used now that jamming had ceased). Panich traveled to Russia frequently and made use of local actors. In fact, by 1993 he was spending even more time in Moscow and St. Petersburg producing plays and films.

Berezhkova also praised the level of the Radio's audience research, which in recent years was able to operate directly with the home audience, often with the cooperation of scholars there:

> In 1991 alone several sociological studies of the audience were conducted by RL in the USSR. The most extensive of them, which encompassed the whole territory of the country, was assigned to the independent public opinion service "Vox Populi," under the direction of Professor Grushin. The survey took place in October 1991. The data col-

lected by the sociologists were not published, but the station reported that the listenership reached over thirty million.[28]

The Russian service received two hundred to three hundred letters each month in 1992. The most interesting were displayed for the Munich staff to read, but it was not possible to answer them. Requests for help in obtaining medicine were turned over to various charitable organizations.

In 1992, Berezhkova also published "'Liberty' as a Recognized Necessity," an interview with dissident satirist and novelist Vladimir Voinovich, who emigrated from Moscow in 1980 and lived outside Munich, where he was a regular freelance contributor to Radio Liberty's Russian broadcasts. The conversation was reproduced in an issue of the *Bulletin of Foreign Broadcasting,* which she edited. In the USSR, Voinovich had written several books sharply satirizing the Soviet system. These were smuggled abroad and published in thirty languages, and in 1974 he was excluded from the Soviet Writers' Union. His most famous book is *The Life and Unusual Adventures of Ivan Chonkin,* the hilarious story of a Soviet G.I. like the Czech good soldier Schweik. Voinovich also worked as a comedy writer for Radio Moscow and wrote many popular songs, one of which became the hymn of the Soviet cosmonauts. After he emigrated, the music editors of Moscow Radio, according to Berezhkova, tried in vain to find a tape of the song in their archives and concluded that it had probably been erased.

Berezhkova told Voinovich that many Soviet listeners first became aware of his banned novels from his frequent appearances on Radio Liberty. When he arrived at the Radio's offices in Munich in December 1980, he was met by a large group of émigré admirers from the Russian desk who immediately urged him to work with them. When he refused, they said that he was making a big mistake and that he would find out that to work at Radio Liberty was "necessary" because it offered him status, money, and the like. He told them: "Then you should rename your station 'Recognized Necessity.'"

However, after a year of teaching Russian literature at Princeton University, Voinovich returned to Munich to live, and then accepted Radio Liberty's invitation to join other émigré writers, such as Viktor Nekrasov, Vladimir Maximov, and Sergei Dovlatov, in the series "Writers at the Microphone." "I tried to talk to them not about the West but about themselves, because I knew that many people here in the Soviet Union have an entirely false idea about their own life." Voinovich told Berezhkova that he modeled his radio talks on "the unforgettable BBC commentator, Anatoly Maximovich Goldberg," mentioned earlier as undoubtedly the best known and beloved of all broadcasters in the Russian language from abroad. He also praised the way Radio Liberty broadcasters Anatoly Kuznetsov, Nekrasov, and Dovlatov handled this genre.

With few exceptions, Voinovich said, his scripts went on the air without any editorial changes. This amazed him, because his former Soviet editors "surprised me all the time not by their political vigilance but by their ability to find and remove from the text precisely those words, lines and paragraphs which made them expressive." But he added that censorship existed at Radio Liberty "like everywhere else."

> There's fear on the part of some circles that somebody will say something wrong, say, a tactless remark about something. Sometimes unbelievable things happened. Some people suddenly started to praise over RL the Ukrainian SS Division "Galichina," which existed during the war. You see, there are all kinds at Radio Liberty.
>
> There are, say, those with nationalistic feelings who try to push through their own points. The censorship that is carried on there is done by very stupid people, but even so it has a positive reason. Here Liberty is often accused of provoking national hatred, but actually they are very careful to see that everything is measured out in doses. Let's say that if there is a conflict between Armenia and Azerbaijan, they make sure that one viewpoint doesn't prevail over the other so that both can be expressed. The station is, after all, built on sound principles. People depart from those principles, but that's another matter. I must say to you though that it's generally an illusion to think that people there are any different from people here. They're the same as they are here.[29]

Voinovich attributed some of his conflicts at Radio Liberty to certain broadcasting taboos:

> Once I wrote an essay (it was in '83 or '84, when disarmament talks were under way). In my essay, an American and a Russian are engaged in the discussions. The American is sober, and the Russian is drunk. And the Russian, well, let's say the "Soviet," looks worse than the American. . . . And the supervisor said to me, "Now look, you've made the American so good and the Soviet so bad." I argued with him and said that I was going to stop working with them. It was a big conflict, but they would not let my material pass.

Voinovich also quoted a passage from one of his plays in which the pro-
tagonist, Otsebyakin, is defending the right of Jews to exist, not only because "we internationalists must be tolerant of all nations" but also because "you have to consider ecology":

> OTSEBYAKIN: I'm thinking of the balance in nature. In nature there
> are no superfluous organisms. If you exterminate one, another will ap-
> pear. Still worse. Take the Chinese, for example: they got rid of spar-
> rows and what happened? Beetles of all kinds started breeding. Mag-
> gots. They ate up all the rice and left nothing for the Chinese. So they
> had to send gold abroad to buy sparrows.
>
> NADYA: I don't know what you're talking about. Jews and sparrows.
> What's the connection?
>
> OTSEBYAKIN: The connection is that if nature can't get along without
> sparrows, maybe she also needs Jews.

Voinovich told Berezhkova that Radio management banned the broadcast:

> There was jamming in those days and they said that if there were no
> jamming the context would be normal, but hearing the word "Jew" un-
> der those conditions people might interpret it as something anti-Se-
> mitic, and we have in Washington a Jewish lobby who would raise such
> a fuss that it would be better not to get mixed up with them, and so on.
> I had a serious talk with Eugene Pell, the president of Radio Liberty and
> Radio Free Europe. Later, when jamming was lifted, they broadcast the
> play in full. So the conflict was settled.[30]

Voinovich's account of this incident shows that management had become supersensitive about the danger of being accused of anti-Semitism.
The fact that his program was eventually aired, when jamming no longer
threatened any misinterpretation of his meaning, validates my previous
critique of those ultranationalist Russians who failed to exercise good
judgment in their choice of program material.

Although he was critical of Radio Liberty for many deficiencies,
Voinovich said: "It has done a great thing in its time. And it was better than
other radio stations. It's another matter that it was not as effective in
Moscow because it was heavily jammed there. . . . But [it] was much more
interesting than [other Western] stations because the information and commentaries concentrated on our local affairs."

Voinovich also told Berezhkova that the role of Radio Liberty was diminishing because other sources were now available:

> You know, the worst days for Radio Liberty will come when this country really becomes free and the need for it will pretty much pass. I even wanted to write a play (it was before perestroika) in which a revolution came and the Soviet Union is replaced, and then the staff of Radio Liberty begins to speak about how the Soviet regime was very good and should be restored immediately. Yes, the putsch was certainly a wonderful time for Radio Liberty, but by and large it's not natural for a radio station somewhere abroad to be the main [medium] for the country. . . .
>
> Yet I have the feeling (and it's now growing stronger) that in our country, in Russia, and in general throughout the former Soviet Union foreign radio will, unfortunately, still be needed. For a variety of reasons. The main reason is that here there is not enough truthful, open, and I would say frank and sincere information. Information is still somehow prepared—often to please certain circles, or perhaps resulting from incompetence. There may not be any censorship, but all the same there is no openness. Maybe there's no openness in people's souls, I don't know.[31]

The question of Radio Liberty's future viability came under serious scrutiny early in 1993, with the arrival of President Bill Clinton in the White House. Both the administration and budget-conscious congressmen were determined to eliminate or curtail drastically many of the subsidized activities now deemed to be vestiges of the Cold War. As Radio Liberty neared its fortieth anniversary, its days seemed numbered.

What's the difference between a
pessimist and an optimist?
    The pessimist says, "Things couldn't get
worse." The optimist says, "Oh, yes they
could!"

 ## RADIO LIBERTY IN THE NEW ERA
OF FREEDOM

If a soothsayer had predicted at the birth of
Radio Liberty in 1953 that forty years later
we would celebrate our anniversary in
Moscow with the blessings of the democratic government of Russia, he would have
been ridiculed as a madman. But there we
were, a small contingent of Radio staff people, Americans and émigrés, and several
BIB members, who were joined by the cultural and political elite of Moscow at the
landmark Central House of Writers for a
gala reception on Saturday, March 20, 1993.

Kevin Klose, the new director of Radio
Liberty since October 1992, invited me to
be a consultant for the forthcoming anniversary. I was asked to select tapes of the
Radio's broadcasts from the early 1950s to
be rebroadcast in full or in part during several weeks of celebration that spring. I
searched in the recording archives of the
New York Programming Center, with the
help of Albert Arkus, who had carefully
preserved everything. We shipped the
appropriate tapes to Aleksandr Perouansky,

a veteran of the Munich Russian service, who had also been recruited from retirement to be the producer of the anniversary series. Gloria and I traveled to headquarters in Munich, where I wrote a retrospective chapter about Radio Liberty's forty years, skillfully translated by Viktor Fedoseyev, which was included in a memorial album for President Yeltsin. Yevgeny Yevtushenko and Vasily Aksyonov also contributed.

Melissa Fleming, RFE/RL's director of public relations, mounted an impressive exhibit of photographs to be displayed in Moscow, and Gloria volunteered her Russian and editorial expertise. On March 18, we all flew to Moscow. Our visas were stamped "Radio Liberty Conference." It was incredible that we were now being openly welcomed after so many decades of enmity.

The Central House of Writers in Moscow is a stately, nineteenth-century mansion that Tolstoy was inspired to fictionalize in *War and Peace* as the residence of the Rostov family. When I first visited there in 1959 during Khrushchev's era, it was the headquarters of the Union of Soviet Writers, a bastion of Communist literary orthodoxy. Thirty-four years passed before I entered that house again. What irony! Here was a retired director of the Radio that for many years had been anathema to the Soviet leadership, a person whom the Soviets had vilified in their controlled newspapers and magazines as an agent of the CIA. Now I shared this mind-boggling experience in a free Russia with colleagues of the Cold War and BIB honchos from Washington, including Steve Forbes, Kenneth Tomlinson, and Karl Rove. Mark Pomar, the BIB's executive director and RL alumnus, was also present.

Among the several hundred guests were liberal members of the legislature, representatives of Yeltsin's government, famous stage and screen stars, and even the former KGB general Oleg Kalugin, who had broken with his secret police bosses a few years earlier and had become a leading reformist. He was now accepted in polite company, even touring the United States and appearing on American television talk shows. This was the very same Kalugin who had visited Radio Liberty's offices in Munich in 1991 and boasted that he had masterminded the bombing of that building ten years earlier. He told the staff that the KGB wanted to frighten the German government into discontinuing RFE/RL's operation on their soil. (As mentioned earlier, his version has been disputed.) At the Moscow reception, he was interviewed by Agence France Presse and said: "Our media face too much censorship for Radio Liberty to stop broadcasting yet."[1]

Boris Yeltsin had accepted our invitation but was unable to attend.

Involved in a bitter struggle against his chief enemies, Aleksandr Rutskoi and Ruslan Khasbulatov, he was preparing a major television speech for that evening. The struggle culminated in October 1993, when Yeltsin fought off an attempted coup d'état by ordering tanks to shell the White House, the same parliament building he had defended in the previous attempted coup of August 1991. However, his press office sent Radio Liberty his congratulatory message: "It would be difficult to overestimate the significance of your contribution to the destruction of the totalitarian regime in the former Soviet Union. No less important are the efforts which you are making today to inform radio listeners in Russia about events in our country and overseas."[2]

Yeltsin's endorsement of Radio Liberty's continuing relevance was especially welcome in early 1993, when the new Clinton administration considered closing RFE/RL under the mistaken impression that the Radios were no longer needed in the post–Cold War era. Further support for the continued operation of the Radios was echoed by many others at the Moscow ceremony. Dr. Sergei Kovalyov, a prominent human rights leader who was imprisoned in the 1970s, said, "It would be wonderful if the U.S. Congress could realize the importance of Radio Liberty and ensure its continued work."[3]

The star of the evening was Mikhail Gorbachev. Even though the former Soviet president no longer wielded any significant political influence, his charisma had not faded. When he entered the dining room, all eyes turned to him, and reporters with camcorders rushed to interview him. When the fuss died down, Gloria and I introduced ourselves, and I told him I was "an old comrade-in-arms of Liberty." I said that in August 1991, when he returned to Moscow from house arrest in the Crimea, we were driving on a highway north of New York City listening to his live radio broadcast: "When you said you heard the latest news of the putsch from Radio Liberty, we almost drove off the road!" Gorbachev laughed, and a photographer captured the moment. (See photo insert.)

A spicy, high-cholesterol Russian buffet was followed by speeches. Gorbachev was flanked by Gene Pell, who would soon step down after eight years as president of RFE/RL, and Steve Forbes, who was about to leave his chairmanship of the Board for International Broadcasting. The former Soviet president lauded the achievements of Radio Liberty and pointed out that in the "confrontational and terribly dangerous times" before his own perestroika reform program began, "Radio Liberty always broadcast much that was essential to people in Russia and in Europe and in the world." (He said nothing about the fact that he kept the jammers on us for more than three years after he came to power.) He added that the station was now "a stabilizing influence in an unstable time" and declared that shutting it down would be "absolutely wrong." He toasted to its continued success: "I would like very much for us to meet on the fiftieth anniversary of Radio Liberty." Then they wheeled in a huge anniversary cake, topped by a miniature Statue of Liberty—wearing earphones!

In a briefing session later with the American executives, Gorbachev learned that the idea of ending the funding for RFE/RL came from "middle-level bureaucrats" who did not understand the importance of the broadcasts to millions of people in countries just emerging from Communist rule. Gorbachev said: "An administration changes, but the bureaucrats don't. You have to be very sharp. I've had my experience—forty years of this."[4] He promised to carry his message personally to leaders in the United States during his forthcoming visit.

The evening's festivities continued in the theater of the Central House of Writers. Popular Russian singers and actors, who had broadcast over Radio Liberty in the recent relaxed times, performed: Bulat Okudzhava, Veronika Dolina, Innokenty Smoktunovsky, and Zinovy Gerdt. Steve Forbes and Kevin Klose addressed the audience. As one of the first members of the Radio's staff, I had been invited to prepare a short speech. Standing in the wings as I waited to be announced, I felt as if I were on another planet. Could this really be taking place?

At stage center against the background of the American flag, the new tricolor of the free Russian Federation, and the Liberty Bell with Radio Free Europe/Radio Liberty emblazoned on it, I addressed the audience in Russian:

> Dear colleagues and guests, I must admit that I feel like some sort of dinosaur. The fact is that I joined Radio Liberty in 1952, six months before the first broadcast. We had prepared a test program that began with the tick-tock of a metronome and a solemn voice that stated "Today Iosif Vissarionovich Stalin is seventy-three years old, so-and-so many days," and after a pause the sepulchral voice intoned, "The time of Stalin is coming to a close."
>
> We planned to go on the air every day with that announcement, but we scrapped the idea because the listeners might be bored hearing it so often, especially if Stalin stayed alive for years. How could we predict that a few hours after we began broadcasting on March 1, 1953, he would have a fatal stroke and die? The birth of RL coincided with the death of

the tyrant, and for the next forty years RL was never silent about things that you people here were forced to be silent about until recently.

To illustrate that cult of silence in the pre-Gorbachev years, I recited my English translation of Aleksandr Galich's popular satirical song "The Gold Prospectors' Little Waltz." In three-quarter time, he says that silence is golden. "That's how you get to be first / That's how you get to be wealthy / That's how you get to be hangmen / Just keep mum, just keep mum, just keep mum." The audience, which included Galich's brother and son, appreciated the tribute to this beloved figure who had broken the silence Soviet censorship had imposed on him and other truth-tellers. Radio Liberty's Moscow bureau recorded my speech and aired it as part of the series during the anniversary period, along with remarks by well-known Russian writers, including Andrei Voznesensky, who spoke about the importance of the Radio.

The exhibit of photographs of famous Americans and Western Europeans at our microphones during the course of four decades of broadcasting was set up in one of the main rooms of the mansion. Also featured were some of the cartoons printed by Soviet media attacking the Radio, such as a CIA mouthpiece squatting on Uncle Sam's money bags. Other caricatures showed a hissing snake coiled around a Radio Liberty microphone, and a quacking duck (like the French *canard*, the Russian word for "duck" also means a lie). By the time the exhibit ended, half the photographs and cartoons had disappeared. Some Muscovites either acquired a unique private collection of Radio memorabilia in their apartments or made a lot of rubles selling them as souvenirs.

Several days after the celebration, a new liberal Moscow daily, *Sevodnya* (Today), published a condensed version of the article I had written for the commemorative album. Called "Forty Years at Liberty," the piece traced the evolution of the Radio from "Liberation" to "Liberty" and from its negative image as the Soviet's public enemy to official acceptance and accolades. In a note accompanying the article, one of their correspondents, Pavel Kryuchkov, who had interviewed me at the reception, quoted my reply to his question concerning my attitude toward the possible termination of the Radio:

> In my opinion, our work has just begun. In America there are enough people who understand that ideas are the most powerful weapon. Enduring democracy, unfortunately, has not yet been established here, and that is precisely the cause for which we have worked throughout all

these years. As for the money, the annual cost of both stations [RFE and RL] can be compared with the cost of one F-16 plane. The sum of 200 million dollars is not all that large, especially compared with the [total] American budget.

How different from the times when the Soviet press used to attack me for my subversive work! Kryuchkov continued:

> In one of Radio Liberty's broadcasts [in the series] "Galich at the Microphone," entitled "Trip to America," the poet describes the first day of his trip [in 1975]: "And then I sang some of my songs, in particular, 'The Gold Prospectors' Little Waltz,' which was translated by my friend, Gene Sosin, who is doing a great deal of work in the history of Soviet songs of protest."
> Eighteen years later, on the stage of the Moscow House of Writers during the days of celebration of RL's fortieth anniversary, Dr. Sosin read that translation of long ago—and the audience, in my opinion, felt why Galich had been happy to sing it: the precision of the translation. Gene Sosin joined the radio station six months before the initial broadcast. During thirty-three years he served in several positions, including director of the New York bureau and senior adviser of Radio Liberty in Munich. . . . With the kind permission of Mr. Sosin and the current leadership of RL, we are publishing excerpts from the article in a special album which will soon lie on the desk of the president of Russia. And we hope that behind the dry account and the American "accent" the reader will sense that inner energy of resistance that has always distinguished this radio station. In the final analysis, the [Liberty] bell in its logo did not appear merely by chance.[5]

While Radio Liberty was being congratulated in Moscow, the controversy in Washington over the fate of Radio Free Europe and Radio Liberty continued. In Munich, the staff experienced months of frustration and plunging morale as rumors and speculation circulated about their future.

Although the *New York Times* had strongly endorsed the Radios before the 1992 election, in April 1993 it supported efforts to reduce the deficit and commented editorially:

> One of the hottest fax wars in Washington rages over the future of Voice of America and its independently operated rivals in Munich, Radio Free Europe and Radio Liberty. The Clinton Administration plans to continue the Voice but phase out the two Munich stations, sav-

ing $644 million over five years. That makes sense. Although the *Times* has supported continuation of the Munich stations in the past, we have now concluded that deficit reduction demands a willingness to sacrifice even worthwhile projects whose prime days have passed. . . .

Only the sourest critic would deny the immense service rendered by the Munich stations. But it is hard to defend the indefinite existence of two broadcast bureaucracies with overlapping functions. Today's fax war is as much about turf as policy.[6]

The *Times* recommended that the Voice of America's foreign language services be expanded and given a sharper edge. Only then would elimination of the Munich radios be justified. However, when the president's decision was finally reached in June, it reflected the tremendous surge of support for RFE/RL both inside the Beltway and from influential U.S. private organizations like Freedom House. On June 15, President Clinton announced that he was proposing to Congress a reorganization of U.S. international broadcasting that would preserve Radio Free Europe and Radio Liberty but place them under a board of governors within the U.S. Information Agency as "Surrogate Broadcasting," together with the Office of Cuba Broadcasting and Radio Free Asia. The Voice of America would also report to the board of governors, but separately. The BIB that had supervised RFE/RL since the mid-1970s would be dissolved within the next two years. Clinton promised that the new structure would result in big savings for the government, without jeopardizing the independence of RFE/RL. The administration also assured Gene Pell that no decisions on specific reductions would be made until the legislative process was completed.

When hard-liners in the parliament engaged in a bitter power struggle against Boris Yeltsin and his government in October 1993, Radio Liberty once again demonstrated its indispensability. Our Russian service was well prepared with fifteen correspondents spread out over Moscow and stringers located throughout Russia. Beginning at 4 P.M. Munich time on October 3, the popular news program "Liberty Live" (broadcast live; the English title was used on the air) continued for thirty-one straight hours, airing approximately four hundred reports to keep listeners informed, as we had done in August 1991.

When the stalemate between the parliamentary faction in the Moscow White House and President Yeltsin began to turn violent, Radio Liberty correspondents were inside the building recording statements by the leaders of the anti-Yeltsin forces, Rutskoi and Khasbulatov. Elsewhere reports were sent about the siege of the Russian television station Ostankino and various demonstrations taking place at Red Square and other strategic spots. Meanwhile, the Washington bureau reported support for Yeltsin from President Clinton and Strobe Talbott, Clinton's special envoy to Russia and the Commonwealth of Independent States, who became deputy secretary of state. Because the Russian national television station and several domestic radio stations were off the air for various periods of time, Radio Liberty was one of the only sources of information for Russians.

Radio Liberty boosted its transmitter power by 1.4 megawatts (that is, 1,400,000 watts) and added eight more frequencies to provide maximum coverage. In Nizhny Novgorod (formerly Gorky), the local station Radio Rendezvous, already an "affiliate station" of Radio Liberty, abandoned its regular broadcasts and carried Radio programs extensively during the crisis. The same was true of other affiliates in St. Petersburg and Ufa. The recently opened Kiev bureau of Radio Liberty in the Ukrainian capital was staffed through the night of October 3–4 in case the Moscow bureau was seized during the revolt, as were other domestic media services in Moscow. The Central Asian and Caucasus services in Munich not only reported the events in their own languages but also advertised the frequencies of the Russian service's special coverage, as did the Baltic services of Radio Free Europe.

The Moscow showdown came just when the Board for International Broadcasting gathered to decide what to cut according to President Clinton's blueprint for reorganizing the Radios. The first broadcasts to be eliminated were RFE's Hungarian service and RL's Radio Free Afghanistan, both of which ceased operation by November 1, 1993. The joint RFE/RL budget was slashed from $210 million to $75 million in fiscal year 1996; the staff of 1,550 was reduced by 50 percent; the New York Programming Center and other bureaus were closed, and plans were drawn up to terminate other RFE languages. Paul Goble was among the RFE/RL executives in Washington who steadfastly persevered in defending the Radios' cause during the difficult years of Clintonian perestroika. For many years he was the State Department's special adviser on the Baltic desk. He served briefly from 1989 to 1990 as deputy (and acting) director of RL research, and after returning to Washington became the Radios' U.S. assistant director for broadcasting. In 1997, he was appointed director of the communications division of RFE/RL. Goble told me that the late Jon Lodeesen deserves great credit for helping to save the Radios during the early 1990s. Lodeesen joined Radio Liberty in Munich in 1969 after serving in the U.S. Embassy in Moscow and in NATO headquarters in Brussels. A policy and pro-gramming executive, he spent the last years of his life in Washington, where he regularly provided various U.S. government offices with unique research and programming materials from Munich that kept the powers-that-be aware of the invaluable contribution of the reorganized Radios in the post-Soviet era.

Sonya Berezhkova successfully defended her carefully researched dis-sertation on Radio Liberty at Moscow State University in 1995. In her con-clusion, she declared:

> At present, when almost one fourth of the planet's population is under the yoke of totalitarian regimes, the unique experience of a surrogate radio broadcaster which RL accumulated can be used in organizing analogous broadcasts to populations of those countries where freedom of the press and human rights are lacking and violated. . . .
>
> Now when the need for surrogate radio broadcasting to Russia has dropped, and the Voice of America exists to carry out alternative broad-casting, there has begun a gradual re-orientation of RL's work. The new role which RL has assumed in the last decade, and is maintaining during the whole "transition" period, consists of helping to establish in Russia and the other former Soviet republics democratic institutions and in par-ticular free and independent information media.
>
> The station secures the flow of intercontinental information in the target area; it contributes to the development of democracy on the ter-ritory of the former USSR; it helps better understanding of democratic values.[7]

The severe budget cuts by Congress made it too expensive to main-tain the Radios in Germany. President Vaclav Havel of the Czech Repub-lic offered RFE/RL, for a nominal rental fee, the former Communist par-liament building near Wenceslas Square in the heart of the capital. Many of the Munich staff retired, and the downsized operation moved to Prague in July 1995. Despite sharply reduced staff and allocation, the Ra-dios benefited from a fresh esprit de corps quite different from the Mu-nich atmosphere, where old enmities and tensions had persisted for years.

I visited RL's new headquarters during the fall of 1996, and spoke with Kevin Klose, who became president of RFE/RL in June 1994, as well as with other American executives of RFE/RL. Robert Gillette, director of broadcasting, and Donald Jensen, his deputy, described current program-ming and the raison d'être for continuing to broadcast to Russia and the other former Soviet republics. The chief archivist of RFE/RL, Leszek Gaw-likowski, took me to the warehouse on the outskirts of Prague, where thousands of program tapes are cataloged and stored, spared from certain destruction due to the foresight of Klose, Gawlikowski, and other staff members in Munich. During the Cold War, RFE/RL had kept very good track of paper files, samizdat, etc., but not tapes. No coherent attention was paid to audio archives. Klose told me:

> When we moved to Prague in 1995, I set as a goal setting up a complete archive of all the tapes of RFE/RL. What you saw is a self-created historic archive which I believe is irreplaceable. Under my leadership we provided to the Polish nation a complete dubbed fresh copy of every tape in the Polish archive which in fact was one of the biggest of the archives. We have engaged in the same kind of activity with regard to the Hungarian service, and we are making available to the people of Hungary as complete a file as we have of the audio tapes. We are dubbing them off in fresh versions, "re-engineered," so they are getting better quality with a life span of forty or fifty years. We had the warehouse surveyed by professional German audio archivists to test it for the dryness of the air, temperature stability—all that is important for preserving the tapes. We've taken off sample tapes dating from the early 1950s; they are nearly perfect, very little deterioration, and I'm very proud we have what we believe is a real asset for the history of the twentieth century.[8]

This audio-history of almost a half-century of broadcasting is now carefully preserved in stacks that run at least one kilometer in length from one end of the warehouse to the other and from ceiling to floor. What a rich treasure awaits enterprising graduate students or researchers who may someday analyze the contents of these tapes, which comprise thousands of hours of what actually went on the air since the early 1950s. But tapes and scripts are a relic of the past since the innovation of state-of-the-art computers now on the desks of every writer and editor. When I asked one Russian editor to show me a recent script, he laughed and called me a "dinosaur from Jurassic Park." He pressed the keys on his computer and played me the program as it had been broadcast and digitally filed.

Editors and writers on the Prague staff described the status of programming. Yuri Handler, director of the Russian service, is a former Soviet dissident who spent time in the gulag before emigrating to the United States in the early 1970s. He first came to work for Radio Liberty in 1973, and he moved to Munich in the 1980s. Radio Liberty, he said, is the largest Russian-language station in the world, with bureaus in Moscow, St. Petersburg, and Washington, and freelancers inside Russia and abroad. In the fall of 1996, the station was preparing to establish a Russian home page for the Internet.

"The age of shortwave is almost over," Handler said. The Russian audience now prefers a clearer signal on AM and FM, and Radio Liberty is competing with other foreign stations like the BBC to attract a wider listenership on those wavelengths. With the cooperation of local stations in several Russian cities—for example, Yekaterinburg, Nizhny Novgorod, Volgograd, and Vladivostok—it is already possible to receive Radio Liberty on medium wave, even in car radios. Agreeing with other members of the Radio's Prague staff, Handler does not consider the media inside Russia to be really free, even if the Soviet control and censorship no longer exist.

Criticism of the strictures on the media by the Yeltsin regime are justified. During the 1996 election campaign, the Kremlin prevented not only the Communist candidate Gennadi Zyuganov but also liberals like Grigory Yavlinsky, Elena Bonner, and Sergei Kovalyov from appearing on television to criticize the president. Aleksandr Solzhenitsyn also complained about censorship of a ten-minute interview with NTV (which he called the "so-called independent station"), where he charged that both of the main contenders, Communist leader Gennadi A. Zyuganov and Yeltsin, were burdened with serious crimes against the interests of the people—one for seventy long years, the other for five. He urged the electorate to vote against both, which would cause the elections to be postponed and allow new candidates to run. The interview was "chopped down to two ragged minutes, and my remarks were rendered incoherent and meaningless."

Gorbachev, who also faces difficulties gaining access to the domestic media, sometimes broadcasts to his former subjects via Radio Liberty. In 1996 he took part in the Radio's observance of the abortive right-wing coup against him. When asked who won and who lost at that time, he replied: "Everyone lost." He has always believed that the Soviet Union could have been saved from disintegration if his moderate approach to reform had continued, but that it was doomed after the Communist putsch of 1991 further alienated the population.

Handler emphasized the need for Congress to continue supporting Radio Liberty even if domestic priorities take precedence:

Could you sign a document guaranteeing the development of Russian democracy? Guaranteeing that no Russian nationalist government will take power in the next ten to fifteen years? I don't think it will happen, but I will not sign because I can't guarantee it. Certain dangers remain: their nuclear arsenal, the fact that Russian public opinion is no longer as friendly to U.S. Even the present government is not one hundred percent friendly.

When I asked about the charge made in recent years that the Russian broadcasts do not serve American interests but reflect the prejudices and parochial viewpoint of Russian citizens working for the Radio, especially in the Moscow bureau, Handler answered that it is difficult for Russian journalists to report like Western journalists. Radio Liberty's task is to help them "to develop democratic instincts."

> If the IMF gives ten billion dollars to the Russian government, it's an investment. We too are making an investment by creating an atmosphere that in the future will make Russia a much more friendly country to the United States. There is no doubt that RL is in the U.S. interests. The best propaganda is where it does not sound like propaganda. We are a professional radio that brings American values to Russia, to help stabilize the situation against violence. It is not our main task to interpret U.S. policy, although the Washington bureau does cover all aspects of American life, for example, the pros and cons of abortion and welfare as they are reflected in the press. It is not our task to praise the U.S.—we cover it objectively, like the *New York Times*. The VOA gives the official American position.[9]

Mario Corti, deputy director of the Russian service, worked in the Italian embassy in Moscow in the 1970s, where he met Soviet dissidents who later came to Rome (usually in transit to America during the détente period). In Moscow he established unofficial ties with dissidents like Pavel Litvinov, Boris Shragin, and Vladimir Voinovich and sent samizdat documents to the West through the Italian diplomatic pouch. After he returned to Italy, he left the diplomatic service but continued his activity in behalf of the Soviet fighters for human rights. He participated in the Rome Sakharov Hearings of 1979 and joined Radio Liberty's samizdat section under Peter Dornan in Munich, where he later took over as chief of that unit. Still later, he joined the combined RFE/RL Research Institute under Ross Johnson, where he worked for several years before moving to Prague with the Russian service. When Corti was in Moscow, he was aware of the impact Radio Liberty had on his dissident friends. They would travel to their dachas outside the city and tape programs to disseminate to others. Even in Moscow, it was sometimes possible to hear the Radio clearly: "On August 21, 1972, the fourth anniversary of the invasion of Czechoslovakia, I tuned in RL on my radio in the Hotel Peking [on Mayakovsky Square not far from the Kremlin]. It was my first day in Moscow. I heard Leonid Finkelstein [broadcasting as Vladimirov] discussing Yevtushenko, who opposed the invasion. It was astonishingly clear."[10] Corti described the composition of current Russian programming: a seven-minute newscast in the morning is followed by three minutes of "thematic news" that alternate during the week: cultural, scientific, economic, sports. Then the popular "Liberty Live" runs for the next two hours.

Lev Roitman, a former lawyer and writer from Kiev, has worked in the Russian service since 1974. For many years he produced feature programs, such as "Events and People" and a roundtable on timely topics that he moderated with Western panelists. Nowadays people inside Russia also participate. Roitman organized a panel on the subject of euthanasia that included a physician at a Moscow cancer institute; Giovanni Bensi, a veteran of the Russian staff who was educated in the Vatican and handled the religious aspects of the subject; and Molly Gordin (Inna Svetlova), who was freelancing from Munich, spoke about the opposition to euthanasia in Germany. The program touched on legal, medical, moral, and religious questions and included the current situation in Australia, where euthanasia is legal, and the United States, where Dr. Jack Kevorkian has caused considerable controversy.

During Yeltsin's recuperation from heart surgery, a roundtable dealt with the Russian public's right to know about the health of elected officials. Participants were Dina Kaminskaya, the well-known former Soviet defense attorney, who now lives in the Washington area; Semyon Mirsky, another Soviet émigré who worked for many years as Radio Liberty's Paris bureau chief and later on the Munich Russian staff; and a Moscow stringer. They discussed the American, French, and Russian approaches to this problem and raised the question of passing a law in Russia making it mandatory to share medical information with the public. Like his colleagues, Roitman emphasized that Radio Liberty promotes democratic values but that the alleged free press in Russia is not yet responsible enough to make superfluous a medium that combines knowledge of domestic issues with the Western perspective.[11]

"Russia Yesterday, Today, and Tomorrow," the oldest running feature program in the Russian service, is produced by Wladimir Tolz, a longtime staff member and specialist in Russian history. In 1996, Radio Liberty commemorated the fortieth anniversary of Khrushchev's secret speech to the Twentieth CPSU Congress, considering it a "turning point for our listeners and for world Communism." Khrushchev's son and grandson, and Gorbachev and even Lavrenti Beria's mistress and son, were quoted. Tolz is already planning a series that will survey the twentieth century, which he calls "Summing Up the Century." Renowned Moscow historian Yuri Afanasyev is cooperating with him in preparing the programs.[12]

Roman Kupchinsky, director of the Ukrainian service, grew up in the United States after his family of Ukrainian refugees immigrated in 1949, and he fought in the American army during the Vietnam War. He is in charge of a "fine network of stringers" in cities throughout Ukraine and often travels to Radio Liberty's Kiev bureau. Now that the broadcasts are heard on medium wave as well as short wave, about 70 percent of the population can hear them. The feedback from the audience is gratifying, and even includes the president of Ukraine. Kupchinsky is friendly with the foreign minister, whom he often visits (always bringing a bottle of scotch). The minister told him that the president of Ukraine telephones to find out what the Radio said when he misses a broadcast. Kupchinsky was surprised to learn from an audience survey in 1995 that 50 percent of the audience is composed of young people from seventeen to forty years of age. "This is the elite and the upcoming elite, and in a few years they will be eager consumers when we go commercial and advertise."

Because Ukraine cannot afford to pay correspondents abroad, Radio Liberty fills that vacuum with a large network of stringers in cities of the West. The Ukrainian program consists of a five-hour day, with two hours in the morning from 6 to 7 o'clock and 8 to 9 o'clock, and three hours in the evening from 8 o'clock to 11 o'clock. The first seven minutes are a newscast live from Prague, and the remainder of the first hour deals with Ukraine and its relations with Russia, and with other former Soviet republics, NATO, and the European Community. "This is important for a nation trying to assert itself. Radio Liberty is trying to drag them into the twenty-first century." The second hour treats international affairs, and the third hour is strictly on domestic issues. Kupchinsky contrasted his Prague staff's motivation to work with the motivation of the majority of the staff in Munich, whose sick days numbered in the hundreds. "These kids here are from Ukraine and earn $35,000 a year where they would get $50 a month at home." As a matter of fact, he added, there are about 40,000 Ukrainians now in Prague who work illegally, earn $300 a month, stay six months, and then go home to pay their bills.[13]

Goulnara Pataridze, director of the Georgian service, was born in Paris in the Georgian émigré community. On the Radio's staff since 1967, she finally visited Georgia in 1992, where she met with the president, Eduard Shevardnadze, Gorbachev's erstwhile foreign minister, who regards Radio Liberty as one of the main sources of information for his citizens and an "absolute necessity." Shevardnadze himself broadcast over the station on one occasion.

Pataridze anticipated that a Radio Liberty bureau would soon open in Tbilisi. (It did.) She is optimistic about the future of Georgia, although she disagrees with Shevardnadze that the nation will be as strong as Western countries in three or four years; she says it will more likely take ten years or more. Most of her staff are recent arrivals from Georgia, and she draws on stringers from inside the country for a major portion of the program, which deals more with current events than with historical themes, because a great deal has already been published in Georgia, including old broadcasts of Radio Liberty.[14]

Tengis Gudava, a young Georgian, is actually a member of the Russian service. He is a former Soviet dissident, having been in the Tbilisi group of Helsinki monitors that was founded in the late 1970s. Gudava covers such topics as Central Asia and the Caucasus, including Chechnya, and political, economic, and cultural problems. He said that the impact of the Radio's broadcasts on him when he was still in Georgia was "super-colossal." It had the greatest influence on his psychological and political maturity: "We should blame Radio Liberty for our becoming dissidents." He called the present post–Cold War period a "cold peace" fraught with uncertainty and danger.[15]

An exciting, innovative project of the Radio is a training program for promising journalists from most of the nations of the former Soviet Union. Bonnie Mihalka, a young American, is in charge of the program. These young people come in groups of eight to ten—thirty-five already in 1996—and work half the time in the various language services and in the studios in addition to formal instruction. (The Voice of America, the BBC, and Deutsche Welle also have trainees but do not allow them to enter the broadcast area.) They are welcomed by the respective directors and their staff as representatives of a coming generation of talented journalists in their countries.[16] Kevin Klose explained to me that he "cut a deal" with the *New York Times* Foundation for Independent Journalism, which has a center for teaching journalism in Central Europe. He invited them to occupy "free digs" in RFE/RL's Prague headquarters in return for access to their training cycle and some trainers. Radio Free Europe and the Foundation operate in coordination with each other, so "we're getting a synergy that's very important. They've done training cycles now for literally hundreds of young broadcast and print journalists."[17]

Quality control of Radio Liberty's broadcasts and the measurement of the listening audience was handled for two years after 1994 by the Open Media Research Institute (OMRI), a nonprofit, public-service center located in Prague and originally supported by philanthropist George Soros. The institute took over the extensive RFE/RL archives, which it maintained and made accessible to the public at large; it regularly published news and analysis of developments in Eastern Europe and the Soviet Union and trained analysts and journalists from the region. OMRI was best known for the "Daily Digest," a six-page compendium of latest news from the target countries, available on Internet.

After 1996 the operation reverted to RFE/RL. The Audience and Opinion Research Department (AOR), later renamed InterMedia, is based in Washington with Gene Parta in Europe as director of research and evaluation for RFE/RL. It supplies American government radios with demographic and psychographic analyses of the listeners, and by means of focus groups and in-depth interviews provides the broadcasters with specific information on reactions to the programming, the personalities at the microphone, and the production quality. It also follows trends in domestic (that is, former Soviet-area) media, tracks trends in public satisfaction with those media, and tracks long-term trends in public opinion with annual surveys, capturing "snapshots" of attitudes during crisis periods. Broadcasters, policymakers, and scholars obtain a deeper understanding of public views and expectations. InterMedia also conducts in-country monitoring of international broadcasts, providing audibility reports and comparison of content and presentation with domestic media.

InterMedia commissioned a Moscow research firm to survey Russian programming for Radio Liberty during the three months from mid-December 1995 to mid-March 1996, to obtain evaluations from seven panelists who were regular listeners to the Russian service in the previous year and who were avid followers of domestic media and current events. The panelists recruited represented geographically dispersed cities and diverse ages and professions.

Three U.S.-based experts provided a parallel evaluation of the same

Radio Liberty programming: Gerd von Doemming, retired, formerly chief of the Eurasian (previously USSR) Division of VOA from 1986 to 1994 and director of Radio Liberty's Russian service in Munich from 1982 to 1985; Dr. Thomas Remington, professor of political science at Emory University in Atlanta, Georgia; and Dr. Ariel Cohen, Salvatori Fellow and senior analyst, Russian and Eurasian Studies, The Heritage Foundation, Washington, D.C.

The in-country panelists listened to the broadcasts at home (whenever possible, those rebroadcast on medium wave), and the expert panelists listened to taped recordings of the broadcasts provided by Radio Liberty. All the panelists completed an evaluation questionnaire for each daily program and for the week's programming as a whole. In addition, the in-country panelists were asked to monitor the quality of reception of Radio Liberty broadcasts during the same week.

InterMedia concluded that the station came across as "a highly professional, objective and innovative source of information on a broad range of political and cultural affairs with relevance to a Russian audience." The in-country panelists and the external control listeners all agreed that the Russian service provided "a geographical and topical diversity of reporting that is unparalleled by any one source available in Russia today." They declared that "the combination of a highly professional creative and editorial staff in Prague, a broad network of skilled domestic correspondents, and access to reporters around the world" allowed the service to present reporting "that is often up-to-the-minute, on-the-spot and in-depth."[18]

During the review period, reporting on the Russian parliamentary elections and on Chechnya stood out for their excellence. The in-country panelists felt that their understanding of topics like the peace process in the Middle East and the Balkans, the problems surrounding military service in Russia, the American presidential primaries, and recent news from the world of science and technology increased considerably. Perhaps even more than news reporting, the panelists believed that it was the very strong cultural and nontopical programming that set the Russian service apart from all other broadcast media. Much of the cultural, scientific, economic, and historical programming reviewed was praised for having a unique approach, a distinctive style, and original and thought-provoking commentary and analysis of events and developments in and affecting Russia. The panelists repeatedly asked that more such programming be included in the schedule. They stressed the need for more views of outside experts and for more background and deeper analysis of issues close to home, such as corruption, lack of legality, ineffective decrees, and obstacles to reform.

The production quality of the broadcasts was also well received. The use of stringers and the quality of language impressed the reviewers; they found many of the programs "easy to listen to and absorb because of the logical formatting, skilled moderation and 'personality' of the contributors." However, shortcomings in production quality mentioned by the panelists included a lack of promotional material informing listeners of upcoming items in the hour and in other programs; delivery that was too slow and monotonous on some occasions and too quick on others; occasional careless editing and language mistakes; and poor use and choice of music at times.

While Radio Liberty was a top-notch news and information service, it was said to be "losing ground as a provider of meaningful commentary and analysis and, in doing so, risks becoming too similar to domestic media." The Radio must make clear distinctions between news and opinion in its programming. While all admired the Russian service's consistent efforts to air a broad range of views, they cautioned that failure to clearly define commentary or to counterbalance commentary with analysis could leave the listener with the impression that the Radio was advocating certain viewpoints. Some of the reports they heard were "somewhat condescending," reflecting their heightened sensitivity to Russia's present image in the post-Soviet era when the country is no longer a superpower.

Gerd von Doemming commented favorably: "These hours are a rich source of information highly tailored to an audience in Russia. . . . The station sounded not like a *surrogate* domestic station but, in both sound and content, like the real thing." Von Doemming did not detect any particular slant or bias, and he "came away with the impression that RL was a reliable news source without any particular ax to grind."[19]

Ariel Cohen was more critical of the broadcasts he reviewed, precisely because they did not appear to him to be taking a firm stand on many vital issues. Although the programs were "timely and reasonably informative," he believed that "U.S. national interests need to guide the broadcasting policy." He recommended increasing the exposure of listeners to Western values and opinions. Making Radio Liberty into another Moscow-centered radio operation misses the point of taxpayer-funded Western broadcasting to the former Soviet Union. Radio Liberty needs to deal more with "human rights, the rule of law, discussions of crime and corruption and their corrosive effect on post-Soviet societies."

It should also fight ethnic prejudice, ultranationalism, economic ignorance, and anti-Western sentiments, and promote religious tolerance and political pluralism. Such a policy focus would promote Russia's integration into the international political, security and economic system, which remains a paramount Western goal. In short, RL needs to more clearly define itself as a bridge between East and West and as the radio of democratic, pro-Western, anti-authoritarian ideas that it was at the peak of its popularity. RL should be careful that stringers do not unintentionally slip a snide, ironic or critical tone against the West.[20]

In March 1996, six of the seven in-country panelists were still evaluating the programs. The sole external control listener who provided a parallel evaluation of the same programming was Sarah Oates, a Ph.D. candidate in political science at Emory University. She had spent eight months conducting research in Russia during 1995–96 and was in Moscow when the programming under review was broadcast.

The in-country panelists were favorably impressed with the timeliness and relevance of the news coverage, especially of Chechnya, and the nontopical programming filled significant gaps left by incomplete coverage in the domestic and other international media. It was the unique cultural, scientific, economic, and historical programming that made the service "truly distinctive." Such series as "Seventh Continent," "Ex Libris," and "Russia Yesterday, Today, and Tomorrow" were singled out. Oates stated that the broadcast on the 1956 Twentieth Congress of the CPSU "presented a fresh and unique perspective on Russian history and culture." Local correspondents were praised as highly professional stringers whose depth of coverage was considered to be one of the Russian service's greatest strengths.

On the negative side, two of the panelists and the external control listener detected instances of what they perceived as "anti-Russian bias." Although these were isolated comments not shared by the majority, they nevertheless suggested that there is a heightened sensitivity to the issue of Russia's image.

Program moderators like Lev Roitman and Inna Svetlova were particularly complimented for their skill in handling their roundtables and choosing issues of vital concern to the public. Roitman's program dealt with the theme "To Whom Does the Land in the Russian Federation Belong?" with Nikolai Shmelev, writer, economist, and corresponding member of the Academy of Sciences of the Russian Federation, and Yuri Chernichenko, a prominent publicist and leader of the Peasant Party of Russia.

Svetlova's *Kontakty* roundtable discussion treated problems surrounding military service in Russia and aired the comments of a press secretary for the Committee of Soldiers' Mothers of Russia; a psychologist; a faculty member of the Moscow City College of Attorneys; a member of the editorial board of the newspaper *Sobesednik;* and the chairman of the State Duma Committee on Defense. This subject of military service struck an emotional chord among the panelists, who appreciated that a full hour of programming was devoted to this pressing and controversial issue but said that a representative of the military should also have been invited. Svetlova was praised for her poise and tactful moderating without imposing her personal position on the participants.

Radio Liberty and its audience were deprived of this uniquely talented and attractive personality when, tragically, Svetlova (Molly Gordin) was shot to death in 1997 while walking from the Prague railroad terminal to the Radio's offices. After the Radios moved from Munich, she continued to live there and commuted to Prague every few weeks for her broadcasts. The motive for her murder is still unclear. For Gloria and me, who were her close friends for thirty years, it was a shocking and irreparable loss.

"Over the Barriers," the cultural program that for many years emanated both from Radio Liberty in New York and from Munich, was now produced by Ivan Tolstoy in Prague. A commemoration of Joseph Brodsky forty days after the poet's death discussed his last works, his final days, and the memorial service held for him in the Cathedral of St. John the Divine in New York, reported by correspondents Aleksandr Genis and Raya Vail. The program received high marks for its journalistic and production quality, which combined poetry, music, and commentary. Unlike most of the native panelists, Oates was not completely satisfied with the program and raised a fundamental question:

> As a tribute it was a tastefully done program on a beloved Russian poet. Yet perhaps these programs are not particularly useful for the modern Russian listener. Does this coverage attract listeners who are struggling to survive in a difficult economic and political situation? Does it better orient them to democratic values, which is the goal of Radio Liberty? I find these questions difficult to answer, but it is an issue that Radio Liberty needs to confront. Can listeners be attracted by having something that is familiar to them—that is, an elegy for a poet—or is it better to present more cutting edge programs in the "Over the Barriers" time slot?[21]

The appropriate emphasis of Radio Liberty programming in recent post-Soviet years is a subject of continuing controversy. Ariel Cohen's criticism of the Radio's lack of American focus was more passionately expressed in 1995–96 by Vladimir Matusevich, mentioned earlier as a long-time member of the Radio's Russian staff and director of the service in Munich from 1987 to 1992. Matusevich has complained to congressmen that Radio Liberty is "turning into a Russian national radio station," declaring:

> Approximately 80 percent of what is broadcast by RL's Russian service is being supplied by freelance contributors, citizens of the Russian Federation. Those freelancers are compiling material not only on Russian topics; they are also doing programs on international politics, including U.S. foreign policy problems. They are taking part in broadcasting, not only as reporters and correspondents but also as moderators and editors.
>
> The U.S. International Broadcasting Act of 1994 defines RL's goal as "promotion of information and ideas, while advancing the goals of U.S. foreign policy." Can journalists of Russia, who live in Russia and are totally dependent on the Russian authorities, be seriously expected to work towards "advancing the goal of United States foreign policy"? It would be immoral to expect or demand that from them.[22]

Matusevich further charged that lack of adequate editorial control by management allowed the Russian contributors to engage in "anti-American propaganda, using American taxpayers' money" and "they were not stopped from claiming to listeners that American policy in the Middle East is dictated by American oil companies" and that those same companies "ordered an exposé from the *New York Times* about an alleged ecological catastrophe in northern Russia (October 24, 1994)." Nor were the Radio Liberty writers in Russia "stopped from accusing Americans of wholesale racism. 'Americans are not interested in adopting children from Asia, Africa and Latin America, but tow-headed Russian children meet the highest standards' (November 18, 1994)."

Matusevich was harsh in his criticism of Radio Liberty's coverage of the war in Chechnya. No correspondents were present during the first six weeks of the war, at a time when the domestic media were demonstrating "a nearly miraculous coming of age of an independent, aggressive and professional Russian journalism." He concluded: "What is now happening to RL is doubly dangerous in light of the difficult and unpredictable situation in Russia. However, it is precisely in the light of that situation that the restoration and maintenance of RL as an influential, alternative, American radio station is of extreme importance to U.S. interests."[23]

Matusevich was not alone. Andrei Sinyavsky, who had frequently broadcast on Radio Liberty from Paris together with his wife, Mariya Rozanova, expressed his deep disillusionment with the Radio's Russian programming in the later 1990s. In his book *The Russian Intelligentsia,* based on a series of lectures at the Harriman (formerly Russian) Institute of Columbia University, the venerable writer and critic declared:

> A virtually unimpeded seizure of foreign territory has begun. What kind of territory? One of the most striking examples is the occupation of the American radio station, Radio Liberty. You will recall how Soviet power fought with it for several decades, how it was unmasked in all the Soviet newspapers, how many times it was infiltrated by Soviet agents, who poisoned and destroyed it, and how the security department of Radio Liberty examined each staff member inside out to check whether he didn't smack of Communism.
>
> And today? Without pain, without blood, without resistance, the American station has virtually ended up in Russian hands, and 90 percent of the time it plays up to the Russian czar [Yeltsin]. Similar things are happening in England with the BBC.[24]

On the other hand, Aleksandr Solzhenitsyn in his book *Russia in Collapse,* published in 1998, criticized Radio Liberty for turning itself into "something like a Chechen radio station" during the two-year war in Chechnya. The implication was clear that Radio Liberty was not backing the Russian side as he would have wished.

Larissa Silnicky, the Radio's chief Washington correspondent for the Russian service, is a native of Odessa who lived for many years in Prague, where she was an interpreter for Dubček at his meetings with Brezhnev and other Warsaw Pact leaders in Bratislava shortly before the invasion of 1968. She left for Israel with her Czech husband, and in the late 1970s they emigrated to the United States. A dedicated member of the Radio Liberty staff for twenty years, Silnicky has covered the American scene and also interviewed scores of Russian official and unofficial visitors from Moscow.

Silnicky says that some of the adverse criticism of Russian programming is valid. It is more important to fulfill the purposes for which Congress and the American taxpayers continue supporting the Radio, instead of trying to be a voice of the Russian people, as it was in the past, when they could not speak freely under the Soviet regime.

> I cannot talk about the Radio in general because I am familiar only with the work of the Russian desk. I don't think that the goal has to be the same for the different desks. In my opinion, because of the quantity and quality of the Russian domestic media, "Svoboda" has to find its own niche to make it attractive and recognizable to Russian listeners. I think that the Radio has to maintain the character of a foreign radio and not to become one of several radio stations. I am a little troubled by the support of the Radio which was expressed by the leaders of those new democracies where we are broadcasting, because journalists are the eyes and ears of democracy, and as a rule leaders who are exposed to criticism from an independent press very rarely love it. I cannot imagine that the president of the United States would formulate his gratitude to some American radio or TV station or newspaper.

Silnicky believes that the focus should be on providing the audience with the perspective of experts on democratic values like human rights, the peaceful aims of NATO, and Western policy. At the same time, "Russians want to hear solid analyses from Americans about what's going on in their country. Radio Liberty's unique contribution should be to offer a dimension lacking in their own media."[25]

Early in 1998, I interviewed the InterMedia director, Mark Rhodes, and the deputy director, Susan Gigli, in Washington. They pointed out that the Russian service of Radio Liberty is not only widely accepted in the Russian Federation but also the dominating foreign medium in all the countries of the newly independent states. Its network of bureaus in the capitals of former Soviet republics includes Yerevan (Armenia), Baku (Azerbaijan), Alma Aty (Kazakhstan), Bishkek (Kyrgyzstan), and Tashkent (Uzbekistan). Gigli said: "If you go to Yerevan, Baku, Alma Aty, Bishkek, most of the people we interviewed—80 to 90 percent—get their information from Russian television, which is very good and very professional. But to get an alternative point of view on NATO enlargement, where are they going to get that? Foreign voices provide that. Besides, big gas and oil moguls are behind Russian TV, and those who pay call the tune."

Rhodes added that Radio Liberty serves as an "insurance policy, keeping local media honest." Listeners want to understand more about global interdependency and their stake in it than domestic journalists can provide with their insufficient training and limited access to sources. As Gigli put it: "They want to know where they fit in the world, what they really need to do to bring their economy and medical standards up. They want pragmatic advice, not Cold War talk, straight, objective news. 'Treat us like grownups; don't talk like superiors.' "[26]

InterMedia gave me several hours of audiotapes of RL Russian programs, and I was able to confirm the validity of the judgments made by recent focus groups that underscore the continuing appeal of the Radio. Later in 1998, Gigli informed me that evaluations of listener panels continue to praise the high quality of the Radio's several language services. She added, however: "It is becoming increasingly difficult to view the Radio as an 'alternative' to domestic media that are becoming increasingly professional, entertaining, and competitive. Rather, it would be more accurate to say that the Radio is now an important 'supplement' to domestic media." As far as Matusevich was concerned, Gigli said that InterMedia had "absolutely nothing to substantiate any of his criticisms. On the contrary, we have evidence to refute his claims that the Radio is anti–United States or anti-Semitic."[27]

The Clinton administration demonstrated its understanding of the importance of RFE/RL when Hillary Rodham Clinton celebrated U.S. Independence Day on July 4, 1996, at the Radios' Prague headquarters, accompanied by President Havel and Madeleine Albright, then U.S. ambassador to the United Nations and later secretary of state. The First Lady's speech was translated into twenty-three languages and beamed to Eastern Europe and the former Soviet Union. She told her listeners:

> Today I am speaking to you from the new headquarters of Radio Free Europe/Radio Liberty in Prague. Not long ago, members of an old-style Soviet parliament filled this room. Today hundreds of independent journalists report the real news from within these walls. Not so long ago, this was a place where ideas were suppressed. Today, it is a place where ideas are given life and a voice that delivers them from the heart of this young democracy to the Baltics in the north, the Balkans in the south, and all the way east to the Pacific Ocean.

Mrs. Clinton also commented on the Russian presidential election: "Tens of millions of people exercised their democratic franchise by voting and opting to shape their future through peaceful free choice. What a hopeful milestone for Russia and us all."[28]

Kevin Klose is convinced that Radio Liberty will continue as a "vital, vibrant part of American foreign policy and American public diplomacy."

In a lengthy interview on C-Span in October 1996, he defended the Radio against opponents who called for its termination as a waste of the taxpayers' money. A foreign policy analyst at the libertarian Cato Institute in Washington, who appeared on the same program, argued:

> We are at a point where we drastically need to shrink government, and we need to get rid of all nonessential functions. During the Cold War this was very relevant and quite important to win the hearts and minds of those in the Communist countries. However, the ideological component is more or less over. . . . They are no longer debating whether democracy and free markets are the way to go. . . . It's a luxury we simply cannot afford to support these programs.
>
> There are now many more opportunities for the private sector to take that role, not only in terms of the media but every time you have business opening and cultural exchanges, any sort of contact whatsoever, you are in fact doing something to promote civil society and American ideals, and that is something that is more properly done by private individuals and private organizations, not the U.S. government.

Klose replied that the Radios were indeed seeking nonfederal support by the end of the 1990s in accordance with the sense of Congress in the law passed in 1994. Meanwhile, he said, it was vital to support the broadcasts. He quoted a letter from Leonid Kravchuk, former president of Ukraine, sent to Bob Dole, then majority leader of the Senate:

> Recent press reports state that the Congress of the United States wants to substantially decrease the budget of Radio Liberty, the motivation being that the Cold War is over and Liberty has no role to play anymore. This reasoning is very wrong. As a former president of Ukraine, I can assure you that Radio Liberty continues to play a very important role in Ukrainian society. Its moderate tone and high quality of information is a vital source of information for us about events taking place in our country and the world. To end its broadcasts now would be a great setback to democratization in Ukraine and other former republics of the USSR.

Klose pointed out that other leaders in Eastern Europe, including the "embattled democratic parliamentary coalition in Belarus," praise Radio Liberty's standard of "openness, of many voices being heard" that cannot be met at present by the local indigenous media, which lacked not only professional journalistic know-how but also sufficient funds.

In 1996, Klose became director of the International Broadcasting Bureau (IBB), which is responsible to the Broadcasting Board of Governors (BBG) established by the 1994 law and supervises U.S. government media such as the Voice of America, Radio Marti, and Internet. RFE/RL and Radio Free Asia are independently funded by grants from the BBG. Klose, still vitally concerned about the fate of RFE/RL, told me early in 1998:

> I think RFE and RL are essential elements in place and powerful in trying to assist democratic and economic transformation in the former Soviet bloc and former Soviet Union. I was in Moscow at Christmas time [1997] with my family and took the opportunity to talk to my friends there from twenty years ago when I was the *Washington Post*'s bureau chief from 1977 to 1981. I asked people, "Do you listen to Western radio?" They are the general Moscow intelligentsia, various age-groups from their late thirties to sixties and seventies, already with careers. They answered that "right after the collapse of Communism in the early 1990s, when we got a stable government with Yeltsin, we basically ceased listening to Western broadcasts or listened less because our own media was growing, our own indigenous Russian media, and it was being taken back from the state." However, in the last year and a half the continuing successful buying-up of all the main media, both print and electronic, by the big new oligarchical combinats—Lukoil, Inkombank, etc., these combinations of banks and energy companies, the hearts of the old Soviet economic empire, which have built themselves into single conglomerates—made people very sensitive to the fact that these newly owned media are starting to spout the line of their owners as opposed to doing independent and objective news and current affairs broadcasting. They have gone back to listen principally to the Russian service of Radio Liberty. That's what they told me, absolutely unanimously.[29]

The current president of RFE/RL, Thomas Dine, succeeded Klose in 1996. In 1998 he shared with me his perspective about the present and future of the Radios:

> As our listeners and the leaders of the countries to which we broadcast tell us, Radio Free Europe/Radio Liberty is needed now more than ever. First, a majority of the countries in our broadcast region are anything but open and free. Governments control the media, brutalize journalists and the political opposition, and attempt to keep their people in the dark. For such countries, our traditional role as a surrogate

broadcaster continues to be vital. And our mission continues to be the promotion of the establishment of truly democratic societies including free speech and a free press.

Second, all of the countries are finding the transition to democracy quite difficult. Democratic values are not understood; institution building will thus evolve over generations. Here RFE/RL plays the role of an alternative prod to change, cooperating with those parts of the media that are free while providing them with an ally against those parts that still are not.

And third, a few of the countries have now made the transition to democracy and have a press that is genuinely free. But even here, the people directly involved tell us that we continue to play a key role, as a model of the best journalistic standards and as an insurance policy against any return to the past. Indeed, every time someone has suggested closing one of our services to these countries, such as the Czech Republic and the three Baltic countries, people and leaders from them have strenuously objected, perhaps the best testimonial to our continuing role.

But as the new century approaches, we at RFE/RL will be playing yet another role: broadcasting to countries like Iran and Iraq that have never been part of our broadcast region before but that definitely need outside assistance to make the transition to democracy and full integration with the international community. And because we are likely to be entrusted with broadcasting to other such countries in the future, RFE/RL may play an even bigger role in the twenty-first century than it has in this one.[30]

★ ★ ★

I am convinced that Kevin Klose and Tom Dine are sound in their judgments. Grigory Yavlinsky, leader of *Yabloko*, a democratic, reformist party, echoes them in his article in *Foreign Affairs*. He observes that the Russian domestic media have become "entirely controlled by the oligarchs, who are part of the government and use their editorial boards and programmers to promote their own selfish agendas. . . . By reading a certain paper or watching a certain television station, a Russian citizen got either one or another robber baron's version of the truth." Yavlinsky added: "Depressingly, the Russian service of Radio Free Europe / Radio Liberty remains Russia's primary supplier of impartial news, just as it was in Soviet times."[31]

The deteriorating state of the economy has intensified growing disillusionment with the Yeltsin regime's flawed version of Western capitalism. Combined with the volatility of Russian politics and the ongoing antagonisms in the "near abroad" nations, these are all factors creating an atmosphere of uncertainty about the future. At the same time, the popularity of the Radio may be increasingly threatened by the rise in anti-American sentiment.

After decades of struggle by the peoples of Russia and the former Soviet republics for a decent life of freedom and peaceful construction—a struggle in which Radio Liberty has played such a significant role—the cherished goal still seems elusive. When RL was in its infancy, we liked to say that our mission would be accomplished if we could preside at our own funeral. But in the words of a Russian song popular among the soldiers in World War II, "It's too early to die / We still have things to do at home."

The Radio must continue as a strong link between the American people and the people of the newly independent states of the former Soviet Union. The glory days of Radio Liberty may be over, but its message still needs to be heard. Radio Liberty must complete its mission of democratic education to help ensure lasting peace in the twenty-first century.

Appendix

More than forty American, Western European, and Russian émigré writers, critics, and scholars responded to Radio Liberty's invitation to commemorate the seventy-fifth anniversary of Fyodor Dostoyevsky's death in 1956 by sending messages to the Soviet audience. In addition, statements were received from other well-known émigrés—a sculptor, a painter, a cellist, a pianist, and a psychiatrist.

Seven contributors are reproduced here. Others included were Yuri Annenkov, M. K. Argus, W. H. Auden, Lyman Bryson, G. V. Deryuzhinsky, John Dos Passos, Clifton Fadiman, James T. Farrell, René Fuelop-Miller, Igor Gouzenko, Granville Hicks, William Hubben, Noemi Eskul Jensen, Joseph Wood Krutch, Kermit Lansner, N. O. Lossky, Jacques Maritain, Arthur Miller, Ernest Nagel, Pierre Pascal, Henri Peyre, Gregor Piatigorsky, Nadia Reisenberg, Ignazio Silone, Ernest Simmons, Isaac Bashevis Singer, Marc Slonim, Harrison Smith, Pitirim Sorokin, I. Z. Steinberg, Fyodor Stepun, Gleb Struve, Lionel Trilling, Henri Troyat, V. S. Yanovsky, Avrahm Yarmolinsky, Boris Zaitsev, Gregory Zilboorg.

STATEMENT OF ALBERT CAMUS

RL ANNOUNCER: Listen now to a letter about Dostoyevsky which we have received from one of the greatest French writers of the younger generation, Albert Camus. Camus has won fame not only for his novels *The Stranger* and *The Plague* and his essays and plays, not only for his own very great literary talent, but also for the clarity, precision, and consistency of his creative outlook. In his own country and far beyond its borders he has gained exceptional respect even from his opponents. All know that he is one of the few who embody the conscience of young France. [In 1957 he won the Nobel Prize for Literature.] Here is what Albert Camus writes:

CAMUS: Several months ago I had a visitor, a very fine young man from the Soviet Union, who greatly surprised me by complaining that few of the works of Russian writers were, as he saw it, translated into French. I gave him more accurate data on this score, saying that we have more and better translations of the works of the great Russian writers of the nineteenth century than of any other writers. The young man from the Soviet Union was especially impressed by my assertion that French literature of the twentieth century would have been quite different were it not for Dostoyevsky. To remove any doubt in his mind, I said: "Look, you are now in the workroom of a French writer who has been in the thick of the intellectual battles of our age. Look there, whose portraits has this writer hung up on the wall?"

He looked up and beamed. I have only two portraits in my room: Tolstoy and Dostoyevsky.

This smile of my young friend was of the kind that makes us forget all the political idiocy and cruelty which are so common in our time and which separate people artificially. I think that this smile had nothing to do with France or Russia but was a response to that creative fervor which knows no national boundaries and which pervades the prophetic works of Dostoyevsky. I read his books when I was twenty years old—and now, twenty years later, the shock that I then experienced is as strong as ever. I consider *The Possessed* in the same category as the *Odyssey, War and Peace, Don Quixote,* Shakespeare's plays—the greatest works of world literature, the crowning achievements of the human spirit.

One reason for my admiration for Dostoyevsky is that he revealed before my eyes the very essence of human nature. Really "revealed." For Dostoyevsky teaches us what we already knew secretly about ourselves but what we refuse to admit openly. A second reason for my admiration developed soon after: insofar as I felt the heavy weight of the tragic events of our times, I valued Dostoyevsky as a person whose insight reached ever to us, and who expressed with incomparable profundity our historical destiny. For me, Dostoyevsky is above all a writer who, long before Nietzsche, was able to trace the outlines of contemporary nihilism, to foresee its monstrous consequences, and to show us how we could save ourselves from it. His main theme is "the spirit of denial and death" (as he himself called it) which demands limitless freedom, a freedom in which "all is permitted" and which leads either to the destruction of everyone or to universal enslavement. Dostoyevsky's personal suffering arose from the fact that he could neither reject this spirit nor accept it. His tragic hope was that mankind would overcome humiliation by humility, and nihilism by renunciation.

The man who wrote that the question of God and immortality is identical with that of socialism, although bearing a different name, this man knew that either all of us will be saved or none at all. But he also knew that universal salvation is impossible as long as we turn our eyes away from the sufferings of *even one single being*. In other words, he could not accept a religion which was not socialistic, in the broadest sense of the word, nor could he accept a socialism which was not religious—again in the broadest sense of the word. In this way he could save the true religion of the future as well as the true socialism of the future, although the contemporary world does not seem inclined to follow him in either respect.

Nevertheless Dostoyevsky's greatness—like Tolstoy's, who said essentially the same thing, only in different words—has not ceased to grow, because the world in which we live will either die or be saved by following precisely that road which Dostoyevsky has shown us. And whether our world dies or is regenerated, Dostoyevsky will be proved right in either case. That is why he reigns in all his grandeur over our literature and our history. That is why, even today, he gives us hope and helps us live.

STATEMENT OF GEORGI ADAMOVICH

RL ANNOUNCER: You will now hear the Russian literary critic Georgi Viktorovich Adamovich on Dostoyevsky. Adamovich has spent many years in Paris. He is one of the most prominent of Russian émigré critics. At present he teaches Russian literature at the University of Manchester in England:

ADAMOVICH: The contradictory, unusually complex, daring, and passionate works of Dostoyevsky were assessed at far less than their true worth by his contemporaries. His works won universal acclaim only in our own time. There is not the slightest doubt that of all writers of the near or distant past Dostoyevsky has exerted the greatest influence on all modern literature, the only exception being Soviet literature. One can appreciate and point out the various formal virtues of his novels, his masterful plot construction, and lastly, the care with which he portrays the social background—the result of his study of Balzac. But if this were all there was to his work, it would leave unexplained the powerful impression he makes on the reader.

The most notable characteristic of Dostoyevsky is his revelation and illumination of man's spirit; he saw in it features which no one had seen hitherto. Dostoyevsky was not merely a remarkable novelist but a kind of Columbus who opened up a new world. The feelings that make up his novels are exceptional, unusual; they are not, however arbitrarily thought up but are shown with faultless psychological insight. In this sense it can be said without any exaggeration that all of modern literature is divided into two periods: Dostoyevskian and post-Dostoyevskian.

Along with this, and to some extent resulting from this, Dostoyevsky seems to me to be questionable as a writer—although this statement does not in the slightest degree cast any reflection on his enormous significance. Rather the other way around: it underlines his significance.

My critical reservation about Dostoyevsky is connected with the question: where do his work and the whole world he has created lead us? Can the new, unknown elements which Dostoyevsky revealed in human nature persist as culture develops or are they a manifestation of morbidity, destined to vanish? More briefly put, is Dostoyevsky's path an impasse or does it really take us into a limitless future?

The question can be phrased much more simply. If Dostoyevsky's life had not been so dreadful, if, for example, he did not have to await execution in Semenovsky Square, if he had not been sent to a hard labor camp—would he have written any differently? Did conditions which cannot be considered normal and natural for a man have any influence on the character of his creative work? And if this influence did exist, does it not therefore follow that Dostoyevsky's works do not hold good for all people?

Similar doubts inevitably arise in connection with *The Idiot* and *The Brothers Karamazov*. The answer is not clear. But there is no doubt that these unanswerable questions provoke the reader to thinking about matters which only a great and brilliant writer can suggest to him. Not to speak of the fact that these questions will force many to review and reappraise the events of our age.

There is, however, one work by Dostoyevsky to which the word "questionable" cannot be applied under any interpretation. Leo Tolstoy regarded it as the best work in all Russian literature, adding in all sincerity, "including Pushkin." This book is *Memoirs from the House of the Dead*. If any one book were to be recommended for careful study by our contemporaries, especially by Russians, then this book is the one to begin with. You won't find a book that is more truthful, or which would inspire a greater and firmer faith in the Russian people, in its inexhaustible spiritual forces and its capacity for preserving the true human character under the most frightful ordeals.

STATEMENT OF FRANÇOIS BONDY

RL ANNOUNCER: You will now hear a letter on Dostoyevsky from the well-known Swiss journalist, François Bondy. Bondy was editor of the literary section of the Swiss newspaper, *Weltwoche*. At the present time he is the editor of the French magazine *Preuves*:

BONDY: That Dostoyevsky's views are still extremely up-to-date, and that the power of his word is great, is most expressively proved by the fact that the Communist dictatorship almost totally banned him for a long time and Soviet textbooks on literature devoted just a few lines to him. And if now the Party regime no longer is able to ignore Dostoyevsky, this proves once again that the thirst for true art and true thought has become very strong among the younger generation of the Russian people.

A dictatorship cannot make use of Dostoyevsky for its propaganda purposes. He condemned any form of compulsion, any form of coercion over man. He foresaw the appearance of a totalitarian state and the forms of a dictatorship which did not exist in his times.

If Dostoyevsky is a thorn in the dictatorship's side, if it is so difficult for the dictatorship to have him serve it, can we, I mean, all those who believe in the free future of his country, rely on him?

Berdyayev and many other outstanding Russian philosophers abroad are still trying to find in Dostoyevsky's works political doctrines which could be applied in practice. I think that these attempts are doomed to failure and that Dostoyevsky's works contain no ready political answers to political questions. André Gide was right when he said: "Dostoyevsky is a man whom one cannot use for one's personal purposes."

True enough, Dostoyevsky cannot be "mobilized" for the defense of any cause. He turned a deaf ear to the ideas of democracy. Political freedom was not his prime ideal. He had no clear political views.

Dostoyevsky's stand was a dual one. And the greatness of his visions is indissolubly connected with the duality of all of his nature. Dostoyevsky is neither a revolutionary nor a counter-revolutionary. He sees both the problems of freedom and the problems of oppression. And this is precisely what Dostoyevsky teaches us: a writer should not be a kind who can be "made use of"; it is not the writer's business to suggest prescriptions and dictate various "trends." The task of a writer is rather not to be made use of, to be "inconvenient," to be an obstacle in the way of various simplifications and ready-made formulae.

Like Dante, Shakespeare, Goethe, or Tolstoy, Dostoyevsky belongs to those writers who transform us. A man who has understood Dostoyevsky ceases to be the one he was before. This change of a man's nature should not be regarded from the utilitarian viewpoint or from the viewpoint of this or that ideology. Dostoyevsky's creative work is richer than any ideology. The point is that his creation is addressed to man who is *spiritually free*. And his creative works help every individual to become spiritually free.

STATEMENT OF BENNETT CERF

RL ANNOUNCER: Here is Bennett Cerf, American publisher of Random House and Modern Library editions:

CERF: As a publisher I am proud to have been able to help bring before the American public for more than a quarter of a century the English translations of Dostoyevsky's works. Hundreds of thousands of copies of *Crime and Punishment, The Brothers Karamazov, The Possessed, The Idiot* and a collection of his most notable short stories have, through Random House and the Modern Library, given English-speaking readers an insight into the character of the Russian people that neither rigid control nor decrees of conformity can ever succeed in changing. The influence of his books in this country has been enormous. They have done more to reveal to us the true nature of the Russian spirit than all the propaganda that has washed and receded from our shores since the Revolution almost forty years ago.

It is a commonplace to say that Dostoyevsky was a great psychologist and a tormented prober into the innermost recesses of the soul. He was that and far more. Uncompromisingly he fought uniformity and he believed with all his heart that the principle of brotherly love was capable of solving the problems of mankind. His trust in the people was as people and not as instruments through whom power could be obtained and used for political purposes.

The emphasis of all his writing, it seems to me, is against the quick and easy solutions that are promised in political slogans and the cold and heartlessly efficient blueprints of a planned society. To him liberty was not at the disposal of an all-powerful, centralized state, but had its origin in the human heart and its fulfillment in an enriched life for all humanity.

Seventy-five years after Dostoyevsky's death his books are in greater demand in America than ever before. The reason is not far to seek. Americans and Russians and people all over the earth have long known and cannot be made to forget that compassion and forgiveness make the whole world kin.

STATEMENT OF SALVADOR DE MADARIAGA

RL ANNOUNCER: We broadcast a letter from one of the most prominent contemporary Spanish writers, an enemy of Franco's regime and an émigré, Salvador de Madariaga. A former ambassador of the Spanish republic, he now lives in Oxford, England. He writes not only in his native language, but—and with equal skill—in French and English. His books about Spain, about the national traits of the Spaniards, Frenchmen, and Englishmen, about Columbus, and the history of Latin America have won him worldwide renown:

DE MADARIAGA: Since the time when I read *The Brothers Karamazov* as a student in Paris this book has become for me the greatest novel of our time and the only one which can be put on the same level with *Don Quixote.* All other novels written by Dostoyevsky appear to me to be only milestones on the way to this greatest among his creative works. The scope of its ideas and the depth of thought, the astounding sincerity, the power of conviction and expressiveness, the poignancy and dramatic cogency of this novel are such as to make it surpass all other works of contemporary literature. I think that the only novelist of the recent past who could be compared with Dostoyevsky is a profoundly humane writer, though, unfortunately, little known outside of Spain, Perez Galdos.

What Galdos has in common with Dostoyevsky is the ability to penetrate to the very depth of the human soul and to present what he sees there in living and vivid images. Galdos differs from Dostoyevsky in that he remains placid while describing the most tragic events. Dostoyevsky's weakness is his constant pessimism which prevented him from endowing Alyosha Karamazov with the same fullness of life with which he endowed Ivan. But Dostoyevsky greatly surpasses Galdos, as well as all others, in the incomparable intensity of creative force and that demonic power which probably only Beethoven and Goya possessed besides Dostoyevsky.

This feature of Dostoyevsky's creative work is based on his ability to concentrate his thought to the utmost. This makes it possible for him to create unforgettable scenes and overwhelming images in a few powerful lines. Let us recall, for example, the legend about the Grand Inquisitor in *The Brothers Karamazov*. This added episode presents in the most concise form an embodiment of the entire epoch of human history. It is more than prophecy—it is a whole revelation of the past, present, and future. And in what a stirring, dramatic form!

The majority of Europeans admit now that the Spanish and the Russian peoples have a certain inner kinship. I have heard that the character of Don Quixote enjoys great popularity among the Russian people. In Spain, everybody reads *The Brothers Karamazov*. If a survey were conducted to find out what books especially interest the readers in Spain, I am sure Dostoyevsky would prove to be the most popular among the foreign writers. And there is nothing strange about it. The Spaniards are attracted by Dostoyevsky's sincerity, by his wish to show without embellishment everything that his inquisitive mind discovers. And of course, what attracts them most is the fact that his creative works are human, that they are not confined to a class or a nation. It is exactly this feature which is especially akin to the spirit of Spanish literature. That is why Dostoyevsky's books are read by everyone in Spain, by the most educated and by the plain people. Our greatest contemporary writer, Unamuno, owed a great deal to Dostoyevsky.

STATEMENT OF SIDNEY KINGSLEY

RL ANNOUNCER: Kingsley is a well-known American playwright of contemporary social conditions in the United States:

KINGSLEY: Today, seventy-five years after his body has been laid to rest, Dostoyevsky is very much alive. Here, in the Western world, one can hardly read a thoughtful, contemporary novel or glance at the book reviews in the Sunday papers without coming upon some direct reference to Dostoyevsky.

There is very good reason for this tremendous renaissance of interest in his work. The central theme of his writings has now become the central theme of the world struggle. Years after his death Lenin wrote that while Hegel had invented the dialectical triad to prove the existence of the soul, Marx had used it to *disprove* the existence of the soul. Dostoyevsky had prophesied this: it was this very problem that obsessed his titanic mind, long before anyone had heard of Lenin.

By turning his eyes inward and examining his own tortured spirit, as no one before or since, Dostoyevsky divined not only that the soul existed, undeniably, but that it was a battleground between the forces of good and evil. He saw that the new religion of irreligion, scientific materialism, in expounding the mechanistic man, was transforming the world into a schizophrenic nightmare. He knew that men could not be reduced to clockwork things. By turning his eyes inward and examining his own tortured spirit, as no one before or since, he knew that men could sooner survive without air than without a moral atmosphere; and that there could be no moral atmosphere without man's recognition not only of his own soul, but of the souls of his fellow men.

The metaphysical conflict Dostoyevsky then depicted has now (as we know too well to our sorrow) grown into the physical conflict by which all the earth is torn today. Thus, on the one hand, we have nations dedicated to the creed that all men are possessed of a soul; and, therefore, of certain unalienable rights which are above and beyond the power of the state; rights which are a matter of individual conscience as between men and their God. On the other hand we have Communism, which asserts that the state is God, and the individual man is at best a machine to be used solely at the whim and will of a few men who are in control of the state, and if at any single moment a man ceases to tick according to their pleasure, he can be stamped upon, crushed and tossed like scrap metal into a junk yard without a qualm.

Mr. Fuelop-Miller, whom you have heard on this program, has pointed out in a splendid and scholarly book that at the time Dostoyevsky wrote *Crime and Punishment* a clerk who was arrested in Moscow justified his crime on the same grounds as Raskolnikov. I should like to add to the record an observation of my own. Some time ago, in writing a play which was called *Detective Story,* I spent many years preparing for it by studying the criminal mind. I talked to criminals in and out of police stations. I got to know many of them intimately and time and time again I have heard them justify themselves in Raskolnikov's *identical words.*

These, mind you, were men who had never heard of Dostoyevsky. Their justification, like Raskolnikov's, is the moral insanity that results when any man regards himself as superman. This pattern is so *typical* in criminal circles that the phrase "Superman" is part of the everyday jargon of the average detective. They can often spot a criminal by the mere fact that he possesses such a philosophy and expresses points of view similar to those of Raskolnikov.

Yes, Dostoyevsky knew his subject well, and for that reason he made it quite clear that in *Crime and Punishment* he was writing a much broader allegory. This, too, we have seen come to pass. In our time we have seen master criminals possess themselves of entire nations, enslave whole peoples, using as an *instrument of power* this identical criminal philosophy. Hitler used it, Mussolini used it, Lenin used it, and in the name of the means justifying their "superior" ends, they have drowned the world in blood. Raskolnikovs, all of them. Unrepentant, unabsolved Raskolnikovs.

And so we see the conflicts of the human heart, which Dostoyevsky explored with so much passion and described with such sensitivity, become in our time the literal battlegrounds of the world; we see the forces he described as good and evil become banners under which the nations of the world march. Let us all, however, take heart from Dostoyevsky's prophetic mind. True, he foresaw the dreadful apocalypses of our time, but after them and coming out of their purgatory, he also saw (and with the clearest of vision), the ultimate and ineluctable triumph of the human soul.

STATEMENT OF MICHAEL KARPOVICH

RL ANNOUNCER: Professor Michael Karpovich of Harvard University is the chairman of the Department of Slavic Languages. He is also the editor of *Novy Zhurnal,* a Russian literary journal published in New York:

KARPOVICH: To me Dostoyevsky is not only a great writer and one of the most profound psychologists in world literature. I see his outstanding merit also in the fact that he makes us face problems, which for everyone of us have a decisive and vital significance. I have in mind not those of his ideas which deal with the issues of Russian and European life of his time, not his political views, not even his thoughts on the historical fate and mission of Russia. All these are debatable and often self-contradictory. Dostoyevsky, the political thinker, is a far lesser Dostoyevsky than the one who in his artistic works raised philosophical, more precisely, ethical problems, which referred to the very essence of human nature and human life. And this he did not as a didactic moralist, not by the way of using dry abstractions, but as a great writer who succeeded in interpreting these problems with the literary images he created. One might say, that in Dostoyevsky's novels ideas are incarnated in their characters, and the characters live in the realm of ideas.

For Dostoyevsky, the fundamental problem was that of human freedom. To him, freedom meant first of all freedom of will, freedom of choice between good and evil. In this moral freedom he saw both the greatest right granted to man by God, and man's greatest responsibility. Everyone must himself make the choice between good and evil, and everyone must carry the responsibility for the choice he has made. Two equally great dangers meet the man on this way. Some people, out of weakness, out of the fear of responsibility, can give up their right to freedom, submit themselves to an authority imposed upon them from the outside, and agree to accept a ready-made truth from other peoples' hands. Others, on the contrary, convinced of their—in fact, more apparent than real—sublime strength, are likely to substitute a proud self-will, an egotistical arbitrariness for a properly understood freedom of will. These people deny the other, in their eyes inferior, men any right to freedom and they forget about their own responsibility not only before men but also before God.

By following the fate of those unforgettable literary characters which Dostoyevsky has created, we can see how in both cases man inevitably comes into a tragic impasse and often to his final doom. It is this central idea of Dostoyevsky which makes him so vitally important and such a modern writer. In our own days, and in my native land in particular, the problem of the freedom of will has become unusually acute. More than ever we have to think of every man's right and duty to make his *own* choice between good and evil, between truth and falsehood—a right and a duty that belong to him alone, not to a state, a nation, a class or a party—as he alone has been created in God's image and likeness.

Notes

INTRODUCTION

1. *Wall Street Journal*, August 26, 1991.

2. In addition to the mass of interview material gathered by the Project, which Western scholars in several disciplines found valuable for their research, two books were published by Harvard University Press: R. A. Bauer et al., *How the Soviet System Works* (1956); and Alex Inkeles et al., *The Soviet Citizen* (1959).

3. Joseph Berliner, Alexander Dallin, Herbert Dinerstein, Robert Feldmesser, Mark Field, Kent Geiger, Sidney Harcave, John Orton, and John Reshetar.

CHAPTER 1: RADIO LIBERTY'S CONCEPTION AND BIRTH

1. Jon Lodeesen, a Russian-speaking RL executive in programming and policy from 1969 in Munich until his untimely death in Washington in 1993, was working on a history of Radio Liberty. In an article "Radio Liberty (Munich): Foundations for a History," *Historical Journal of Film, Radio, and Television* 6, no. 2 (1986), he wrote that the idea of an American-sponsored radio station in Germany dates back at least to 1946. General Lucius Clay, then military governor of the American occupation zone, objected to a State Department initiative as contrary to the "spirit of the quadripartite government." Clay changed his mind later. The article is a valuable source of information and insights on the evolution of Radio Liberty, as are hundreds of other documents in the voluminous Jon S. Lodeesen Papers, deposited in the Georgetown University Library Special Collections Division, a gift of Peggy Jean Lodeesen, 1996.

2. Other members of the board in the early years of Amcomlib included Mrs. Oscar Ahlgren, former president of the American Federation of Women's Clubs; John R. Burton, banker; Hon. Charles Edison, former secretary of the navy and former governor of New Jersey; J. Peter Grace, industrialist; Allen Grover, vice-president, Time Inc.; H. J. Heinz II, industrialist; Henry V. Poor, counsel for the New York State Division of Housing; Dr. John W. Studebaker, educator; William L. White, newspaper publisher; and Philip H. Willkie, banker.

3. See Anatole Shub, "Papa Knew Best," *New Leader,* September 9–23, 1991.

4. Boris Shub, *The Choice* (New York: Duell, Sloan & Pearce, 1950).

5. Denicke fled the Soviet Union in 1917 and lived in Germany, where he wrote prolifically for anti-Communist publications. When the Nazis came to power in 1933, he emigrated to France and later to the United States. He became a consulting historian for such organizations as Harvard's Russian Research Center and the United States Information Agency under the name of George Denicke.

6. In 1959, Goul succeeded Mikhail M. Karpovich, who had been editor since 1946. Karpovich was in Washington as the press attaché of the Russian Provisional Government in 1917; later he became a venerated Harvard professor.

7. Other members of the NYPS included Vyacheslav K. Zavalishin, Viktor F. Rossinsky, and Vladimir S. Varshavsky. For more on Goul, see John Glad, *Conversations in Exile* (Durham, N.C.: Duke University Press, 1993). For Varshavsky and Goul, see Gleb Struve, *Russkaya Literatura v Izgnanii* [Russian Literature in Exile] (Paris: YMCA-Press, 1984). For Denicke, see Leopold Haimson, *The Making of Three Revolutionaries* (New York: Cambridge University Press, 1988).

8. See Michael Scammell's magisterial biography, *Solzhenitsyn* (New York: W. W. Norton, 1984), 765–69, where he describes the Russian author as a longtime admirer of Schmemann through his Radio Liberty broadcasts. Scammell writes: "It may even have been a broadcast of Schmemann's that inspired Solzhenitsyn to compose his 'Lenten Letter.'" The letter, written early in 1972, was a sharp criticism of the Russian Orthodox church, which he accused of preaching to émigrés to foster love for the church while remaining silent at home and selling out to the state. Father Schmemann was deeply impressed with the letter when it reached the West, and he began his Easter sermon over Radio Liberty by comparing Solzhenitsyn with the Old Testament prophets, who "could not experience peace and self-satisfaction, who swam, as they say, against the tide, told the truth, proclaimed the heavenly judgment over all untruth, weakness, and hypocrisy. . . . And now this forgotten spirit of prophecy has suddenly awakened in the heart of Christianity. We hear the ringing voice of a lone man who has said in the hearing of all that everything that is going on—concessions, submission, the eternal world of the church compromising with the world and political power—all this is evil. And this man is Solzhenitsyn."

Solzhenitsyn heard the broadcast and later wrote that he was "profoundly moved to hear that my favorite preacher had given me his approval. This in itself was my spiritual reward for the letter, and for me, conclusive confirmation that I was right." Scammell observes that from then on Solzhenitsyn began to speak out more boldly, seeing "'the finger of God' in events that befell him and regarding himself as a 'sword' in the 'Hand of the Highest'" in opposing his enemies. After Solzhenitsyn was exiled in 1974, he and Schmemann met and became friends, although the priest later criticized the writer's ultraconservative views.

See also Serge Schmemann's remarks concerning his father's Radio Liberty broadcasts in *Echoes of a Native Land: Two Centuries of a Russian Village* (New York: Knopf, 1997), 16–18.

9. In Russian: "*Vy zhertvoyu pali v bor'be rokovoi, / V lyubvi bezzavetnoi k narodu, / Vy otdali vsyo, chto mogli, za nego, / Za zhizn' ego, chest' i svobodu.*"

10. Alec Nove, in his *Glasnost in Action: Cultural Renaissance in Russia* (Boston: Unwin Hyman, 1989), 4, recalls this excision of Beria and describes the BSE's elimination of an entry on an eminent medical scientist named Zelenin. As the volume with the letter Z was

going to press, he was arrested. "A hasty substitution occurred: Zelenin was replaced by a short note on *Zelenaya lyagushka*, 'green frog,' thereby providing the only known instance of a professor being turned into a frog. Readers will be glad to know that Zelenin was released, and the 'green frog' disappeared from subsequent editions of the encyclopedia!"

11. James Critchlow, *Radio Hole-in-the-Head/Radio Liberty* (Washington, D.C.: American University Press, 1995).

12. *London Sunday Times,* December 21, 1952. Berlin added that Weidle's pages on St. Petersburg "are perhaps the best ever devoted to that immortal city."

13. See Laszlo Dienes, "Gaito Gazdanov," *Harvard Magazine,* January–February 1998, 48.

14. Other non-Russian desk chiefs who served for many years included Torossian (Armenian), Akber (Azerbaijani), Cvirka (Belorussian), Khodarov (North Caucasian), Josefoglu (Tatar-Bashkir), Zunnun (Turkestani), and Dobriansky (Ukrainian). In New York: Gustav Burbiel (Ukrainian) and Jan Zaprudnik (Belorussian).

CHAPTER 2: WE ARE ON THE AIR!

1. Author's collection.

2. Isaac Don Levine, Isaac Patch, and other Americans strove mightily during the early 1950s to coalesce these disparate groups of Soviet émigrés, following the model of the Eastern European émigrés working with Radio Free Europe's parent organization, the Committee for a Free Europe. But it was much more difficult and frustrating to convince basically incompatible Russian and non-Russian groups, and the Coordinating Center did not survive for long. The Russian signatories of the Wiesbaden declaration were Boris Nicolaevsky for the League of Struggle for Freedom of the Peoples, with headquarters in New York; Victor Baidalokoff for NTS, the National Labor Union, in Limburg, West Germany; Boris Yakovlev for SBONR, the Union of Struggle for the Liberation of the Peoples of Russia, in Munich; Professor Serge Melgunov for the Union of Struggle for the Freedom of Russia, in Paris. Also signing were representatives of the Georgian National Council in Paris; the Azerbaijan Committee of National Unity in Ankara; the North Caucasian Anticommunist Union in Munich; the Belorussian Democratic Republican Union in Paris; the Armenian Union of Freedom Fighters in Stuttgart; and the Turkestan National Committee in Munich. The Ukrainian émigrés, then embroiled in political disputes with the Russians, joined later. See Isaac Patch, *Closing the Circle* (Wellesley, Mass.: Wellesley College, 1996); and the Jon S. Lodeesen Papers, gift of Peggy Jean Lodeesen, 1996, Special Collections Division, Georgetown University Library.

3. Author's collection.

4. Ibid.

5. The other North Caucasian languages were Avar, Adyge, Karachai-Balkar, and Ossetian. In 1954, Radio Liberty printed a brochure produced by all the non-Slavic desks to commemorate the first anniversary of their broadcasts. Its fifty pages reproduced the texts in English translation of representative commentaries in each language. They dealt primarily with the Communist repression of their peoples' ethnic and cultural identities and expressed the hope of eventual "liberation from the Communist dictatorship in the Kremlin."

6. Author's collection.

1. Author's collection.

2. Kennan wrote that Kelley assembled in his division "the best library on Soviet affairs in the United States." During the negotiations over recognition of the Soviet Union in the early 1930s, Foreign Minister Maxim Litvinov "paid him the bitter compliment of saying that the division had better records on the history of Soviet diplomacy than did the Soviet foreign office itself." George F. Kennan, *Memoirs, 1925–1950* (Boston: Little, Brown, 1967), 84. Kelley was named vice-president of the Radio Liberty Committee when Amcomlib's name was changed in July 1964. His duties in Munich included maintaining relations with West German government officials. When he died in 1977, he bequeathed his collection of rare coins from the Byzantine and early Greek periods to the American Numismatic Society. The collection, which he quietly and systematically built up during his years in the foreign service, was estimated at half a million dollars, according to the Department of State newsletter of April 1977.

3. Meyer's memoir, *Facing Reality: From World Federalism to the CIA* (New York: Harper & Row, 1980), includes a chapter on Radio Free Europe and Radio Liberty from his vantage point as chief of the CIA's International Organizations Division. For most of the period from 1954 until the early 1970s, when the CIA's connection was terminated, Meyer was responsible for providing policy guidance and support for both Radios. "In dealing with these two organizations, our basic principle was to give the top American management the widest possible autonomy and to delegate to them the responsibility for day-to-day decision-making."

Meyer describes how the CIA worked out an arrangement with the Department of State under which they cooperated in drafting an annual guideline for each country to which the Radios broadcast. In times of crisis, they relied on the American management to ensure implementation, but as a check each month his staff reviewed one day's taped broadcasts, chosen on a random basis, to identify mistakes in tone and content. "Journalists and historians in the past have commented on the dangerous degree of freedom that these private radios seemed to exercise in influencing U.S. relations with the Soviet bloc. In fact, this missing link did not exist, and our control function, although not publicly evident, served to keep the broadcasts responsive to official policy."

"My staff and I saw our job as one of protecting the integrity and credibility of the Radios within the broad guidelines laid down," said Meyer. He related how pressures to distort the purpose of the Radios came occasionally from within the CIA. "Ingenious schemes to use the Radios in disinformation campaigns against particular Communist leaders were raised from time to time, and my answer to all such proposals was negative. Compromise of the reputation for reliable accuracy that the broadcasts had come to enjoy was not worth the ephemeral and dubious advantage that might be gained by the use of false information."

Meyer also states that Allen Dulles's faith in the thirst of educated Soviet citizens for knowledge led him to convince skeptical Congressional committees to supplement Radio Liberty's budget by more than $5 million for the construction of the powerful shortwave transmitter base in Spain, which Howland Sargeant proposed.

4. In an interview in Prague in October 1996, Richard Cummings, for many years RFE/RL's security officer in Munich, reaffirmed for me that the KGB was almost surely involved in Fatalibey's murder.

5. Volodya was born Zhabinsky, but his pen name was Yurasov; his American name

was Vladimir Rudolph. Shortly after he arrived in the United States from Munich in 1951, he was "discovered" for Radio Liberty by Robert Dreher, a Soviet area specialist in the CIA who had served as a naval officer in Moscow. Rudolph impressed Dreher as the kind of "decent Russian" who would be an asset to the future radio station. After Volodya was hired, Dreher himself joined Amcomlib in New York as head of the radio division in the early years.

The Rudolph family gave me scores of Volodya's radio scripts and reminiscences, one of which describes his confidential meeting—and all-night pub-crawling—with Yevgeny Yevtushenko and Andrei Voznesensky in New York in 1961. Both poets praised his writing in émigré publications, which they read in Moscow, and in guarded language let him know that they had heard him on Radio Liberty and urged him "not to make counterrevolutionaries" of them when he broadcast about them. Voloyda lived to witness his rehabilitation in reprints of his poetry and a laudatory biography in Moscow magazines during Gorbachev's era.

6. Excerpts from the writers' messages are from the Amcomlib booklet *A Free Voice at the Soviet Writers' Congress*, 1955.

7. One of the exiles wrote a poem in reply to Pushkin's message, assuring him that their grievous labors were not in vain and that "from the spark there will ignite a flame." This phrase became popular among the Russian revolutionaries at the end of the nineteenth century, and the Social Democrats, led by Lenin and Plekhanov, chose *Iskra* (Spark) as the title of their underground newspaper.

8. *A Free Voice at the Soviet Writers' Congress*, 1955.

9. These letters are in the author's collection.

CHAPTER 4: A BRIDGE OF IDEAS BETWEEN WEST AND EAST

1. The Americans who sent messages were Harold Willis Dodds, president of Princeton University; Buell G. Gallagher, president of the College of the City of New York (CCNY); Henry T. Heald, chancellor of New York University; Millicent C. McIntosh, president of Barnard College; George N. Shuster, president of Hunter College; Vannevar Bush, president of the Carnegie Institute of Washington; James T. Babb, librarian of Yale University; George S. Counts, professor of education at Teachers College, Columbia University; Joel H. Hildebrand, president of the American Chemical Society; H. J. Muller, professor of zoology, Indiana University and Nobel Prize laureate in Physiology and Medicine, 1946; Wendell M. Stanley, professor of biochemistry, University of California and Nobel Prize winner in Chemistry, 1946; Conway Zirkle, professor of biology, University of Pennsylvania.

2. Excerpts from messages are from the Amcomlib booklet *A Free Voice at the Moscow University Bicentennial*, 1955.

3. Amcomlib booklet *A Free Voice Salutes the Rebels of Vorkuta*, 1955.

4. Excerpts from messages on Dostoyevsky are in the author's collection.

5. Letter from Boris Shub to the author, January 13, 1956.

6. Harvey Breit, "In and Out of Books," *New York Times Book Review*, February 26, 1956.

7. When Singer died in July 1991, I sent his statement on Dostoyevsky to the *Forward*, the English language Jewish weekly. Singer had published his stories regularly in the Yiddish newspaper of the same name for many years before he attained world fame as a Nobel Prize laureate. The editors printed it and credited Radio Liberty with having broadcast it to the Soviet Union in Yiddish. For the 150th anniversary of Dostoyevsky's birth in 1971, the Radio rebroadcast Singer's message, along with others from the 1956 series.

1. The CIA apparently obtained it from the Israeli secret service Mossad, which was in contact with a Polish Communist Party functionary. Ray Cline, then a high official in the Agency's Directorate for Intelligence, judged the text to be genuine and urged its publication. See Thomas Powers, *The Man Who Kept the Secrets: Richard Helms and the CIA* (New York: Knopf, 1979), 80.

2. John Gunther, *Inside Russia Today*, 2nd ed. (New York: Harper & Row, 1962), 246.

3. Amcomlib "Policy Position Papers, June 1956 (For Internal Use Only)," author's collection. This forty-four-page report distilled the thinking of American and émigré staff members, outside consultants, and the Munich Institute for the Study of the USSR. With more than thirty years of hindsight, one can appreciate the sound analyses and suggestions contained in these papers. In addition, the views of three specialists were quoted concerning the propaganda potential for Radio Liberty broadcasts: Robert F. Byrnes, professor of history at Indiana University; journalist and author William Henry Chamberlin, one of our trustees; and Charles W. Thayer, the first director of VOA's Russian service. In order to conduct periodic surveys of expert opinion on events in the Soviet Union, Sargeant had one of his staff executives, Donald Dunham, a former diplomat, act as liaison with such State Department Russian experts as Francis Stevens and with U.S. academic and émigré specialists.

4. See Gene Sosin, "Trotsky Redux," *New Leader*, September 3, 1990. Pegged to the fiftieth anniversary of his assassination, the article was devoted to excerpts from Sedova's Radio Liberty message.

5. Full text in the author's collection.

6. Tape in the author's collection.

7. Ibid.

8. Sergei Khrushchev, *Khrushchev on Khrushchev* (Boston: Little, Brown 1990), 208–9.

9. Nikita Khrushchev, *Khrushchev Remembers: The Last Testament*, trans. and ed. Strobe Talbott (Boston: Little, Brown, 1974), 77.

10. Nikita Khrushchev, *Khrushchev Remembers*, trans. and ed. Strobe Talbott (Boston: Little, Brown, 1970), 412–13.

11. Ibid.

12. Tape in the author's collection.

13. Ibid.

14. Text in the author's collection.

15. Tape in the author's collection.

16. As cultural counselor of the U.S. Embassy in Moscow from 1967 to 1969, Yale Richmond listened frequently to Radio Liberty. In a letter dated December 11, 1969, from Howland Sargeant to Henry Loomis, then deputy director of the USIA, Sargeant expressed his gratitude for the valuable data Richmond provided about the jamming of the Radio. "As a result of his efforts, we were in a good position to evaluate our various frequencies and to adjust them accordingly." Sargeant added that Richmond "was able to tell us that our signal could be heard in the heart of Moscow," and that he "also provided RL from time to time with expert programming judgments." Richmond was succeeded by McKinney Russell, an alumnus of Radio Liberty who worked in the news department in Munich during the early years before serving with distinction in the U.S. foreign service. He was also helpful in giving Radio Liberty useful information about reception inside the Soviet Union.

17. See Sig Mickelson, *America's Other Voice: The Story of Radio Free Europe and Radio Liberty* (New York: Praeger, 1983).

18. Wilbur Schramm, "A Communications Research Man Looks at Radio Liberation," Munich, August 1957, author's collection.

19. They included Terence Catherman, Paul Cook, Richard Davies, J. T. Kendrick, William Luers, Walter Stoessel, Malcolm Toon, and Hans Tuch.

20. Text in the author's collection.

21. Ibid.

22. Tape in the author's collection. In 1996, on the eve of the Russian runoff election between Boris Yeltsin and Gennadi Zyuganov, Radio Liberty interviewed me about Mrs. Roosevelt's 1958 message and rebroadcast her tape. Kevin Klose, then president of RFE / RL, presented a copy to Hillary Rodham Clinton when the First Lady visited the Radios' new headquarters in Prague on July 4, 1996 (see Chapter 14). Mrs. Clinton had revealed a few weeks earlier that she carried on imaginary conversations with Mrs. Roosevelt in the White House, aided by a "spiritual adviser." I was pleased that she received her distinguished predecessor's real voice through my own medium—the tape recorder. See Gene Sosin, "Eleanor's Russia," *Forward*, July 5, 1996.

CHAPTER 6: LIBERATION TO LIBERTY

1. See Gene Sosin, "The Children's Theater and Drama in Soviet Education," in Ernest J. Simmons, ed., *Through the Glass of Soviet Literature* (New York: Columbia University Press, 1953).

2. See Joshua Rubenstein, *Tangled Loyalties: The Life and Times of Ilya Ehrenburg* (New York: Basic Books, 1996).

3. Some of the books dealing with the Radio give 1964 as the date of the name change, confusing it with Amcomlib's change to Radio Liberty Committee.

4. For a discussion of RFE's role in the events of 1956, see Michael Nelson, *War of the Black Heavens: The Battles of Western Broadcasting in the Cold War* (Syracuse, N.Y.: Syracuse University Press, 1997); and George Urban, *Radio Free Europe and the Pursuit of Democracy: My War Within the Cold War* (New Haven: Yale University Press, 1998).

5. Script in the author's collection.

6. *New York Times*, April 21, 1965.

7. Roscoe Drummond, *New York Herald Tribune*, July 24, 1962.

8. Roy A. Medvedev and Zhores A. Medvedev, *Khrushchev: The Years in Power* (New York: Columbia University Press, 1976), 146–47.

9. Telex from Bertrandias to Sosin, March 23, 1962, author's collection.

10. Two other women in the New York office who contributed significantly to the formulation of the Radio's programming policy were Cathryn Donohoe and Joan Beecher Malukoff. Joan was a descendant of Harriet Beecher Stowe; she later became a commentator on the Russian service of Voice of America.

11. The quotes concerning the Cuban missile crisis appeared in a Radio Liberty broadside printed a few weeks later, titled "Radio Liberty Reports on the Cuban Crisis to the Peoples of the Soviet Union." By juxtaposing a day-by-day summary of the Radio's broadcasts alongside that of the Soviet press and radio, the omissions and distortions of the latter were highlighted.

12. Letters in author's collection. For a concise survey of Radio Liberty's efforts to ascertain the composition and opinions of its Soviet audience, see R. Eugene Parta, "Soviet Area Audience and Opinion Research (SAAOR) at Radio Free Europe / Radio Liberty," in K. M. Short, ed., *Western Broadcasting over the Iron Curtain* (New York: St. Martin's Press, 1986), 227–44. David Anin (Azarchs) and George Perry were for many years executives with SAAOR.

CHAPTER 7: PROGRAMS AND CONFERENCES IN THE 1960s

1. See S. Frederick Starr, *Red and Hot: The Fate of Jazz in the Soviet Union* (New York: Oxford University Press, 1983), 270–75.

2. *New York Herald Tribune*, June 16, 1963. Starr, *Red and Hot*, 271, describes an all-night jam session at the Hotel Astoria in Leningrad in 1962, where members of the Goodman group, including Zoot Sims and Bill Crow, met Gennadi Golshtein and "other top musicians of the city."

3. Gene Sosin, "The Role of Radio Liberty," in John Boardman Whitton, ed., *Propaganda and the Cold War* (Washington, D.C.: Public Affairs Press, 1963), 96.

4. Author's collection.

5. *Neva*, no. 5, 1966.

6. Among Cantril's works is *The Invasion from Mars*, subtitled "A Study in the Psychology of Panic." First published in 1940 by Princeton University Press and in 1966 by Harper & Row, the book reproduces the script of the famous CBS radio broadcast on Halloween 1938 of Orson Welles's adaptation of *The War of the Worlds*, by H. G. Wells. Cantril analyzed the reaction of the American public to the broadcast as symptomatic of their panicky mood on the eve of World War II.

7. *New York Times*, March 21, 1964.

8. Ibid., November 30, 1961.

9. Author's collection.

10. *Belaya kniga po delu A. Sinyavskogo i Yu. Danielya* [White Book on the Case of A. Sinyavsky and Yu. Daniel], comp. Aleksandr Ginzburg (Frankfurt-am-Main: Possev, 1967), 177. The book appeared in a pocket-size edition to facilitate distribution inside the USSR. Publication of samizdat works abroad came to be known as *tamizdat* ("published over there"), and thousands of copies of dissident writings made their way back to the homeland with the help of Western organizations and individuals. Isaac Patch, *Closing the Circle*, devotes a chapter to his "Book Program," undoubtedly one of the most successful enterprises among those seeking to transmit ideas into the Soviet Union. With Howland Sargeant's backing and annual CIA funding, Ike ran the Bedford Publishing Company (separate from Radio Liberty) with a staff in New York, and highly qualified representatives in London, Paris, Rome, and Munich. Patch praises the efforts of his colleagues there: Joan Balcar, Betty Carter, Morrill (Bill) Cody, Bob Shankland, Jack Stewart, Ludmilla Thorne, and Helene Zwerdling. Not only dissidents' documents, but also hundreds of thousands of carefully selected Western books translated into Russian, reached Soviet intellectuals primarily via journalists, scholars, doctors, lawyers, and others who traveled to Moscow, and Soviet tourists who obtained them during trips abroad. Solzhenitsyn's wife, Natasha, informed Patch that during the years preceding his exile they regularly "received Western books through an intermediary who was supplied by us."

11. Ibid., 245. Sinyavsky served most of his sentence and was released in June 1971. He

emigrated to France in 1973 with his wife, Mariya Rozanova, and their son. He taught Russian literature at the Sorbonne until his retirement in 1994, and he broadcast frequently over Radio Liberty. He died in January 1997.

12. Speech at RL–New York University conference, "Communicating with the Soviet Peoples," November 19, 1965, author's collection. See "The Shortwave Audience in the USSR: Methods for Improving the Estimates," in *Communication Research* 9 (October 1982), 581–606.

13. Transcript of confidential colloquium at RL-NYU conference, November 20, 1965, author's collection.

14. Ibid.

15. As national security adviser, Brzezinski urged Carter to strengthen Radio Free Europe and Radio Liberty, and the new president's "Report on International Broadcasting," submitted to Congress in March 1977, called for eleven additional 250-KW transmitters. Brzezinski later wrote: "While the Radio should not be used to foment insurrections in the East, it should, in my judgment, serve as an instrument for the deliberate encouragement of political change." Quoted in Robert M. Gates, *From the Shadows: The Ultimate Insider's Story of Five Presidents and How They Won the Cold War* (New York: Simon & Schuster, 1996), 95.

16. Scott memorandum to Sargeant, June 1966, author's collection.

CHAPTER 8: THE MUNICH YEARS, 1966–1970

1. Pavel Litvinov, *Dear Comrades* (Amsterdam: Alexander Herzen Foundation, 1971).

2. Author's collection.

3. Marietta Chudakova, *Russkaya Mysl'*, September 21–27 and September 28–October 4, 1995. Belinkov's books are being published in post–Soviet Russia thanks to Natasha's devotion and persistence.

4. For the transcript of the conference, see Robert Farrell, ed., *Studies on the Soviet Union*, 11:2 (Munich: Institute for the Study of the USSR, 1971).

5. Author's collection.

6. Ibid.

7. Ibid.

8. Script in author's collection.

9. In an interview with Abraham Brumberg in *Encounter* (June 1977), Amalrik said: "Foreign broadcasts in Russian play an enormous role. It is the only alternative information available to millions of Soviet citizens. The role of the radio is growing for two reasons. One is simply physical: the number of transistor radios in the Soviet Union keeps on growing. And second, the activity of the Soviet dissidents is itself continually growing, and the growth of that activity is communicated and becomes widely known."

10. Oleg Tumanov, *Tumanov: Confessions of a KGB Agent*, trans. David Floyd (Chicago: Edition Q, 1993).

11. Oleg Kalugin, *The First Directorate: My 32 Years in Intelligence and Espionage Against the West* (New York: St. Martin's Press, 1994), 194–97. Kalugin alleges that Tumanov assisted in the bombing plans, and he describes the re-defection of Tumanov to Moscow in 1988 and his subsequent denunciation of Kalugin as a traitor.

12. Author's collection.

1. *New York Times,* March 19, 1967.

2. *Washington Post,* May 4, 1969. Cord Meyer, *Facing Reality,* 132–33, reviews the *Ramparts* revelations and the work of the Katzenbach report to President Johnson that recommended that no federal agency should provide any covert financial assistance or support, direct or indirect, to any of the nation's educational or private voluntary organizations. However, the Johnson administration decided that since the two Radios "were not private and voluntary as defined by the Katzenbach report but rather government proprietaries established by government initiative and functioning under official policy direction," they were still eligible for covert CIA funding. They were permitted to survive through a process called "surge funding," pending a future decision by Congress. Meyer adds that the responsible Congressional committees "accepted this compromise arrangement, but not without a struggle. Richard Helms, as director of the CIA, proved to be as able and persuasive an advocate before Congress on the subject of the Radios as Allen Dulles had been, but the going was not always easy."

3. Author's collection.

4. *Congressional Record,* July 30, 1971.

5. Ibid.

6. Joseph G. Whelan, *Radio Liberty: A Study of Its Origins, Structure, Policy, Programming, and Effectiveness* (Washington, D.C.: Library of Congress Congressional Research Service, February 29, 1972). The quotations by Whelan in the following pages are from this report.

7. *New York Times,* February 21, 1972.

8. *Congressional Record,* March 8, 1972.

9. Reprint in author's collection.

10. Speech in U.S. Senate, March 6, 1972, author's collection.

11. Author's collection.

12. Alexeyeva emigrated to the United States in 1977 after active work in Moscow as one of the founders of the Helsinki Watch Group (see Chapter 11). She regularly broadcast on Radio Liberty and on Voice of America, and although often critical about some of the RL content, she played an important role in the 1980s in publicizing Radio Liberty's influence.

13. Author's collection.

14. They included Rudolf L. Tökés, Kendall Bailes, George Kline, Alexander Dallin, Robert V. Daniels, Edgar Lehrman, and Leon Lipson from American universities; and Peter Reddaway, Leonard Schapiro, Max Hayward, and Martin Dewhirst from British universities. In addition, two recent Soviet Jewish émigrés, Leonid Rigerman and Boris Tsukerman, who had been leading activists in the human rights movement in Moscow, wrote strong letters supporting Radio Liberty.

15. Author's collection.

16. Ibid.

17. "A Setback for Liberty," *Washington Post,* February 26, 1972.

18. The debate in the Senate on the passage of S.1914, providing for the establishment of the BIB and the continuation of assistance to Radio Free Europe and Radio Liberty, was printed in the *Congressional Record* for September 6, 1973. It makes for fascinating reading, as all the arguments pro and con are aired with eloquence and passion. The principal advocates for the Radios were Senators Percy, Buckley, Javits, Goldwater, Thurmond, and Humphrey. The principal supporters of Senator Fulbright's anti-Radio position were Sen-

ators Church, Symington, and Pastore. The bill was passed by a wide margin. For a discussion of the managerial conflicts between the new Board for International Broadcasting and the Radios that continued for several years, see William A. Buell, "Radio Free Europe/Radio Liberty in the Mid-1980s," in Short, *Western Broadcasting*, 69–97.

19. "Sargeant wanted to stay on and become the first president of the merged Radios. Bill Durkee [then president of RFE] wanted out and said he would support Sargeant's candidacy, but insisted that the top position in Munich go to an RFE person. The BIB decided, however, that the new president should come from the outside. This left Howland with no choice but to leave." (Letter to the author from Ralph Walter, former director of RFE, November 14, 1996.)

20. Author's collection.

CHAPTER 10: THE TRANSITION PERIOD, 1971–1975

1. The quotations from the London conference on the following pages are from Boiter's memorandum of April 23, 1971, "The Future of Samizdat: Significance and Prospect."

2. Sosin telex to Boiter and Van Der Rhoer, October 28, 1971.

3. Script in author's collection.

4. *New York Times*, February 12, 1972.

5. Ibid., April 3, 1972.

6. Scammell, *Solzhenitsyn*, 286, relates that in January 1974 Solzhenitsyn went to his dacha in Peredelkino "to listen to the excerpts from *The Gulag Archipelago* that were already being broadcast by Radio Liberty. Although that station was still jammed, the readings could be heard with complete clarity, and for once he sacrificed part of his rigid schedule to listen to his own creation."

7. *New York Times*, February 12, 1972.

8. Fifty years after he was murdered, Mikhoels was honored in Moscow. See *New York Times*, January 14, 1998.

9. I obtained the tape thanks to Professor Herbert Paper, then of the University of Michigan and now at Hebrew Union College, Cincinnati, Ohio.

10. Quoted in *Zaklinaniye Dobra i Zla: Aleksandr Galich* [Incantation of Good and Evil] (Moscow: Progress, 1991), 293. The 500-page book is a collection of articles and reminiscences of his friends, and selections from his prose and poetry. It was compiled by Nina Kreitner, the stepdaughter of Galich's brother Valeri Ginzburg, a well-known cinematographer. Kreitner was also responsible for the production of Galich's songs by Melodiya, the Soviet Ministry of Culture's recording company. She has worked tirelessly to preserve and glorify Galich's memory.

11. Ibid., 201.

12. The quotes are from Ronalds's summary of October 1973, author's collection.

13. As early as the mid-1960s, I was active in the American human rights advocacy movement on behalf of Soviet Jews. In my lectures, I described the desperate plight of the millions in the Soviet Union who were treated as second-class citizens, denied access to the best educational institutions, discriminated against in seeking employment in certain professions, forbidden to practice their religion freely, and accused of disloyalty to the Soviet regime because of their growing determination to seek a haven in Israel. I also told these audiences about the efforts of Radio Liberty to reach Soviet Jews with messages of support from the West and broad dissemination of samizdat petitions.

For many years, Gloria and I have been members of the board of directors of the New York Association for New Americans (NYANA), a major Jewish organization that helps resettle Soviet Jews emigrating to the United States to join their relatives. We interviewed hundreds of Soviet refugees who expressed their admiration for Radio Liberty's broadcasts both on general themes and on the violation of their rights in the Soviet Union. During visits to Israel, most recently in 1996, we met many more new arrivals, who were almost without exception enthusiastic in their praise for the Radio.

One well-known refusenik, mathematician Evgeny Lein, told me that his sentence to the gulag had been reduced from four years to two years, thanks to the glare of publicity on his case by Radio Liberty, which caused embarrassment to the KGB. Lein expressed his profound gratitude to the Radio as "not only a source of information but an animating source that gave us hope of not being buried alive." (Interview, Jerusalem, May 26, 1996.)

CHAPTER 11: FROM STAGNATION TO GLASNOST AND PERESTROIKA, 1976–1985

1. BIB annual report, 1977.
2. Ibid.
3. BIB annual report, 1976.
4. Author's collection.
5. Ibid.
6. Memorandum from James Critchlow to BIB: "Problems of the Radio Liberty Russian Service," January 2, 1981.
7. Percy letter to Shakespeare, April 9, 1984, author's collection.
8. William Korey, "Flouting American Ideals," March 1984, author's collection.
9. *Newsweek,* November 28, 1983.
10. *Newsweek,* December 5, 1983.
11. *New Republic,* February 4, 1985.
12. *New Republic,* February 18, 1985.
13. Ibid.
14. *Washington Post,* March 11, 1985.
15. *Washington Post,* March 27, 1985. The *August 1914* program was one of those evaluated by a panel of recent émigrés selected by Radio Liberty. Five were Jewish and three were Russian; most of them had a higher education and were professional people. Three of the Jewish listeners objected to the program, with varying degrees of intensity: a thirty-six-year-old mathematician said that "anti-Semitism oozed from every word" and that the program would "reinforce the current notion in the USSR that responsibility for the revolution lies with the Jews, and that if we were only rid of the Jews, everything would be fine." Another panelist, a thirty-five-year-old computer programmer, said that the writer's comparison between Stolypin and Bogrov "increases the impression of anti-Semitism." A third Jewish evaluator, a forty-eight-year-old biochemist, said the program was interesting but placed "too much emphasis on Bogrov's Jewishness."
16. *New York Times,* November 13, 1985.
17. See Pyotr Grigorenko, *Memoirs,* trans. Thomas P. Whitney (New York: W. W. Norton, 1982).
18. Interview in Prague, October 3, 1996.

CHAPTER 12: THE SOVIET ERA DRAWS TO A CLOSE

1. See Gloria Donen Sosin, "The Nobel Prize-Winner Nobody Knows," *New York Times* (Westchester), January 3, 1988; "Goodbye Brodsky," *Forward,* February 2, 1996.

2. BIB annual report, 1988, 68.

3. See Gene Sosin and Gloria Donen Sosin, "Today's Soviet Hero Made His Statement with Satire," *International Herald Tribune,* July 25, 1989.

4. Among the American scholars Shragin interviewed were James Billington, Robert V. Daniels, Victor Erlich, Richard Pipes, Marshall Shulman, Robert C. Tucker, and Adam Ulam.

5. Interviews with Toomas Ilves and Paul Goble, Washington, D.C., August 1996.

6. *Shortwaves,* September 1989.

7. *Shortwaves,* July 1991.

8. Ibid.

CHAPTER 13: FROM GORBACHEV TO YELTSIN

1. *Shortwaves,* August–September 1991.

2. Scott Shane, *Dismantling Utopia: How Information Ended the Soviet Union* (Chicago: Ivan R. Dee, 1994), 266.

3. Quoted in *Russia at the Barricades: Eyewitness Accounts of the August 1991 Coup,* ed. Victoria E. Bonnell, Ann Cooper, and Gregory Freidin (Armonk, N.Y.: M. E. Sharpe, 1994), 289.

4. Ibid., 296. See also *Crisis Compendium: Analyses of Media Use in the USSR During the Coup Attempt,* prepared by Media and Opinion Research, RFE/RL Research Institute, January 1992.

5. Mikhail Gorbachev, *The August Coup: The Truth and the Lessons* (London: Harper-Collins, 1991), 27.

6. *Shortwaves,* August–September 1991.

7. Ibid.

8. Ibid.

9. Ibid.

10. Elena Bonner in *Radio Svoboda: August 19–21* (Moscow: NIKO, 1992), 3. Author's translation.

11. *Shortwaves,* October 1991.

12. Ibid.

13. Jack F. Matlock Jr., *Autopsy on an Empire* (New York: Random House, 1995), 634-47. See also Robert V. Daniels, *Russia's Transformation: Snapshots of a Crumbling System* (Lanham, Md.: Rowman & Littlefield, 1998).

14. *Shortwaves,* December 1991.

15. BIB annual report, 1992.

16. Ibid.

17. *Shortwaves,* August–September 1992.

18. Ibid., January 1992.

19. Letter from S. Berezhkova, author's collection.

20. *Vestnik Moskovskogo Universiteta,* no. 2, 1993, 52–62.

21. *Byulleten Inoveshchaniya,* no. 1, 1992, 16–17.

22. Ibid., 17.

23. Ibid., 17–18.

24. *Washington Post,* July 23, 1991.

25. *Byulleten,* 20–21.

26. Ibid., 22–23.

27. Ibid., 27.

28. Ibid., 28–29.

29. *Byulleten Inoveshchaniya,* no. 3, 1992, 3.

30. Ibid., 4.

31. Ibid., 6–7.

CHAPTER 14: RADIO LIBERTY IN THE NEW ERA OF FREEDOM

1. *Shortwaves,* April 1993.

2. Ibid.

3. Ibid.

4. Ibid.

5. *Sevodnya,* March 30, 1993.

6. *New York Times,* April 26, 1993. On the other hand, four other leading newspapers took a strong editorial stand in favor of the Radios: the *Wall Street Journal,* the *Washington Post,* the *Los Angeles Times,* and the *Baltimore Sun.*

7. Sofya Borisovna Berezhkova, *Radio "Svoboda" v Sisteme Mezhdunarodnogo Radioveshchaniya Na Russkom Yazyke* (1988–1994) [Radio Liberty in the System of International Radio Broadcasting in Russian (1988–1994)] (diss., Moscow State University, Faculty of Journalism, 1995), 165–66.

8. Interview, Washington, D.C., January 28, 1998.

9. Interview, Prague, October 6, 1996.

10. Interview, Prague, October 7, 1996.

11. Interview, Prague, October 9, 1996.

12. Interview, Prague, October 6, 1996.

13. Interview, Prague, October 8, 1996.

14. Interview, Prague, October 10, 1996.

15. Interview, Prague, October 11, 1996.

16. Interview, Prague, October 10, 1996.

17. Interview, Washington, D.C., January 28, 1998.

18. RFE/RL Russian Programming: Internal Monitoring Panel and External Control Listener Reviews, December 1995, i–iv.

19. Ibid., 29–30.

20. Ibid., 34–35.

21. Ibid., March 1996, 1–19.

22. Vladimir Matusevich, "From Radio Liberty to Radio Garden Ring Road," 1995, manuscript, in author's collection. In 1998, Matusevich resumed his attack on RL's Russian programming in an article printed in Moscow's *Nezavisimaya Gazeta* (February 24).

23. Ibid., 20.

24. Andrei Sinyavsky, *The Russian Intelligentsia,* trans. Lynn Visson (New York: Columbia University Press, 1997), 81.

25. Conversations in Washington, D.C., August 1996, January 1998, July 1998.

26. Interview in Washington, D.C., January 27, 1998.

27. E-mail, June 26, 1998.

28. Transcript of broadcast, July 4, 1996, author's collection.

29. Interview, Washington, D.C., January 28, 1998. Klose became president and CEO of National Public Radio in November 1998.

30. E-mail, June 10, 1998. NPR interviewed me in October 1998 at the time of the inauguration of Radio Free Iraq.

31. Grigory Yavlinsky, "Russia's Phony Capitalism," *Foreign Affairs* 77 (May–June 1998): 67–79.

Bibliography

Alexeyeva, Ludmilla. *Soviet Dissent: Contemporary Movements for National, Religious, and Human Rights*. Middletown, Conn.: Wesleyan University Press, 1985.

———. *U.S. Broadcasting to the Soviet Union*. New York: Helsinki Watch Committee, 1986.

Alexeyeva, Ludmilla, and Paul Goldberg. *The Thaw Generation: Coming of Age in the Post-Stalin Era*. Boston: Little, Brown, 1990.

Amalrik, Andrei. *Notes of a Revolutionary*. Translated by Guy Daniels. New York: Knopf, 1982.

———. *Will the Soviet Union Survive Until 1984?* New York: Harper & Row, 1981.

Andrew, Christopher, and Oleg Gordievsky. *KGB: The Inside Story of Its Operations from Lenin to Gorbachev*. New York: HarperCollins, 1990.

Babyonyshev, A.; R. Lert; and E. Pechuro, comps. *Sakharovskii Sbornik* [Sakharov Collection]. New York: Khronika Press, 1981.

Bauer, R. A.; A. Inkeles; and C. Kluckhohn. *How the Soviet System Works: Cultural, Psychological, and Social Themes*. Cambridge, Mass.: Harvard University Press, 1956.

Belinkova, N., ed. *Novy Kolokol* [The New Bell]. London: N.p. 1972.

Berezhkova, Sofya Borisovna. *Radio "Svoboda" v Sisteme Mezhdunarodnogo Radioveshchaniya Na Russkom Yazyke (1988–1994)* [Radio Liberty in the System of International Radio Broadcasting in Russian (1988–1994)]. Diss., Moscow State University, Faculty of Journalism, 1995.

Board for International Broadcasting. *Annual Reports*. Washington, D.C., 1974–94.

Bohlen, Charles. *Witness to History, 1929–1969*. New York: W. W. Norton, 1973.

Bonnell, Victoria E.; Ann Cooper; and Gregory Freidin, eds. *Russia at the Barricades: Eyewitness Accounts of the August 1991 Coup*. Armonk, N.Y.: M. E. Sharpe, 1994.

Bonner, Elena. *Alone Together*. Translated by Alexander Cook. New York: Knopf, 1986.

———. Introduction in *Radio Svoboda, August 19–21*. Moscow: NIKO, 1992.

Brumberg, Abraham, ed. *In Quest of Justice*. New York: Praeger, 1970.

Brzezinski, Zbigniew. *The Grand Failure: The Birth and Death of Communism in the Twentieth Century.* New York: Charles Scribner's Sons, 1989.

Bukovsky, Vladimir. *To Build a Castle: My Life as a Dissenter.* Translated by Michael Scammell. New York: Viking Press, 1979.

Chalidze, Valery. *To Defend These Rights.* New York: Random House, 1974.

Cohen, Stephen F., and Katrina van den Heuvel. *Voices of Glasnost: Interviews with Gorbachev's Reformers.* New York: W. W. Norton, 1989.

Coleman, Fred. *The Decline and Fall of the Soviet Empire: Forty Years That Shook the World, from Stalin to Yeltsin.* New York: St. Martin's Press, 1996.

Critchlow, James. *Radio-Hole-in-the-Head/Radio Liberty.* Washington, D.C.: American University Press, 1995.

Daniels, Robert V. *The End of the Communist Revolution.* New York: Routledge, 1993.

———. *Russia's Transformation: Snapshots of a Crumbling System.* Lanham, Md.: Rowman & Littlefield, 1998.

Dobrynin, Anatoly. *In Confidence.* New York: Times Books, 1995.

Dulles, Allen. *The Craft of Intelligence.* Westport, Conn.: Greenwood Press, 1963.

Dunlop, John B. *The Rise and Fall of the Soviet Empire.* Princeton, N.J.: Princeton University Press, 1993.

Eisenhower, Susan. *Breaking Free: A Memoir of Love and Revolution.* New York: Farrar Straus Giroux, 1995.

Farrell, Robert, ed. *Studies on the Soviet Union,* II:2. Munich: Institute for the Study of the USSR, 1971.

Frank, Vasily, ed. *Pamyati Viktora Franka* [In Memory of Victor Frank]. Munich: N.p. 1974.

Gates, Robert M. *From the Shadows: The Ultimate Insider's Story of Five Presidents and How They Won the Cold War.* New York: Simon & Schuster, 1996.

Gerstenmaier, Cornelia. *The Voices of the Silent.* Translated by Susan Hecker. New York: Hart, 1972.

Ginzburg, Aleksandr, comp. *Belaya kniga po delu A. Sinyavskogo i Yu. Danielya* [White Book on the Case of A. Sinyavsky and Yu. Daniel]. Frankfurt-am-Main: Possev, 1967.

Glad, John. *Conversations in Exile.* Durham, N.C.: Duke University Press, 1993.

Gleason, Abbott. *Totalitarianism: The Inner History of the Cold War.* New York: Oxford University Press, 1995.

Gorbachev, Mikhail S. *The August Coup: The Truth and the Lessons.* London: HarperCollins, 1991.

———. *Memoirs.* New York: Doubleday, 1995.

Grigorenko, Pyotr. *Memoirs.* Translated by Thomas P. Whitney. New York: W. W. Norton, 1982.

Gunther, John. *Inside Russia Today.* Second edition. New York: Harper & Row, 1962.

Haimson, Leopold. *The Making of Three Revolutionaries.* New York: Cambridge University Press, 1988.

Hayward, Max. *Writers in Russia, 1917–1978.* Edited and with an introduction by Patricia Blake. New York: Harcourt Brace Jovanovich, 1983.

Inkeles, Alex et al. *The Soviet Citizen.* Cambridge, Mass.: Harvard University Press, 1959.

Israelyan, Victor. *Inside the Kremlin During the Yom Kippur War.* University Park, Pa.: The Pennsylvania State University Press, 1995.

Johnson, Priscilla, and Leopold Labedz, eds. *Khrushchev and the Arts: The Politics of Soviet Culture, 1962–1964.* Cambridge: M.I.T. Press, 1965.

Kaiser, Robert. *Russia: The Power and the People.* New York: Atheneum, 1976.

Kalugin, Oleg. *The First Directorate: My 32 Years in Intelligence and Espionage Against the West.* New York: St. Martin's Press, 1994.

Kaminskaya, Dina. *Final Judgement: My Life as a Soviet Defence Lawyer.* Translated by Michael Glenny. London: Harvill Press, 1983.

Keep, John. *Last of the Empires: A History of the Soviet Union, 1945–1991.* New York: Oxford University Press, 1995.

Kennan, George F. *Memoirs, 1925–1950.* Boston: Little, Brown, 1967.

———. *Sketches from a Life.* New York: Pantheon Books, 1989.

Khrushchev, Nikita. *Khrushchev Remembers.* Translated and edited by Strobe Talbott. Boston: Little, Brown, 1970.

———. *Khrushchev Remembers: The Last Testament.* Translated and edited by Strobe Talbott. Boston: Little, Brown, 1974.

Khrushchev, Sergei. *Khrushchev on Khrushchev.* Boston: Little, Brown, 1990.

Klose, Kevin. *Russia and the Russians: Inside the Closed Society.* New York: W. W. Norton, 1984.

Koch, Stephen. *Double Lives: Spies and Writers in the Secret Soviet War of Ideas Against the West.* New York: The Free Press, 1994.

Krasnov, Vladislav. *Soviet Defectors: The KGB Wanted List.* Stanford, Calif.: Hoover Institution Press, 1985.

Kreitner, Nina, comp. *Zaklinaniye Dobra i Zla: Aleksandr Galich* [Incantation of Good and Evil: Aleksandr Galich]. Moscow: Progress, 1991.

Laqueur, Walter. *The Dream That Failed.* New York: Oxford University Press, 1994.

———. *The Long Road to Freedom.* New York: Charles Scribner's Sons, 1989.

Lein, Evgeny. *Lest We Forget: The Refuseniks' Struggle and World Jewish Solidarity.* Jerusalem: Jerusalem Publishing Centre, 1997.

Lisann, Maury. *Broadcasting to the Soviet Union: International Politics and Radio.* New York: Praeger, 1975.

Litvinov, Pavel, ed. *The Trial of the Four.* London: Longmans, 1972.

Lodeesen, Jon. *Jon S. Lodeesen Papers.* Georgetown University Library Special Collections Division, Washington, D.C., 1996.

Matlock, Jack, Jr. *Autopsy on an Empire.* New York: Random House, 1995.

Medvedev, Roy. *Khrushchev.* New York: Anchor Press/Doubleday, 1983.

Medvedev, Roy, and Giulietto Chiesa. *Time of Change: An Insider's View of Russia's Transformation.* New York: Pantheon Books, 1989.

Medvedev, Roy A., and Zhores A. Medvedev. *Khrushchev: The Years in Power.* New York: Columbia University Press, 1976.

Meerson, M., and B. Shragin, eds. *The Political, Social, and Religious Thought of Samizdat.* Belmont, Mass.: Nordland, 1977.

Meyer, Cord. *Facing Reality: From World Federalism to the CIA.* New York: Harper & Row, 1980.

Mickelson, Sig. *America's Other Voice: The Story of Radio Free Europe and Radio Liberty.* New York: Praeger, 1983.

Mickiewicz, Ellen. *Changing Channels: Television and the Struggle for Power in Russia.* New York: Oxford University Press, 1997.

Nahaylo, Bohdan, and Victor Swoboda. *Soviet Disunion: A History of the Nationalities Problem in the USSR.* New York: The Free Press, 1990.

Naylor, Thomas H. *The Gorbachev Strategy.* Lexington, Mass.: Lexington Books, D.C. Heath, 1988.

Nekrich, Alexander. *The Punished Peoples.* Translated by George Saunders. New York: W. W. Norton, 1978.

Nelson, Michael. *War of the Black Heavens: The Battles of Western Broadcasting in the Cold War.* Syracuse, N.Y.: Syracuse University Press, 1997.

Nove, Alec. *Glasnost in Action: Cultural Renaissance in Russia.* Boston: Unwin Hyman, 1989.

Orlova, Raisa. *Memoirs.* Translated by Samuel Cioran. New York: Random House, 1983.

Palazchenko, Pavel. *My Years with Gorbachev and Shevardnadze.* University Park, Pa.: The Pennsylvania State University Press, 1997.

Panfilov, Artyom. *Radio SShA v psikhologicheskoi voine* [U.S. Radio in Psychological Warfare]. Moscow: Mezhdunarodnye otnosheniya, 1967.

———. *Za kulisamy "Radio Svoboda"* [Behind the Scenes with Radio Liberty]. Moscow: Mezhdunarodnye otnosheniya, 1974.

Parta, R. Eugene; John C. Klensin; and Ithiel de Sola Pool. "The Shortwave Audience in the USSR: Methods for Improving the Estimates, in *Communication Research,* 9, no. 4. Beverly Hills, Calif.: Sage Publications, 1982.

Patch, Isaac. *Closing the Circle.* Wellesley, Mass.: Wellesley College, 1996.

Popov, Nikolai. *The Russian People Speak.* Syracuse, N.Y.: Syracuse University Press, 1995.

Potok, Chaim. *The Gates of November: Chronicles of the Slepak Family.* New York: Knopf, 1996.

Powers, Thomas. *The Man Who Kept the Secrets: Richard Helms and the CIA.* New York: Knopf, 1979.

Pryce-Jones, David. *The Strange Death of the Soviet Empire.* New York: Henry Holt, 1995.

Reddaway, Peter, ed. and trans. *Uncensored Russia: The Human Rights Movement in the Soviet Union.* London: Jonathan Cape, 1972.

Remnick, David. *Lenin's Tomb: The Last Days of the Soviet Empire.* New York: Random House, 1993.

———. *Resurrection.* New York: Random House, 1997.

Report of the Presidential Study Commission on International Radio Broadcasting: The Right to Know. Washington, D.C.: U.S. Government Printing Office, 1973.

Reznik, Semyon, ed. *Sakharovskiye Slushaniya: Chetvyortaya Sessiya Lissabon Oktyabr 1983* [International Sakharov Hearings: Fourth Session, Lisbon, October 1983]. London: Overseas Publications Interchange Ltd., 1985.

Rothberg, Abraham. *The Heirs of Stalin: Dissidence and the Soviet Regime, 1953–1970.* Ithaca, N.Y.: Cornell University Press, 1972.

Rubenstein, Joshua. *Soviet Dissidents: Their Struggle for Human Rights.* Boston: Beacon Press, 1980.

———. *Tangled Loyalties: The Life and Times of Ilya Ehrenburg.* New York: Basic Books, 1996.

Sakharov, Andrei. *My Country and the World.* Translated by Guy Daniels. New York: Knopf, 1975.

———. *Sakharov Speaks.* Edited by Harrison Salisbury. New York: Vintage, 1974.

Satter, David. *Age of Delirium: The Decline and Fall of the Soviet Union.* New York: Knopf, 1996.

Scammell, Michael. *Solzhenitsyn.* New York: W. W. Norton, 1984.

Schmemann, Serge. *Echoes of a Native Land: Two Centuries of a Russian Village.* New York: Knopf, 1997.

Schroeter, Leonard. *The Last Exodus.* New York: Universe, 1974.

Shane, Scott. *Dismantling Utopia: How Information Ended the Soviet Union.* Chicago: Ivan R. Dee, 1994.

Shanor, Donald R. *Behind the Lines: The Private War Against Soviet Censorship.* New York: St. Martin's Press, 1985.

Sharansky, Natan. *Fear No Evil.* New York: Random House, 1988.

Shipler, David K. *Russia: Broken Idols, Solemn Dreams.* New York: Times Books, 1983.

Short, K. R. M., ed. *Western Broadcasting over the Iron Curtain.* New York: St. Martin's Press, 1986.

Shragin, Boris. *The Challenge of the Spirit.* Translated by P. S. Falla. New York: Knopf, 1978.

Shub, Anatole. *The New Russian Tragedy.* New York: W. W. Norton, 1969.

Shub, Boris. *The Choice.* New York: Duell, Sloane & Pearce, 1950.

Sinyavsky, Andrei. *The Russian Intelligentsia.* Translated by Lynn Visson. New York: Columbia University Press, 1997.

———. *A Voice from the Chorus.* Translated by Kyril Fitzlyon and Max Hayward. London: Collins and Harvill Press, 1976.

Sinyavsky I Daniel Na Skame Podsudimykh [At the Trial of Sinyavsky and Daniel]. New York: Rausen, 1966.

Smith, Gerald Stanton. *Songs to Seven Strings.* Bloomington: Indiana University Press, 1984.

Smith, Hedrick. *The New Russians.* New York: Random House, 1990.

———. *The Russians.* New York: Quadrangle Books, 1976.

Sosin, Gene. "The Children's Theater and Drama in Soviet Education." In *Through the*

Glass of Soviet Literature, ed. Ernest J. Simmons. New York: Columbia University Press, 1953.

——. Introduction to Albert L.Weeks, *The Troubled Détente.* New York: New York University Press, 1976.

——. "Magnitizdat: Uncensored Songs of Dissent." In *Dissent in the USSR,* ed. Rudolf L. Tökés. Baltimore: Johns Hopkins University Press, 1975.

Starr, S. Frederick. *Red and Hot: The Fate of Jazz in the Soviet Union.* New York: Oxford University Press, 1983.

Stites, Richard. *Russian Popular Culture.* New York: Cambridge University Press, 1992.

Struve, Gleb. *Russkaya Literatura v Izgnanii* [Russian Literature in Exile]. Paris: YMCA Press, 1984.

Svirsky, Grigory. *Hostages: The Personal Testimony of a Soviet Jew.* Translated by Gordon Clough. New York: Knopf, 1978.

Tumanov, Oleg. *Tumanov: Confessions of a KGB Agent.* Translated by David Floyd. Chicago: Edition Q, 1993.

Urban, George. *Radio Free Europe and the Pursuit of Democracy: My War Within the Cold War.* New Haven: Yale University Press, 1998.

Urban, George, ed. *Détente.* New York: Universe Books, 1976.

Reve, Karel van het, ed. *Dear Comrade: Pavel Litvinov and the Voice of Soviet Citizens in Dissent.* New York: Pitman, 1979.

Vlady, Marina. *VLADIMIR ou le vol arrêté.* France: Fayard, 1987.

Voinovich, Vladimir. *The Life and Extraordinary Adventures of Private Ivan Chonkin.* Translated by Richard Lourie. New York: Farrar Straus Giroux, 1977.

Wettig, Gerhard. *Broadcasting and Détente.* London: C. Hurst, 1977.

Whelan, Joseph G. *Radio Liberty: A Study of Its Origins, Structure, Policy, Programming, and Effectiveness.* Washington, D.C.: Library of Congress Congressional Research Service, 1972.

Whitton, John Boardman, ed. *Propaganda and the Cold War: A Princeton University Symposium.* Washington, D.C.: Public Affairs Press, 1963.

Wohl, Josephine, and Vladimir Treml, comps. *Soviet Unofficial Literature, Samizdat: An Annotated Bibliography of Works Published in the West.* Durham, N.C.: Duke University Center for International Studies, March 1978.

Yurasov, Vladimir. *Parallaks* [Parallax]. New York: Novoye Russkoye Slovo, 1972.

Index

Bogoraz, L., 190
Bogrov, Dmitri, 181, 185, 286
Bohlen, Charles, 19, 31
Boiter, Albert, 76, 151, 154, 164, 285
Bolshaya Sovetskaya Entsiklopediya (BSE), 7
Bolsheviks, 3, 16, 20, 22–23, 25, 42, 44–45, 66, 178. *See also* October (Bolshevik) revolution
Bolshoi Theater (Moscow), 83
Bondy, François, 164, 268–69
Bonner, Elena (wife of Andrei Sakharov), xv, 173, 190, 220–23, 247
Borodin, Alexander, 23
Bourdeaux, Michael, 152
Brainerd, Gretchen, 143
Brandeis University, 146
Brandt, Willy, 186
Bratislava, 258
Breit, Harvey, 51–52
Brezhnev, Leonid, xv, 121, 167, 171–72, 193, 258
Brezhnev regime, 111–12, 117–18, 129, 156–57, 159, 166–68, 187, 192, 198
Brignola, Nick, 102
British Broadcasting Corporation. *See* BBC
Broadcasting Board of Governors (BBG) funding, 262
Brodsky, Joseph, 198–99, 256
Bronfenbrenner, Urie, 28–29
Brookmeyer, Bob, 102
Brothers Karamazov, The (Dostoyevsky), 49, 268, 270–71
Browder, Earl, 132
Brown, George, 66
Brumberg, Abraham, 21, 152, 163
Bryson, Lyman, 265
Brzezinski, Zbigniew, 113, 115, 283
Buckley, James L., 180–81, 183–84, 194
Buckley, William F., Jr., 184–85
Buell, William A., 285
Bukharin, Nikolai Ivanovich, 3, 21
Bulganin, Nikolai Alexandrovich, 58, 65, 67
Bulletin of Foreign Broadcasting (Radio Moscow), 228, 232
Bunch, John, 102
Bunin, Ivan, 11, 114, 163
Burbiel, Gustav, 277
Burks, Richard, 145–46
Burton, John R., 275
Bush, George, 224
Bush, Keith, 206
Bush, Vannevar, 279
Byrnes, Robert F., 280

California Institute of Technology, 93
Camus, Albert, 49, 265–67
Cancer Ward, The (Solzhenitsyn), 191
Cantril, Hadley, 107, 282
Cape, Jonathan (publishers), 125
Carleton University, 175
Carlos (terrorist), 193
Carter, Betty, 282
Carter, Jimmy, 115, 167, 171, 283
Case, Clifford, 29, 77, 104, 132, 134–36
Castro, Fidel, 29, 90
Cathedral of St. John the Divine (New York), 256
Catherman, Terence, 281
Catholic War Veterans, 50
Cato Institute (Washington), 261
Caucasus, 24–25, 204, 224, 251
CBS (Columbia Broadcasting System), 115, 185, 204
    "In the Pay of the CIA: An American Dilemma" (1971), 132
    "60 Minutes" program, 185–87
Center for Middle Eastern Studies (Harvard University), 175
Central Asia, 224, 244, 251
Central House of Writers (Moscow), 238, 240
Central Intelligence Agency. *See* United States government: Central Intelligence Agency, 49, 269–70
Chaliapin, Fyodor, 118
Chamberlain, Neville, 9
Chamberlin, William Henry, 2, 280
Chanukah, 166
Charles Scribner's Sons (publishers), 34
Chas Pik (Rush Hour), 212
Chechnya, 226, 251, 253, 255, 257–58
Chekhov, Anton Pavlovich, 42, 84
Chernenko, Konstantin, 168, 187, 194
Chernichenko, Yuri, 255
Chernobyl (nuclear accident), 195–96, 198, 202, 227
Chicago White Sox, 103
China (People's Republic of China), 139, 142
Chinese Communists, 92
Choice, The (Shub), 3
Christian Science Monitor, 30, 110
Christianson, Geryld B., 179
Chronicle of Current Events, 153
Chukovskaya, Lidia, 191
Chukovsky, Kornei, 118
Church, Frank, 285
Chute, B. J. (Joy), 88
CIA (Central Intelligence Agency). *See* United States government

Heritage Foundation, The, 253
Herzen, Alexander, 5, 42, 106, 152
Herzen Foundation, Alexander, 126
Hewitt, Don, 186–87
Hicks, Granville, 49, 265
Hillenbrand, Martin J., 135
Hitler, Adolf, 9, 35, 69, 90, 129
Hoffman, George, 175
Holzman, Elizabeth, 186
Hotel Peking (Moscow), 249
Hubben, William, 265
Hughes, John, 225
Hughes, Langston, 88
Humphrey, Gordon, 196
Humphrey, Hubert, 77, 284
Hungary, 60, 69–70, 205, 229, 246
Hungarian revolution (1956), 18, 68, 79, 86
"Hymn to Free Russia" (Grechaninov), 23

Idiot, The (Dostoyevsky), 268, 270
Ilves, Toomas, 211
Inasaridze, Carlo, 11
Ingster, Boris, 49
Inkombank, 262
Inside Russia Today (Gunther), 56
Institute of Sociological Research, 203–4
Institute for the Study of the USSR (Munich), 31, 121, 129
InterMedia (formerly RFE/RL Audience and Opinion Research Department), 252–53, 259–60. *See also* Audience Research Department; Audience and Opinion Research Department (AOR)
International Broadcasting Bureau (IBB), 262
International Herald Tribune, 85. See also *New York Herald Tribune*
International Ladies Garment Workers' Union, 67
International PEN. *See* PEN
International Rescue Committee, 108
International Research and Exchanges (IREX), 164
International Telecommunications Union (ITU), 201
Internet, 252, 262
Ionin, Leonid, 217
Isar River (Munich), 33, 169
Iskra (Spark), 279
Israel, 117, 119–20, 129, 147, 161, 167, 201, 258
Italian diplomatic service, 248
Ivanov, Anatoly, 188
Ivanov, Nikolai, 205
Izvestiya, 13, 20, 37, 77–78, 97–98, 124

James, Daniel, 58
jamming, 14. *See also* Radio Liberty: jamming of by Soviet Union
Javits, Jacob, 284
jazz, 101–2
"Jazz at Liberty" album, 102
Jensen, Donald, 245
Jensen, Noemi Eskul, 265
Jerusalem, 119
Jews. *See* Soviet Jews
Jews, persecution of, 84
Johns Hopkins University, 146
Johns Hopkins University Press, 188
Johnson, Lyndon B., 1, 77, 133, 284
Johnson, Ross, 248
Jonathan Cape (publishers). *See* Cape, Jonathan
Josefoglu (Tatar-Bashkir desk chief), 277
Judaism, 53, 129
Jurasas, Jonas, 192

Kabachnik, Galya, 160
Kabachnik, Victor, 160
Kabakov, Aleksandr, 205
Kaganovich, Lazar, 92
Kaiser, Robert, 158–59
Kaledin, Sergei, 205
Kalinin Bridge (Moscow), 217
Kalugin, General Oleg, 128, 192–93, 210, 238, 283
Kamenev, Lev Borisovich, 21
Kaminska, Ida, 167
Kaminskaya, Dina, 192, 249
Karaganda camp, 46
Karas, Leonid, 33
Karpovich, Mikhail M., 273–74, 276
Kartashev, Mikhail, 221
Kassof, Allen, 164
Katzenbach, Nicholas, 133
Katzenbach report, 284
Kazakhstan, 46, 259
Kazan, 4
Kelley, Robert F., 31, 116, 278
Kendrik, J. T., 281
Kennan, George F., 1, 19, 31, 278
Kennedy, Caroline, 91
Kennedy, Edward, 91
Kennedy, Jacqueline, 91
Kennedy, John F., 29, 77, 91, 96–97, 107
Kennedy, John F., Jr., 91
Kennedy, Robert F., 91
Kerensky, Alexander, 3, 23, 90
Kevorkian, Jack, 249

Library of Congress report. *See* Whelan,
    Joseph G.
Liebknecht, Karl, 66
Life, 83
Limburg (West Germany), 277
Lincoln, Abraham, 90
Lipson, Leon, 284
Literaturnaya Gazeta, 62, 124
Lithuania, 99, 172, 196, 208, 224
Lithuanian language broadcasts, 171–72
Litvinov, Maxim, 278
Litvinov, Maya, 188
Litvinov, Pavel, 117–18, 188, 190, 248
Lodeesen, Jon S., 244–45, 275
Loewenthal, Richard, 164
Loftus, John, 185
Lomonosov, Mikhail V., 42
London, 65, 85, 121–26
London conference on *samizdat*, 151–54
London conference on Soviet censorship,
    121–25
London School of Economics, 176
London Sunday Times, 10
Loomis, Henry, 75
Los Angeles Times, 288
Lossky, N. O., 265
Loy, Myrna, 49, 90
Lubyanka prison (Moscow), 105
Luce, Henry R., 132
Luers, William, 281
Lukoil, 262
Luxemburg, Rosa, 66
Luzhniki sports complex (Moscow), 209
Lvov (L'viv) (Ukraine), 39, 211
Lvov, Arkady, 167
Lyndon B. Johnson School of Public Affairs
    (University of Texas), 146
Lyons, Eugene, 2, 30
Lyubimov, Yuri, 192, 205

Madariaga, Salvador de, 49, 270–71
Madison Square Garden (New York), 69
magnitizdat, 187–88
Magnitogorsk (Urals), 131
Malamuth, Charles, 108
Malenkov, Georgi Maksimilianovich, 9, 21,
    92
Malukoff, Joan Beecher, 281
Mandelshtam, Nadezhda, 191
Mann Auditorium (Tel Aviv), 161
Mantle, Mickey, 103
Mao Tse-tung, 92
Maritain, Jacques, 265
Mariupol (Ukraine), 207

Markov, Sergei, 218
Marx, Karl, 220, 272
Massachusetts Institute of Technology
    (MIT), 75, 112, 115, 164, 173, 202
Matlock, Jack F., Jr., 208, 224
Matlock, Rebecca, 208
Matusevich, Wladimir, 177, 206, 221, 230,
    257–58, 260, 288
Matveyeva, Novella, 188
Maximov, Vladimir, 159, 177, 179, 190, 192,
    232
Mayakovsky Square (Moscow), 219, 249
McCarthy, Joseph, 51
McGiffert, Colonel S. Y. (Steve), 87
McIntosh, Millicent C., 279
McMaster University conference on *samizdat,*
    154
Meader, Vaughn, 91
Meany, George, 46
Medvedev, Roy, 92
Medvedev, Zhores, 92
Mehnert, Klaus, 164
Melgunov, Serge, 277
Melnikov, Yuri. *See* Von Schlippe, Yuri
Melodiya, 285
Memoirs from the House of the Dead (Dos-
    toyevsky), 268
Mensheviks, 3, 50, 66
mergers. *See* Radio Liberty
Meri, Lennart, 210–11, 229
Metropole Hotel (Moscow), 83
Meyer, Cord, 32, 95, 284
MGB. *See* KGB
Michener, James, 182
Mickelson, Sig, 169, 149, 180
Middle East, 253, 257
Mieli, Renato, 164
Mihalka, Bonnie, 251
Mikhoels, Natalia, 162
Mikhoels, Solomon, 162, 285
Mikoyan, Anastas Ivanovich, 58, 91
Miliukov, Pavel N., 42
Miller, Arthur, 49–52, 190, 265
Minsk, 38, 186
Mironov, Andrei, 217
Mirsky, Semyon, 249
Mogilev (Moldavia), 39
Moiseyev dancers, 81
Moldavia, as Moldova, 224, 226
Moldavia, 39, 222
Moldova. *See* Moldavia
Molotov, Vyacheslav Mikhailovich, 92
Monat, Der, 66
Moscow, 1–2, 4–6, 23, 30, 38, 41, 50, 57, 63,

66, 70, 81, 83, 85, 90, 97, 121, 124, 126, 132, 134, 153, 161–62, 167, 202–3, 206–7, 217, 219, 223, 226, 232, 238, 241, 248–49, 262

"Moscow Appeal," 190

Moscow City College of Attorneys, 256

Moscow Institute of Aviation, 124

Moscow News, 204

Moscow Party Committee, 206

Moscow Radio and Television Committee, 122

Moscow Radio, 215

Moscow State University (MGU), 42–44, 81, 99, 122, 124, 159, 218, 227–28, 245

Moscow Writers' Union, 36. *See also* Union of Soviet Writers

Mosely, Philip E., 118, 143–44

Moskva, 122

Mossad (Israeli secret service), 280

Muller, H. J., 279

Munich, 2–4, 8, 10–11, 13, 21, 27, 29–31, 33, 37, 49, 51, 68, 71, 74–75, 121, 134, 232, 245

Muslims, 201

Mussolini, Benito, 273

MVD. *See* KGB

Naby, Eden, 175

Nagel, Ernest, 265

Nagorno-Karabakh (Azerbaijan), 204, 226

Nahaylo, Bohdan, 211

Nardi, Sulamith, 119

Nash, Ogden, 104

National Broadcasting Company. *See* NBC

National Labor Union (NTS), 160, 277

National Public Radio (NPR), 289

National Students Association, 133

NATO (North Atlantic Treaty Organization), 250, 259

Nazis, 8, 71, 19, 179, 185

NBC (National Broadcasting Company), 194, 217

Negev desert, 201

Neizvestny, Ernst, 192

Nekrasov, Viktor, 163, 192, 232

Nekrich, Aleksandr, 192

Neva, 106

Nevozvrashchenets (The Defector), 205

New Leader, The, 7, 58, 62, 66–67

New Republic, The, 182–83

New Review, The. See Novy Zhurnal

New School, The, 68

New York City, 3, 23, 28, 32, 34, 37, 41, 52, 62, 68, 78, 90, 273

New York Association for New Americans (NYANA), 286

New York Herald Tribune, The, 64, 91. See also *International Herald Tribune*

New York Program Section (NYPS), 3, 6, 87

New York Public Library, 22

New York Times, 5, 45, 51, 58, 61, 63, 90, 93, 108, 133, 137–38, 140, 155, 158–59, 185, 188, 204, 230, 242–43, 251, 257

New York Times Book Review, 51, 108

New York Times Magazine, 121

New York University conferences, 112–15, 118, 279

New York Yankees, 103

Newsweek, 180–81

Nezavisimaya gazeta (Moscow), 217, 230

Nicholas II (Czar), 176, 181

Nichols, Lewis, 108

Nicolaevsky, Boris, 7, 22, 57, 277

Nietzsche, Friedrich, 266

Nixon, Richard M., 29, 133, 138–39, 146, 157–58

Nixon administration, 134

Nizhny Novgorod. *See* Gorky

Nobel Prizes, 64, 87, 93, 123, 173, 198, 209, 222, 229, 266, 279

North Atlantic Assembly, 171

North Atlantic Treaty Organization. *See* NATO

North Caucasian Anti-Communist Union, 277

North Ossetia, 226

Novak, Robert, 133, 137

Nove, Alex, 276

Novikoff, Michael M, 43–44

Novodevichy Cemetery, 155

Novosti press agency, 203

Novy Mir, 47–48, 122, 158

Novy Zhurnal (The New Review), 4, 114, 273

Nozhkin, Mikhail, 188

Nureyev, Rudolph, 163

NYPS, 21, 22

Oates, Sarah, 255

Obolensky, Valerian (Zhuk), 28, 67, 96, 108, 110, 131

October (Bolshevik) Revolution (1917), 34, 63, 73, 98, 190

Odessa, 43, 167, 197, 207–9, 258

Office of Cuba Broadcasting, 243

Okudzhava, Bulat, 188, 240

Olesha, Yuri, 5, 88

Olympic Games in Munich (1972), 164

OMRI. *See* Open Media Research Institute

Shalamov, V., 191
Shane, Scott, 217
Shankland, Bob, 282
Sharansky, Natan. *See* Shcharansky, Anatoli
Shazar, Zalman (b. Rubashov), 119–20
Shcharansky, Anatoli (later Natan Sharan-
    sky), 167, 198
Shcharansky, Avital, 167
Shepilov, Dmitri, 72
Shevardnadze, Eduard Amvrosiyevich, 251
Shevchenko, Taras Hryhorovych, 25
Shmelev, Nikolai, 205, 255
Shollenberger, Lewis, 109
Shortwaves, 221
Shragin, Boris, 183, 188–90, 192, 207, 248
Shragin, Natasha (Sadomskaya), 188
Shub, Anatole (Tony), 21, 66
Shub, Boris, xviii, 3–4, 6–8, 10, 18, 21–22, 28,
    41, 48–50, 66, 71, 85, 87, 89–90, 103–4,
Shub, David Natanovich, 3, 4, 22
Shub, Libby, 90
Shulman, Colette, 113, 161
Shulman, Marshall, 113, 287
Shultz, George, 193
Shushkevich, Stanislav, 224
Shuster, George N., 279
Siberia, 22, 41, 53, 90, 98, 118, 215
Sigua, Tengis, 230
Silnicky, Larissa, 258–59
Silone, Ignazio, 49, 265
Silvers, Phil, 95
Simis, Konstantin, 192
Simmons, Ernest J., xvi, 265
Simon, George T., 102
Sims, Zoot, 102, 282
Sinclair, Upton, 34, 49
Singer, Isaac Bashevis, 49, 52–53, 265, 279
Sinyavsky, Andrei (Abram Tertz), 87–88, 107,
    111–12, 117–19, 151, 191–92, 258,
    282–83, 289
Sinyavsky, Mariya (Rozanova), 258, 283
Six-Day War (Middle East), 117, 162, 166
"60 Minutes" program. *See* CBS
Sizov, Igor, 38
Slonim, Marc, 87–88, 124, 265
Slonim, Tanya, 124
Smelyakov, Y., 158
Smith, Harrison, 265
Smith, Hedrick, 158–59
Smoktunovsky, Innokenty, 240
Sobesednik (Interlocutor), 206, 256
Social Democrats, 279
Social Science Research Council, 82
Socialist Party, 39

Socialist Revolutionaries (SRs), 7
Sokolov, Maxim, 230
Sokolov, Mikhail, 85, 216, 230
Solidarity movement (Poland), 173, 191, 201
"Solidary Sunday" demonstrations in New
    York, 167
Solzhenitsyn, Aleksandr Isayevich, xvi, 5, 45,
    92, 116, 123–24, 127, 147, 155, 158–59,
    177, 179, 81–85, 188, 190–91, 191, 209,
    247, 258, 276, 282, 285, 286
Solzhenitsyn, Natasha, 282
Sorbonne, 119
Sorensen, Robert, 107
Sorensen, Theodore, 107
Sorensen, Thomas, 107
Sorokin, Ptirim, 265
Soros, George, 252
Sosin, Debbie, 110, 129, 199
Sosin, Donald, 110, 129, 199
Sosin, Gene. *See also* Radio Liberation; Radio
    Liberty
    London conference on Soviet censorship,
        121–25
    in Munich office, 117–29
    in New York office, 116, 129, 131–94
    and New York Program Section (RL), 3, 6
    panel on Soviet policy, 108
    in Prague, 245
    joins Radio Liberation, 27
    retires from Radio Liberty, 194, 196
    in Salzburg for symposium on East-West
        affairs, 163–66
    and Soviet Jews, 129, 285
    in Soviet Union, 82–85, 92, 197, 207, 219,
        237–42
    in Spain, 87
    speech at Radio Liberty's 40th anniversary,
        240
    and update of Gunther's *Inside Russia
        Today*, 56
Sosin, Gloria Donen, xvi, 28, 87, 149, 160–61,
    163, 188, 197, 199, 207
Sotsialisticheski Vestnik (Socialist Herald), 7
Sovetskaya Molodyozh (Soviet Youth), 205
Soviet Academy of Sciences, 93
Soviet Area Audience and Opinion Research
    (SAAOR), 200, 202–4
Soviet Jews, 66, 117, 125, 129, 142, 166–68,
    285
Soviet Writers' Congresses, 34–35, 37, 41
Soviet Writers' Union. *See* Union of Soviet
    Writers
St. Petersburg. *See* Leningrad
Stalin, Josef Vissarionovich, xv, 1, 3, 7, 9, 19,

Walesa, Lech, 173, 191, 229
Wall Street Journal, 288
Wallace, Mike, 185–87
Walter, Ralph, 285
Warren, Robert Penn, 37
Washington, D.C., 28, 30, 121, 129, 161, 190, 259
Washington Post, 133–34, 158, 183–84, 229, 262
Watergate scandal, 157–58
Wattenberg, Ben, 182–84
Wayne State University, 145
Weidle, Wladimir, 10, 277
Welles, Orson, 282
Wells, H. G., 282
Weltwoche, 268
Wenceslas Square (Prague), 245
West Germany, 4, 35, 73
Whelan, Joseph G., 136–42, 154–55, 166
White Guard, 37, 50
White House (Moscow), xv, 216, 218, 239
White, William L., 275
Whitney, Thomas P., 8
Whitton, John Boardman, 105
Wick, Charles Z., 203
Wiesbaden declaration, 277
Wiesel, Elie, 185
Wilder, Thornton, 34
Williams, Manning, 8, 10
Williams, Spencer, 98
Willkie, Philip H., 275
WMCA radio (New York), 186
Woche, Die, 164
Wolfe, Bertram, 62, 96, 156–57
Woods, Phil, 102
World's Fair (Brussels, 1958), 73
Wrangel, Baron Peter, 178
"Writers at the Microphone" series, 232–33
Writer's Union (Soviet). *See* Union of Soviet Writers
Writers' Congress. *See* Soviet Writers' Congresses
Wyle, Frederick, xvii

Yabloko, 263
Yakovlev, Alexander, 194
Yakovlev, Boris, 277
Yakushev, Alexei, 124
Yale University, 105
Yalta conference, 19

Yanayev, 220–21
Yankee Stadium (New York), 103
Yankelevich, Tanya, 221
Yankelevich, Yefrem, 191
Yanovsky, V. S., 265
Yarmolinsky, Avrahm, 265
Yavlinsky, Grigory, 247, 263
Yazov, 217
Yedigaroff, André, 95
Yekaterinburg (formerly Sverdlovsk) (Urals), 174, 227, 247
Yeltsin, Boris, xv, 21, 47, 205–6, 210–11, 217–18, 221, 224, 229, 238, 239, 243–44, 249, 258, 281
Yeltsin regime, 247, 263
Yeltsin, Nina, 227
Yerevan (Armenia), 259
Yermilov, V., 47–48
Yesenin, Sergei, 153
Yevtushenko, Yevgeny, 238, 249, 279
Yezhov, 155
Yunost, 125
Yurasov, Vladimir. *See* Zhabinsky, Vladimir

Zaitsev, Boris, 34, 36–37, 49, 265
Zamyatin, Yevgeni, 5, 22, 88
Zaprudnik, Jan, 277
Zasulich, Vera, 3
Zavalishin, Vyacheslav K., 276
Zelenin, 276–77
Zenzinov, Vladimir, 7
Zhabinsky, Vladimir (Volodya; RL name Vladimir Yurasov; American name Vladimir Rudolph), 4–6, 33, 278–79
Zhdanov, Andrei, 155
Zhdanov Palace of Young Pioneers, A. A. *See* Anichkov palace
Zhelev, Zhelyu, 229
Zhvanetsky, Mikhail, 219
Zilboorg, Gregory, 265
Zinoviev, Grigory, 21
Zionists, 85
Zirkle, Conway, 279
Zorin, Valery, 96
Zorza, Victor, 76, 126
Zoshchenko, Mikhail, 22
Zunnun (Turkestani desk chief), 277
Zwerdling, Helene, 282
Zyuganov, Gennadi A., 247, 281